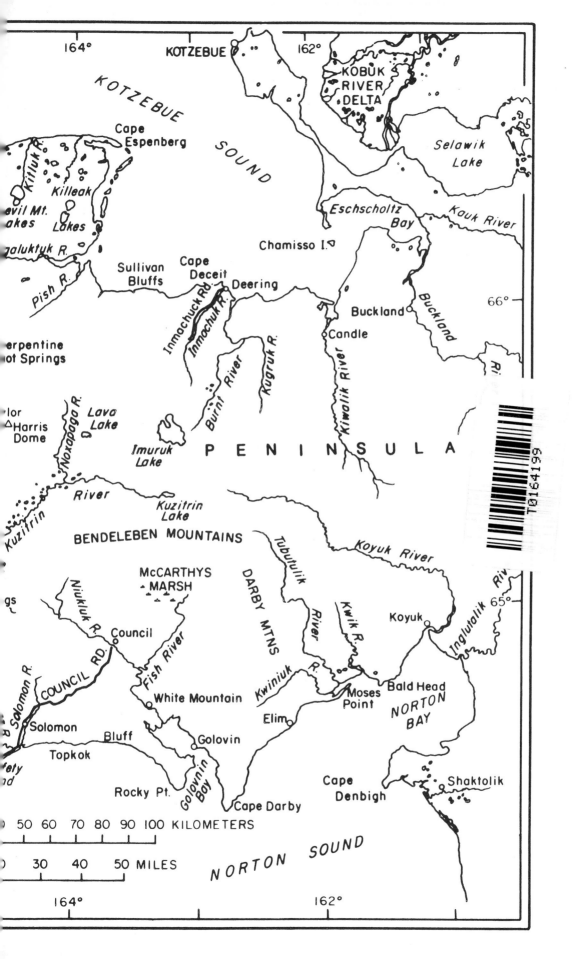

BIRDS
OF THE
SEWARD PENINSULA, ALASKA

Their Biogeography, Seasonality,

and Natural History

Brina Kessel

University of Alaska Press

Library of Congress Cataloging-in-Publication Data

Kessel. Brina.
    Birds of the Seward Peninsula, Alaska.

    Bibliography: p.
    Includes index.
    1. Birds—Alaska—Seward Peninsula.   I. Title.
QL684.A4K47 1989   598.29798'6   89-5030
ISBN 0-912006-29-3 (alk. paper)

Printed in the United States of America by Heath Printers,
    on 60# Hammermill Lustre Offset Opaque Cream White.

The paper used in this publication meets the minimum requirements of
American National Standard for Information Services—Permanence of Paper
for Printed Library Materials,   ANSI Z39.48-1984.

Typeset by Robert C. Emmett.

Publication coordination, design and production by Robert C. Emmett.

DEDICATED

to the memory of

Alfred M. Bailey,

Dwight Tevuk,

and

Arthur Nagozruk

who contributed so much
to our early knowledge
of the birds
of the Seward Peninsula.

Contents

List of Illustrations

Illustrations by John C. Pitcher   *Page*

List of Tables

List of Figures

BIRDS
OF THE
SEWARD PENINSULA, ALASKA

Introduction

Alaska's Seward Peninsula, named after William Henry Seward,[*] possesses a diverse and fascinating avifauna. Birds of three major biomes—tundra, taiga, and marine—are present, and a varied topography provides 21 major habitats, ranging from saltwater habitats and those of the terrestrial wet lowlands to dry alpine summits (see below). In addition, the geographic position of the Peninsula relative to Eurasia, the Bering Land Bridge, and the North American Arctic and subarctic facilitates the occurrence of a number of species of special biogeographic interest.

Until the mid-1960s, the avifauna of the Seward Peninsula had largely escaped the attention of ornithologists. Prior to that time, the only major study of the birds of the Peninsula was that of Alfred M. Bailey (1943, 1948, 1971), who spent 6 April-4 August 1922 about Wales and vicinity and who continued to obtain data from the area in subsequent years through the activities of Dwight Tevuk and Arthur Nagozruk, Wales residents who had been his field assistants in 1922.

A few bird notes are available from the Seward Peninsula prior to Bailey's visit (Nelson 1887; Grinnell 1900a, b; McGregor 1902; Anthony 1906), and some additional reports appeared between 1922 and the mid-1960s: Hill (1922, 1923), Thayer (1951), Cade (1952), Kenyon and Brooks (1960), and Peyton (1963). I was struck, however, by the dearth of avifaunal knowledge about this potentially fascinating region on my first visit in 1966 and thus initiated my studies in 1967. Concurrent with my studies, interest in the birds of the Seward Peninsula increased rapidly. The Alaska Department of Fish and Game initiated studies of the State's raptor populations (Roseneau 1972, Swartz et al. 1975, and various unpublished notes and reports), environmental impact studies were carried out under the impetus of the 1971 Alaska Native Claims Settlement Act (Noble and Wright 1977, Melchior 1979, Wright 1979), seabird studies were conducted under the National Oceanic and Atmospheric Administration's Outer Continental Shelf Environmental Assessment Program (Drury 1976a, b; Drury and Steele 1977; Steele and Drury 1977; Drury et al. 1978; Biderman and Drury 1978; Connors 1978; Divoky 1979; Flock and Hubbard 1979; Ramsdell and Drury 1979, Schamel et al. 1979; Drury et al. 1981; Woodby and Divoky 1983; Springer and Roseneau 1985; Springer et al. 1985a, b; Murphy et al. 1986; Springer et al. 1987; Murphy et al. in prep; and, extralimitally, Shields and Peyton 1977, 1979); and, concomitantly, others have undertaken more limited studies, have become interested in birds as a part of their local environment, or have visited the Peninsula just to enjoy birding there (Flock 1972, 1975; Springer 1974; Walker 1977; and much unpublished data utilized in the following annotated list).

---

[*]Seward, U. S. Secretary of State, engineered the "Treaty of Cession of Russian America to the United States," transferring Alaska to the USA in 1867.

Acknowledgments

Many people and several organizations contributed over the years to this study of the birds of the Seward Peninsula. Their combined support was extensive and varied and was essential to the success of the study and its culmination in this book.

Of great value was the friendship and assistance of the villagers and townspeople of the Peninsula. Special assistance was provided by Gilford Barr and Alfred Karman and their families of Deering, Clarence and Faye Ongtowasruk and Frank and Evelyn Oxereok of Wales, Marvin and Nita Thomas of Buckland, and Alex Weyiouana of Shishmaref.

In Nome, colleagues at the Alaska Department of Fish and Game, especially John J. Burns, Carl A. Grauvogel, and Robert A. Pegau, encouraged and facilitated my work in numerous ways; and the staff of the Alaska Department of Highways, especially Chuck Lewis, Maintenance Supervisor, arranged for reliable ground transportation. Skilled pilots from several flight services, especially Buck Maxson, formerly of Kotzebue, and Jim Isabelle of Teller Air Service, got me into—and out of—otherwise inaccessible field sites.

In several years I was accompanied in the field by colleagues who not only helped gather observational data but also enlivened camp life. Here, special mention is due William L. Foster, Daniel D. Gibson, Hugh E. Kingery, Stephen O. MacDonald, and Fritz G. Scheider.

Many individuals provided previously unpublished data for this book. I am grateful for their valuable contributions, and they are credited below for their specific observations. In addition, John J. Burns, Bruce Conant, John I. Hodges, James G. King, Rodney J. King, David G. Roseneau, Douglas L. Schamel, Jeffery D. Walters, Douglas A. Woodby, and John M. Wright were especially helpful and patient in responding to my many requests for supplemental information.

The black and white illuminations of typical Seward Peninsula birds were creatively done by John C. Pitcher.

Daniel D. Gibson helped tremendously by reading the entire manuscript and making many suggestions that improved its accuracy and clarity. The book was also improved through the suggestions of Thomas K. Bundtzen, David M. Hopkins, Sylvia "Tass" Kelso, Edward C. Murphy, David G. Roseneau, and Alan M. Springer, who each read selected parts of the manuscript.

Portions of the study were partially financed by the Sycamore Tree Trust, the U. S. National Park Service, and the University of Alaska Fairbanks.

I express my deep appreciation to all the above sources for the assistance so generously provided.

General Description of the Region

The Seward Peninsula is a roughly rectangular land mass that projects westward from the mainland of west-central Alaska and forms the eastern edge of the Bering Strait, which separates the Bering and Chukchi seas (Figures 1 and 2). Its eastern boundary, for the purposes of this treatise, is at approximately 161⁰ West Longitude and is formed by the Koyuk River and its East Fork and the Buckland River and its West Fork. Thus defined, the land mass of the Seward Peninsula is approximately 52,000 km² (20,000 mile²), which is four times the size of the state of Connecticut.

Physiography

The Seward Peninsula was recognized by Wahrhaftig (1965) as a distinct physiographic province of Fenneman's (1946) Intermontane Plateaus Physiographic Division of the North American Cordillera. Relative to avian distribution, the Seward Peninsula can be subdivided into six physiographic units:

1. Highlands.—The Highlands are a composite of the only truly rugged mountainous terrain of the Peninsula: the York, Kigluaik, Bendeleben, and Darby mountains (Figure 2). Formed mostly of Precambrian and early Paleozoic metamorphic rocks, they have igneous cores of intruded granite, which form some of the highest peaks. Maximum elevations are Mt. Osborn in the Kigluaik Mountains at 1437 m (4714 ft), Mt. Bendeleben in the Bendeleben Mountains at 1137 m (3730 ft), Brooks Mountain in the York Mountains at 883 m (2898 ft), and a 998-m (3273-ft) unnamed peak in the Darby Mountains. These mountain systems and adjacent uplands were the only portions of the Seward Peninsula to be glaciated during the Pleistocene (Kaufman and Hopkins 1986).

2. Southern Uplands.—The Southern Uplands include the low, rolling hills south of Grantley Harbor and Teller and the more or less gentle slopes south of the Kigluaik and Bendeleben mountain systems. About half of the Southern Uplands have been glaciated, including much of the area between the Kigluaiks and Norton Sound (ibid.). Vegetative cover is predominantly a mesic tundra of Dwarf Shrub Meadow,* with Dwarf Shrub Mat* developing at the higher elevations and on exposed ridges and slopes. Areas of Medium Shrub and Tall Shrub thickets* are common along the major river drainages and on protected foothill slopes. Eastward, beginning in the Niukluk River drainage, Coniferous Forest and Woodland habitats* occur on

---

*These vegetative types are described more fully under Avian Habitats.

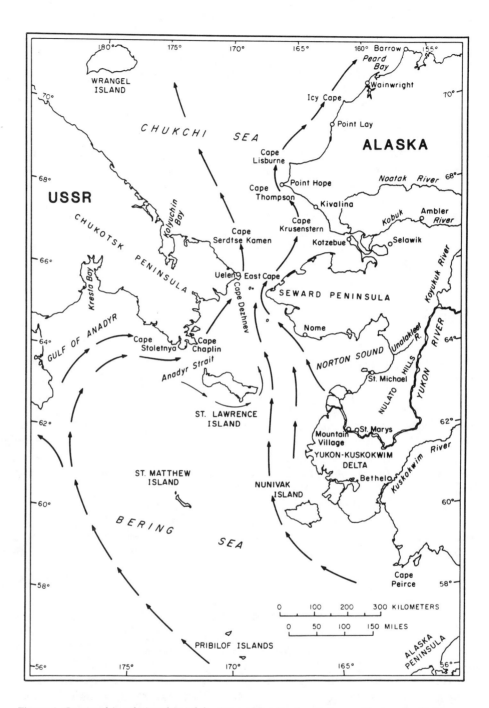

Figure 1. Geographic relationship of the Seward Peninsula relative to Alaska, the Union of Soviet Socialist Republics, and the Bering and Chukchi seas. The arrows track the northward movement of the three main Bering Sea water masses—Anadyr, Bering Shelf, and Alaskan Coastal waters (after Coachman et al. 1975).

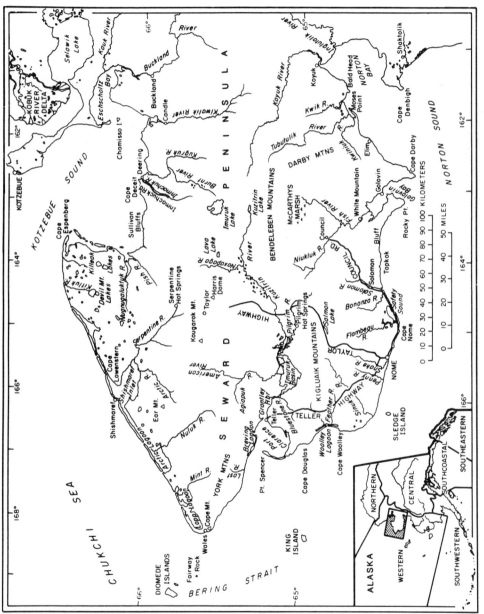

Figure 2. Map of place names and major geographic features of the Seward Peninsula, Alaska. The inset shows Kessel and Gibson's (1978) six biogeographic regions of Alaska, which are also used in this work. "Interior Alaska" is the portion of Central Alaska between the crests of the Alaska and Brooks mountain ranges.

adequately drained and protected sites. Surficial deposits underlying the vegetation in the unglaciated areas consist of alluvium in the valley bottoms and regolith, rock mantle broken and moved by frost action, on the slopes and summits. Glacial morainal deposits predominate on lower slopes and in valley bottoms in the glaciated area. Elevations generally range from about the 30-m (100-ft) contour adjacent to the coastal lowlands up to 660 m (2000 ft).

3. Northern Uplands.—The Northern Uplands extend the entire length of the Peninsula north of the Kuzitrin and Koyuk river valleys, from the foothill slopes of Cape Mountain and the York Mountains to Granite Mountain (65°26'N, 161°14'W) and the Buckland River. These uplands have an extensive rolling topography, again with mesic tundra predominating. As in the Southern Uplands, surficial deposits consist largely of alluvium in the valley bottoms and broken regolith moved by frost action on slopes and summits. Wind-blown silt and redeposited silt mixed with organic material cover lower slopes and fill valleys in much of the eastern two-thirds of the region; glacial deposits are extensive in the western third (D. M. Hopkins in litt.). Elevations get somewhat higher than in the Southern Uplands, reaching a maximum elevation of 875 m (2870 ft) on Kougarok Mountain. A characteristic series of disconnected ridges, domes, and low, flat-topped mountains—predominantly recrystallized limestone and barren or vegetated by sparse Dwarf Shrub Mat—extends east-west across these uplands.

4. Interior Lowlands.—Interior Lowlands include the flat, broad, poorly drained valley bottoms and tectonic depressions of the Peninsula, the most extensive of which are the Kuzitrin-Noxapaga lowlands, Pilgrim (Kruzgamepa)-Kuzitrin lowlands and Imuruk Basin, and McCarthys Marsh (upper Fish River flats); less extensive lowlands occur in places along the Agiapuk, Niukluk, and Koyuk rivers. These interior basins are covered with surficial alluvial deposits of silt, sand and gravel, or glacial deposits (Hudson 1977), and they are characterized by numerous ponds and sluggish drainage systems and by extensive Wet Meadow vegetation. Medium Shrub and Tall Shrub thickets and occasional tree-sized Balsam Poplar (*Populus balsamifera*) stands occur along the raised, well-drained banks of the river channels.

5. Coastal Lowlands.—The low-lying coastal wetlands less than 30 m (100 ft) in elevation, including river deltas, lagoons, spits and barrier strips, and beaches and tidal flats constitute the Coastal Lowlands. The most extensive of these lowlands is an essentially continuous strip along the northwest coastline from Wales, around Cape Espenberg, to the mouth of the Nugnugaluktuk and Pish rivers. Major lowlands also occur at the mouth of the Buckland River, at Breving Lagoon ("Brevig Lagoon"), from Point Spencer along a narrow coastal strip to the region of the mouth of the Sinuk River, at Safety Sound ("Safety Lagoon") and Taylor Lagoon, in the Fish River delta-Golovnin Lagoon ("Golovin Lagoon") area and Moses Point flats (Kwiniuk-Tubutulik-Kwik river deltas), and at the mouth of the Koyuk River. More restricted coastal lowlands occur along the lower reaches at the mouths of other rivers, such as the Kiwalik, Inmachuk, and Goodhope rivers, and the Snake and Nome rivers and Hastings Creek. Most of the southern Coastal Lowlands are underlain by alluvial or beach deposits, but ancient glacial deposits cover a large part of the coastal plain

areas between the Sinuk and Solomon rivers. Surficial deposits in the northern coastal plain between Wales and Kotzebue Sound consist of ancient sand dunes that have been modified by the melting of ground ice and that are partly mantled by the deposits of ancient thaw lakes (D. M. Hopkins in litt.). The older, more stabilized deposits are vegetated primarily by Wet Meadow tundra, although drier sites may support either Dwarf Shrub Meadow or Dwarf Shrub Mat types of vegetation. Beach Rye (*Elymus arenarius*) Grass Meadow vegetation occurs on exposed beach deposits above the reach of regular tidal inundations.

6. Coastal Cliffs.—Sea cliffs provide unique habitats for nesting seabirds and for a few raptors and ravens. These cliffs are formed of erosion-resistant bedrock. Those used by breeding birds along the mainland coast and on Chamisso Island are mostly of metamorphic rock. The major offshore islands—Sledge, King, and Little Diomede islands, and Fairway Rock—are granitic masses.

The bedrock geology of the Seward Peninsula is complex and varied (see Hudson 1977) and has a lengthy history, beginning with the Precambrian Era, of marine sedimentation, consolidation, metamorphism, and uplift, intrusions of granitic masses, volcanic activity, horizontal thrust faulting, and erosion, and, in the mountains, glaciation. Sainsbury et al. (1970:2502) stated,

> The Seward Peninsula consists principally of metamorphic rocks of Precambrian age, or less metamorphosed pelitic and carbonate rocks of late Precambrian age, and of thick carbonate rocks of Paleozoic age. These rocks are intermixed in extensive thrust plates of two ages: the earlier (eastward thrusting) is probably pre-middle Cretaceous, and the later (north-ward thrusting) is older than 74 m.y. Stocks and batholiths of granitic rocks, containing alkalic rocks locally, and gneissic phases intruded the older thrust plates, whereas stocks of biotite granite with associated tin and beryllium deposits intruded the younger thrust sheets. Extensive andesitic volcanic rocks on the eastern Seward Peninsula are of Late Jurassic to Early Cretaceous age; they grade upward into graywackes and siltstones of Cretaceous age which are tightly folded. Tertiary rocks are coal bearing and deformed and crop out in small areas; they are most probably of late Tertiary age. Extensive volcanic fields of latest Tertiary to Holocene age cover large areas of the central and eastern Seward Peninsula. Marine terraces older than Sangamon are warped, and a range-front fault along the Kigluaik Mountains offsets moraines of Wisconsin age.

A less technical description is provided by Hopkins and Hopkins (1958:106):

> The bedrocks of Seward Peninsula are much more like those of the Chukot-ski Peninsula in Siberia than those of adjoining parts of the Alaskan mainland. Most of the peninsula is underlain by schist or slate. Limestone underlies the York Mountains and several other large upland areas. Granite is common in the Kigluaik, the Bendeleben, and the Darby Mountains, and small bodies are present elsewhere. Sandstone, shale, and conglomerate

of Cretaceous age extend from Norton Bay to the southeast corner of Kotzebue Sound. Basalt lavas of Pleistocene age cover about 1,000 square miles near Imuruk Lake and a smaller area along the Koyuk River near Haycock, and volcanic ash covers several hundred square miles near Devil Mountain. Most of the lowlands and coastal plains in the southern part of the peninsula are underlain by coarse gravel, whereas most of those in the northern part are underlain by thick [greater than 1.5 m] deposits of silt.

The bedrock of the Peninsula is largely covered by unconsolidated surficial deposits, the result of frost action, rain, wind, and glaciers. Exposed bedrock, however, is the dominant feature of the rugged mountains of the highlands; rock cliff faces are present at sites along rivers and the coastline; and resistant outcrops and granite tors are widely distributed through the uplands. Late Tertiary and Quaternary volcanic rock is a conspicuous feature in the Imuruk Lake-Lava Lake area, and unconsolidated volcanic breccia, scoria, tuff, and cinder deposits occur about the old volcanic vents now forming Killeak Lakes, Devil Mountain Lakes, and White Fish Lake. Barren ridges and domes, of recrystallized limestone and metavolcanic rock, occur across the Northern Uplands.

Climate and Other Environmental Factors

The climate of the Seward Peninsula is rigorous, with brief, cool summers and cold, relatively dry winters. Climate in the interior portions of the Peninsula is continental, with relatively wide temperature fluctuations, both seasonal and diurnal, and relatively low amounts of precipitation, cloud cover, and fog. In coastal areas the climate is continental during the period of winter sea ice coverage, but maritime during the ice-free season, with less extreme temperatures and more atmospheric moisture and precipitation. Generally, the weather in the southern portions of the Peninsula is more stormy than in the northern portions, since some of the low pressure systems of the main storm track that moves east-northeastward across the Bering Sea (Selkregg 1977) are deflected by the mountains from reaching the northern Peninsula (National Ocean Service 1985).

Temperature and precipitation records for various sites are summarized in Table 1. Since most of the permanent towns and villages are located on or near the coast, most weather records are from the coastal environment. Council, where data were collected primarily from 1938 to 1942, is the only interior site from which year-round records are available.

While there is considerable geographic and temporal variation, mean .summer temperatures average about 10°C (50°F), with means slightly above 10°C prevailing in the southeast portions of the Peninsula (where spruce trees are thus able to grow [see Wolfe and Leopold 1967]) and somewhat below 10°C farther west (where tundra occurs). Winter temperatures show the same general pattern of geographic variation, with an overall average of about -16°C (3°F).

Except for surface layers, most of the soils of the Peninsula are permanently frozen to depths ranging from 5 to more than 80 m (Hopkins 1955). During summer, depending on exposure, soil types, and insulative vegetative cover, thaw may extend to depths of 30-300 cm. Permafrost functions as a percolation barrier, resulting in much of the ground during the summer being saturated with moisture. Overlying soils are also maintained at relatively cool temperatures, restricting plant growth.

Annual precipitation ranges from about 20 cm (8 inches) at Shishmaref to probably over 100 cm (40 inches) in the mountains north of Nome (Selkregg 1977); August is the month of the greatest and most frequent precipitation (Environmental Data Service 1971). Annual snowfall varies from 76 to 100 cm (30 to 40 inches) along the north coast to probably 250 cm (100 inches) in the mountains north of Nome (Selkregg 1977). Fresh snow begins to fall on some of the higher summits by mid-August, but does not begin to accumulate in the lowlands until almost the first of November. Most seasonal snow has melted by mid- to late June. Most recording stations west of Nome have reported at least a trace of snowfall every month of the year. Since most birds have selected nest sites prior to final snow melt, localities where snow melt is late, such as in draws and depressions and on north-facing slopes, are largely devoid of breeding birds.

Winds are generally from southerly directions during the summer (June, July, and August) and northerly the remainder of the year. Wind speeds are not excessive, with monthly means ranging from 16 to 19 kph (10 to 20 mph) at Nome and 22 to 35 kph (13 to 22 mph) at Tin City. Speeds are lowest during the summer months and highest during fall and winter. Severe windstorms, exceeding 113 kph (70 mph), have been recorded at Nome during all months from October through March (Environmental Data Service 1971, 1977).

Diurnal tidal ranges are small around the shores of the Seward Peninsula: 49 cm at Nome, 43 cm at Port Clarence, and 82 cm at the mouth of the Kiwalik River in Kotzebue Sound (National Ocean Service 1985). Water levels are influenced more by winds than tides. Offshore winds may lower levels 60 to 90 cm, whereas storms have raised levels over 4 m (14 ft) (ibid.), causing flooding by salt water of otherwise freshwater and terrestrial coastal habitats.

Sea ice surrounds the Seward Peninsula during winter. The extent and timing of ice coverage fluctuates considerably among years, due primarily to large-scale changes in atmospheric circulation in winter, i.e., whether upper air flow is from the Pacific Ocean to the south or the Arctic to the north (Niebauer 1981). Coverage is of greater duration and extent in Kotzebue Sound than Norton Sound. Generally, young ice forms in bays and sheltered areas in October, although waters of Norton Sound are easily navigable through November. Navigation among the ice floes becomes difficult in early December and is usually suspended from late December to mid-May (National Ocean Service 1985). Ice coverage, except in areas of shore-fast ice, is seldom solid; it is formed of fields, cakes, and floes, separated by leads and polynyas, with the ice kept in motion primarily by winds. Coverage is most complete during February and March, when the sea is seven-eighths or more covered by ice (Potocsky 1975). Ice becomes less compact about the Peninsula during late March and April; and, when rivers begin to break up in May (earliest at the base of the Peninsula), they break out and clear the ice away from their mouths and adjacent shorelines, making available a critical habitat for migrant waterbirds. Breakup is not complete until late

Table 1. Temperature and precipitation summary for localities on the Seward Peninsula, Alaska. Data from Environmental Data Service (1971, 1977) analyzed after Selkregg (1977).

	Period of Record yr	Mean Annual Precipitation cm (inches)		Mean Annual Snowfall cm (inches)		Daily mean temperatures °C (°F) Summer (JN, JL, AU) Minimum	Maximum	Winter (DE, JA, FE) Minimum	Maximum
Candle	6-20	21.8	(8.6)	91	(36)	2 (36)	17 (63)	-29 (-20)	-17 (02)
Shishmaref	22	20.3	(8.0)	84	(33)	1 (33)	12 (54)	-24 (-12)	-14 (07)
Wales	25-30	28.7	(11.3)	104	(41)	1 (33)	11 (51)	-24 (-11)	-13 (09)
Tin City	15-22	46.0	(18.1)	175	(69)	1 (34)	9 (49)	-25 (-13)	-14 (07)
Teller	22	29.2	(11.5)	127	(50)	3 (37)	14 (57)	-23 (-09)	-13 (09)
Nome	30-60	42.4	(16.7)	138	(54)	6 (42)	12 (54)	-19 (-03)	-11 (13)
Golovin	1-5	25.7	(10.1)	97	(38)	4 (40)	16 (60)	-19 (-02)	-7 (19)
Moses Point	24	48.0	(18.9)	102	(40)	6 (42)	16 (61)	-21 (-06)	-13 (09)
White Mountain	17	37.6	(14.8)	147	(58)	5 (41)	16 (61)	-22 (-07)	-9 (15)
Council	6	35.6	(14.0)	117	(46)	3 (38)	18 (64)	-23 (-09)	-9 (15)

Table 1. Temperature and precipitation summary for localities on the Seward Peninsula, Alaska.(cont.)

	Extreme annual temperatures						
	Minimum			Maximum			
	°C	(°F)	mo, yr	°C	(°F)	mo, yr	
Candle	-51	(-60)	JA 1919	29	(85)	JL 1918 & AU 1911	
Shishmaref	-44	(-48)	FE 1947	26	(78)	JL 1946	
Wales	-42	(-44)	FE 1955	24	(75)	JL 1926	
Tin City	-42	(-44)	FE 1955	24	(75)	JL 1966	
Teller	-43	(-45)	FE 1952	28	(82)	JN 1957	
Nome	-44	(-47)	JA 1919	30	(86)	JL 1968 & 1977	
Golovin	-40	(-40)	JA 1943	27	(80)	JN 1942	
Moses Point	-45	(-49)	FE 1956	31	(87)	JN 1957	
White Mountain	-48	(-55)	JA 1925	32	(89)	JL 1936 & AU 1926	
Council	-43	(-45)	JA 1940	30	(86)	JL 1939	

June along the south shore of the Peninsula and the Bering Strait and until early July or later along the north shore. Table 2 gives the dates of ice freeze-up and breakup for various localities of the Seward Peninsula and shows the wide range of annual variation.

Vegetation

The vegetation of the Seward Peninsula belongs to three different zones, according to Young's (1971) floristic zonation for arctic regions. Spruce trees and associated taiga vegetation extend onto the southeastern quarter of the Peninsula. The remainder of the vegetation is tundra, and most of it falls into Young's floristic Zone 4, the relatively rich "low arctic." The western tip of the Peninsula, however, falls into Zone 3—a primarily coastal zone, transitional between the floristically depauperate "high arctic" zones and Zone 4. In the western third of the Northern Uplands, barren landscapes extend down to the 200-m level, and the mesic tundra is limited to the lower and more protected and moist slopes. Here, also, shrubbery is restricted to sheltered ravines and gullies, where some shrubs may get as high as 2 m (medium shrub), but most are shorter than 1.5 m; only dwarf shrubs (less than 0.4 m) are found at the western extremity of the northern uplands. Based on observed distributions and growth patterns of cottongrass (*Eriophorum vaginatum*), Mountain or Green Alder (*Alnus crispa*), and Dwarf Birch (*Betula nana*), D. M. Hopkins (in litt.) suggested that the break between the two zones on the Seward Peninsula comes at about 166° W—an approximate longitude corroborated by bird distributions (see below).

Young (1971) presented convincing evidence that the distributions of arctic plants are largely the result of current environmental conditions rather than historical and distributional factors. He found a strong correlation between his floristic zonations and the amount of summer warmth available for physiologic processes (aggregate of mean temperatures above 0°C)—but not with other environmental factors (i.e., annual mean temperature, mean annual precipitation, day length, and soil type or other edaphic features).

Vegetation, as it affects birds, is described below under Avian Habitats. Scientific and vernacular names follow Hultén (1968).

Table 2. Dates of freeze-up and breakup of rivers and sea ice, Seward Peninsula, Alaska (National Ocean Service 1985).

	Waters	Period of Record (yr)	Breakup Dates			Freeze-up Dates		
			Average	Earliest	Latest	Average	Earliest	Latest
Moses Point	Kwiniuk River	6	24 MY	2 MY 51	11 JN 49	20 OC	1 OC 51	2 NO 52
Golovin	Golovnin Bay	6	23 MY	13 MY 40	14 JN 39	2 NO	8 OC 42	19 NO 37
White Mountain	Fish River	24	21 MY	5 MY 40	2 JN 37	14 OC	27 SE 31	9 NO 25
Solomon	Solomon River	10	20 MY	1 MY 42	30 MY 45	29 OC	10 OC 40	29 NO 48
Council	Niukluk River	12	17 MY	27 AP 40	31 MY 52	30 OC	13 OC 20	9 NO 40
Nome	Norton Sound	50	29 MY	28 AP 42	28 JN 48	12 NO	13 OC 18	13 DE 47
Teller	Grantley Harbor	16	7 JN	12 MY 36	18 JN 39	10 NO	13 OC 42	26 DE 50
Wales	Bering Strait	16	8 JN	15 MY 47	30 JN 49	3 DE	8 OC 48	8 JA 51
Shishmaref	Chukchi Sea	18	22 JN	30 MY 36	8 JL 33	10 NO	6 OC 39	18 DE 34
Deering	Inmachuk River	4	4 JN	11 MY 43	30 JN 41	23 OC	3 OC 46	4 NO 41
Candle	Kiwalik River	8	18 MY	5 MY 43	27 MY 27	17 OC	10 OC 42	23 OC 43

Avian Habitats

Following are brief descriptions of the major avian habitats of the Seward Peninsula, based on a classification of Alaska's avian habitats by Kessel (1979).

Lacustrine Waters and Shorelines

This habitat includes all fresh or brackish surface waters of lakes and ponds (except the small pools found in wet meadows) and their immediate shorelines. The origins of these waterbodies on the Peninsula are varied (D. M. Hopkins in litt.). The vast majority are thaw lakes caused by melting ground ice. In the mountainous areas, many, such as Salmon Lake, are moraine dammed. Imuruk Lake and Imuruk Basin, as well as Grantley Harbor and Port Clarence, are the result of crustal down-warping. Killeak and Devil Mountain lakes are maar lakes formed in old volcanic vents. Many of the waterbodies in the deltas and coastal marshes, including the long, linear lakes at Cape Espenberg and on the barrier strip off Lopp Lagoon, are caused by oxidation of peat in areas of ponded drainages (ibid.). The Lacustrine Waters and Shorelines habitat is the primary breeding habitat for loons, waterfowl, and phalaropes.

Fluviatile Waters and Shorelines

All flowing surface waters and their immediate shorelines, except drains and rivulets too small or shallow for swimming birds, are included in this category. The habitat is used extensively by breeding Harlequin Ducks and Red-breasted Mergansers, Glaucous and Mew gulls, and American Dippers.

Nearshore Waters

Protected marine waters, such as inlets, lagoons, and bays are combined under this category. Examples include Shishmaref Inlet ("Shishmaref Lagoon"), Lopp and Arctic lagoons, Port Clarence, Grantley Harbor, Safety Sound, Golovnin Lagoon and Golovnin Bay, and the open mouths of such rivers as the Buckland and Nugnugaluktuk. This habitat is used primarily by loons, waterfowl, and gulls. It is an especially critical habitat in spring for migrant waterfowl that arrive when most habitats are covered with ice and snow; open water is usually first available at the mouths of rivers, whether they open into lagoons or river-mouth bays, and early migrants concentrate at these restricted locations.

Inshore Waters

This category includes the exposed coastal waters of Norton Sound and Kotzebue Sound, large embayments that are relatively shallow (less than 25 m) and are strongly influenced by discharges from coastal rivers, especially the Yukon and Kobuk rivers, respectively. Upper water layers are relatively warm in summer and have relatively low salinities (Fleming and Heggarty 1966, Coachman et al. 1975, Niemark 1979), and zooplankton are fewer, less diverse, and of different species than in the Offshore Waters (English 1966, Cooney 1977, Niemark 1979). Inshore Waters are used extensively for feeding by fish-eating birds and those feeding on benthic invertebrates, e.g., loons, eiders, scoters, Harlequin Ducks, Red-breasted Mergansers, Pelagic Cormorants, *Larus* gulls, Black-legged Kittiwakes, Arctic Terns, Common Murres, and Horned Puffins.

Offshore Waters

The Offshore Waters of the Seward Peninsula are composed of continental shelf water originating south of St. Lawrence Island (Bering Shelf Water) and oceanic water originating along the continental slope (Anadyr Water) (Coachman et al. 1975). These waters are generally colder and more saline than the Inshore Waters, which originate along the mainland coast of Alaska (Alaska Coastal Water). All three water masses flow northward over the Bering Sea shelf and through the Bering Strait into the Chukchi Sea (Figure 1). Inshore Waters and Offshore Waters are separated by a relatively stable north-south front between the lower-density coastal water and the higher-density shelf and oceanic waters, a front that occurs between the mouth of Norton Sound and St. Lawrence Island and parallels the southwest and northwest coasts of the western end of the Peninsula. Auklets and Thick-billed Murres are heavy users of this habitat, where they feed on the relatively rich zooplankton and benthic invertebrate communities of the northern Bering Shelf.

Sea Ice Edge

Ice edges are present in the vicinity of the Seward Peninsula during periods of fall freeze-up and spring thaw of the ice pack, and during the winter whenever open leads develop. The food-rich interface between the sea water and these edges attracts alcids, particularly murres, Glaucous and Slaty-backed gulls, Ivory and Ross' gulls, Black Guillemots, and migrant eiders and Oldsquaws.

Beaches and Tidal Flats

Unvegetated shorelines subject to regular tidal inundations compose this habitat. Most beaches of the Seward Peninsula are gentle slopes of gravel, sand, silt, or mud, although some below coastal cliffs are rocky. Tidal flats occur at the mouths of most of the major rivers, both in lagoons and along the coast, and at many lagoon inlets. Arctic Terns and Common Eiders sometimes use the upper beaches for nesting, but the heaviest use of beaches and tidal flats is by loafing and feeding shorebirds, gulls, and waterfowl. Use of this habitat is especially high during the postbreeding and fall migration periods (Connors 1978, Woodby and Divoky 1983), although it is also used by local populations during the breeding season.

Coastal Cliffs and Block-fields

Bedrock coastal cliffs and erosional deposits of rock and rubble form this unique habitat for breeding seabirds (Figure 3). The mainland cliffs include Bluff and Bald Head ("Cape Isaac"), composed of Paleozoic recrystallized limestone; Cape Darby, of Precambrian schist and marble; Rocky Point and Topkok, of Precambrian "York Slate" (carbonaceous and siliceous metasedimentary rocks); Cape Riley, of Precambrian argillaceous and dolomitic limestone; the south face of the York and Lost River terraces, of Silurian and Ordovician recrystallized limestone; Cape Mountain, of Cretaceous granite; Sullivan Bluffs, of Mississippian limestone, marble, and subordinate shale; and Cape Deceit, Precambrian calcareous schist. The major offshore islands—Sledge, King, and Little Diomede islands, and Fairway Rock—consist of granite and granite rubble. Chamisso Island in Kotzebue Sound is of Paleozoic recrystallized limestone, similar to Bluff and Bald Head.

Figure 3. Coastal cliffs at Cape Deceit, 23 June 1973. Used for nesting by raptors, kittiwakes, murres, and Cliff Swallows.

Pelagic Cormorants, Glaucous Gulls, and Horned Puffins nest at most of these cliffs, whereas Black-legged Kittiwakes and murres usually nest only at the larger ones—Bluff, Sullivan Bluffs, Cape Deceit, Chamisso Island, and those of the offshore granitic islands. Thick-billed Murres, auklets, and Tufted Puffins occur mainly on the coastal cliffs and islands in or near the Offshore Waters habitat.

Figure 4. Inland Cliff and Block-field habitat west of Big Creek in the eastern Kigluaik Mountains, 21 June 1977. Used for nesting by raptors, Say's Phoebes, Water Pipits, and Rosy Finches.

Inland Cliffs and Block-fields

Exposed, vertical cliffs of bedrock, rock scree slopes, and fractured lava flows constitute this inland habitat, which predominates in the Highlands mountain systems and in much of the Quaternary lava flow area about Imuruk and Lava lakes (Figures 4-6). This habitat is also conspicuous throughout the Northern and Southern uplands, where erosion-resistant outcrops, mostly of metamorphic rock, are common and where rivers have carved cliff faces from bedrock along their banks. Granitic tors are a conspicuous feature at Ear Mountain, Cape Mountain, in the Serpentine Hot Springs area, at Asses Ears north of Imuruk Lake, and on the uplands along the Taylor Highway between Pilgrim and Kuzitrin rivers.

The Inland Cliffs and Block-fields habitat is the primary habitat for most of the large raptors and for Say's Phoebes and Cliff Swallows; it is used extensively by Common Ravens, Northern Wheatears, and Snow Buntings; and some Canada Geese nest on river bluffs and in the lava block-fields.

Figure 5. Inland Cliff and Block-field habitat, Serpentine Hot Springs, 2 July 1971. Used for nesting by raptors, Say's Phoebes, Cliff Swallows, ravens, robins, and Snow Buntings.

Figure 6. Block-field of fractured lava at Lava Lake, 10 July 1973. Used for nesting by Canada Geese, Rough-legged Hawks, Northern Wheatears, and Snow Buntings; and, where there is low shubbery, by Yellow Wagtails, American Tree Sparrows, White-crowned Sparrows, and redpolls.

Alluvia

Unvegetated alluvial deposits of rocks, gravel, sand, and silt occur along mountain streams and along most of the major river systems, providing habitat for nesting Semipalmated Plovers, Spotted Sandpipers, Wandering Tattlers, Glaucous, Herring, and Mew gulls, and Arctic Terns (Figure 7). Waterfowl and other shorebirds use river bars for loafing and feeding.

Figure 7. Alluvial rock and gravel 50 km up the Nome River, 23 June 1977. Habitat used by Harlequin Ducks, Red-breasted Mergansers, Semipalmated Plovers, Wandering Tattlers, Spotted Sandpipers, Ruddy Turnstones, Arctic Terns, and gulls.

Subterranean Soil

Cutbanks of silt along river banks are used by nesting Bank Swallows.

Salt Grass Meadow

A habitat subject to periodic tidal inundations and vegetated with *Puccinellia* spp., *Carex subspathacea*, and *C. ramenskii* occurs in some areas, usually just above tidal flats in lagoons and at the heads of shallow bays and inlets. Tidal pools and unvegetated surfaces may be interspersed with the vegetated meadows, forming a Salt Grass Meadow-Pond habitat complex. Salt Grass Meadow is commonly used for nesting and feeding by Brant, Emperor Geese, Black Turnstones, Glaucous Gulls, and Sabine's Gulls and for foraging and resting by other waterfowl and shorebirds. The Salt Grass Meadow-Pond complex is of prime importance to postbreeding and migratory shorebirds. An estimated 250,000-350,000 shorebirds use this habitat along the lagoon barrier strip off Shishmaref Inlet and northeast of there, during mid- to late August (Connors and Connors 1985), as do many waterfowl, especially Brant (ibid., R. J. King pers. comm.)

Wet Meadow

Characterized by a high moisture content in the substrate, Wet Meadow exists primarily on flat or gently sloping, poorly drained sites (Figure 8). Some sites, such as the low centers of polygons or the edges of ponds, may have standing water over the substrate; and often substantial amounts of moss (primarily *Drepanocladus* spp.) are present. Graminoids are the dominant vascular vegetation, with *Carex aquatilis*, *Arctophila fulva*, and *Eriophorum angustifolium* being diagnostic, as is *Potentilla palustris*. This habitat occurs extensively throughout both the Coastal Lowlands and Interior Lowlands and wherever poor drainage conditions exist in the uplands, such as along rivulets and streams, around lakes and ponds, on flat summits and passes, etc. Frequently this habitat occurs in a mosaic with ponds and intervening ridges, forming a habitat complex referred to below as Ridged Wet Meadow-Pond habitat complex.

Pectoral Sandpipers, Long-billed Dowitchers, and Red-necked Phalaropes are characteristic breeders in the Wet Meadow habitat, as are Red Phalaropes and Dunlins in the coastal areas.

Figure 8. Wet Meadow habitat on the Kuzitrin River flats, 22 June 1977. Used for feeding and cover (and when drier for nesting) by loons, grebes, waterfowl, and some sandpipers.

Figure 9. Dwarf Shrub Meadow habitat of tussock-forming sedge surrounding tundra
lake in the flats along the lower Inmachuk River, 21 June 1973. Used by Willow
Ptarmigan, Short-eared Owls, American Tree Sparrows, Savannah Sparrows, and
Lapland Longspurs. The lake contained an apparently nesting Pacific Loon, Canada
Geese, Northern Pintails, Greater Scaup, Oldsquaws, and Black and Surf scoters
when the photo was taken.

Dwarf Shrub Meadow

Dominated by sedges, Dwarf Shrub Meadow occupies a wide range of substrate
moisture, but is generally more mesic than Wet Meadow (Figures 9 and 10). The dominant sedges are tussock-forming, with *Eriophorum vaginatum* dominating the
damper flat areas and lower slopes and *Carex bigelowii* the more sloping and otherwise better-drained sites (Racine and Anderson 1979). Dwarf shrubs (less than
0.4 m in height) are interspersed in varying amounts among the sedges; the most
common shrubs are *Betula nana, Empetrum nigrum, Ledum palustre, Vaccinium
uliginosum*, and *Salix planifolia pulchra*.

Dwarf Shrub Meadow is probably the most widespread avian habitat on the Seward
Peninsula, occurring from the mesic edges of coastal flats, over much of the extensive, rolling Southern and Northern uplands, and up the flanks of the mountain
systems. The varied vegetative patterns found in this habitat—hummocks, exaggerated
sedge tussocks, polygons, solifluction terraces, peat rings, etc.—are the result primarily
of seasonal frost action (Hopkins and Sigafoos 1951; Johnson et al. 1966). Generally,
the dwarf shrub component of this habitat is associated with the raised relief of these
formations, either because of a drier substrate or because of protection from winds.

The Lapland Longspur is the most abundant species in this habitat, followed by
the Western Sandpiper. Semipalmated Sandpipers also use this habitat extensively
where unvegetated substrates of mud, silt, or sand are nearby.

Grass Meadow

Two types of Grass Meadow occur on the Seward Peninsula. Meadows of _Calamagrostis canadensis_ are limited in extent and appear to be of little significance in avian distribution. They are found at sites that apparently are quite wet in early spring, e.g., old lake bottoms, near late-melting snow banks, as well as along wet drainage ways and in disturbed areas (old mining activities, eroded slopes, etc.). Beach Rye (_Elymus_) meadow is primarily a strand community found at the upper edges of most beaches around the Seward Peninsula, and it is extensive in sand dune areas and along some of the lagoon barrier strips. _Elymus_ meadow is used only lightly by birds, although it often provides the only nesting cover along coastal beaches or in estuaries. A few waterfowl, Semipalmated Sandpipers, Glaucous Gulls, Arctic and Aleutian terns, Lapland Longspurs, and a few Savannah Sparrows use this habitat for nesting.

Figure 10. Dwarf Shrub Meadow habitat with relief of hummocks and ridges that support a denser growth of dwarf shrubs, Sinuk River drainage, 25 June 1977. Used by Whimbrels, Bar-tailed Godwits, Western Sandpipers, and Savannah Sparrows; hummocks are used for perching and sometimes for nest sites by jaegers and owls.

Dwarf Shrub Mat

Dwarf Shrub Mat is dominated by low, woody plants less than 0.4 m high, often matted and prostrate in form (Figures 11 and 12). Varying amounts of lichen, sedge, grass, and forb may be present, and much of the ground may be bare. Typical taxa include _Empetrum nigrum, Ledum palustre, Vaccinium vitis-idaea, Betula nana, Salix reticulata, Salix rotundifolia, Loiseleuria procumbens, Saxifraga oppositifolia_, and _Dryas_ spp. This habitat occurs on many of the xeric sites throughout the Peninsula, from raised windblown ridges in the coastal lowlands, to the expos-

Figure 11. Dwarf Shrub Mat habitat on xeric limestone dome west of Kougarok Mountain, 23 June 1974. Used by Red Knots and Horned Larks, and, where less exposed, by Lesser Golden-Plovers, Ruddy Turnstones, Water Pipits, Lapland Longspurs, and Snow Buntings.

Figure 12. Dwarf Shrub Mat habitat on mesic substrate along the Taylor Highway, 19 June 1977. Used for breeding by redpolls and for feeding by many of the sparrows (e.g., American Tree, Golden-crowned, and White-crowned sparrows) and the Yellow Wagtail from adjacent low shrub habitats.

ed slopes, ridges, and domes of the uplands and highlands, and in the lava block-fields. This habitat incorporates the barrens or rock deserts of Porsild (1951), the dwarf shrub tundra of Racine and Anderson (1979), and alpine or dry tundra and rock-cushion fellfield of others.

This habitat supports a distinctive, but sparse, avifauna; the more exposed sites are used only for feeding, and then only on relatively calm days. Characteristic birds include Lesser Golden Plover, Ruddy Turnstone, Red Knot, Baird's Sandpiper, Horn-ed Lark, Water Pipit, Rosy Finch, and Lapland Longspur.

Low Shrub Thicket

Closed, open, or sparse stands of shrubs 0.4-1.1 m high occur throughout the Penin-sula (Figure 13). Where environmental conditions are too harsh for taller shrubs, these low shrubs form a unique habitat along small drainageways and in protected draws, even as far west as Wales and Shishmaref Inlet. The main plant components are willows (especially *Salix planifolia pulchra* and *S. glauca*) and Dwarf Birch (*Betula nana*). Willow Ptarmigan, Savannah Sparrows, and American Tree Sparrows use this habitat almost wherever it occurs; while less widespread, both White-crowned and Golden-crowned sparrows also use low shrubs extensively.

Figure 13. Low Shrub Thicket habitat of willow along the lower Inmachuk River, 21 June 1973. Primary habitat for American Tree, Golden-crowned, and White-crowned sparrows, and, if near sedge openings, for Willow Ptarmigan and Savannah Sparrows.

Figure 14. Medium Shrub Thicket habitat of willow in moist draw along the Taylor Highway, 18 June 1977. Primary nesting habitat for Arctic Warblers, Orange-crowned and Wilson's warblers, Gray-cheeked Thrushes, and Fox Sparrows.

Medium Shrub Thicket

Closed, open, or sparse stands of shrubs 1.2-2.4 m high constitute this habitat (Figure 14). It occurs over much of the Peninsula, but forms more extensive and robust stands in Young's floristic Zone 4 than in Zone 3. In Zone 3 this habitat is restricted to protected ravines, bowls, deep or leeward draws, etc. These thickets are formed either from the same willow species (plus *S. lanata richardsonii*) as form the Low Shrub Thickets, or from alder, *Alnus crispa*, or Dwarf Birch. Medium shrubs form an important and unique avian habitat, and it is the most productive one on the Peninsula. Birds found regularly in this habitat, but seldom—if ever—in low shrubs, include Gray-cheeked Thrush, Fox Sparrow, Wilson's Warbler, Arctic Warbler, and Orange-crowned Warbler.

Tall Shrub Thicket

Closed, open or sparse stands of shrubs 2.5-4.9 m high are limited in extent, occurring only in Young's Zone 4. The most important type in this habitat is dominated by the Alaska or Feltleaf Willow (*Salix alaxensis*), which occurs mainly in narrow bands along watercourses or in disturbed areas (Figure 15). Medium shrubs usually flank the narrow band of tall shrubs, and many of the medium shrub birds make regular use of the tall shrubs, too, especially for song and observation perches. Blackpoll Warblers and Northern Waterthrushes are found only in this habitat, however, and Yellow Warblers are four times more frequent in this habitat than in other shrubs.

Alder reaches tall-shrub stature in places on the eastern half of the Peninsula; it is a relatively barren habitat, used primarily by the medium shrub birds. The only birds that exhibit a selective preference for alder are Varied Thrushes, which seem attracted to the dense cover, and redpolls, which feed extensively on the seeds.

Small, open patches of tall shrub-sized Balsam Poplar (*Populus balsamifera*) are scattered about the uplands and Interior Lowlands (see below) and a few scattered willows grow to tree heights (5 m or over), but neither of these phenomena appear to influence avian distribution on the Peninsula.

Figure 15. Tall Shrub Thicket habitat of willow, Milepost 56 Taylor Highway, 21 June 1973. Primary habitat for Alder Flycatchers, Blackpoll and Yellow warblers, and when near water, for Northern Waterthrushes and Rusty Blackbirds.

Deciduous Forest and Woodland

The only deciduous forests on the Seward Peninsula are of Balsam Poplar (Figures 16 and 17). Tree-sized (5 m or over) poplars are largely restricted to raised, xeric river banks in the Interior Lowlands. Small stands, some with old, dying, and fairly large trees (up to 10 cm dbh), were present on the inner elbows of the Fish River in McCarthys Marsh in 1973. Stands of several hundred trees or more, with heights of 9 m (30 ft) and 30-40 cm dbh, occur along the Fox River tributary of the Fish River and the Bear Creek and American Creek tributaries of the Niukluk River. Similar stands, most of somewhat lesser stature, occur at intervals along the banks of the Kuzitrin and Pilgrim rivers. The most impressive forest is an extensive stand of tall trees at Pilgrim Hot Springs, many of which were 30 cm dbh or larger in 1971, and under which was an extensive ground cover of such warm-soil plants as *Heracleum*

Figure 16. Deciduous Forest and Woodland habitat of Balsam Poplars along Bear River, Milepost 71.5 Council Road, 2 July 1977. Primary habitat for Bohemian Waxwings at 163°42'W on the Seward Peninsula.

Figure 17. Deciduous Forest and Woodland habitat of Balsam Poplars along the Pilgrim River at Milepost 60 Taylor Highway, 21 June 1977. The largest tree trunk was 41 cm (16 inches) dbh. Gyrfalcons raised two young in the raven's nest in 1966.

lanatum, Ribes triste, and 1.2-m-high ferns, *Dryopteris dilatata*.

In addition to these tree-sized stands of Balsam Poplar, very small patches of small plants (mostly less than 5 m tall and 3-8 cm dbh) that form open Tall Shrub Thickets, occur at scattered localities in both the Southern Uplands and Northern Uplands: several spots on the slopes above the Nome River, on the outwash of Basin Creek at the Nome River, several places on the slopes along the upper Inmachuk River, and on the creek bed at Serpentine Hot Springs. Racine and Anderson (1979) found that one 4.5-cm-diameter stem on the Inmachuk River was 42 years old!

Largely because of the small size and isolated nature of the poplar forests on the Seward Peninsula, they serve almost entirely as an auxiliary habitat for birds that are already present because of other habitats—especially the tall shrub birds and the medium shrub birds that also use tall shrubs. Varied Thrushes, which favor dense cover, use poplar stands extensively when they are available, and Bohemian Waxwings seemed to restrict their activities to this habitat at the western extremity of their range in 1977 along Bear Creek and Fox River west of Council.

Coniferous Forest and Woodland

Spruce forests, an extension of the interior Alaska taiga, occur on slopes and along well-drained river banks in the Southern Uplands as far west as the Niukluk and Fish river drainages (Figures 18 and 19). The stature of the forests varies with local environmental conditions, and the size and density of trees generally decrease from

Figure 18. Coniferous Forest and Woodland habitat on the Fish River flats near White Mountain, 3 July 1972. Note the restriction of the White Spruce to the warmest, best-drained substrates along the riverbed.

Figure 19. Coniferous Forest and Woodland habitat of White Spruce, with Medium Shrub Thicket of Dwarf Birch in the foreground, along the Fox River at Milepost 68 Council Road, 3 July 1977. Many coniferous forest birds extend their range to the geographic limits of this habitat.

east to west. Spruce forests are extensive north and northwest of Koyuk; on the south and southwest-facing slopes the tallest and densest stands are composed of White Spruce (*Picea glauca*) 9-12 m (30-40 ft) tall, with some up to 46 cm (18 inches) dbh. Forests about Elim are only slightly less in extent and stature, with many spruce in the densest stands reaching 25-30 cm dbh and a few getting to 46 cm dbh. Both of these localities have some Paper Birch (*Betula papyrifera*) mixed among the White Spruce, some young and some very old, and some Black Spruce (*Picea mariana*) occur on the less well-drained sites.

Stands are more open in the Niukluk and Fish river drainages. Forests about Council and a tongue of forest that reaches up the Fox River to 163°43′ W near the Council road are open, with canopy coverages of 10% or less, but many trees reach 25 cm dbh (one dead trunk in 1977 was 35 cm dbh). Spruce stringers along the river banks in McCarthys Marsh in 1973 were 9-11 m tall and 33-46 cm dbh. A few scattered, sentinel spruce get up the Niukluk River to 65°03′ N. A few spruce also straggle into the headwaters of the Koyuk River and adjacent Kugruk River and the west fork of the Buckland River.

Alder and, to a lesser extent, willow shrubs form an understory in many of the spruce forests. Ground cover consists largely of lichens and mosses.

Birds of the coniferous forest community follow the spruce forests and woodlands to their extremities. In a patch of woodland at 163°42′ W along the Fox River on 3 July 1977, I recorded the Gray Jay, Boreal Chickadee, Ruby-crowned Kinglet, Yellow-rumped Warbler, Pine Grosbeak, White-winged Crossbill, and Dark-eyed Junco.

Comparative Avian Densities

All birds that were seen or heard during all my field expeditions in the various parts of the Seward Peninsula were enumerated and recorded, and the duration or distance (or both) covered in each observational period was documented, as was a general description of habitats traversed. Unfortunately, many transects crossed mosaics of habitats, and often counts were not stratified by habitat. In retrospect, however, it has been possible to extract from my field notes a number of counts made in adequately delineated habitats and to thus obtain relative population density figures for several of the more extensive habitats of the region.

The number of birds recorded per unit of time has been used as the comparative unit of measure, since stationary counts were included. True density figures are not available, since transect widths were not standardized nor were compensations made for differences in detectability among the various bird species. Also, as censuses were never duplicated (except some in subsequent years), counts are simply the total number of birds seen or heard in these habitats and cannot be directly correlated to number of breeding pairs. The counts were made between late June and mid-July and hence are essentially of local individuals, though not necessarily breeders. Non-breeders are a particularly important population component in wetland habitats utilized by waterfowl and shorebirds.

The total numbers of birds recorded per hour in the respective habitats are given in Table 3. The bird numbers for Dwarf Shrub Mat habitat and the Salt Grass Meadow-Pond habitat complex may be a bit inflated compared to the other habitats, because the terrain is more easily traversed so more area can be covered and hence more birds seen per unit time.

In spite of this probable upward bias, and in spite of the fact that a few birds associated with damper alpine habitats were included in the totals, the Dwarf Shrub Mat habitat supported the lowest avian density of all habitats for which data were available—only 12.2 birds/h, and many of these were only foragers from other nesting habitats.

Wetland habitats supported the highest population densities, though many of the birds using these habitats were either nonbreeding or postbreeding birds. Counts showed highest densities in the Ridged Wet Meadow-Pond complex (97.4/h) and the Salt Grass Meadow-Pond complex (107.2/h), but they included flocks of pintails, Brant, Canada and Greater White-fronted geese, and other waterfowl and many shorebirds, including feeding flocks of Semipalmated and Western sandpipers, Dunlins, Bar-tailed Godwits, and Long-billed Dowitchers. As early as late June, sandpipers begin to gather in littoral areas for feeding, and their numbers gradually increase as failed breeders, postbreeders, and juveniles leave the breeding territories. Nesting densities in these wetland habitats are not high, however; most average 1.0-3.4 nests/ha, although densities of up to 9 nests/ha have been found on Cape Espenberg (Table 3).

Away from the wetland complexes, highest densities of birds occurred in the shrub thickets. Among these thickets, Low Shrub Thicket habitat had the lowest density (40.1 birds/ha) and the Medium Shrub Thicket habitat had the highest (69.3 birds/ha). In spite of the fact that medium-height shrubs are often closely associated (adjacent or intermixed) with tall shrubs and the fact that medium shrub birds readily utilize tall shrubs, actual census counts in the Tall Shrub Thicket habitat showed somewhat

Table 3. Avian densities in various habitats, Seward Peninsula, Alaska (Number of birds per unit time or area).

	Tall Shrub	Medium Shrub	Low Shrub	Dwarf Shrub Meadow	Wet Meadow/ Dwarf Shrub Meadow mosaic	Wet Meadow	Dwarf Shrub Mat	Salt Grass Meadow-Pond complex	Grass Meadow
Kessel (this study) Overall, 153 h*	62.7/h	69.3/h 56.1/h	40.1/h	24.6/h	97.4/h	-	12.2/h	107.2/h	-
Wright (1979)									
Arctic River, 53 ha*	-	4.8 pr/ha	-	2.2 pr/ha	2.4 pr/ha	3.4 pr/ha	-	-	-
Kitluk River, 35 ha	-	3.1 pr/ha	-	2.2 pr/ha	1.4 pr/ha	1.0 pr/ha	1.8 pr/ha	1.8 pr/ha	0
Schamel et al. (1979) Cape Espenberg, 333 ha									
1976	-	-	-	-	1.4 nests/ha	7.7 nests/ha	-	-	
1977	-	-	-	-	2.1 nests/ha	9.0 nests/ha	-	-	2.1 nests/ha
Connors (1978)									
Wales, 25 ha	-	-	-	-	1.2 pr/ha	-	-	-	-
Shishmaref Barrier Strip, 17-18 AU 1977, 13,000 ha	-	-	-	-	-	-	-	50.0 birds/ha	-

* Total effort in all habitats, either time spent (h) or area censused (ha)

lower densities (62.7 birds/ha). In Interior Alaska, Tall Shrub Thicket is the most productive woody avian habitat (Spindler and Kessel 1980). Several factors may account for the slightly lower avian density in Tall Shrub Thicket on the Seward Peninsula compared to Medium Shrub Thicket. Of the two basic types of tall shrubs on the Peninsula (see above), the riparian *Salix alaxensis* has an open growth form that provides scant cover and the hillside stands of *Alnus crispa* have low levels of primary productivity (Spindler and Kessel 1980). Also, none of the birds with preferences for tall shrubs in the taiga are abundant as far west as the Seward Peninsula—Alder Flycatcher, Yellow Warbler, Blackpoll Warbler, Northern Waterthrush, and Rusty Blackbird—and only one, the Yellow Warbler, is even common.

Densities in the Dwarf Shrub Meadow habitat, the most extensive tundra habitat of the Peninsula, were intermediate (24.6/ha), but low compared to shrub thickets.

At the mouths of the Arctic and Kitluk rivers, Wright (1979) found that shrub thickets had the highest nesting densities of the habitats he censused. He combined the Low Shrub and Medium Shrub thickets and, with repeated censuses of a total of 10.8 ha at three sites, found average nesting densities ranged from 2.6 to 4.8 pairs/ha. In comparison, a weighted average of my counts in Low Shrub and Medium Shrub thickets showed 56.1 birds/h. In censuses of a total of 52 ha at three sites of "Tussock Shrub" (= Dwarf Shrub Meadow), Wright also found intermediate nesting densities—2.2 pairs/ha.

Avian Species Abundance

The relative abundance of the terrestrial bird species during summer on the Seward Peninsula as a whole has been derived from the total numbers of individuals of each species that I counted during the course of field work between 1967 and 1977. During this time, a "transect," consisting of approximately 1140 km (710 miles) by foot, 1415 km (880 miles) by automobile, 370 km (230 miles) by boat, and 320 stationary counts, was made over representative regions and habitats of the Peninsula. Complete counts were kept of every independent bird (not individuals of dependent broods) of each species seen or heard. While regions and habitats undoubtedly were not visited in exact proportion to their representation on the Peninsula, attempts were made to visit all habitats in all physiographic regions, and the total counts provide a fair approximation of the overall comparative or relative abundance of each species. Tables 4-7 list, in decreasing order of abundance, the more numerous species of various groupings of terrestrial birds. The **actual** numbers listed in the tables are meaningless in themselves; they are included solely for their **comparative** significance.

Numbers and relative abundance of seabirds have been derived from colony counts, obtained primarily from other observers (see Table 8).

Relative abundance rankings are heavily weighted toward large, conspicuous birds, which are more visible so that greater proportions of the total population are seen than are those of small or inconspicuous birds. For example, cranes, robins, and Wilson's Warblers are all considered fairly common breeders on the Peninsula on the basis of the numbers I recorded, yet the total numbers of both robins and Wilson's Warblers on the Peninsula are probably far greater than those of cranes. Overall, I have ranked 16 species as abundant on the Seward Peninsula and 23 species as common (Table 9).

On a more refined scale, at a given locality, habitat availability and its degree of utilization largely determine the relative abundance of otherwise generally distributed species. Most birds on the Peninsula are relatively stenophilic in their habitat preferences, and their presence at a given site can be equated to the availability of specific habitats. Other birds, such as the Glaucous Gull, robin, and redpolls, are euryphilic, utilizing a relatively wide range of habitats.

Tables 10-12, derived from a total of 289 hours of observation in the more extensive habitats or habitat complexes of the Peninsula, compare the use of these habitats by different species of birds and thus indicate broadly the birds' habitat preferences. These data, as well as species-specific habitat density data from Connors (1978), Schamel et al. (1979), and Wright (1979) are included in the accounts in the Annotated List of Species.

35

Table 4.   Comparative abundance ratings of the most numerous waterfowl on the Seward Peninsula, Alaska.

Species	No. recorded
Northern Pintail	3186
Oldsquaw	1551
Brant	1475 *
Common Eider	966
Canada Goose	709
Greater Scaup	662
American Wigeon	520
Tundra Swan	454
Red-breasted Merganser	381
Black Scoter	304
White-winged Scoter	297
Green-winged Teal	236
Emperor Goose	116
Greater White-fronted Goose	111
Surf Scoter	88

*Mostly inshore coastal migrants

Table 5.   Comparative abundance ratings of the most numerous
             shorebirds on the Seward Peninsula, Alaska.

Species	No. recorded
Western Sandpiper	2869
Semipalmated Sandpiper	2312
Red-necked Phalarope	1637
Bar-tailed Godwit	1286
Dunlin	1070
Red Phalarope	681
Lesser Golden-Plover	555
Common Snipe	377
Long-billed Dowitcher	358
Whimbrel	280
Black Turnstone	262
Pectoral Sandpiper	153
Semipalmated Plover	147
Ruddy Turnstone	122
Hudsonian Godwit	85
Wandering Tattler	81
Baird's Sandpiper	76
Rock Sandpiper	62
Spotted Sandpiper	45
Bristle-thighed Curlew	43
Red Knot	26
Black-bellied Plover	13
Least Sandpiper	8

Table 6.   Comparative abundance ratings of the most numerous
            Laridae on the Seward Peninsula, Alaska, excluding
            coastal cliff colonies.

Species	No. recorded
Glaucous Gull	3147
Arctic Tern	2144
Black-legged Kittiwake	1262
Long-tailed Jaeger	810
Mew Gull	615
Parasitic Jaeger	380
Sabine's Gull	298
Aleutian Tern	193
Pomarine Jaeger	94

Table 7.   Comparative abundance ratings of the most numerous,
            ubiquitous shrub thicket birds and the sparrows of the
            Seward Peninsula, Alaska.

Species	No. recorded
Common Redpoll, including "Hoary"	3980
Lapland Longspur	2812
Savannah Sparrow	2083
American Tree Sparrow	1994
Gray-cheeked Thrush	1543
Yellow Wagtail	1351
White-crowned Sparrow	1188
Fox Sparrow	1157
Arctic Warbler	580
Yellow Warbler	573
Northern Waterthrush	388
American Robin	377
Golden-crowned Sparrow	322
Wilson's Warbler	317
Varied Thrush	296
Blackpoll Warbler	269
Willow Ptarmigan	173
Orange-crowned Warbler	141

Table 8. Numbers of adult seabirds in Coastal Cliffs and Block-Fields habitat, Seward Peninsula, Alaska.

	Pelagic Cormorant	Glaucous Gull	Black-legged Kittiwake	Murre sp.	Common Murre	Thick-billed Murre
Bald Head[1]	X	X		X		
Cape Darby	325-450[2]	290[3]				
Rocky Point[2]	415-900	380				
Square Rock[2]	15-18	24-26	800-1500		4000-6000	50
Bluff	100-170[2]	75-200[2]	700-12,500[18]		12,300-70,000[19]	500[2]
E. Topkok[3]	59	32				
Topkok Head[2]	320-385	304				
Sledge Island[2]	300-500	45	1000-2500		2000-2500	400-700*
Cape Riley	100[3]		75[20]			
York-Lost River Terraces	175 nests[14]	X[4]	X[4]			
Cape Mountain	20[8]		X[8]			
Fairway Rock[2]	25	125	650	4000	X[11]	X[12]
King Island[2]	100	100	6000	76,000	38,000	38,000
Little Diomede Island[2]	140	160	20,000	60,000	25,000	35,000
Rex Pt—Sullivan Bluffs	40[2]	35[2]	550[2]-1040[9]	2550[6]-3000[9]	1600[9]	1400[9]
Toawlevic Point	12[9]	48[9]	280[2]-500[9]	1300[2]-6500[9]	3250[9]	3250[9]
Cape Deceit	5[13]	100[7]	300[7]	1700[9]-4396[6]	100+[7]	500[7]
Ninemile Point area		14[9]-80[8]	5[8]	5[8]		
Motherwood Point area	1[9]	54[9]	X[8]	X[8]		
Puffin and Chamisso islands	0[9]-9[8]	68[9]-155[8]	3300[9]-4000[8]	10,700[9]-15,320[8]	11,260[8]	4060[8]
Totals (rounded)	2300-3000	1900	43,000-50,000	192,000-250,000		

Table 8. Numbers of adult seabirds in Coastal Cliffs and Block-Fields habitat, Seward Peninsula, Alaska. (cont.)

	Pigeon Guillemot	Parakeet Auklet	Crested Auklet	Least Auklet	Horned Puffin	Tufted Puffin
Bald Head[1]					X	
Cape Darby					575[2]	51[2]
Rocky Point[2]	3				190-210	6
Square Rock[2]					70-400	1-6
Bluff	2-4	50-75[2]			600-3000[2]	10[2]
E. Topkok[3]	13-15				31	
Topkok Head[2]	8-10				50-180	30-35
Sledge Island[2]		85-165**			160	15
Cape Riley	X[16]				100[3]	2[16]
York-Lost River Terraces					X[4]	X[4]
Cape Mountain	X[5]				X[5,8]	
Fairway Rock[2]	100	500	10,000	15,000	75	1000
King Island[2]	940	35,000	35,000	85,000	10,000	1000
Little Diomede Island[2]	275	15,000	100,000	600,000	10,000	1000
Rex Pt—Sullivan Bluffs					70[9]	X[8]
Toawlevic Point					400[9]	X[8,10]
Cape Deceit	X[8]				300-500[7]	X[10,15,17]
Ninemile Point area	X[8]				40[9]	
Motherwood Point area					40[9]	
Puffin and Chamisso islands					12,800[9]-14,500[8]	20[8,9]
Totals (rounded)	1400	51,000	145,000	700,000	35,500-40,500	3200

Table 8. Numbers of adult seabirds in Coastal Cliffs and Block-Fields habitat, Seward Peninsula, Alaska. (cont.).

X   Present

*   Thick-billed Murres outnumbered Common Murres 5:3, 21-22 June 1968 (D. G. Roseneau unpubl. notes)

**   1000+ pairs, 21-22 June 1968 (D. G. Roseneau unpubl. notes)

1   Local residents of Elim and Koyuk

2   Drury et al. 1981:Tables 13, 14, 17 [1975-1978]

3   Steele and Drury 1977:Table 5 [1976]

4   M. Lenarz pers. comm. [July-August 1972]

5   Bailey 1943 [June-July 1922]

6   Schamel et al. 1979 [9 July 1978]

7   Kessel and Gibson pers. obs. [23 June and 29 July 1973]

8   Sowls et al. 1978

9   Nelson and Sowls 1985 [mid-August 1981]

10   G. Barr pers. comm.

11   D. R. Paulson unpubl. notes (no Thick-billed Murres seen 11 July 1978)

12   Bailey 1925, 1943 (only Thick-billed Murres seen 25-27 June 1921)

13   J. M. Wright pers. comm. [4 July 1978]

14   R. J. King pers. comm. [1982]

15   Hudson 1957 [7-8 August 1956]

16   D. A. Woodby unpubl. notes [first week July 1980]

17   J. D. Walters unpubl. notes [mid-July-Aug 1984-86]

18   See Table 15 [1975-1987]

19   See Table 16 [1975-1985]

20   D. G. Roseneau pers. comm. [9 July 1969]

Table 9.   List of abundant and common bird species of the Seward Peninsula, Alaska.

Abundant	Common
Northern Pintail	Red-throated Loon
King Eider*	Snow Goose*
Oldsquaw	Brant*
Semipalmated Sandpiper	Canada Goose
Western Sandpiper	Greater Scaup
Red-necked Phalarope	Common Eider
Glaucous Gull	Sandhill Crane*
Arctic Tern	Lesser Golden-Plover
Common Murre	Bar-tailed Godwit
Least Auklet	Pectoral Sandpiper*
Crested Auklet	Dunlin
Gray-cheeked Thrush	Red Phalarope
American Tree Sparrow	Long-tailed Jaeger
Savannah Sparrow	Mew Gull
Lapland Longspur	Black-legged Kittiwake
Common Redpoll	Thick-billed Murre
	Parakeet Auklet
	Horned Puffin
	Arctic Warbler
	Yellow Wagtail
	Yellow Warbler
	Fox Sparrow
	White-crowned Sparrow

* This abundance occurs only during migration

Table 10.   Abundance of bird species in two wetland habitat complexes of the Seward Peninsula, Alaska: Ridged Wet Meadow-Pond complex, primarily from coastal lowlands, and Salt Grass Meadow-Pond complex (Number of birds per hour of observation).

Species	Ridged Wet Meadow-Pond complex (51.0 h)*	Salt Grass Meadow-Pond complex (8.0 h)*
Glaucous Gull	10.5	8.8
Northern Pintail	10.1	11.6
Common Eider	7.9	1.9
Oldsquaw	6.5	5.1
Semipalmated Sandpiper	6.4	7.6
Red-necked Phalarope	6.0	11.9
Dunlin	5.9	9.1
Red-throated Loon	5.4	0
Western Sandpiper	5.1	4.8
Red Phalarope	5.0	12.0
Arctic Tern	4.2	9.0
Lapland Longspur	4.2	0
Greater Scaup	2.1	0.3
Long-billed Dowitcher	2.0	5.9
Savannah Sparrow	1.9	0
Pectoral Sandpiper	1.8	0
Pacific Loon	1.5	0
Canada Goose	1.4**	0
Parasitic Jaeger	1.4	0.4
Sandhill Crane	1.3	0
Sabine's Gull	1.2	2.5
Emperor Goose	1.0	2.3
Greater White-fronted Goose	0.7**	0.1
Ruddy Turnstone	0.6	1.0
Lesser Golden-Plover	0.6	0
Bar-tailed Godwit	0.4	6.3
Long-tailed Jaeger	0.4	0
Brant	0.2	2.0
Black Turnstone	0.2	2.8
Whimbrel	0.2	0

* Total hours of observation
** All Interior Lowlands

Table 11.   Abundance of bird species in various shrub habitats of the Seward Peninsula, Alaska (Number of birds per hour of observation).

Species	Dwarf Shrub Mat (77.2 h)**	Dwarf Shrub Meadow (22.3 h)	Low Shrub Thicket (14.8 h)	Medium Shrub Thicket (17.9 h)	Tall Shrub Thicket (20.5 h)
Common Redpoll, including "Hoary"	1.0	0.6	3.7	11.6	9.1
Lapland Longspur	2.0	6.9	8.8 *	4.3 *	0.2
Savannah Sparrow	0.3	1.5	8.1	5.9 *	1.2 *
American Tree Sparrow	<0.1	1.8	5.7	7.3 *	5.6 *
Gray-cheeked Thrush			0.8	7.6	8.2
Fox Sparrow			1.1	7.4	5.7 *
White-crowned Sparrow			1.9	3.0 *	5.2 *
Wilson's Warbler			0.1	1.5	1.7
Western Sandpiper	0.6	3.4	1.0	0.2	
Semipalmated Sandpiper	0.1	3.9			
Arctic Warbler				5.1	0.8
Yellow Warbler			0.1	1.4	5.9
Northern Waterthrush				0.1	2.2
Blackpoll Warbler				0.1	1.9
American Robin	0.4		0.2	0.7	1.4
Yellow Wagtail	0.14	0.3	6.6	0.7	1.3 *
Golden-crowned Sparrow			1.1	2.4 *	0.4
Varied Thrush					0.8
Orange-crowned Warbler				1.5	0.9
Lesser Golden-Plover	1.1	1.4			
Bar-tailed Godwit		1.3			
Whimbrel		1.3			
Willow Ptarmigan		0.5	1.0	0.2	
Long-tailed Jaeger	0.6	0.9			

*   Number biased upward by birds seeking elevated lookouts when disturbed by intruders and by lower-height shrubs usually being intermixed with or adjacent to taller height classes

**   Total hours of observation

Table 12.   Abundance of bird species in alpine tundra and Dwarf Shrub Mat
of the Seward Peninsula, Alaska (77.2 h of observation).

Species	No. birds/h
Lapland Longspur	2.0
Snow Bunting	2.0
Water Pipit	1.8
Lesser Golden-Plover	1.1
Common Redpoll, including "Hoary"	1.0
Western Sandpiper	0.6
Northern Wheatear	0.5
Long-tailed Jaeger	0.5
Red-throated Pipit	0.4
Baird's Sandpiper	0.4
Rock Sandpiper	0.4
American Robin	0.4
Savannah Sparrow	0.3
Horned Lark	0.3
Yellow Wagtail	0.1
Ruddy Turnstone	0.1
Rock Ptarmigan	<0.1
Rosy Finch	<0.1
American Tree Sparrow	<0.1

Patterns of Distribution

Bird distribution is a dynamic phenomenon, changing over time in response to many interrelated factors. The present-day distribution is only a "snapshot" in a continuing evolution of a species' range and is the culmination of the species' (and its ancestor's) responses to both historical and contemporary factors. The most determinant historical factors relative to the avifauna of the Seward Peninsula are (1) the geographic centers of evolution of the various taxa (i.e., where families, genera, species, and subspecies differentiated) and (2) the earth's geologic history from the Tertiary to the present, especially in terms of timing relative to events in avian evolution. Of the contemporary factors, usually the most influential are habitat availability, current population centers, and migration routes.

Historically, three land masses that were disconnected and reconnected at several times during the Tertiary were major differentiation centers for avifaunas of the Northern Hemisphere: Eurasia, North America, and South America (Mayr 1946). The Bering Land Bridge that intermittently connected Eurasia with North America, most recently in the Pleistocene, was especially significant to the avifauna of the Seward Peninsula, since the Peninsula formed a part of this connection. When exposed, this land mass provided a passageway for the exchange of land and freshwater birds between Eurasia and North America but served as a barrier to the movement of seabirds between the Pacific and Arctic oceans; the influence was reversed when the land bridge was inundated by raised sea levels.

The effectiveness of these barriers varies among species and species groups. In spite of flight capabilities, the dispersal of some avian taxa may be blocked by certain geographic features. Other taxa are not blocked, however, or are differentially retarded in their dispersal. Some seabirds regularly cross land masses during migration (e.g., Brant, eiders, Parasitic Jaeger), and some land birds likewise cross large expanses of ocean (e.g., Short-eared Owl, Savannah and Golden-crowned sparrows, crossbills). The regular crossing of the northern Bering Sea by some land and freshwater migrants that otherwise do not cross oceanic expanses, however, indicates that these species established their migration routes across the region when the Bering Land Bridge was present. The Emperor Goose, for example, first moves eastward in spring from its wintering grounds in the Aleutian Islands and the Alaska Peninsula into Bristol Bay before heading north and then northwestward across the Bering Sea (Eisenhauer and Kirkpatrick 1977). Sandhill Cranes cross a wide expanse of the northern Bering Shelf when migrating in spring to breeding grounds in the Anadyr-Chukotsk Peninsula region (Kessel 1984). Snow Geese sometimes cut directly across the western end of the Seward Peninsula and the southern Chukchi Sea on a direct flight to nesting grounds on Wrangel Island (Flock 1972). Such passerines as the Arctic Warbler, Bluethroat, White and Yellow wagtails, and Red-throated Pipit from Asia and the Gray-cheeked Thrush from North America undoubtedly used the land bridge, with its tundra-steppe vegetation, as they developed their migration patterns between the two continents.

Zoogeographic Affinities

Based primarily on the apparent differentiation centers of the encompassed taxa, five contemporary avifaunal elements are represented on the Seward Peninsula. Determination of these historical differentiation centers is based on multiple lines of historical and contemporary evidence (e.g., see Mayr 1946, Darlington 1957, Fay and Cade 1959), with current centers of breeding abundance being primal evidence at the subspecific level and for most species. The five avifaunal elements can be referred to as Old World, North American, South American, Panboreal (after Mayr 1946) and Beringian.

The first three elements represent taxa that evolved in the three major land masses mentioned above. The birds of the Panboreal element are widely distributed circumboreal or nearly circumboreal taxa, so well represented in both the Old World and North America that their differentiation centers cannot be determined. In fact, some forms have apparently moved back and forth between the regions, and families and genera have had secondary differentiation centers on one or the other land masses. This Panboreal element is particularly prevalent in the tundra and taiga regions, undoubtedly because of the recurring presence of the Bering Land Bridge, which facilitated historical mixing of land faunas when present and oceanic faunas when inundated.

The Bering Land Bridge also provided conditions whereby the Bering Sea area became a regional differentiation center for a Beringian avifaunal element, separating populations at various geologic times and permitting genetic changes in isolated refugia that gave rise to new taxa. Both physical and climatic conditions provided isolating mechanisms for evolving Beringian forms. During cold periods, the exposed Bering Land Bridge, with its tundra-steppe vegetation, was at times isolated from continental populations by glaciers and ice sheets; and during warmer interglacials, the waters inundating the Strait separated both Beringian and Panboreal forms. The unique Beringian element has been discussed relative to the Pribilof Islands by Palmer (1899), Nunivak Island by Swarth (1934), Aleutian Islands by Murie (1959), and St. Lawrence Island by Fay and Cade (1959).

Of the regularly occurring breeding birds and visitants on the Seward Peninsula today (Table 13), 47% are of North American derivation and only 6% are Old World; another 15% are Panboreal. It is thus apparent that the Bering Strait, when present, is a significant barrier to the dispersal of many birds. Populations of a number of Panboreal taxa have become separated at the Bering Strait and have become isolated enough to differentiate at least to the subspecific level on the respective sides of the Strait. This subspecific differentiation, most of which has probably occurred since the most recent flooding of the Strait 10,000-14,000 years ago, accounts in large part for the high proportion of North American forms on the Seward Peninsula.

Birds of the Beringian element make up the second largest group (30%) on the Peninsula. This high representation reflects the position of the Peninsula as part of the continental land mass that forms the land bridge during glacial periods. The small number of birds of South American affinity is expected in view of the distance and climatic barriers involved.

A different zoogeographic pattern is shown by the birds that reach the Seward Peninsula only on a casual or accidental basis (Table 14). Here, most birds are either Old World or North American, essentially equally represented. As much as anything, this situation seems to reflect the wanderings of birds that have never bred and migrants that get lost, overfly their normal breeding ranges, or are displaced by severe weather, lack of food resources, or other environmental factors. Under these circumstances, the distances from normal ranges to the Seward Peninsula are equal, whether over land or sea.

Contemporary Distribution Patterns

Superimposed on the major historically derived distribution patterns on the Seward Peninsula are some patterns mediated by contemporary factors. The most obvious factor is that of habitat availability. One of the main reasons for the distinctiveness of the avifauna of the southeastern quadrant of the Peninsula is the presence of taiga vegetation, which allows forest birds, particularly those of coniferous woodlands, to breed in this portion of the Peninsula (e.g., Spruce Grouse, Northern Goshawk, Great Horned Owl, Gray Jay, Black-capped and Boreal chickadees, Ruby-crowned Kinglet, Varied Thrush, Bohemian Waxwing, Yellow-rumped Warbler, Dark-eyed Junco, Pine Grosbeak). In the Northern Uplands, Alder Flycatchers, Blackpoll Warblers, and Rusty Blackbirds get only as far west as the Inmachuk River, beyond which there is an absence of Tall Shrub Thicket of sufficient density to provide proper nesting habitat. Similarly, Orange-crowned and Yellow warblers and Northern Waterthrushes are limited by growths of Medium Shrub Thicket, which are scarce west of Serpentine Hot Springs.

Overall, as pointed out under Vegetation, 166° W is an approximate dividing line between Young's (1971) floristic Zone 3 to the west and Zone 4 to the east. The comparatively harsh conditions in Zone 3 restrict growth of shrubbery, so birds of tall and medium shrubs are correspondingly rare or absent west of 166° W. The distribution of some species appears to be even more directly related to climate. The cold soil may prevent the Bank Swallow from nesting successfully in Zone 3, and dependence on flying insects for food may limit nesting by the Say's Phoebe and Cliff Swallow this far west. Most land birds, including ptarmigan and redpolls, desert this region in winter.

The relatively high densities of Wandering Tattlers in the western Southern Uplands is apparently the result of available habitat provided by the morainal deposits left by Pleistocene glaciations.

The proximity of the base of the Peninsula to the range peripheries of a number of North American bird species enables them to extend their breeding ranges onto the base of the Peninsula. In addition to the forest birds mentioned above, several shrub and waterbirds fit this category: Northern Shoveler; American Wigeon; Lesser Yellowlegs; Solitary, Spotted, and Least sandpipers; Alder Flycatcher; Northern Waterthrush; Lincoln's Sparrow; and Rusty Blackbird. Associated with the extension of the breeding ranges of some of these shrub and waterbirds is an apparent dispersal

Table 13. Zoogeographic affinities of the Seward Peninsula avifauna. Listings include all regularly occurring breeders and visitants, even if very rare, but exclude regular transient migrants and Southern Hemisphere breeders. For purposes of illustrating affinities, relationships are carried to the subspecific level, based primarily on assumptions made from a review of recent literature.

Panboreal

Gavia stellata
Anas platyrhynchos platyrhynchos
Anas acuta acuta
Anas clypeata
Somateria spectabilis
Clangula hyemalis
Melanitta perspicillata
Mergus serrator
Falco rusticolus
Pluvialis squatarola
Arenaria interpres interpres
Phalaropus lobatus
Phalaropus fulicaria
Stercorarius pomarinus
Stercorarius parasiticus
Stercorarius longicaudus
Rissa tridactyla
Xema sabini
Sterna paradisaea
Nyctea scandiaca
Asio flammeus flammeus
Riparia riparia riparia
Plectrophenax nivalis nivalis

Old World

Gavia arctica viridigularis
Anas penelope
Charadrius morinellus
Cepphus grylle mandtii
Luscinia svecica svecica
Oenanthe oenanthe oenanthe
Motacilla alba ocularis
Anthus cervinus
Carduelis flammea flammea

Beringian

Gavia adamsii
Fulmarus glacialis rodgersii
Phalacrocorax pelagicus
Chen canagica
Branta bernicla nigricans
Aythya marila nearctica
Somateria mollissima v-nigra
Somateria fischeri
Polysticta stelleri
Histrionicus histrionicus
Melanitta nigra americana
Lagopus lagopus alascensis
Lagopus mutus nelsoni
Pluvialis dominica fulva
Heteroscelus incanus
Numenius tahitiensis
Limosa lapponica baueri
Arenaria melanocephala
Aphriza virgata
Calidris canutus rogersi
Calidris mauri
Calidris ruficollis
Calidris melanotos
Calidris ptilocnemis tschuktschorum
Limnodromus scolopaceus
Larus argentatus vegae
Larus schistisagus
Larus glaucescens
Larus hyperboreus barrovianus
Sterna aleutica
Uria aalge inornata
Uria lomvia arra
Cepphus columba columba
Brachyramphus brevirostris
Synthliboramphus antiquus
Cyclorrhynchus psittacula

Table 13. Zoogeographic affinities of the Seward Peninsula avifauna. (cont.)

Beringian

Aethia pusilla
Aethia cristatella
Fratercula cirrhata
Fratercula corniculata
Eremophila alpestris arcticola
Phylloscopus borealis kennicotti
Motacilla flava tschutschensis
Anthus spinoletta pacificus
Plectrophenax hyperboreus
Calcarius lapponicus alascensis
Leucosticte arctoa tephrocotis

South American

Empidonax alnorum
Sayornis saya yukonensis/saya

North American

Gavia immer
Gavia pacifica
Podiceps auritus cornutus
Podiceps grisegena holboellii
Cygnus columbianus columbianus
Anser albifrons frontalis
Branta canadensis parvipes/taverneri
Anas crecca carolinensis
Anas americana
Aythya valisineria
Melanitta fusca deglandi
Bucephala clangula americana
Bucephala albeola
Pandion haliaetus carolinensis
Circus cyaneus hudsonius
Accipiter gentilis atricapillus
Buteo lagopus sanctijohannis
Aquila chrysaetos canadensis
Falco columbarius bendirei
Falco peregrinus anatum/tundrius
Dendragapus canadensis osgoodi
Grus canadensis canadensis
Pluvialis dominica dominica
Charadrius semipalmatus
Tringa flavipes
Tringa solitaria
Actitis macularia

Numenius phaeopus hudsonicus
Limosa haemastica
Calidris pusilla
Calidris minutilla
Calidris bairdii
Calidris alpina pacifica
Gallinago gallinago delicata
Larus philadelphia
Larus canus brachyrhynchus
Larus argentatus smithsonianus
Alle alle alle
Bubo virginianus algistus/lagophonus
Surnia ulula caparoch
Aegolius funereus richardsoni
Ceryle alcyon caurina
Picoides pubescens nelsoni
Tachycineta bicolor
Hirundo pyrrhonota hypopolia
Perisoreus canadensis pacificus
Corvus corax principalis
Parus atricapillus turneri
Parus hudsonicus hudsonicus
Cinclus mexicanus unicolor
Regulus calendula calendula
Catharus minimus minimus
Catharus ustulatus almae
Catharus guttatus guttatus
Turdus migratorius migratorius
Ixoreus naevius meruloides
Bombycilla garrulus pallidiceps
Lanius excubitor borealis/invictus
Vermivora celata celata
Dendroica petechia amnicola
Dendroica coronata hooveri/coronata
Dendroica striata
Seiurus noveboracensis
Wilsonia pusilla pileolata
Spizella arborea ochracea
Passerculus sandwichensis anthinus
Passerella iliaca zaboria
Melospiza lincolnii lincolnii
Zonotrichia atricapilla
Zonotrichia leucophrys gambelii
Junco hyemalis hyemalis
Euphagus carolinus carolinus
Pinicola enucleator leucura/alascensis
Loxia leucoptera leucoptera

Table 14. Zoogeographic affinities of Seward Peninsula birds occurring as casual or very rare migrants and casual or accidental visitants.

Old World

Cygnus cygnus
Anser fabalis
Anas crecca crecca/nimia
Anas formosa
Aythya fuligula
Mergus merganser merganser
Charadrius mongolus
Charadrius hiaticula
Tringa glareola
Xenus cinereus
Numenius phaeopus variegatus
Numenius madagascariensis
Limosa limosa melanuroides
Calidris temminckii
Calidris ferruginea
Philomachus pugnax
Larus ridibundus
Rhodostethia rosea
Sterna hirundo longipennis
Cuculus canorus canorus
Cuculus saturatus horsfieldi
Jynx torquilla chinensis
Delichon urbica lagopoda
Luscinia calliope
Turdus obscurus
Motacilla lugens
Anthus trivialis trivialis
Pyrrhula pyrrhula cassinii

Panboreal

Oceanodroma leucorhoa leucorhoa
Anas strepera strepera

South American

Trochilidae
Contopus borealis
Contopus sordidulus

North American

Cygnus buccinator
Branta bernicla hrota
Aythya collaris
Aythya affinis
Mergus merganser americanus
Haliaeetus leucocephalus alascanus
Accipiter striatus velox
Falco sparverius sparverius
Fulica americana americana
Charadrius vociferus
Bartramia longicauda
Calidris himantopus
Tryngites subruficollis
Larus thayeri
Columba fasciata monilis
Zenaida macroura marginella
Colaptes auratus auratus
Progne subis subis
Tachycineta thalassina lepida
Hirundo rustica erythrogaster
Sitta canadensis
Agelaius phoeniceus arctolegus
Molothrus ater

Beringian

Oceanodroma furcata furcata
Heteroscelus brevipes
Calidris tenuirostris
Calidris ptilocnemis quarta
Brachyramphus marmoratus
      marmoratus

route from the taiga of the southeastern portion of the Peninsula, northward up the Fish and Niukluk river valleys, through the low pass between the Bendeleben and Kigluaik mountains, and into the Pilgrim and Kuzitrin river drainages to Imuruk Basin. Red-necked Grebes and White-winged Scoters nest in Imuruk Basin in concentrations not found anywhere else on the Peninsula, and the densities of Varied Thrushes, Blackpoll Warblers, and Rusty Blackbirds are unique along this route, with these species extending as far west as trees or tall shrubs extend down the Pilgrim and Kuzitrin rivers.

At the western end of the Peninsula, a similar geographic proximity to Asia accounts for the presence of some species there and not farther east. Regular breeders include Arctic Loon, Rufous-necked Stint, and Red-throated Pipit; and many casual and accidental visitants from Asia get only as far east as the Bering Strait region of the Peninsula, e.g., Tufted Duck, Common Ringed Plover, Wood Sandpiper, Oriental Cuckoo, Eurasian Wryneck, Siberian Rubythroat, Eye-browed Thrush, Brown Tree-Pipit.

Finally, a basic distribution pattern influenced primarily by food resources is that of the seabirds of the Coastal Cliffs and Block-fields. Auklets, which feed primarily on planktonic invertebrates, especially the large copepods, nest on islands in the Offshore Waters in Bering Strait—where Anadyr and Bering Shelf waters flow over the northern Bering Shelf, carrying oceanic and shelf zooplankton and nutrients and creating an environment of high productivity. Birds nesting on cliffs along the Inshore Waters of Norton Sound and southern Kotzebue Sound, however, are primarily fish-eaters, depending largely on the Sand Lance (*Ammodytes hexapterus*) and Saffron Cod *(Eleginus gracilis)*, e.g., Black-legged Kittiwake, Common Murre, and Horned Puffin. While these fish-eaters also nest on the offshore islands, they predominate in Norton Sound and Kotzebue Sound. The Crested and Least auklets are restricted to the Strait region, and the more generalized-feeding Thick-billed Murre, Parakeet Auklet, and Tufted Puffin are more numerous there than in Inshore Waters.

Seasonal Patterns of Avian Activities

S easonal phenomena on the Seward Peninsula show considerable variation, both temporal and geographic. Annual variations in climatic conditions, particularly those in spring that affect the timing of breakup of the sea ice in Norton and Kotzebue sounds and Bering Strait and the breakup of the rivers, ponds, and lakes and those that affect the timing of snow melt and the availability of nesting substrates onshore, play a significant role in determining arrival times of spring migrants and subsequent nesting chronologies. These events may vary annually by two or more weeks in response to spring environmental conditions (3-4 weeks in kittiwakes and murres at Bluff), and they tend to be about two weeks later in the Bering Strait region and along the Chukchi Sea coast than in Norton Sound and Eschscholtz Bay. Thus, the following overview of seasonal activity patterns in the avifauna is necessarily generalized, and it tends to emphasize timing in seasonally early years.

Among the first signs of spring on the Seward Peninsula are the arrivals of migrant Snow Buntings, cliff-nesting raptors, and seabirds that utilize leads and polynyas in the sea ice. Migrant Snow Buntings, moving up the Bering Sea coastline, may arrive as early as 1 March, and some Golden Eagles may return by mid-March. King Eider migration is underway by early April, the first migrant murres and Glaucous Gulls arrive by mid-April, and Kittlitz's Murrelets shortly thereafter.

By late April-early May, as the sea ice becomes less compact and warming daytime temperatures result in puddle formation and the start of river breakup, a number of other species begin to arrive, including more seabirds (Pelagic Cormorant, Common and Spectacled eiders, Oldsquaw), waterfowl (Tundra Swan, Canada Goose, Northern Pintail), and other raptors (Rough-legged Hawk, Northern Harrier, and probably Short-eared Owl) and land birds (Sandhill Cranes and several passerines, including American Robin, Northern Shrike, Common Redpoll, and probably Horned Lark, Ruby-crowned Kinglet, Bohemian Waxwing, Yellow-rumped Warbler, American Tree Sparrow, Fox Sparrow, Lapland Longspur, and Rusty Blackbird). These early migrants are mostly predators or birds that can subsist on seeds and berries from the preceding fall or on nonflying insects.

Some resident upland birds begin to nest in April, with ravens and jays laying eggs as early as the first week of April. Gyrfalcons and Golden Eagles may have eggs by mid-April, as may early nesting redpolls.

Most migrants arrive in May—the loons, most of the rest of the waterfowl, all the shorebirds and other larids, and most passerines. The sea ice continues to deteriorate, rivers break up, ice melts at the edges of ponds and lakes, and enough snow melts to expose a variety of habitats and sites for nesting. Because of ice conditions, most alcids do not arrive until late May or early June (Horned Puffin). The last land birds arrive at about this time, too—the Alder Flycatcher and Bank Swallow from Interior

Alaska and the Arctic Warbler, Bluethroat, White Wagtail, and Red-throated Pipit from Asia.

May is also the month when most species begin nesting, although the above-mentioned late-arriving passerines and many of the seabirds (Yellow-billed Loon, Black Scoter, Red-breasted Merganser, Red Phalarope, terns, murres, guillemots, auklets, and puffins) do not begin egg-laying until June—the auklets and puffins not until the end of June.

For most bird species, June is occupied with nesting activities, mostly incubation of eggs and caring for young. By late June, however, postbreeding flocks of redpolls are forming, and some shorebirds have already begun postbreeding movements (e.g., male Pectoral Sandpipers, female phalaropes, female Semipalmated and Western sandpipers, and failed breeders of several additional species). Flocks of postbreeding male ducks also begin to form by the end of June, and some drakes begin molting.

July is the month in which most young shorebirds and passerines fledge, as do many of the raptors and some of the larids (jaegers, terns, Mew and Sabine's gulls). Flocks of postbreeding shorebirds, first adults and, later, juvenals, gather at productive feeding sites in the Coastal Lowlands; and flocks of mostly juvenal sparrows and pipits become conspicuous in the uplands by the end of the month. July is also a period of heavy molt in most species of waterfowl, and there is a major exodus from the region of several species of shorebirds (Semipalmated Sandpiper, turnstones, and phalaropes). On the sea cliffs, the latest nesters (Parakeet Auklet and Tufted Puffin) do not lay until early July, whereas the eggs of the earlier species (kittiwakes, murres, and guillemots) hatch during the month.

In August the young of most waterfowl and loons fledge, as do those of cranes and Glaucous Gulls. Waterfowl populations increase at staging sites in coastal wetlands for feeding preparatory to migration. Shorebird flocks, predominated by juvenals, continue to utilize feeding sites in the coastal wetlands, with passage migrants from farther north (especially Dunlins and golden-plovers) in late August replacing the many local birds that leave on migration during the month. The main exodus of tattlers, Spotted Sandpipers, and Whimbrels occurs in August; and the larids that fledged in July leave the Peninsula during late July and the first half of August. Crane and goose migration begins in mid-August, first with the departure of failed and nonbreeders. Many passerines, especially the insectivorous species, depart on fall migration during August.

Most auklets and puffins hatch during August, although the earlier sea cliff species fledge during the month (cormorants, kittiwakes, guillemots). The main exodus of murres from the cliffs occurs during August.

Overall, September is the peak month of fall migration. Most of the remaining shorebirds (e.g., golden-plovers, Dunlin, juvenal dowitcher, Common Snipe) and passerines (e.g., American Robin, Varied Thrush, American Tree Sparrow, Lapland Longspur, Rusty Blackbird) depart, leaving only redpolls, Snow Buntings, and occasional shrikes among the migrant passerines by the end of the month. Crane migration peaks in mid-September, and the peak of waterfowl departures occurs during the month—except for most Black Scoter chicks, which do not even fledge until the second week of the month, and Red-Breasted Merganser chicks, which do not fledge until the last third of the month. Most auklets and puffins leave the sea cliff colonies during September, the Parakeet Auklet and Tufted Puffin not until the last half of September.

A few migrant seabirds and waterfowl remain until mid- or late October (Yellow-billed Loon, Pelagic Cormorant, Short-tailed Shearwater, Tundra Swan and sea ducks, and a few alcids [Kittlitz's Murrelet and Parakeet Auklet] and gulls [Herring Gull and Black-legged Kittiwake]). A few Pelagic Cormorants, Spectacled Eiders, and Snow Buntings may remain into early November, and a few migrant Glaucous Gulls and offshore Thick-billed Murres, King and Common eiders, and redpolls until late November. Thereafter, only residents and winter visitants remain.

Evidence suggests that at least 26 species may overwinter on the Peninsula:

Common Eider	Downy Woodpecker
King Eider	Gray Jay
Oldsquaw	Common Raven
Gyrfalcon	Black-capped Chickadee
Spruce Grouse	Boreal Chickadee
Willow Ptarmigan	Dipper
Rock Ptarmigan	Northern Shrike
Glaucous Gull	Snow Bunting
Ivory Gull	McKay's Bunting
Thick-billed Murre	Pine Grosbeak
Black Guillemot	White-winged Crossbill
Great Horned Owl	Common Redpoll
Snowy Owl	Boreal Owl

Annotated List of Species

As of June 1988, 215 species of birds had been recorded from the Seward Peninsula. In addition, three other species are discussed below as "hypothetical," because their occurrence in the region has been inadequately documented. Of the 215 known species, 155 occur regularly, as residents, migrants, or breeders; the others (28%) have occurred only occasionally, mostly as casual or accidental visitants or very rare migrants. Most species are present only during the summer or during the spring and fall migration periods; about 26 species may endure the winter conditions of the Peninsula (see above).

The status and distribution of all of these species on the Peninsula are described in the following species accounts. In addition, for regularly occurring species, the following topics are addressed insofar as available data permit: habitat preferences, wintering locations relative to the Seward Peninsula, seasonal chronologies, breeding biology, food, and, as appropriate, miscellaneous notes on other topics of interest, such as systematics, plumage coloration, or unique behavior.

In describing the distribution of a given species, I have used the physiographic and habitat units delineated above. Geographic place names follow Orth (1967), with local names indicated within quotation marks. In describing status, I have followed the terminology of Kessel and Gibson (1978):

resident—a species present throughout the year.

migrant—a seasonal transient between wintering and breeding ranges; in spring, includes species that have overshot their normal breeding range.

breeder—a species known to breed; prefixed by "possible" or "probable" if concrete breeding evidence is unavailable.

visitant—a nonbreeding species; also, in fall, a species not directly en route between breeding and wintering ranges.

abundant—species occurs repeatedly in proper habitats, with available habitat heavily utilized, and/or the region regularly hosts great numbers of the species.

common—species occurs in all or nearly all proper habitats, but some areas of presumed suitable habitat are occupied sparsely or not at all and/or the region regularly hosts large numbers of the species.

fairly common—species occurs in only some of the proper habitat, and large areas of presumed suitable habitat are occupied sparsely or not at all and/or the region regularly hosts substantial numbers of the species.

uncommon—species occurs regularly, but utilizes little of the suitable habitat, and/or the region regularly hosts relatively small numbers of the species; not observed regularly even in proper habitats.

rare—species within its normal range, occurring regularly but in very small numbers. "Very" rare is used for a species that occurs more or less regularly, but not every year, and usually in very small numbers.

casual—a species beyond its normal range, but not so far but what irregular observations are likely over a period of years; usually occurs in very small numbers.

accidental—a species so far from its normal range that further observations are unlikely; usually occurs singly.

I quantified the overall relative abundance status of the more numerous summer visitants and breeders according to the following scale, based on my own counts (see Avian Species Abundance): Abundant, 1500-4000 birds counted; Common, 550-1350 birds; Fairly Common, 240-520 birds; Uncommon, 11-195 birds. Assignment of abundance ratings for the less numerous species and at other seasons was more subjective. For breeding seabirds, I used the totals of the colony counts in Table 8 and based the abundance terms on the following scale: Abundant, 130,000-1,000,000+ birds; Common, 30,000-90,000; Fairly Common, 2300-10,000 birds; Uncommon, 500-1900 birds; Rare, 100 or fewer birds.

The use of "extralimital" in the species accounts refers to locations beyond the boundaries of the Seward Peninsula, as delimited for the purposes of this study; most of these locations are shown on the map in Figure 1. Supplemental data from extralimital sites were useful in determining seasonal chronologies for the Peninsula.

In referring to plumages of birds, the "basic" plumage (after Humphrey and Parkes 1959) is that gained by a complete molt and replacement of juvenal feathers. It may be worn throughout the year, or in birds with two or more molts a year, it is replaced, usually through partial molts, by an "alternate" plumage, which may be the breeding plumage of adult birds ("definitive alternative plumage") or the intermediate plumages of subadult birds.

Age classes used for waterfowl chicks are those of Gollop and Marshall (1954), i.e., Class I = downy young with no feathers visible under ideal field conditions; Class II = partly feathered when viewed from the side; and Class III = fully feathered but still incapable of flight; a, b, and c further denote developmental stages within these classes.

Brackets placed about the title of a species account denote the occurrence of this species as "hypothetical." Brackets are sometimes used, also, to distinguish comments or interpretations of mine when they have been imposed on or added to data provided by others.

The sample variance of a statistical mean, when possible to calculate or when provided in references, is presented as its standard deviation and follows the data mean (±SD). The mode is given in some data sets, when this statistic provides additional information of interest.

Several abbreviations are used throughout the species accounts: ANRS for the Alaska Nest Record Scheme, NWR for National Wildlife Refuge, and, for museums from which specimens are cited—DMHN, Denver Museum of Natural History; MCZ, Museum of Comparative Zoology, Harvard University; MVZ, Museum of Vertebrate Zoology, University of California at Berkeley; USNM, U. S. National Museum of Natural History;

UAM, University of Alaska Museum; UF, Florida State Museum, Gainsville.

Considerable unpublished data have been used in this work. In citing sources of these data, I have tried to denote their nature as follows:

pers. comm.—information received verbally

in litt.—data received by a letter that usually contains one to several records, sometimes short lists

unpubl. notes—usually more comprehensive notes, either raw field notes or compiled field lists

unpubl. data—a comprehensive record file, usually covering a number of years of data

MS—prepared manuscript of which only a few copies may have been duplicated and distributed.

The written data sources are on file at the University of Alaska Museum, as are the photos that have been cited as documentary evidence. Reports that have been duplicated and distributed, although not necessarily refereed, such as those by state and federal agencies, are listed below in Literature Cited.

When giving an overview of the food habits of predators, I have used only generalized mammal names. More specifically, the main mammalian prey on the Peninsula includes the Snowshoe Hare (*Lepus americanus*), Tundra Hare (*Lepus othus*), Arctic Ground Squirrel (*Spermophilus parryii*), Northern Red-backed Vole (*Clethrionomys rutilus*), Tundra Vole (*Microtus oeconomus*), Singing Vole (*Microtus miurus*), Brown Lemming (*Lemmus sibericus*, sensu lato), Collared Lemming (*Dicrostonyx nelsoni*), Arctic Fox (*Alopex lagopus*), and Red Fox (*Vulpes vulpes*).

Red-throated Loon—*Gavia stellata*

The Red-throated Loon is a common breeder on the Seward Peninsula and is the most numerous of the five species of loons. It occurs throughout the Peninsula where suitable wetlands are present, both in the lowlands and uplands, but it is most abundant in the Coastal Lowlands. Greatest densities occur at Cape Espenberg, where, in 45 km of hiking during 3-5 July 1973, D. D. Gibson and I counted 363 birds and where Schamel et al. (1979) found densities of 0.6 nests/10 ha in 1976, 0.8 nests/10 ha in 1977, and estimated that there was a total of 174 nests in 1977. Substantial populations are also present on the coastal barrier strip off Lopp Lagoon (34 birds, mostly paired, in 10-km hike northeast of "Third Inlet," 4 July 1974, and 41 birds in 19-km hike southwest of "First Inlet," 10 July 1974, both Kessel pers. obs.) and on the river delta areas at the north edge of Imuruk Basin (89 birds, many paired on small ponds, in about 80 km of boat travel, 25-29 June 1971, Kessel pers. obs.).

During the breeding season, Red-throated Loons usually nest at small, shallow, freshwater ponds, fringed by Wet Meadow habitat. Nesting ponds average less than 0.5 ha in size (Davis 1972, Petersen 1976, Bergman and Derksen 1977). These ponds, which thaw earlier in spring than other waterbodies, can be used by this species, because, compared to other loons, it can become airborne over a shorter stretch of water, even from land (Palmer 1962, Davis 1972), and it does not depend on its nest pond for food. On the other hand, breeding success is best when territories include several waterbodies (Davis 1972), which may in part explain why, on the Seward Peninsula, Red-throated Loons nest in greatest densities where wetlands studded with small ponds are adjacent to large waterbodies, i.e., the ocean, large lagoons, bays, and basins. Even within Imuruk Basin, densities are greater close to the open waters of the Basin than toward the uplands at the north edge of the Basin and up the Kuzitrin River, and this loon is more numerous in the pond areas at the mouth of the Buckland River and on the lower estuarian islands of that river than farther up the estuary. In the interior of the Peninsula, nesting sites usually are not far from a river or large lake. When on the ocean, summer or winter, the Red-throated Loon uses primarily Nearshore Waters and inner Inshore Waters.

Red-throated Loons winter in coastal waters along the entire Pacific Coast of Alaska, and they are uncommon in winter in the Aleutian Islands and along the north coast of the Alaska Peninsula (Gabrielson and Lincoln 1959, Gill et al. 1981). The Seward Peninsula population probably moves northward in spring along Alaska's Bering Sea coastline; and the first migrants arrive at the Peninsula about the second week of May (earliest, one, 9 May 1983, near Nome, J. D. Walters unpubl. notes; 11 May 1980, Nome, D. A. Woodby in litt.; one, 12 May 1988, Deering, J. D. Walters unpubl. notes). Environmental conditions cause considerable annual variation in arrival dates, and arrivals in the Bering Strait and from Wales to Cape Espenberg are apparently somewhat later than in Norton Sound and Eschscholtz Bay, often not appearing until after 20 May. Movement continues until mid-June through the Bering Strait.

Nesting is delayed until sufficient ice has melted to allow occupation of nesting ponds, an event that can vary annually by a week or more and occurs earlier at the base of the Peninsula than elsewhere. Breeding age in Red-throated Loons is unknown but is probably 2 yr (Palmer 1962, Cramp 1980a). After breeding pairs occupy their nesting ponds, the female is apparently physiologically incapable of laying eggs for another 11-13 days (Petersen 1976). The nest is variously located along the shoreline of a pond, on a small island, or on platforms of aquatic vegetation in littoral sedge zones. The nest is formed from mud, mosses, sedges, and other vegetation found in the immediate vicinity of the nest. As elsewhere, most clutches on the Seward Peninsula consist of two eggs, although some contain only one. In two-egg clutches, the second egg is laid about 48 h after the first. Incubation begins with the laying of the first egg and lasts an average of 27 days (range 24-29 days) (Bundy 1976), with chicks hatching about 24 h apart (Davis 1972). Replacement clutches may be laid if earlier eggs are destroyed (Davis 1972, Bundy 1976, Schamel and Tracy 1985). Both parents incubate and care for the young (Petersen 1976, Cramp 1980a). In the Shetland Islands (Bundy 1976), young of 18 broods fledged at an average age of 43 days (range 38-48 days), but fledging of two broods on the Yukon-Kuskokwim Delta was reported at 55 and 58 days (Petersen 1976). The survival success of the second egg of a clutch may be low. Of 19 successful nests that started with two-egg clutches in the Shetland Islands, both eggs hatched in only seven nests, and in only two were both chicks successfully fledged (Bundy 1976). Also, at Storkersen Point on the Beaufort Sea, one chick each from nine two-chick broods failed to survive to 15 days of age (Bergman and Derksen 1977).

In the Norton Sound area, including the Seward Peninsula coastline (D. A. Woodby in litt.), and on the Yukon Delta, egg-laying may begin by the fourth week of May (Petersen 1976, Woodby and Divoky 1983). In the former area in 1980 and 1981, Woodby and Divoky (1983) reported egg-laying 24 May-12 June (peak 29 May), hatching 19 June-11 July (peak 24 June), and fledging 31 July-21 August (peak 4 August). At Cape Espenberg, where breakup is later, egg-laying did not begin until 3 June in 1978 and 1979 (D. Schamel pers. comm.). Thus, hatching would have begun about 30 June and fledging between 12 and 24 August.

Throughout the year, Red-throated Loons feed almost entirely on small fish, although they may take some invertebrates (Palmer 1962). During breeding they fly from their small ponds to larger waterbodies, often the ocean, for feeding and later to bring fish back to their chicks. The chicks feed on crustaceans and aquatic insects for 3-4 days after hatching, but consume fish thereafter (Palmer 1962).

Birds begin leaving the Peninsula soon after the young have fledged, and local population levels have dropped substantially by early September. Red-throated Loons are rare after mid-September (one, 14 September 1986, Deering, J. D. Walters unpubl. notes; two, 19 September 1977, Cape Espenberg, Schamel et al. 1979). Somewhat later dates at Wales suggest the presence of more northern migrants moving through the Bering Strait during September, and a few migrants undoubtedly con-continue to move through as late as October, since, to the north in the Chukchi Sea, fully grown young were reported at Wainwright 23-24 September 1921 (Bailey 1948), peak flights past Icy Cape were not over until mid-September 1980 (Lehnhausen and Quinlan 1981), and this species has been reported at Cape Thompson as late as 12 October [yr?] (Williamson et al. 1966) (latest, male collected, 24 October 1935, extralimitally at St. Lawrence I, Murie 1936).

Arctic Loon—*Gavia arctica*

The Arctic Loon is a locally rare breeder on the Seward Peninsula. The eastern Siberian form of this species, *G. a. viridigularis*, has been found nesting in Alaska only about Lopp Lagoon near Wales. Little has been added to our knowledge of this species since Bailey (1948) summarized its status, including nine nestings at Wales between 1923 and 1934, although I was able to view in detail an incubating bird on the barrier strip near the "First Inlet" of Lopp Lagoon on 10 July 1974. Bailey (1948) reported egg dates between 24 June and 6 July. This loon is a casual spring migrant and summer visitant at other coastal locations (male, Nome, 20 August 1905, A. H. Dunham, MCZ 248760; one, on Norton Sound east of Nome, 10 June 1974, D. D. Gibson and others unpubl. notes; pair, Safety Sound, 29 June 1980, T. G. Tobish in litt.; two or three with 15+ Pacific Loons, off Cape Nome, 17 June 1987, P. D. Vickery in litt.).

Pacific Loon—*Gavia pacifica*

A fairly common breeder on the Peninsula, the Pacific Loon is less abundant overall than the Red-throated Loon but is more evenly distributed. It occurs widely throughout both the lowlands and uplands, where suitable wetlands are present. In the Coastal Lowlands it is generally outnumbered 2:1 by the Red-throated Loon, but elsewhere it frequently outnumbers the Red-throated Loon and often occurs at locations where the latter is rare or absent. This differing distribution pattern is not only noticeable on the Seward Peninsula as a whole, but at more local levels, such as in the wetlands of the Buckland, Koyuk, and Kuzitrin rivers, where the Pacific outnumbers the Red-throated above the mouths and lower estuaries of these rivers.

As many observers have noted, breeding Pacific Loons favor larger waterbodies than Red-throated Loons (average, 1.8 ± 0.2 ha [range, 0.3-9.6 ha], Yukon-Kuskowim Delta, Petersen 1976; average, 3.0 ± 8.4 ha [range, 0.7-12.1 ha], Storkersen Point, Bergman and Derksen 1977), and these larger waterbodies tend to be deeper and have larger expanses of open water. On the coast, Pacific Loons use the Nearshore and Inshore waters.

This loon winters along the entire Pacific Coast of Alaska, although it is uncommon in winter from Kodiak Island (MacIntosh 1986) westward through the Aleutians (Byrd et al. 1974). Spring migrants in the southern Bering Sea, at Cape Peirce (Petersen and Sigman 1977) and the Yukon-Kuskokwim Delta (Petersen 1976), average almost 2 weeks later than Red-throated Loons, but they lag by only a week when they reach the Seward Peninsula. The first migrants may arrive at the base of the Peninsula by mid-May (earliest, first seen, 11 May 1977, extralimitally at the Akulik-Inglutalik R delta, Shields and Peyton 1979; eight birds, 12 May 1981, Buckland R delta, Eldridge 1982), but farther west at Wales and Shishmaref they are usually not reported until the last few days of May. Migration is evident along the coast throughout June, with a peak occurring 16-23 June (Bailey 1925, Drury 1976b). Judging from the time constraints of the breeding season, these latter migrants must be nonbreeders. Although a loose flock of 40+ Pacific Loons that I watched loafing and feeding off Cape Nome on 20 June 1972 could have been a communal fishing flock of breeders instead of migrants (see Sjölander 1978), flocks of 60 and 45 birds moving west along the Norton Sound coastline on 2 July 1975 (Drury 1976b) were probably nonbreeder migrants; by this time, even breeders on Alaska's North Slope have occupied their nesting lakes.

Pacific Loons do not begin breeding until they are 2-3 yr old (Cramp 1980a); once paired, they apparently remain mated for life (Sjölander 1978). Birds occupy the nesting ponds as soon as enough water is available to allow birds to take off from the surface. Since the larger, deeper waterbodies do not melt as early as the smaller ones, nesting usually begins later than in the Red-throated Loon. In late years, however, when breakup occurs abruptly, both species may begin nesting simultaneously (see Petersen 1976). Nests and nest locations are similar to those of the Red-throated Loon, although substrates tend to be somewhat drier and use of vegetative platforms less frequent, and sites are usually immediately adjacent to deep water. The male selects the site, which is often one that has been used previously, and the nest is made by the bird on the site stretching out and pulling in nearby materials and forming them around its body (Sjölander 1978). Seven to 11 days may elapse between occupation of nesting ponds and the laying of the first egg (Petersen 1979). Two eggs constitute the usual clutch (Bergman and Derksen 1977, Petersen 1979), although occasionally only one egg is laid (Davis 1972). Eggs are laid at 2-day intervals, with incubation beginning when the first egg is laid; incubation lasts 28-30 days, with hatching asynchronous (Cramp 1980a). Pairs will renest if first clutches are destroyed (Sjölander 1978). Both sexes incubate and care for the young (Petersen 1976; Sjölander 1978);

Sjölander (1978) found that the female averaged 84% of the incubation effort. Young may remain in the nest for decreasing amounts of time during their first 4 days (ibid.). The young fledge at 62-63 days of age (Petersen 1976, Sjölander 1978) but continue to receive some food from the parents for at least another week—after which, over a period of 2-3 weeks, they become increasingly independent of the parents (Sjölander 1978). Even when both chicks hatch (37% on Yukon-Kuskokwim Delta, Petersen 1979), usually only one survives; this 50% mortality occurred in 12 two-chick broods at Storkersen Point (Bergman and Derksen 1977) and in 21 such broods on the Yukon-Kuskokwim Delta (Petersen 1976), but in Sweden 3 of 18 two-chick broods survived to fledging (Sjölander 1978).

Egg-laying may begin by late May in Norton Sound, but many Pacific Loons do not lay until mid-June, especially in the western and northwestern portions of the Peninsula. In Norton Sound in 1980 and 1981, Woodby and Divoky (1983) reported egg-laying 27 May-21 June (peak 31 May), hatching 23 June-19 July (peak 28 June), and fledging 22 August to about 19 September. At Wales, however, "an early set" of eggs was collected on 15 June 1936 (Bailey 1948); at Kitluk River the first chick was not observed until 10 July 1977 (J. M. Wright unpubl. notes); and in Shishmaref Inlet, the first chick was not seen until 14 July 1976, and a pair with a "very young chick" was found on 13 August 1976 (Noble and Wright 1977). With a developmental period of at least 90 days from the beginning of incubation to fledging, many young would not fledge until mid-September or later; e.g., 15 birds were still on Cape Espenberg on 22 September 1977 (Schamel et al. 1979), indicating that fledging was still not complete. If ponds begin to freeze before the young fledge, the flightless young are capable of propelling themselves overland for some distance to other nearby wetlands (Bergman and Derksen 1977), including, presumably, nearby coastlines.

The diet of Pacific Loons consists primarily of fish, but, especially during the breeding season, they consume significant quantities of aquatic invertebrates (Palmer 1962, Cramp 1980a). While breeding, adults may feed on their nesting ponds, but some pairs may fish in nearby rivers and large lakes, and, in the Coastal Lowlands, many fly to Nearshore and Inshore waters to feed. Young are fed mostly invertebrate prey obtained from the brood-rearing ponds (Bergman and Derksen 1977), although some fish may be carried back to the young from larger waterbodies, including the ocean. Families may shift waterbodies during brood-rearing, apparently to reach better food resources (ibid.).

The first fall migrants, probably non- or failed breeders, become noticeable in early August. At the Akulik-Inglutalik River delta, movement started about 6 August 1976, and large flocks were common during mid- and late August (Shields and Peyton 1977). Successful breeders begin leaving the Peninsula as soon as the young fledge, so most Pacific Loons have departed coastal Norton Sound by the third week of September— and a week later from farther west and northwest (latest, one, 2 October 1983, Deering, J. D. Walters unpubl. notes; but, extralimitally, two immature males, 29 October 1935, St. Lawrence I, Murie 1936).

Common Loon—*Gavia immer*

The Common Loon is a rare migrant and summer visitant and a rare possible breeder on the Seward Peninsula (earliest, two, 21 May 1983, Wales, M. L. Ward unpubl. notes;

latest, one, 18 October 1970, Bering Strait, Watson and Divoky 1972). Spring migration continues through mid-June, and thereafter occasional summering birds may occur anywhere along the coastal Inshore Waters of the Peninsula.

The presence of a pair of Common Loons on a fairly large lake at McCarthys Marsh on 17 July 1973 suggests possible breeding. While the birds appeared healthy, the distal third of the lower mandible of one was broken off and the upper mandible was fractured. A family of Yellow-billed Loons occupied this same lake.

Yellow-billed Loon—*Gavia adamsii*

Overall, the Yellow-billed Loon, locally known as the "King Loon," is an uncommon migrant and breeder on the Peninsula; but it is a fairly common breeder in the northern half, especially north of about 66° N. It occurs where appropriate waterbodies are present in both the uplands and lowlands, including at Agnes and Lava lakes in the Northern Uplands and near the junction of Noxapaga and Kuzitrin rivers in the Interior Lowlands (Kessel pers. obs.). It seems most numerous, however, where an assemblage of suitable lakes occurs at the junction of Coastal Lowlands with uplands (e.g., at the foot of Potato Mt, south of Mint R, every pond "of any size had its pair of Yellow-billed Loons" during the second week of July 1922 [Bailey 1925:28]; and, in the wetlands just northeast of North Killeak Lake on 30 June 1973, along a 13-km transect, D. D. Gibson and I saw six pairs of Yellow-billed Loons as well as six pairs of Pacific and one pair of Red-throated loons). In contrast, the Yellow-billed Loon is a comparatively rare breeder at such coastal wetlands as Cape Espenberg, those in the immediate vicinity of Shishmaref Inlet, and those seaward of Lopp Lagoon. Only two breeding localities are known in the Southern Uplands: one to two breeding pairs nested annually at Salmon Lake from 1967 through 1976, and a pair with a several-day-old chick was on a lake in McCarthys Marsh on 17 July 1973 (Kessel and Gibson unpubl. notes). Throughout the summer, occasional Yellow-billed Loons occur in the Inshore Waters of the Bering Strait region, i.e., from near Nome around the coast to Cape Espenberg.

For breeding, Yellow-billed Loons select medium- to large-sized lakes, similar to those used by Pacific Loons, but averaging larger. Nesting ponds northeast of North Killeak Lake ranged from about 6 ha to 81 ha, whereas each side of the partial isthmus across Salmon Lake exceeds 400 ha. Most waterbodies used southeast of Barrow, Alaska, were 30-50 ha (range 20-150 ha) (Sjölander and Ågren 1976). The 81-ha lake northeast of North Killeak Lake contained a pair of Yellow-billed Loons and two pairs of Pacific Loons on 30 June 1973.

The Yellow-billed Loon winters along the Pacific coasts of Alaska and Asia (American Ornithologists' Union 1983); it is uncommon in Southcoastal Alaska as far west as Kodiak Island (MacIntosh 1986) and rare in the Aleutians (Kessel and Gibson unpubl. data). Spring migrants apparently begin arriving in the vicinity of the Seward Peninsula toward the end of the third week of May (earliest reported, "few," 22-23 May 1965, Nome, S. J. Young unpubl. notes; but, extralimitally northward in the Chukchi Sea, one, 19 May 1986, Kotzebue, Selawik NWR unpubl. notes; one, 22 May 1922, Wainwright, Bailey 1925; and two, 24 May 1954, 32 km north of Icy

Cape, R. A. Ryder unpubl. notes). Movement continues until mid-June, with the peak occurring between about 27 May and 7 June. Since almost the entire population of this Beringian species apparently passes through the Bering Sea, it is puzzling that no large numbers have been reported passing through the Bering Strait, as have been reported farther north along leads in the Chukchi Sea (Bailey 1925, Palmer 1962). Perhaps migrants cut unobserved across the unpopulated western part of the Seward Peninsula (and across the Chukotsk Peninsula?). The largest group of Yellow-billed Loons reported from the Seward Peninsula was a loose flock of 60 birds on 12 June 1966 on the waters of Shishmaref Inlet, which still contained considerable ice (J. G. King in litt.). Whether this group was composed of late migrants or of breeders awaiting the breakup of inland lakes is unknown.

Generally, the spring arrival of the Yellow-billed Loon approximates the time of thawing along the shorelines of the larger ponds and lakes, and pairs can occupy their nesting lakes soon after arrival. As with other species of loons, nests are placed on small islets, on peninsulas, or on the main shorelines of waterbodies; the nest is built by the sitting bird pulling surrounding materials toward it and forming them around its body; and both parents incubate and care for the young (Sjölander and Ågren 1976). Yellow-billed Loons probably begin laying shortly after occupying their nesting lakes in spring, as does the closely related Common Loon (in Common Loons, 5 days in Iceland, Sjölander and Ågren 1972; and 4 days in one clutch in Saskatchewan, Yonge 1981). The usual clutch size is two eggs (Bailey 1948, Sjölander and Ågren 1976). Incubation is estimated to be 27-29 days (Sjölander and Ågren 1976), and, judging from the somewhat smaller Common Loon (Barr 1973), fledging probably occurs at 12 weeks of age. As in other loons, the second chick of a brood usually disappears within a few days of hatching (Sjölander and Ågren 1976).

Back-dating from observed events indicates that egg-laying on the Seward Peninsula begins in early June (pair with "very young downy" chick, 5 July 1969, Salmon Lake, Kessel pers. obs.) and continues through mid-June (several-day-old chick, 17 July 1973, McCarthys Marsh, above), and perhaps later farther west (Bailey [1943] estimated 1 July as the average date for fresh eggs at Wales). Most fledging, then, should occur from mid-September through the first week of October. The larger, deep lakes used by Yellow-billed Loons freeze later than smaller ones and thus allow a few more days for fledging of late-hatched chicks.

The diet of these loons consists largely of fish (Cramp 1980a), although Sjölander and Ågren (1976) found in northern Alaska that young took about 15% plant materials. Food is obtained from the nesting lake if resources are adequate, but, if necessary, adults will fly 5-8 km to other waterbodies to get fish (Bee 1958, Sage 1971).

Fall migration begins in early September, when groups of one to three adults have been observed moving southward along the Chukchi Sea coast (total of 13 birds, 4 and 5 September 1973, Cape Espenberg, D. D. Gibson and G. J. Divoky pers. comm.; seven "highly-plumaged birds," in ones and twos, 6 September 1973, observed from a plane as they flew southwest along protected lagoons between the Arctic Circle and Wales, ibid.; and, several daily, 4-13 September 1921, seen during a boat trip extralimitally between Wainwright and Icy Cape, "all going south, flying fairly close to the water and a couple of hundred yards offshore," Bailey 1925:26). These early September migrants may be successful breeders that have abandoned their nearly grown broods, as occurs with at least some Common Loons (see Yonge 1981:101).

Peak fall departures, both on the Peninsula and farther north, are closely associated with the actual time of fledging of the young, beginning about mid-September, with families leaving the nesting ponds of the Seward Peninsula almost as soon as the young can fly. At Wainwright Inlet, Chukchi Sea, there was an exodus of a very large group of these loons on the night of 20 September 1921 (Bailey 1925). The latest fall record is 11 October [yr?] extralimitally in the Chukchi Sea at Cape Thompson (Williamson et al. 1966), but probably occasional birds, especially late-hatched young, remain in the Bering Strait region throughout October.

Horned Grebe—*Podiceps auritus*

The Horned Grebe is a very rare migrant and summer visitant on the Peninsula, on both inland Lacustrine Waters and coastal Inshore Waters; there has been no indication of breeding.

On the basis of extralimital records (Kessel and Gibson unpubl. data), this grebe can be expected to occur on the Peninsula any time between mid-May and early October. To date, it has been recorded on the lower Koyuk and Flambeau rivers (one, 26-28 August 1980, and three, 4 September 1980, respectively, both D. A. Woodby unpubl. notes), offshore from Nome (two in basic plumage, 7 June 1986, D. E. Wolf in litt.), in a pond off Milepost 6 Teller Highway (two, 10 August to end of month, 1968, D. G. Roseneau and W. R. Tilton unpubl. notes), in a pond near the Pilgrim River at Milepost 61 Taylor Highway (one, 7 July 1967, Kessel pers. obs.), offshore near Deering (three, 1 August 1914, Hersey 1916), and at Wales (pair, 22 June 1940, Bailey 1943; one, 24 June 1966, J. J. Burns pers. comm.).

The Horned Grebe is a fairly common breeder in Interior Alaska, but it is rare at the western edge of the taiga and becomes increasingly rare beyond treeline.

Red-necked Grebe—*Podiceps grisegena*

The Red-necked Grebe is an uncommon but widespread breeder throughout the uplands and Interior Lowlands of the Seward Peninsula, although its local abundance varies considerably. It is fairly common in Imuruk Basin, where S. O. MacDonald and I counted 53 adults, many in pairs on isolated ponds, and found several nests with eggs 25-29 June 1971; it was particularly common about the lower reaches of the Kuzitrin River. Other than this concentration, the Red-necked Grebe is most numerous in the Fish-Niukluk and mid- and upper Kuzitrin-Pilgrim river drainages—a route along which it probably extended its breeding range to Imuruk Basin. It is rare in the Coastal Lowlands.

In addition to Imuruk Basin, I have seen concrete breeding evidence from Lava Lake (adult sitting on nest continually 6-12 July 1973), McCarthys Marsh (adult with one large chick, 17 July 1973), and on the Pilgrim River flats at Milepost 62 Taylor Highway (pair carrying chicks on back, 9 July 1969).

Summer habitat consists almost entirely of medium-sized, inland Lacustrine Waters that contain emergent vegetation, e.g., *Hippuris, Carex, Arctophila*, but bays of larger lakes that contain emergents are also used. Only occasional birds, probably non- or failed breeders, are seen on coastal waters at this season.

Red-necked Grebes winter on salt water along both coasts of the Pacific Ocean, with some wintering in the Aleutian Islands (American Ornithologists' Union 1983) and occasionally north to the Pribilof Islands (Preble and McAtee 1923). The source of migrants to the Seward Peninsula is unknown, i.e., whether they come up the coast from the southern Bering Sea or arrive overland from Interior Alaska, but their distribution pattern on the Peninsula suggests the latter. While migrants in early years may arrive by mid-May (extralimital first dates, 9 May [yr?], Arctic Village, Gabrielson and Lincoln 1959; 9 May 1978, Ambler, D. K. Wik in litt.), in most years they do not arrive until the last one-third of May (two, 21 May 1983, Wales, M. L. Ward unpubl. notes; one, 22 May 1978, Wales, Flock and Hubbard 1979; one, 22 May 1983, Nome, and five, 25 May 1985, Deering, J. D. Walters unpubl. notes).

Breeders, which apparently mature at 2 yr of age (Cramp 1980a), occupy their nesting lakes immediately upon arrival (pair, 23 May 1983, in melted edge of Salmon Lake, J. D. Walters unpubl. notes). Nests are placed on low or submerged hummocks, islands, or spits or on platforms built out in emergent vegetation. In Interior Alaska, the average size of 16 clutches was 4.1 ± 0.9 eggs (range 2-6 eggs)(ANRS); this figure may be low, since evidence indicates a loss of some eggs during incubation, and these data were obtained from various ages of clutches. Eggs are laid on consecutive days, and incubation apparently begins before the clutch is complete. Incubation is by both sexes (Palmer 1962), and the eggs are covered by vegetation when neither parent is on the nest. Incubation lasts 22-23 days (Palmer 1962), and unhatched eggs frequently remain in the nest. Both parents care for the young, which seldom exceed two per brood. The age at fledging is unknown, but one chick reported by Palmer (1962) had not fledged at 72 days of age.

These data, combined with observed events, suggest that egg-laying on the Seward Peninsula begins during the first few days of June, and it continues in the population for a period of about 2 weeks. Renesting results in even later clutches. Hatching begins during the first few days of July, and, given a fledging period of approximately 11 weeks, the first young would fledge during the second week of September. Broods should continue to fledge throughout the remainder of the month. Red-necked Grebes were "fairly common" on the Fish River delta 6-10 September 1980 (D. A. Woodby unpubl. notes).

During August, birds begin appearing at ponds not used for nesting or along the coast, probably the result of dispersal after failed nesting attempts. Fall departure is diffuse, occurring throughout September as the families fledge (latest, one each, 6 October 1984 and 12 October 1985, off Cape Deceit, J. D. Walters unpubl. notes).

Northern Fulmar—*Fulmarus glacialis*

The fulmar is an uncommon spring and fall visitant and rare summer visitant in the Offshore Waters of the Seward Peninsula. It is the only breeding procellariid in Alaska, nesting as far north as the St. Matthew-Hall-Pinnacle island group (Sowls et al. 1978). Farther north along the Siberian coastline, there is a breeding colony at Cape Stoletnya, apparently one at Cape Dezhnev, and possibly one near Checham village on the north coast of the Chukotsk Peninsula (Portenko 1972).

Fulmars winter as far north as the ice-free waters of the Bering Sea (Shuntov 1972). Cruises into the sea ice in March have found them within the ice front (Divoky 1977), including one perched on an ice hummock between Nunivak and St. Matthew islands on 20 March 1968 (Irving et al. 1970).

While a few birds may reach the northern Bering Sea in late April (two, 25 April 1978, off Gambell, St. Lawrence I, E. P. Knudtson in litt.; specimen collected, 28 April 1942, off Wales, Bailey 1943), most spring observations, both at St. Lawrence Island and in the Bering Strait, have been between the last few days of May and mid-June (first seen in the Bering Strait 19 May 1964 ["quite numerous," J. L. Burns unpubl. notes], 23 May 1973 [one, C. A. Grauvogel unpubl. notes], 27 May 1922 [pair collected, Bailey 1943], and 29 May 1958 [one, Kenyon and Brooks 1960]). During the first half of June they have been variously reported in the Strait as "seen daily" during the first week of June in 1922 (Bailey 1943:82), "numerous and constantly in view" on 13 June 1958 (Kenyon and Brooks 1960:458), and "fairly common over ocean during storms" between 3 and 16 June 1978 and when 30 were seen on 6 June and 40 on 15 June 1978 (D. R. Paulson unpubl. notes).

In view of these dates of greatest abundance and the facts that (1) all birds collected in late May and early June by Bailey (1943) had been "belly-picked" [had incubation patches] and (2) an adult male collected 1.5 km north of Gambell on 28 May 1973 (UAM 2625) had well-developed testes, it is likely that most of these birds are partaking in the "pre-laying exodus" (as described by Hatch 1979) from breeding colonies on the Chukotsk Peninsula. This assumption is supported by extrapolations from known breeding chronologies farther south. The facts that peak hatching at St. Matthew Island occurs during the last week of July-first week of August (B. E. Lawhead pers. comm.) and that mean incubation time is 48.4 days (Hatch 1979) would place peak egg-laying in mid-June. Thus, the pre-laying exodus, which Hatch (1979) found to last an average of 19.7 days (range 9-30 days) at the Semidi Islands, would occur during the first half of June in the Bering Sea, the period of greatest fulmar abundance in the Bering Strait.

Nonbreeders (and failed breeders?) range regularly in small numbers in summer from the Bering Strait to as far north as the ice edge in the Chukchi Sea (Bailey 1948, Shuntov 1972, Watson and Divoky 1972), although there are few mid-summer (July-early August) records for the Bering Strait itself. Two birds were seen on Fairway Rock on 26 July 1946 (Gabrielson and Lincoln 1959) and again on 11 July 1978 (D. R. Paulson in litt.), and a single bird was seen north of Cape Espenberg on 5 July 1898 (Grinnell 1900a).

Fulmars feed primarily by "surface seizing" (Ashmole 1971), i.e., by sitting on the ocean and grabbing prey items at or near the surface. Squid are prominent in the diet of Bering Sea birds; other items include crustaceans, especially euphausiids, jellyfish, and varying amounts of fish (Preble and McAtee 1923, Hunt et al. 1981a). Fulmars are opportunistic feeders and are locally known in the Bering Strait as "walrus birds," because they congregate on the ice in spring about the kills and butchering activities of hunters of sea mammals (Bailey 1943, Kenyon and Brooks 1960). They also take offal from around fishing vessels (Fisher 1952).

Numbers increase again in the Bering Strait region in late August-early September (abundant in the vicinity of East Cape on the Chukotsk Peninsula and in Bering Strait, 26 August-6 September 1928, Jaques 1930; thousands passed Gambell, 5 September

1975, P. D. Martin in litt.), and some birds are still present in mid-October (seen throughout the day during cruise through the Strait on 18 October 1970, Watson and Divoky 1972; one specimen from near St. Michael on 15 October 1879, Nelson 1887).

Both light and dark color morphs of this species occur in the region, although most birds are light-colored (Jaques 1930, Kenyon and Brooks 1960, Swartz 1967, Watson and Divoky 1972).

Short-tailed Shearwater—*Puffinus tenuirostris*

The Short-tailed Shearwater is a fairly common spring and fall migrant and an uncommon summer visitant in the Offshore Waters of the Seward Peninsula. Known as the "mutton-bird" where it breeds on the islands of southwestern Australia, it spends its nonbreeding season in the oceanic waters of the Northern Hemisphere, ranging to 71° N or beyond in the northern Chukchi Sea (Jaques 1930, Bailey 1948, Watson and Divoky 1972, Divoky 1984).

It takes only about 6 weeks for the postbreeding birds to travel from southern Australia to the Bering Sea (Serventy et al. 1971), with the first birds crossing into the Bering Sea as early as the end of April (Shuntov 1972, Hunt et al. 1981b, Gould et al. 1982). The majority move into the Bering Sea in May and June, and they are the most abundant bird species in the Bering Sea from June through September (Hunt et al. 1981b).

While they also occur regularly in lesser numbers throughout the Chukchi Sea in summer, there are relatively few reported observations from the waters of the Seward Peninsula, most from the Bering Strait. The first birds arrive in the region during the third week of June (14 June 1987, one over surf off Nome River mouth, M. W. Schwan unpubl. notes; 15 June 1978, four flying offshore of Wales during a storm, D. R. Paulson unpubl. notes; 23 June 1922, two, near Wales, Bailey 1943; 23 June 1972, one, near Nome, UAM 3269). D. G. Roseneau (unpubl. notes) saw one off Rocky Point in Norton Sound on 20 July 1969; Grinnell (1900a) took an emaciated specimen at the mouth of Kotzebue Sound, 6 km offshore from Cape Blossom, on 4 July 1899; Jaques (1930:361) reported shearwaters as "very abundant in Bering Straits, July 27, and off East Cape [Siberia], July 31 [1928]"; and J. D. Walters (unpubl. notes) recorded observations of one to eight birds in southern Kotzebue Sound near Deering, including two dead birds washed ashore, between 30 August and 10 September 1983.

Shearwater numbers continue to increase in the northern Bering Sea and the Chukchi Sea into August, although some adults apparently begin to move southward as early as the end of August (Shuntov 1972). They were "extremely abundant" from north of the Chukotsk Peninsula to the Bering Strait between 24 August and 4 September 1928 (Jaques 1930), an assemblage of over 200,000 shearwaters was in the same area on 8 September 1976 (Gould et al. 1982), "thousands" flew along the south and west coasts of St. Lawrence Island in the last few days of August 1956 and 1957 (Fay and Cade 1959), and "tens of thousands" traveled westward along the north shore of St. Lawrence Island on 5 September 1975 (P. D. Martin in litt.). Several flocks of 10,000-26,000 shearwaters were recorded in the southern Chukchi Sea during surveys 4-6 October 1976 (Gould et al. 1982), and birds were still present in numbers in the Bering Strait on 18 October 1970, when Watson and Divoky (1972) reported 12 sightings of groups of less than five birds to flocks of up to 100.

Most shearwaters leave the Bering Sea during September and October (Hunt et al. 1981b), but stragglers have been recorded as far north as Barrow as late as any water exists, even to mid-November (Gabrielson and Lincoln 1959).

In the Bering Sea, diets of Short-tailed Shearwaters consist of over 70% euphausiids (*Thysanoessa*) in summer and over 60% large hyperiid amphipods (*Parathemisto libellula*) in fall, and some squid and small fish (average 25 mm) (Hunt et al. 1981a, Sanger 1986). These items are obtained primarily by pursuit plunging, with some surface seizing (Hunt et al. 1981a).

Fork-tailed Storm-Petrel—*Oceanodroma furcata*

An abundant breeder in the Aleutian Islands (Murie 1959, Sowls et al. 1978), the Fork-tailed Storm-Petrel is a very rare summer and fall visitant in marine waters of the Seward Peninsula. It forages abundantly in the southern Bering Sea, but decreases in abundance progressively with latitude and is uncommon north of 58° N (Gould et al. 1982).

The type specimen for the species was collected on Captain Cook's last voyage, "on the ice between Asia and America," when the vessel was north of Bering Strait (Stresemann 1949:251), "perhaps on 13 July 1779." Nelson (1887:64) reported obtaining several specimens at St. Michael, "usually during October," and he stated that, "Two specimens were taken in Kotzebue Sound by Eskimo during my residence at Saint Michaels. . . ." He also wrote (loc. cit.) "During the cruise of the Corwin, in 1881, these petrels were seen on several occasions in Bering Straits and about Saint Lawrence Island, and in Plover Bay, Siberia." A female was collected near Nome on 7 October 1913 (J. Koren unpubl. notes). The only recent report of the species is of four birds in the Strait west of Wales at 65°37′ N, 168°29′ W, on 14 September 1975 (Gould et al. 1982).

Leach's Storm-Petrel—*Oceanodroma leucorhoa*

The Leach's Storm-Petrel is accidental in the region. The only record is of a dead bird that washed ashore at Nome after a severe storm in June 1968 (UAM 5383). The species, which breeds in the Aleutian Islands and forages over deep oceanic waters, is rare over the southern edge of the Bering Sea Shelf to about 57° N (Gould et al. 1982).

Pelagic Cormorant—*Phalacrocorax pelagicus*

Pelagic Cormorants are fairly common breeders about the Seward Peninsula, occurring at most of the coastal cliffs of the region, including southern Kotzebue Sound (Table 8). The largest numbers are at the inshore cliffs along the northern coast of Norton Sound, where Drury (1976a) estimated that 30-40% were non-breeders. They nest in individual pairs or small groups on sheer cliff faces and pinnacles or on isolated rocks and sea stacks, placing their bulky grass nests on open or covered ledges and in shallow crevices. Like other cormorants, they are birds of Inshore Waters, usually feeding within a few kilometers of their colonies (Swartz 1966, Hunt et al. 1981b). When farther from shore, they are usually associated with ice or floating debris (Gabrielson and Lincoln 1959, Ramsdell and Drury 1979).

This cormorant winters regularly in the Aleutian Islands and in the southern Bering Sea as far north as the Pribilof Islands (Preble and McAtee 1923, Gabrielson and Lincoln 1959), and it is sometimes found in leads and polynyas in the ice farther north (a small flock off St. Matthew I, 7 February 1970, G. E. Hall unpubl. notes; overwintering of a few near the south coast of St. Lawrence I reported by local residents, Fay and Cade 1959; overwintering of a few in leads about Diomede I, especially at north end, reported by local residents, Kenyon and Brooks 1960; but none reported by Irving et al. [1970] or Divoky [1977] during their March cruises within the ice front).

The Pelagic Cormorant is an early spring migrant. Earliest arrival records are late April for both St. Lawrence Island (Fay and Cade 1959, Searing 1977) and the Bering Strait region (one, 20 April 1967, flying near King I, J. J. Burns unpubl. notes; present, 25 April 1953, Little Diomede I, Kenyon and Brooks 1960; first seen, 26 April 1922, and common by end of month, Wales, Bailey 1943; one, 26 April 1965, outlet of Bonanza R, J. J. Burns unpubl. notes). Migration apparently continues throughout May (5 May to 9 June 1976 at Cape Peirce north of Bristol Bay, peaking 12 May, Petersen and Sigman 1977; 7 May to about 21 May 1924 at Dall Point, Yukon-Kuskokwim Delta, Brandt 1943; first arrived at Cape Thompson on 8 May 1960 and 21 May 1961, Swartz 1966), and birds do not come to the cliffs in any numbers until the latter half of May (large numbers not at Little Diomede cliffs until 18 May 1953, Kenyon and Brooks 1960; first at Little Diomede cliffs on 20 May 1977, Biderman and Drury 1978).

Commencement of nesting varies annually and among colonies, apparently in response to the time of snow melt on cliff faces (M. H. Dick MS) and probably the melting of the sea ice near the colonies. Timing appears closely similar to that at St. Lawrence Island (cf. Searing 1977) but almost 2 weeks earlier than at Cape Thompson (cf. Swartz 1966, Springer and Roseneau 1977). Based on lengths of incubation and nestling periods and back-calculations, some egg-laying about the Seward Peninsula may occur as early as late May, and it continues through June. Clutch sizes at 22 nests at Bluff in 1977 averaged 3.6 eggs, range 1-6 eggs, mode 3-4 (Drury et al. 1978). Incubation begins during egg-laying and lasts for 27 or 28 days, and hatching is asynchronous (M. H. Dick MS, Swartz 1966). The nestling period for two chicks at Cape Peirce in 1970 was 49-50 days (M. H. Dick MS), and at Cape Thompson in 1960, chicks stayed in one nest for 52-60 days (Swartz 1966). At Bluff, hatching began in late June and fledging in early August in 1976 and 1978, but not until a week or more later in 1977 (Steele and Drury 1977, Drury et al. 1978, Ramsdell and Drury 1979). Fledging may continue into mid-September.

Asynchronous hatching serves to adjust brood sizes to annual environmental conditions, i.e., when parents are unable for any reason to provide sufficient food for all chicks, the later-hatched, smaller siblings die early in the nestling period

(M. H. Dick MS), thus decreasing brood size and tending to improve the chances of survival for the remaining chicks. Chicks may or may not be able to fly when they reach the water, often climbing and flapping clumsily from the cliffs (M. H. Dick and L. S. Dick MS). Adults continue to attend and feed the young for several weeks after they leave the nest (ibid.).

The food of Pelagic Cormorants consists primarily of fish, with lesser amounts of crustaceans, especially shrimp (Preble and McAtee 1923, Swartz 1966). They obtain their prey both from the benthos and, by pursuit diving, from the water column.

Departure from the colonies is gradual, with numbers declining as failed breeders, nonbreeders, and fledged young disperse (M. H. Dick MS). In the north, late breeders are among the last seabirds to leave the colonies in fall, often remaining until forced out by environmental conditions. Both adults and young were still present in the water below Bluff when observers left on 11 October 1976 (Steele and Drury 1977). Two birds were seen flying over water about 24 km south of Wales on 18 October 1970 (Watson and Divoky 1972), and 22 were on the water below Cape Deceit on 19 October 1985 and two were there on 24 October 1987 (J. D. Walters unpubl. notes). Farther north at Cape Thompson, adults and fledglings were present in near maximum numbers on 27 September 1960, although many apparently departed thereafter during a period of stormy weather; the last bird of the season was recorded on 17 October 1960 (Swartz 1966). Adults and young were still present when observers left on 3 October 1961 (Swartz 1966). At St. Lawrence I, a single bird remained along the edge of the sea ice at Northeast Cape on 19 November 1964 (Thompson 1967), and several were still present at North Punuk I on 4 December 1981 when observers departed (B. P. Kelly unpubl. notes).

Tundra Swan—*Cygnus columbianus*

The Tundra or Whistling Swan is a fairly common, widely distributed summer visitant and breeder on the Seward Peninsula, occurring throughout almost all of the lowlands and uplands of the region, wherever suitable wetlands are present. It is rare as a breeder in the outer fringes of the Coastal Lowlands (e.g., Cape Espenberg and seaward of Lopp Lagoon), relatively uncommon on lower river deltas, and fairly common but widely scattered at interior lakes throughout the middle and upper drainages of the Kuzitrin and Pilgrim rivers and at such upland sites as Lava, Agnes, and Salmon lakes. It is most abundant, however, where numerous lakes occur in the zone between the lowlands and the lower-elevation uplands, an abundance pattern that coincides with that of the less widely distributed Yellow-billed Loon—and, more often than not, I have found swans occupying the same lakes as Yellow-billed Loons.

Estimated numbers on the Peninsula increased from an average of 489 ± 329 birds during 1956-1967 (J. G. King in litt.) to 1730 ± 390 birds during 1970-1981 (U. S. Fish and Wildlife Service 1978-1987), an increase paralleling a similar continental increase (see Palmer 1976). Unusually large numbers of flocked birds in 1981 and 1982 were followed by a doubling of territorial birds in 1982 and 1983 (about 4900 birds), and numbers subsequently remained at 4000 territorial birds through 1986 (ibid.).

Tundra Swans use Lacustrine Waters for breeding, usually waters with some Wet Meadow around the shoreline, some embankments, and surrounded by Dwarf Shrub Meadow/Mat tundra. It is amazing how inconspicuous these large white birds can be, even in small waterbodies, when they hunker down in shoreline vegetation and against banks and nearby shrub thickets. Small flocks of nonbreeding summer visitants use similar habitats, but they tend to remain in the more extensive wetlands, including McCarthys Marsh, the relatively protected lower river deltas (e.g., Fish, Agiapuk, Nugnugaluktuk, and Buckland river deltas), and the flats inland from Safety Sound and Woolley Lagoon.

Tundra Swans of the region winter in central California, and their migration route takes them through Nevada, Utah, Idaho-western Montana, up the eastern side of the Rocky Mountains, and through southern Yukon Territory and Interior Alaska to their summering grounds in Western Alaska (R. J. King pers. comm., M. A. Spindler pers. comm.). As early season migrants, their arrival time on the breeding grounds is strongly affected by spring environmental conditions and may vary by a week or more among years. In early years, the first swans may arrive by late April (earliest, 22 April 1944, extralimitally at Mountain Village, H. C. Kyllingstad unpubl. notes; 26 April 1978, Nome River mouth, Beltz School unpubl. notes), but most first arrivals over the years have been reported during the first week of May. Most breeders have arrived by mid-May. Since Western Alaska is a migration terminus for Tundra Swans and arriving breeders go directly to breeding territories, only small groups are seen as swans arrive in May. Flocks of nonbreeders arrive later and are conspicuous during the last half of June as they congregate in bays, lagoons, and river estuaries (400+ birds on 15 June 1981, Safety Sound [J. L. Dunn pers. comm.]; 60 on 15 June 1951 [Alaska Game Commission 1951], 175 on 24 June 1970 [Kessel pers. obs.], and 100 on 26 June 1976 [Noble and Wright 1977], all at the mouth of the Serpentine R; about 80 on June 1973, Nugnugaluktuk R estuary [Kessel and D. D. Gibson unpubl. notes]; 700 on 27 June 1982, Golovnin Bay [R. J. King pers. comm.]).

Landscapes are still largely frozen when pairs arrive at their territories, and the timing of ice and snow melt is a major factor in annual swan productivity, with late springs resulting in fewer nesting swans and smaller clutches (Lensink 1973). The usual age at first breeding appears to be 4 yr, although pairing may begin at 2 yr (Cramp 1980a). Nests consist of a mound of vegetation, placed on a relatively dry, elevated site that becomes snow-free early, i.e., an upland hummock or hillock, usually near a lake edge, or on a shoreline bank. Egg-laying begins as soon as environmental conditions permit, with early clutches begun by mid-May (about 10 May 1980 at Koyuk and on 17 May 1981 on the Fish R delta, Woodby and Divoky 1983; about 11 May 1983, based on a pipping egg in a 4-egg clutch on 18 June at Cape Woolley, R. and B. Mearns unpubl. notes; and about 12 May 1973, back-dated from a 3-4-week-old chick on 12 July at the junction of the Noxapaga and Kuzitrin rivers, Kessel pers. obs). Laying in the population extends for about a month, judging from the size of cygnets I have seen in July and the recently hatched young on 11 July 1922 at Mint River (Bailey 1943).

Clutch sizes of 354 nests on the Yukon-Kuskokwim Delta, 1963-1971, varied from 3.3 ± 0.7 eggs (late season) to 5.0 ± 1.1 eggs (early season), with a range of 1-7 eggs and annual modes varying from 3 to 5 eggs (Lensink MS). Eggs are laid on alternate days (Cramp 1980a, Hawkins 1986). Incubation is by both sexes, with the female contributing considerably more effort than the male (60-81%); the male's time is devoted to territorial defense and to covering the eggs while the female is off the nest (Scott 1977, Hawkins 1986). Incubation lasts 31-32 days (Hawkins 1986), and most clutches on the Peninsula have hatched by mid-July. Time to fledging is unknown; it has variously been given as 40-45 days (Dement'ev and Gladkov 1952) and an estimated 9-10 weeks (Palmer 1976). Forty-five days appears probable for the Seward Peninsula birds, since Woodby and Divoky (1983) reported that most young had begun to fly by late August-early September. Drury (1976b) counted 18 flightless broods on 26 September 1975, however, at the mouth of the Fish River. Occasional late broods fail to fledge before freeze-up, especially during abbreviated summers.

Flocks of nonbreeders break up and disperse to molt during July. Breeders also begin molt during July, while on their territories caring for their young.

Food of the Tundra Swan consists primarily of vegetable matter, either submerged plants obtained by tipping or terrestrial vegetation taken by grazing or grubbing. Items include stems and leaves, seeds, and fleshy roots (Palmer 1976). *Potamogeton* corms are used extensively in the Kotzebue Sound region (W. R. Uhl pers. comm.).

Nonbreeders begin to congregate again in late August after they have regained flight. The Fish River delta-Golovnin Bay area is a major late summer and fall staging site for these premigratory nonbreeders and later for paired birds and families. Apparently most of the Seward Peninsula population (i.e., 1600 swans) was in this area on 10 September 1981 (Woodby and Divoky 1983), and 1200 adults were there on 26 September 1975 (Drury 1976b); 524 birds were still in the Golovnin area on 1 October 1976 (Drury et al. 1981). Most swans have departed on migration by early October (latest, five, 8 October 1966, near mouth of Sinuk R, J. J. Burns unpubl. notes; one flying juvenal, 8 October 1984, Deering, J. D. Walters unpubl. notes; six families, 11 October 1977, extralimitally on the Yukon-Kuskokwim Delta, Yukon Delta NWR unpubl. data).

Whooper Swan—*Cygnus cygnus*

The Whooper Swan is a very rare June visitant in the Seward Peninsula-Kotzebue Sound region. Two were seen with 16 Tundra Swans at Wales on 11 June 1975 by P. G. DuMont (Kessel and Gibson 1978). Extralimitally in the Kotzebue Sound region, a yellow-billed swan was seen at Selawik in June 1965 by P. E. K. Shepherd, and two Whoopers were seen with 30 Tundra Swans on the Noatak River delta on 19 June 1967 by H. K. Springer (ibid.). This Old World swan is an uncommon winter visitant in the western and central Aleutian Islands (ibid.).

Trumpeter Swan—*Cygnus buccinator*

The only record of Trumpeter Swan for the Seward Peninsula is based on a set of four eggs at the Chicago Field Museum of Natural History that was collected 60 km "northeast of Cape Nome" on 28 June 1902 by W. E. Bryant (Banko 1960). This swan is normally a bird of forested regions but is a casual breeder west of the taiga of Interior Alaska (Hansen et al. 1971).

Bean Goose—*Anser fabalis*

A casual spring migrant in Western Alaska, a Bean Goose was identified by H. K. Springer at Safety Sound on 9 June 1974 (Kessel and Gibson 1978).

Greater White-fronted Goose—*Anser albifrons*

White-fronted geese are uncommon migrants and summer visitants and rare breeders on the Seward Peninsula, which lies between two major breeding grounds for the species—eastern Kotzebue Sound and the Yukon-Kuskokwim Delta (Gabrielson and Lincoln 1959). A female was flushed from a nest with six eggs 12 km northeast of Wales on 18 June 1977 (D. A. Woodby pers. comm.); and on an aerial survey J. G. King (pers. comm.) saw two broods on the lower Pish River on 14 July 1986 and another on Kaguerk Creek, Arctic Lagoon, on 15 July 1986. I was told by Elim residents that "pink-foots" nest in the marsh near Bald Head, but I have no further details to support the statement. Pairs, whose breeding status is unknown, and small flocks of 10-20 birds may occur at almost any Peninsula wetland during the summer, but they are more frequent, though still uncommon, in areas adjacent to Kotzebue Sound or northeastern Norton Sound than elsewhere. The former appear to be an extension of the population in eastern Kotzebue Sound, whereas the latter are mostly prestaging fall migrants.

The Seward Peninsula birds belong to the population of white-fronts that winters in central and eastern Mexico and migrates north in the Central Flyway through Louisiana and Texas, Saskatchewan and Alberta, and Interior Alaska to reach northwest Alaska (C. J. Lensink 1969, MS). In most years, they reach Interior Alaska at Fairbanks 21-24 April (Kessel unpubl. data), and, depending on weather conditions, probably reach the Peninsula about a week later (earliest reported, five birds, 4 May 1988, Deering [J. D. Walters unpubl. notes], and two birds, 5 May 1951, Moses Point [Alaska Game Commission 1951]; birds, but extralimitally, 28 April 1955 at Selawik [Shepherd 1955] and 29 April 1951 upriver from Selawik [Alaska Game Commission 1951]). Most reports of spring migrants on the Peninsula have not been until the third week of May and probably represent the later-arriving nonbreeders.

Summer visitants molt during July (two flightless flocks, 16 and 19 birds, respectively, in pond area at headwaters of the Burnt R, 13 July 1973, Kessel and D. D. Gibson unpubl. notes), and flocks have begun to gather at fall staging areas by mid-August (60 birds, 13-18 August 1980, Fish R flats, D. A. Woodby unpubl. notes).

Fall migration is under way by the third week of August and most have left by early September (latest, eight birds, 19 September 1977, Moses Point, and 75 birds, 22 September 1978, Koyuk R flats, R. J. King pers. comm.).

Snow Goose—*Chen caerulescens*

Snow Geese are common migrants and rare summer visitants on the Seward Peninsula. According to Palmer (1976:133), they "have nested...in the Wales area," but no documentation is provided. During migration, depending on environmental conditions, they may largely bypass or overfly the Peninsula or may land and utilize Coastal Lowlands, especially river estuaries. Sites often used in spring for resting and feeding include the Koyuk-Akulik-Inglutalik River flats (about 5000 birds during spring 1977, Shields and Peyton 1979; 640 birds on 8 May 1980 and 800 birds on 18 May 1981, Woodby and Divoky 1983), Cape Spencer-Port Clarence area (large concentrations usual, Gabrielson and Lincoln 1959, Teller residents pers. comm.), Buckland River estuary (690 birds on 12 May and 920 on 19 May 1981, Eldridge 1982), and Kiwalik Lagoon (700 birds on 19 May 1981, ibid.); other estuaries in northern Norton Sound and southern Kotzebue Sound are used but with less consistency and by fewer birds. In fall, the Cape Woolley-Sinuk River area is a favored site (200-350 birds 1-4 October 1966, J. J. Burns unpubl. notes; 100 birds, 9 September 1980, D. A. Woodby unpubl. notes), although some use is also made of the spring sites mentioned above (see Woodby and Divoky 1983).

The Snow Geese that migrate through the Seward Peninsula region apparently winter primarily in the Frazer River and Skagit River deltas of British Columbia and Washington state, respectively, and in central California and breed on Wrangel Island, USSR (Sladen and Kistchinski 1977). It seems likely that the Kotzebue Sound birds arrive via Interior Alaska, whereas those in Norton Sound probably consist of both coastal and interior migrants. Many observers have reported migrant flocks flying across the Bering Strait in both spring and fall; J. J. Burns (unpubl. notes) commented that in spring "they often fly low over the ice in formations similar to those of eiders." Radar echos recorded on the morning of 19 May 1970 at Tin City were apparently caused by a movement of Snow Geese traveling diagonally across the western tip of the Peninsula from the Port Clarence area, passing at least 18 km northeast of Tin City, and heading directly toward Wrangel Island (Flock 1972).

In early seasons, the first spring migrants may arrive at the eastern end of the Peninsula by the first week of May (earliest, 21 birds on 6 May 1981 and 640 birds on 8 May 1980 at Koyuk, Woodby and Divoky 1983; but extralimitally, 29 April 1943 at Mountain Village, Gabrielson and Lincoln 1959, and 3 May 1976 at Ambler on the Kobuk R, D. K. Wik in litt.), but in most years they are not reported on the Peninsula until the second week of May (10 May 1962, one near Cape Woolley, and 10 May 1967, "lots" flying west past Nome, J. J. Burns unpubl. notes; 12 May 1981, 691 birds in Buckland River estuary and 86 birds at Kiwalik Lagoon, Eldridge 1982). Peak numbers moved through the Akulik-Inglutalik delta area 11-21 May 1977 (Shields and Peyton 1979), but farther west the main movement of breeders usually occurs during the last third of May. In the very late spring season of 1964, a major movement occurred in the Bering Strait on 3 June, when small flocks of 20-40 birds passed west over the Diomede Islands throughout most of the day (J. J. Burns unpubl. notes); and, concomitantly, the main spring arrival at Wrangel Island began on 4 June 1964 (Uspenskii 1965).

In most years the peak passage of breeders takes only a few days, but significant numbers of birds, probably nonbreeders, continue to migrate past the Peninsula through mid- or even late June (flock of twelve, 22 June 1922, Wales, Bailey 1943; flock of five, 26 June 1977, Cape Espenberg, Schamel et al. 1979). Occasional late June and early July stragglers may remain on the Peninsula throughout the summer (e.g., one, 4 July 1977, Safety Sound, Kessel pers. obs.; one, first week of July 1980,

Breving Lagoon, D. A. Woodby unpubl. notes; six, 15 July 1980, Fish R flats, D. A. Woodby unpubl. notes; an adult, 21 July 1985, mouth of Pish R, R. J. King pers. comm.; one flightless bird, about 26 July 1898, probably near Eschscholtz Bay, Grinnell 1900a).

Fall migration of non- or failed breeders is under way by late August (28 August 1977, flock of 18 birds stayed one day at Cape Espenberg, Schamel et al. 1979; 29 August 1975, three birds at base of Point Spencer spit, Drury 1976b), but the main fall passage does not occur until the last week of September and the first week of October (8 October 1966, flocks still present in Cape Woolley-Sinuk R area, J. J. Burns unpubl. notes).

The Snow Goose that occurs on the Seward Peninsula is the western form, sometimes called the "Lesser" Snow Goose (*C. c. caerulescens*). Its dark-color morph, the "Blue" Goose, has been recorded on the Peninsula only once: A blue phase bird was seen with three white morphs on the ice off the Kitluck River mouth on 29 May 1977 (J. M. Wright pers. comm.). Since the early 1960s, occurrences of the blue morph have been increasing in western North America (Dzubin 1979), including Alaska (Kessel and D. D. Gibson unpubl. data), and a male was photographed on Wrangel Island during summer 1973 (Palmer 1976).

Emperor Goose—*Chen canagica*

A Beringian endemic, the Emperor Goose is an uncommon breeder on the Seward Peninsula, nesting in the Coastal Lowlands from Lopp Lagoon around the coast to Cape Espenberg and the Nugnugaluktuk-Lane-Pish river region. In addition, it is an uncommon migrant in the Bering Strait region and a rare migrant and summer visitant along the northern Norton Sound coastline. In the late 1960s, J. G. King estimated that fewer than 500 pairs were breeding on the Peninsula (Eisenhauer and Kirkpatrick 1977). During 18-25 June 1951, Thayer (1951) calculated that Emperor Geese were 11% of the waterfowl on the lower Serpentine River; but when I visited 24-26 June 1970, they were only about 6% of the waterfowl at the combined Serpentine and Arctic river deltas, and they constituted about the same percentage on the delta of the Arctic River in mid-June 1976 (Noble and Wright 1977).

The Emperor Goose breeds primarily in pond-studded lowlands at the lower extremities of rivers that drain either into large lagoons (e.g., Mint, Arctic, and Shishmaref rivers) or directly into the sea (e.g., Kitluk and Pish rivers), but some nest in wetlands on coastal barrier strips (e.g., off Lopp Lagoon and at Cape Espenberg). They frequently feed on nearby Salt Grass Meadow and mudflats and in shallow brackish and salt waters.

This goose winters primarily in the Aleutian and Commander islands (Eisenhauer and Kirkpatrick 1977), but it also extends eastward along the north coast of the Alaska Peninsula to Nelson Lagoon (Gill et al. 1981) and even Port Heiden (Headley 1967) if enviromental conditions permit and along the Pacific coast into Southcoastal Alaska (Isleib and Kessel 1973, Forsell and Gould 1981). In spring it migrates along the coastline, sometimes cutting across major bays, to reach its main breeding grounds on the Yukon-Kuskokwim Delta, where an estimated 80-90% of the world population breeds (Eisenhauer and Kirkpatrick 1977). It has been known to reach here by the first week of May (ibid.), but its modal date of arrival is 12 May, with arrivals peaking 14-15 May (King and Dau 1981).

Apparently the main population of Seward Peninsula breeders migrates across the mouth of Norton Sound from the Yukon Delta to reach the Cape Woolley-Port Clarence area and Wales, since few are seen along the south shore of the Peninsula east of Port Clarence (see Woodby and Divoky 1983). Spring migrants occasionally arrive in early May (earliest, 3 May 1951, Shishmaref, Alaska Game Commission 1951; 7 May 1984, Nome, M. Wassmann, Beltz School unpubl. notes; 9 May [yr?], extralimitally at Cape Thompson, Williamson et al. 1966), but in most years first migrants do not arrive until after 15 May, peaking about 20-25 May (common, 20 May 1977, Kitluck R, J. M. Wright unpubl. notes; 62 birds, 23 May 1983, Wales, M. L. Ward unpubl. notes). The few groups of 1-5 birds reported during the second week of June and early July along the northern Norton Sound coastline are apparently nonbreeders (e.g., one, 11 June 1950, Sledge I, Cade 1952; one to three birds almost annually 8-29 June, Safety Sound, Woodby and Divoky 1983 and Kessel and D. D. Gibson unpubl. data; five, 9 July 1983, base of Point Spencer spit, Woodby and Divoky 1983). It is possible that these birds, as well as some failed breeders, join others at the major molting areas on St. Lawrence Island to molt (see Jones 1972, Eisenhauer and Kirkpatrick 1977).

Breeding birds are paired when they arrive on their nesting grounds and are physiologically capable of nesting almost as soon as they arrive, if environmental conditions permit (Headley 1967, Eisenhauer and Kirkpatrick 1977). The female selects the nest site, often one that has been used previously (Eisenhauer and Kirkpatrick 1977). Preferred sites are raised shorelines of small ponds or hummocks, which have growths of grasses or sedges for screening; and most are immediately adjacent to pond edges, although occasional sites may be 12-15 m away. The female hollows out a bowl in the substrate, so that the edge of the final nest will be level with the ground surface, and she lines it with grass and down (Headley 1967). Egg-laying begins as soon as the nest is completed, and eggs are usually laid daily until the clutch is complete (Eisenhauer and Kirkpatrick 1977). The mean clutch size calculated from 30 Peninsula nests reported from various sources over the years is 5.2 eggs, range 3-9 eggs. The relatively few data from the Peninsula tend to corroborate the observations of Eisenhauer and Kirkpatrick (1977) that clutches are larger in seasonally early years than in later ones (see especially Thayer [1951] with five clutches averaging 7.0 eggs in 1951 and Schamel et al. [1979] with means of 5.1 eggs in eight nests in 1977 but only 4.3 eggs in ten nests in the relatively late year of 1976). A clutch of 11 eggs at the Serpentine River on 23 June 1951 (Thayer 1951) probably included some eggs "dumped" by a second hen. As with other geese, the female alone incubates, while the male usually remains nearby and defends the nest site— although he may join other males and nonbreeders at nearby feeding sites (Eisenhauer and Kirkpatrick 1977). The modal length of incubation is 24 days (Headley 1967, Eisenhauer and Kirkpatrick 1977). Chicks are usually brooded for 12-24 h before they leave the nest and then are accompanied by both parents after leaving the nest (Eisenhauer and Kirkpatrick 1977). Fledging has been variously reported as occurring as early as 48 days (Headley 1967) and between 50 and 60 days (Mickelson 1975).

Using the above chronologies and back-dating from observed hatching dates indicates that egg-laying on the Seward Peninsula may begin during the last few days of May (8-egg clutch hatched 26 June and 7-egg clutch hatched 28 June 1951, Serpentine R, Thayer 1951), but peak laying in most years appears to be during the first week of June. Fresh eggs have been reported at Wales, however, as late as 26 June 1972 (C. Ongtowasruk pers. comm.) and 20 June-10 July 1922 (Bailey 1943). Thus, depending somewhat on the year, peak hatch occurs during the first third of July, and most young should fledge during the fourth week of August and the first week of September.

Emperor Geese are primarily vegetarians, feeding mostly by grazing on sedges and grasses in summer and sometimes consuming crowberries (*Empetrum*) in fall (Headley 1967, Eisenhauer and Kirkpatrick 1977). On the coast, especially on their wintering grounds, they depend to a large extent on eelgrass (*Zostera*) and sea lettuce (*Ulva*)(Headley 1967). Geese feeding at bay edges and on tidal flats during summer take some animal matter, especially molluscs and crustaceans (Eisenhauer and Kirkpatrick 1977).

Molting by breeders begins about 2 weeks after the young have hatched, and adults take 4-5 weeks to regain flight; unsuccessful and nonbreeders molt 2-4 weeks earlier (Eisenhauer and Kirkpatrick 1977).

Fall migration of non- and failed breeders begins by mid-August (7 August 1980, 21 birds at the base of Point Spencer spit, and 16 August 1980, 10 birds at Cape Woolley, Woodby and Divoky 1983), and migration of families begins shortly after both adults and young can fly in late August. Many birds are still on the breeding grounds, however, as late as 20 September (latest, 21 September 1940, juvenal birds taken at Wales by D. Tevuk, Bailey 1943; 22 September 1977, seven still present when observers left Cape Espenberg, Schamel et al. 1979), and occasional late families probably linger into early October.

Brant—*Branta bernicla*

Brant are common migrants and rare summer visitants and breeders on the Seward Peninsula, where their overall breeding distribution is similar to that of the Emperor Goose, apparently because of the proclivity of both species for the Salt Grass Meadow-Pond habitat complex. Brant seldom nest near Wales and Lopp Lagoon (C. Ongtowasruk and other Wales residents pers. comm., Bailey 1925), but a few nest on low islands and flats at the mouths of rivers draining into Arctic Lagoon (Pinguk R, C. Ongtowasruk pers. comm.; Upkuarok Ck [= "Opkawaruk R"], Bailey 1929, 1943) and Shishmaref Inlet (Serpentine R, Thayer 1951; Arctic R, Noble and Wright 1977), on Cape Espenberg (Schamel et al. 1979), on islands just off the coast in western Kotzebue Sound (J. C. Bartonek pers. comm.), and on small islands in the vicinity of the Nugnugaluktuk River estuary (40 + nests, 28 June 1982, R. J. King pers. comm.; 400 + nests, 8 June 1983, J. I. Hodges in litt.). In addition, at the mouth of the Buckland River, F. G. Scheider and I found an emaciated Brant dead on a nest with one egg at Igloo Point on 24 June 1975 and one of a pair on a nest on the east side of the river mouth on 25 June 1975.

More than 40,000 birds pass the Peninsula during migration (39,500 estimated passing Icy Cape, Chukchi Sea, in spring 1980, Lehnhausen and Quinlan 1981; plus others flying inland up the Kobuk, Grinnell 1900a, and probably Noatak rivers). While the accumulating evidence indicates that many spring migrants, especially the breeders, overfly the Peninsula, a number migrate along the coastline, where some stop to rest and feed in the Coastal Lowlands. About 3000 used the extralimital Akulik-Inglutalik River delta during spring 1977, 1800 on 25 May (Shields and Peyton 1979); at least 4000 used the Golovnin area in 1981, including about 1500 on 18 May, and lesser numbers in 1980 and 1981 used wetlands at Moses Point, Safety Sound, the Cape Woolley-Port Clarence area, and Breving Lagoon (Woodby and Divoky 1983); small numbers also use the river estuaries along the Kotzebue Sound coastline (Eldridge 1982), and undoubtedly also in Arctic Lagoon and Shishmaref Inlet. In fall, the Norton Sound wetlands are little used (Shields and Peyton 1979; Woodby and Divoky 1983), whereas those along the northwest coast may be heavily used (5900 birds along southern shore of Shishmaref Inlet and in the northeast "narrows" of Arctic Lagoon on 18 September 1977, R. J. King pers. comm.; 15,000 on barrier strip off Shishmaref Inlet and to the northeast on 6 September 1978, Connors and Connors 1985).

While a few Brant winter on the coastlines of Southwest and Southcoastal Alaska (Gabrielson and Lincoln 1959, C. P. Dau pers. comm.), most from western North America and eastern Siberia winter in Baja California (Bellrose 1980). Izembek Lagoon at the western tip of the Alaska Peninsula, with its vast beds of eelgrass, serves as a staging area in both spring and fall for most of these Brant. An estimated 30-50% of these birds nest on the Yukon River Delta, with the first usually arriving there 11 May and migration peaking 15-18 May (King and Dau 1981). Arrivals at the Seward Peninsula are only a few days later (earliest, 5 May 1951, Shishmaref, Alaska Game Commission 1951; 8 May 1980, Nome, T. Willoya, Beltz School unpubl. notes; 12 May [yr?], Kotzebue Sound, Gabrielson and Lincoln 1959; twelve, 12 May 1981, on aerial survey between Shishmaref and Cape Espenberg, Eldridge 1982; four, 13 May 1965, Cape Nome, J. J. Burns unpubl. notes), with the main movement of breeders over the years occurring sometime between about 18 May and 31 May. Non-breeding subadults continue to move northward throughout June and into mid-July (30 flying past Wales on 18 July 1978, D. R. Paulson unpubl. notes), in all likelihood heading to the molting grounds north of Teshekpuk Lake on Alaska's North Slope (King and Hodges 1979, Derksen et al. 1979).

The possibility that spring migrants may fly overland across the Peninsula was first suggested by Bailey (1925), based entirely on the small number of Brant he saw in Bering Strait in spring 1922. Direct evidence for such a shortcut includes:(1) a report by R. D. Jones of flocks of hundreds heading east and northeast from Safety Sound (Lehnhausen and Quinlan 1981), (2) a description of migrants moving into Golovnin Lagoon from the southeast (D. A. Woodby in litt.) and then leaving toward the northwest during the last half of May 1981 (Woodby and Divoky 1983), (3) observations of more than 3700 birds in numerous flocks moving north past Utica Creek and down the Inmachuk River toward Kotzebue Sound 23-28 May 1978, including 2975 birds in ten flocks of 175-400 individuals each on 27 May (J. M. Wright unpubl. notes), and (4) the fact that Brant arrive at about the same time in mid-May in Norton Sound and Kotzebue Sound, but usually not until the last third of May in the Bering Strait region.

Breeding data from the Seward Peninsula are few, but back-dating from known hatching dates shows that egg-laying may begin by late May (based on a usual laying rate of one egg per day and an average incubation period of 24 days [Barry 1967]). Spring breakup can delay laying for a week or more, however; and laying in the population may continue over a 2-week period (Bellrose 1980). Fifteen clutches in the Serpentine-Arctic River area averaged 5.0 eggs (Thayer 1951, Noble and Wright 1977). Hatching was under way at the mouth of the Serpentine 26 June-4 July 1951 (Thayer 1951), and the first chick hatched at Arctic River on 30 June 1976 (Noble and Wright 1977). Given a period to fledging of 40-45 days (Barry 1967), Seward Peninsula goslings should be fledging from the second week of August to early September.

Brant are almost entirely vegetarians, and while on the breeding grounds, they mostly graze on sedges and grasses on Salt Grass Meadow and later in the summer may feed on *Potamogeton* spp. and occasionally take berries from the tundra (Barry 1967, Mickelson 1975, Palmer 1976, M. H. Dick and L. S. Dick MS).

Fall migration begins in mid- to late August, soon after the molting adults and goslings gain flight. At this time it is also possible that a few molted subadults could already be returning south from molting grounds in the Teshekpuk Lake region (Derksen et al. 1979, Lehnhausen and Quinlan 1981). A flock of 20 Brant was at the mouth of the Buckland River on 26 August 1981 (Eldridge 1982), 300 flew over the base of Point Spencer spit on 29 August 1977 (Drury 1976b), a few arrived at Cape Espenberg during the last week of August in both 1976 and 1977 (Schamel et al. 1979), and a major movement of many flocks of 200-300 birds each migrated past Wales 6-8 September 1973, including all night on 8 September (D. D. Gibson unpubl. notes). Migration peaks in mid-September (flocks passed Nome 10-16 September 1967, J. J. Burns unpubl. notes; 6700 birds in the lagoons along the northwest coast on 18 September 1977, R. J. King pers. comm.) and most have passed through by the end of the month (latest, 150 on 10 October and four on 12 October 1985, over Deering, J. D. Walters unpubl. notes).

The usual form of Brant on the Peninsula is *B. b. nigricans*, but a specimen of the light-bellied Atlantic form, *B. b. hrota*, was collected at Wales on 19 June 1924 by A. Nagozruk (Bailey 1943).

Canada Goose—*Branta canadensis*

The Canada Goose is a common migrant and summer visitant and a fairly common, widespread breeder on the Seward Peninsula. Some 20,000 of these geese use the Peninsula during summer, judging from fall counts (see below). They occur primarily in the Northern and Southern uplands and in the Interior Lowlands, where, for example, I have seen evidence of significant numbers breeding at McCarthys Marsh; throughout the entire Lava Lake-Noxapaga-Kuzitrin-Pilgrim river drainages and Imuruk Basin; in the wetlands northwest, north, and northeast of North Killeak Lake, and in the Burnt and Inmachuk river drainages. R. J. King (pers. comm.) also noted scattered pairs along the Pish River in late June 1982. A few nest in the Coastal Lowlands; here, they are usually somewhat inland from exposed coastlines, such as in the wetland flats of rivers back from their entrances into lagoons, but one pair nested on the relatively exposed coastal tundra at Cape Espenberg in 1976 (Schamel et al. 1979) and territorial birds were resident at Igloo Point in Eschscholtz Bay on

24 June 1975 (Kessel pers. obs.). The species is absent as a breeder west of about 166°15′ W and rare in the Norton Sound region (three nests in 2 yr, 1980 and 1981, on the Fish R delta, Woodby and Divoky 1983; none at head of Norton Bay, 1976 and 1977, Shields and Peyton 1977, 1979).

Small flocks of 5-35 nonbreeders may summer on any of the Seward Peninsula wetlands, but the uplands from Noxapaga River to Imuruk Lake and the headwaters of the Burnt River and to Kuzitrin Lake appear to be a favored summering and molting area for these nonbreeders (e.g., 100+, Imuruk L, 25 June 1973; 72 in four groups, upper Burnt R, 13 July 1973; about 150, Sand L area south of Imuruk L, 15 July 1973, and 225+, Kuzitrin L, 22 July 1973, all Kessel and D. D. Gibson unpubl. notes). A flock of 445 birds was on South Killeak Lake on 21 July 1985 (R. J. King pers. comm.).

The Canada Geese of the Seward Peninsula and Kotzebue Sound region belong to the population that migrates both spring and fall through Interior Alaska, Yukon Territory, and central British Columbia to and from wintering grounds in eastern Washington and Oregon and near the mouth of the Columbia River (Johnson et al. 1979, King and Hodges 1979, C. J. Lensink pers. comm.). Few migrants are seen along the east coast of Norton Sound (Steele and Drury 1977, Shields and Peyton 1979, Woodby and Divoky 1983), indicating that the Alaska Peninsula-Bering Sea migrants stop for the summer farther south in the Yukon-Kuskokwim Delta region.

Arrival of the first birds in spring is closely associated with the time that mean daily temperatures reach about 2°C (35°F) (Lincoln and Peterson 1979), which can vary annually by a week or more. The first migrants usually reach the Peninsula during the first week of May, but a few may arrive by late April (earliest, two, 25 April 1980, Kuzitrin R flats off Taylor Highway, D. Kost, Beltz School unpubl. notes; two, 27 April 1987, and one, 29 April 1986, Deering, J. D. Walters unpubl. notes; two, 2 May 1951, Deering, Alaska Game Commission 1951; also, extralimitally, first seen 28 April 1955, Selawik, Shepherd 1955, and one, 28 April 1983, Kotzebue, S. Hills unpubl. notes). Most of the breeding population usually has arrived by 20 May. Few spring migrants have been reported as far west as Wales, and these have been recorded during the third week of May or later, which indicates that they are nonbreeders.

While a few yearlings may attempt nesting (Mickelson 1975), the minimum successful breeding age is 2 yr and many do not breed until 3 yr (Bellrose 1980). Breeders arrive on their nesting grounds paired and apparently have already copulated (Mickelson 1975). The female selects the nest site, which is near water and has cover for the nest but a view of the surrounding landscape (Bellrose 1980). Nests on the Peninsula are placed on raised sites near some open water in Wet Meadow or Dwarf Shrub Meadow habitat or on bluffs along large creeks and rivers, e.g., Iron Creek, upper Kougarok River, Bluestone River—a habitat they share with Gyrfalcons and Rough-legged Hawks, often using old nests of the latter as a substrate. About a dozen breeding pairs nested on the canyon walls of the Bluestone River in June 1968 and 1969 (D. G. Roseneau unpubl. notes).

Nests consist of an indentation in the substrate, lined with vegetation pulled from the immediate surroundings by the female; down from her breast is added to the nest, beginning about the time the third egg is laid and continuing through incubation (Palmer 1976). In arctic forms of the Canada Goose, eggs are usually laid at the rate of one per day (MacInnes 1962, Mickelson 1975). Over their entire North

American range, clutch size averages 5.1 eggs (Bellrose 1980). Clutches from 7 nests on the Bluestone River cliffs averaged 5.9 ± 1.2 eggs (range 4-8 eggs) (ANRS), whereas clutches from 15 nests of this same subspecies on the Yukon Delta averaged 4.8 ± 1.1 eggs (range 4-7 eggs) (Yukon Delta NWR unpubl. data). Incubation begins with the laying of the last egg (MacInnes 1962, Palmer 1976), and, based on the similar-sized *B. c. hutchinsii* of the central Canadian Arctic (MacInnes 1962), incubation in the Seward Peninsula birds is probably 24-25 days. The female alone incubates, while the male stands guard nearby; both parents care for the young, which leave their nest within a day of hatching (Bellrose 1980). Fledging probably occurs at about 50 days of age, based on *B. c. minima* at 40-46 days (Mickelson 1975) and on *B. c. hutchinsii* at 52-60 days (C. D. MacInnes in Bellrose 1980).

Using the above data to back-date from observed events shows that egg-laying on the Seward Peninsula may begin by 20 May (four eggs of a six-egg clutch pipped on 17 June 1969 at the Bluestone R, D. G. Roseneau, ANRS) and continues until about 8 June. Hatching occurs from mid-June through the first week of July (nest of six eggs hatched 6 July 1976, Serpentine R, Noble and Wright 1977), and fledging occurs from the first week of August (young flying by 4 August 1976, Serpentine R, Noble and Wright 1977) to about 25 August.

Adult breeders molt their flight feathers when the young are 1-2 weeks old and regain flight about the time the young begin flying; non- and failed breeders may begin molt earlier (Bellrose 1980), apparently by early July on the Peninsula. Flightless adults predominate in the Peninsula population from the second week of July through the end of that month.

Canada Geese feed almost exclusively on plant matter, grazing on short sedges and grasses and taking seeds of these plants when they become available; some insects are taken, especially when the chicks are young, and berries are utilized in late summer (Mickelson 1975). Fall flocks of several thousand Canada Geese were reported by Woodby and Divoky (1983) on Dwarf Shrub Meadow at the southwest side of Golovnin Lagoon, apparently feeding extensively on crowberries (*Empetrum nigrum*) and blueberries (*Vaccinium* sp.).

Fall movement begins as soon as molters have regained flight, and numbers begin increasing by mid-August in the Coastal Lowlands, especially in river estuaries and on deltas within lagoons. Concentrations from several hundred to several thousand Canada Geese may occur at a number of these coastal wetlands between late August and the end of September. In southern Kotzebue Sound, for instance, R. J. King counted 2500 at the mouth of the Nugnugaluktuk River on 25 August 1981, and 3845 at Kiwalik Lagoon and 4732 at the Buckland River estuary on 26 August 1981 (Eldridge 1982). In Norton Sound, in late August aerial surveys in both 1975 and 1977, 650-850 Canada Geese were counted along the coast between Point Spencer spit and the Sinuk River (Drury et al. 1981), 1500 were in Safety Sound on 23 September 1975 (Drury 1976b), and from Moses Point to the wetlands in the vicinity of Koyuk there were about 2350 birds in late August 1977 and 975 on 1 October 1976 (Drury et al. 1981). Also, there were over 1000 birds in the vicinity of Koyuk on 23 September 1980 and 28 August 1981 (Woodby and Divoky 1983). The vicinity of Fish River delta-Golovnin Lagoon is the major staging area in Norton Sound, however. There were 5700 Canada Geese there in late August 1977, 3860 on 9 September 1976, and 4300 on 1 October 1976 (Drury et al. 1981), and almost 2000 there on 10 September 1980 and 5 September 1981 (Woodby and Divoky 1983). The total number of Canada Geese counted along the Norton Sound coastline from the base of Point Spencer spit to the head of Norton Sound in late August 1977 was about 9100, and from Golovnin Bay to the head of Norton Sound on 1 October 1976 was about 5300 (Drury et al. 1981).

With the possible exception of some of the birds at the Buckland River estuary, these fall concentrations appear to be of local origin, with the summering birds from the interior of the Peninsula forming the core of the fall aggregations on the Fish River-Golovnin staging area. On 21 August 1967, J. J. Burns (unpubl. notes) watched flocks of 15-25 birds, "flying really high," move down the Niukluk River toward Golovnin Bay, and Woodby and Divoky (1983) reported that on 9 September 1980 flocks entered Golovnin Lagoon from the northwest, i.e., down the Fish River into which the Niukluk River flows. The geese staging at estuaries and lagoons in southern Kotzebue Sound apparently migrate eastward along the coast and into Interior Alaska via the Koyukuk River drainage, whereas those along the south coast of the Peninsula apparently fly eastward over Koyuk into the Yukon River drainage.

As shown by the above numbers and dates, the major fall migratory movement occurs from late August throughout September. Thereafter, numbers drop precipitously, and the large number reported along the coast on 1 October 1976 (Drury et al. 1981) is unusually late (latest, flocks of 75 and 130 birds on 5 October, 12 on 7 October, and 85 on 8 October 1984, and one on 12 October 1985, all flying eastward past Deering, J. D. Walters unpubl. notes).

The Canada Goose of the Seward Peninsula is an intermediate-sized form, recognized as *B. c. taverneri* by Delacour (1951, 1954) but subsumed under *B. c. parvipes*, the "Lesser" Canada Goose, by Palmer (1976). The tiny "Cackling" Goose, *B. c. minima*, may be a very rare migrant on the Peninsula, since three members of a group were collected at Wainwright, Chukchi Sea, on 5 July 1922 (Bailey 1948). Also, five "small-sized" Canada Geese were seen at the Nome River on 8 June 1974 by H. K. Springer and A. Bernecker (unpubl. notes), and several flocks of "very small-dark-bellied Canada Geese" in September 1975 were reported by Drury (1976b) from Safety Sound and Bluff.

Green-winged Teal—*Anas crecca*

A fairly common, widespread breeder on the Peninsula, the Green-winged Teal is most abundant in the uplands and the Interior Lowlands. It is rare during the breeding season in the Coastal Lowlands (nest with six eggs in 1976 at Cape Espenberg, Schamel et al. 1979) and uncommon to rare west of about 166°W, although some spring migrants and summer visitants have been reported west to Wales (e.g., maximum of 19 teal, 28 May 1978, Flock and Hubbard 1979; 1-2 birds seen periodically, 9 June-21 August 1977, D. A. Woodby and K. V. Hirsch unpubl. notes; 2-8 seen almost daily 20 May-12 June 1983, M. L. Ward unpubl. notes). Pairs are scattered widely during breeding, and they make extensive use of woody cover, occurring most frequently where shrub thickets are juxtaposed with either lacustrine or fluviatile waters or wet meadows. Numbers increase in the Coastal Lowlands as the summer progresses and postbreeding birds congregate for molting and premigratory staging.

Banding return data (Hansen 1960, McKnight 1962) suggest the probability that teal from the Peninsula winter in the Pacific Coast states from southern British Columbia to Baja California and in the Central Flyway in New Mexico, Texas, and Oklahoma and migrate northward in spring through the interior of western Canada and Alaska to reach the Seward Peninsula.

The first spring migrants arrive during the second week of May (earliest, 7 May 1978, extralimitally at Kotzebue, D. P. Harrington in litt.; 10 May 1983, Nome, and 10 May 1988, Deering, J. D. Walters unpubl. notes), but most do not arrive until the third week of the month—3 weeks later than in Interior Alaska at Fairbanks. Nesting begins soon after arrival, however, resulting in breeding chronologies only slightly later than those in eastern Interior Alaska.

Most Green-winged Teal, as other dabbling ducks, breed in their first year (Palmer 1976). Most nests in Interior Alaska and on the Seward Peninsula are placed on relatively high, dry sites and are well concealed under shrubs; they may be as far as 90 m from water (ANRS, McKnight 1962), although most are closer. Nests are shallow bowls lined with dried graminoids, and down is added during egg-laying and incubation. Clutch size in 18 nests from Interior Alaska and the Seward Peninsula (ANRS and other sources) averaged 8.2 ± 1.9 eggs (range 5-12 eggs). Eggs are laid at the rate of one per day, and incubation begins with the laying of the last egg, resulting in synchronous hatching (Cramp 1980a). The length of incubation has not been well documented in the literature, but is often given as 21-23 days; one nest of 7 eggs northeast of Fairbanks (R. B. Weeden, ANRS) took 26 days to hatch, however, and Palmer (1976) reported incubation times of 23-24 days in captivity. The females lead the newly hatched chicks to nearby waterbodies, where they remain until fledging at about 25-30 days (Cramp 1980a).

The main egg-laying period on the Seward Peninsula is during the last few days of May and the first third of June, judging from the few available data on egg and hatching dates (two eggs in nest on 30 May 1978, Inmachuk R, J. M. Wright unpubl. notes; six 1-wk-old chicks on 2 July 1981, Fish R delta, D. A. Woodby in litt.). Most observations of young downies have been during the first third of July. Hatchings after mid-July are most likely from renestings begun after destruction of earlier nests. Fledging in the population is well under way by the second week of August.

Green-winged Teal are predominantly vegetarians, feeding mostly on the seeds and foliage of aquatic or wet meadow plants. The small amounts of animal matter consist largely of insects, but other invertebrates are consumed as available (Palmer 1976).

The drakes leave the breeding females during late egg-laying or early incubation and congregate on ponds with other males (e.g., 10 males on a small tundra pond near Cape Lowenstern ["Seven-mile Point"], Shishmaref Inlet, 24 June 1970, Kessel pers. obs.). There is a gradual shift during the summer of these birds, plus failed breeders, toward coastal pond areas, where they become locally common in August (60-75 birds, 5-6 August 1977, Cape Espenberg, Schamel et al. 1979; 50 on lakes near the Flambeau R on 19 August 1975, and 20-35 between Bonanza R and Taylor Lagoon 11 August-22 September 1975, Drury 1976b). Fledged families may join these staging groups during August and early September, but many probably initiate migration directly from their rearing wetlands. Migration occurs throughout September, with teal becoming uncommon after mid-September (latest, two, 23 September 1977, Cape Espenberg, Schamel et al. 1979; 30 still present, 1 October 1976, vicinity of Koyuk, Drury et al. 1981).

The usual form of the Green-winged Teal on the Seward Peninsula is *A. c. carolinensis*, but a male "Eurasian" Green-winged Teal, *A. c. crecca/nimia*, on a small pond at the Nome airport on 9 May 1983 was observed closely by J. D. Walters (unpubl. notes), and a similar male was photographed extralimitally at Kotzebue on 21 June 1986 by R. Johnson (identified from photo by D. D. Gibson).

Baikal Teal—*Anas formosa*

A casual spring migrant from the Old World, the Baikal Teal has been recorded several times in the Bering Strait region: at King Island, A. Nagozruk collected two males on 23 and 25 May 1931, respectively (Bailey 1933), and at Wales, D. Tevuk collected a pair on 8 June 1942 (Bailey 1943) and another male on 22 June 1944 (Bailey 1948).

Mallard—*Anas platyrhynchos*

The Mallard is a rare migrant and summer visitant and very rare breeder on the Peninsula. It is widely distributed but is most numerous at the base of the Peninsula, where it is locally uncommon during migration in the river delta-lagoon areas of the Koyuk, Kwiniuk, Fish, Buckland, and Kiwalik rivers. The average total population estimates of 2600-5700 Mallards on the Peninsula, from U. S. Fish and Wildlife Service breeding population surveys (King and Lensink 1971, U. S. Fish and Wildlife Service 1978-1987), seem excessive; they were extrapolated from too few data, and these numbers are probably reached only in years when drought in the prairie breeding grounds forces some duck populations farther north than usual (see Northern Pintail, below).

As with the other dabbling ducks of the Seward Peninsula, the Mallards appear to be an extension of the populations of Interior Alaska, migrating overland through Alaska, through western Canada, primarily via interior British Columbia, and wintering mostly in the Pacific Flyway, especially in the Puget Sound area of British Columbia and Washington (hypothesized from data provided by Hansen 1960 and McKnight 1962). It is not known whether any Seward Peninsula birds are among the overwintering populations in Interior Alaska (Kessel unpubl. data) and Southcoastal Alaska (Isleib and Kessel 1973, Forsell and Gould 1981), or possibly even in the Aleutian Islands (Murie 1959).

Weather permitting, the first migrants probably reach the Peninsula by late April-early May (extralimitally, 16 April 1943 and 23 April 1944 at Mountain Village, H. C. Kyllingstad in litt.; 4 May 1988 at Deering, J. D. Walters unpubl. notes; 11 May 1941 at Wales, Bailey 1943). Most early season records have been mid-May or later, however, and probably represent nonbreeders.

Apparent residents, usually only one or two birds, have remained at localities throughout the summer (Wales in 1977 and 1978, D. A. Woodby and K. V. Hirsch unpubl. notes and D. R. Paulson unpubl. notes, respectively; Cape Espenberg in 1977, but not 1976, Schamel et al. 1979), but few incidents of breeding have been reported.

A brood of four half-grown chicks was reported along the Serpentine River on 17 July 1951 (Thayer 1951), and a brood was on a pond on the Teller Highway near Nome on 23 June 1977 (H. K. Springer pers. comm.). In addition, extralimitally on the Inglutalik River at the head of Norton Bay, a hen with seven chicks was present on 20 June 1976, and a hen with four chicks was there on 2 August 1976 (Shields and Peyton 1977). Given these brood dates and an average incubation time of 28 days (range 26-30) (Bellrose 1980), egg-laying must have begun by mid-May. With a fledging period of 40-43 days in Alaska Mallards (ibid.), young should be flying by the first week of August.

From mid- to late August, numbers begin to increase in the coastal wetlands of both eastern Kotzebue Sound (M. A. Spindler pers. comm.) and eastern Norton Sound, where numbers peak during the last half of September (Woodby and Divoky 1983). The origin of these staging birds is unknown, but only a few could be from the Peninsula. Migration occurs throughout September, and most birds have departed by the end of the month (latest report, four, 21 September 1980, Safety Sound, D. A. Woodby unpubl. notes), although a few undoubtedly linger into early October.

Northern Pintail—*Anas acuta*

An abundant migrant and breeder, the Northern Pintail is the most common species of waterfowl summering on the Peninsula; it is more than twice as numerous as the next most abundant species, the Oldsquaw (Table 4). Populations on the Peninsula have increased over the last 30+ yr (Figure 20), in contrast to the striking decline of continental populations since 1969 (Conant and Roetker 1987). Between 1978 and 1987, in years without an influx of drought-displaced ducks (see below), an average of $141,700 \pm 33,100$ pintails have been present; numbers more than double in years of severe prairie droughts (U. S. Fish and Wildlife Service 1978-1987). Pintails are widely distributed throughout both the Coastal and Interior lowlands and the Northern and Southern uplands, with greatest densities in the wetlands along the lower reaches of rivers that enter lagoons or that flow through extensive estuaries before discharging into protected bays. They favor open habitats with shallow waterbodies, usually with some exposed mud banks, gravel bars, or beaches for loafing spots.

While the pintail is an uncommon to rare winter visitant along the entire Pacific coastline of Alaska, most, if not all, of the Seward Peninsula birds belong to the population that migrates through Interior Alaska, southern Yukon Territory, and western Canada—via either interior British Columbia or east of the Rocky Mountains—to wintering grounds in Washington, Oregon, California, and Mexico, and to the Gulf Coast states of Texas and Louisiana (see banding returns in Hansen 1960, including 73 from Kotzebue Sound).

Arrival of the first spring migrants at the Seward Peninsula coincides with the first thawing of puddles, a time that can vary annually by more than a week. In early years, the first pintails arrive at the end of April (earliest, male, 27 April 1983, Nome, J. D. Walters unpubl. notes; seen, 30 April 1980, Nome, B. Murray, Beltz School unpubl. notes), but in most years they do not arrive until 3-9 May—and after mid-May at the western end of the Peninsula. The peak of migration occurs about a week after the first birds appear, and movement continues through May. A few pintails con-

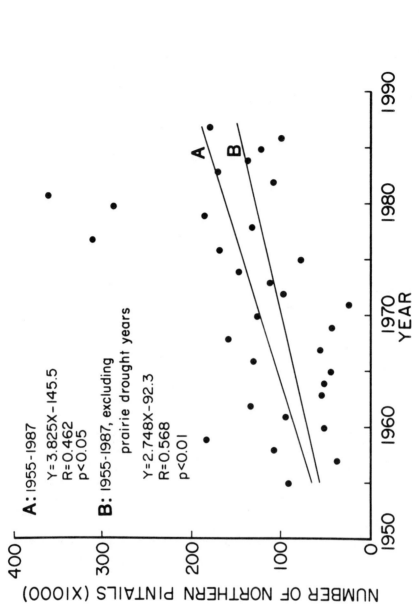

Figure 20. Estimated numbers of Northern Pintails on the Seward Peninsula 1955-1987. Data are based on aerial samples of 72.5 km² (28 mi²) of wetlands made during the U. S. Fish and Wildlife Service annual waterfowl breeding population surveys. The fitted regression lines show an overall increase in population levels, with or without prairie drought years (courtesy J. I. Hodges, USFWS, Juneau, AK).

tinue migration across the Bering Strait to breed in northeastern Siberia (Henny 1973).

Under normal conditions, pintails breed during their first year. Pair formation begins on the wintering grounds (Palmer 1976), and most birds are paired by the time they reach Alaska. The female selects a relatively dry site for her nest, often in Dwarf Shrub Meadow, where the nest is placed against a tussock or at the base of a dwarf shrub. Nests are also commonly in grass-sedge meadow, including *Elymus* meadow, and sometimes on Dwarf Shrub Mat. Pintails select nest sites farther from water than most other ducks, although most sites are within 90 m of water and average 35 m (Bellrose 1980). A nest in the Nome River valley was almost 2 km from the nearest water, however—high on a hill in the only available clump of willows and surrounded by rocky tundra (D. G. Roseneau and W. R. Tilton, ANRS).

The nest consists of a depression lined with dried vegetation from the immediate vicinity and with down from the hen's breast. Eggs are laid at the rate of one per day. On a continent-wide basis, 1276 clutches averaged 7.8 eggs, with a range of 3-14 eggs (Bellrose 1980). Sixteen clutches from the Seward Peninsula (varied sources) averaged 6.1 ± 1.6 eggs, range 3-8 eggs. Incubation begins with the laying of the last egg and takes 22-23 days (R. W. Fuller in Bellrose 1980). Renesting occurs if clutches are lost during incubation (Smith 1968).

Egg-laying may begin in mid-May (about 10 eggs, 24 May 1979, Nome, N. Levinson, Beltz School unpubl. notes; 8 eggs, 26 May 1977, Kitluk R, J. M. Wright unpubl. notes) but peaks during the fourth week. Some laying continues until late June, the latest undoubtedly renesting attempts (a few paired birds are present through June, Kessel pers. obs.; nest of newly hatched chicks, 10 July 1967, Safety Sound, K. Hahn pers. comm.). Hatching usually begins 10-11 June (but "about June 3," 1949, near Elephant Point, Eschscholtz Bay, Alaska Game Commission 1949). The young leave the nest almost as soon as all are hatched and dried, and the hen takes them to nearby wetlands where they remain until fledging. Fledging in Alaska pintails takes 36-43 days (Bellrose 1980), so the first chicks of the season should be flying soon after mid-July (reported flying 26 July 1951, Serpentine R, Thayer 1951; brood of four Class IIIa chicks, 17 July 1973, McCarthys Marsh, Kessel pers. obs.), and most should be fledged by mid-August.

Pintails generally feed in shallow water, taking food at the surface or tipping up to stretch their long necks for deeper items; they also surface feed at water edges and on intertidal flats. Largely vegetarians, they feed predominantly on seeds of pond-weeds, sedges, grasses, smartweeds, etc., but they also take vegetative parts of plants, especially new growth (Palmer 1976). *Potamogeton* corms are important food items in Kotzebue Sound, especially in spring and fall (W. R. Uhl pers. comm.). Ducklings feed mostly on invertebrates, and adults also take them opportunistically (Palmer 1976). In fall, pintails sometimes feed on tundra berries (Nelson 1887).

Drake pintails desert the females early in incubation and soon thereafter repair to nearby wetlands, forming flocks with other postbreeding males. Paired birds are still fairly common as late as mid-June, but are scarce by the end of the month (two pairs on flats northeast of North Killeak L, 30 June 1973, Kessel pers. obs.). Male flocks become increasingly common after mid-June, and many drakes are in heavy wing and body molt by the last week of June. Molting is heaviest in the population during the first half of July, during which time flocks of drakes, nonbreeders, and failed females occur in many of the wetlands throughout the Peninsula. Many flocks are small, but some are large: about 300 molting males on 9 July 1951 in a shallow pond 10 km up the Serpentine River (Thayer 1951); 200 flightless males on 5 July 1973 on a small pond at the tip of Cape Espenberg (Kessel and D. D. Gibson unpubl. notes); flocks of 120 and 300 on 3 July 1974 in riverine ponds at the northeast end of Lopp Lagoon (Kessel pers. obs.); and up to 1000 molting birds on 11 July 1977 on a lake 5 km up the Kitluk River (J. M. Wright unpubl. notes). The drakes, although still in basic ("eclipse") body plumage, begin to regain flight in late July. Breeding hens apparently leave their broods at about the time the chicks are ready to fledge and do not undergo major molting until then, i.e., until late July-early August.

Migratory movement begins in early August, as soon as the drakes begin to regain flight, e.g., large numbers arrived at east Norton Bay about 2 August 1976, and numbers increased throughout the month (Shields and Peyton 1977); and 1250 pintails were in the Nugnugaluktuk River estuary on 8 August 1981 (Eldridge 1982). Premigratory flocks continue to form locally as young fledge and later-molting adults regain flight, and migration continues throughout August and September. Migration peaks during the second week of September (Shields and Peyton 1979, Woodby and Divoky 1983), and most birds have departed by the end of the month. About 800 pintails were still present along coastal Norton Bay on 1 October 1976 (Drury et al. 1981), however, and it is likely that a few remain until freeze-up (some remained at St. Michael until 8-10 October, according to Nelson [1887]).

Periodically, drought conditions in the prairie pothole country of southern Canada and north-central United States cause large numbers of ducks to bypass this normally prime breeding area and continue northward into northern Canada, Alaska, and even northeastern Siberia (Hansen and McKnight 1964, Smith 1970, Henny 1973, Derksen and Eldridge 1980). While a number of species of prairie-breeding ducks are forced northward during these droughts (Hansen and McKnight 1964), the Northern Pintail appears affected to the greatest degree, perhaps because of its preference for shallow waters, which can disappear completely during severe droughts. Drought years that have caused significant influxes of prairie ducks to Alaska include 1949, 1959, 1961, 1968, 1977, 1980, and 1981. In 1981, some 361,000 pintails were estimated to be on the Seward Peninsula (U. S. Fish and Wildlife Service 1978-1987). While some of the drought-displaced ducks may attempt to breed in Alaska, many apparently do not, and overall productivity is low (Hansen and McKnight 1964, Derksen and Eldridge 1980). A flock of 10,000 nonbreeding pintails was present on Safety Sound on 7 June 1980 (U. S. Fish and Wildlife Service 1978-1987). There is often a lag effect following a severe drought year, whereby population levels remain above normal for at least a second year, possibly because of homing to the previous year's breeding sites (see Hansen and McKnight 1964, Henny 1973).

Northern Shoveler—*Anas clypeata*

The Northern Shoveler is an uncommon migrant and summer visitant and a rare breeder on the Seward Peninsula. It is widely distributed and can be expected almost anywhere freshwater pond-Wet Meadow habitat exists, even as far west as Wales (pair, 21 May 1969, W. L. Flock in litt.; seen, 10 June 1977, D. A. Woodby and K. V. Hirsch unpubl. notes; pair, 30 May 1978, D. R. Paulson unpubl. notes; two pairs, 11 June

1981, T. G. Tobish in litt.; male, 30 May, and 1-2 birds, 8-13 June 1983, M. L. Ward unpubl. notes, in litt.) and the Chukchi Sea coast (male, 5-16 June 1976, Arctic R delta, Noble and Wright 1977; pair, 20 May, and a west-flying flock of 15 birds, 28 May 1977, Kitluk R, J. M. Wright unpubl. notes). Numbers fluctuate widely from year to year, but generally shovelers are most numerous at the east end of the Peninsula, in the wetlands along southern Kotzebue Sound and along Norton Sound, and in years of prairie drought. In addition to occasional small groups of nonbreeders, one to six pairs of shovelers have been seen each year (22 pairs in the drought year of 1981) during the U. S. Fish and Wildlife Service (1978-1987) aerial breeding population surveys of wetlands in the western half of the Peninsula. Preferred habitat of shovelers is open, marshy areas with relatively shallow water that has abundant aquatic vegetation and soft mud bottoms and that has open, dry resting areas and surrounding dry meadows for nesting (Palmer 1976).

Occasional shovelers winter along the length of the Pacific coastline of Alaska (Kessel and Gibson 1978, Forsell and Gould 1981), but returns of birds banded in Interior Alaska (Hansen 1960, McKnight 1962) indicate that this population, and hence most probably the Seward Peninsula birds, migrates through interior western Canada and joins others from northwest Canada and Alberta to winter in California and along the west coast of Mexico. The first spring migrants usually arrive by mid-May (earliest, two, 4 May 1988, and one, 10 May 1987, Deering, J. D. Walters unpubl. notes; and extralimitally, one, 2 May 1986, Kotzebue, Selawik NWR unpubl. notes, and male, 6 May 1981, and 30+ birds, 8 May 1980, at ice edge at Shaktoolik, (D. A. Woodby in litt.). Migration continues through May.

Except at the Fish River delta in the prairie drought year of 1981 (when eight broods ranging in age from 1-2 wk to near fledging were seen on 3 and 4 August [D. A. Woodby in litt.]), breeding records for the Peninsula are few. Following the 1968 prairie drought year, a brood of four 1-week-old ducklings was found near the Kuzitrin River bridge on 5 July 1969 (D. R. Roseneau and G. E. Hall pers. comm.), and on 9 July 1969 I watched a hen with four downies at Safety Sound. In addition, a female I watched on a small pond near Buckland on 24 June 1975 and another that flew on several occasions across a marshy area in McCarthys Marsh on 17 July 1973 were probably breeders. In 1980, another drought year, five 3-day-old chicks were seen at Nome on 3 July and four 3-wk-old chicks at Safety Sound on 19 July (D. A. Woodby in litt.), and chicks were seen at Moses Point on 27 July (D. A. Woodby unpubl. notes). Back-dating from the 1969 brood observations indicates that egg-laying was under way by late May, and the first egg of a nine-egg clutch was laid on 29 May 1981 at the Fish River delta (D. A. Woodby in litt.).

Shovelers are filter feeders, taking in water at the tip of their spatulate bills and expelling it through the fine lamellae at the base, straining out food items. They take both phyto- and zooplankton from water surfaces and stretch their necks under water to sweep over the surface of bottom muds for many types of seeds and small invertebrates; they seldom up-end while feeding and seldom feed on dry shores (Palmer 1976).

Some summer flocking of drakes occurs on the Peninsula, but the source and composition of these flocks is unknown, i.e., whether local or not and whether of non-breeders, postbreeders, or both. On 25 June 1975 a flock of 30 shovelers, mostly males, loafed at a pond on the east side of the Buckland River estuary (Kessel and

F. G. Scheider pers. obs.); and on 26 and 30 June 1977, 35-40 birds were near the mouth of the Flambeau River in Safety Sound (J. O. Biderman in litt.).

Fall departures probably begin by mid-August, as soon as molting adults and fledged young can fly well, and most shovelers have left by mid-September (latest, "a few," 10-16 September 1980, Moses Point, D. A. Woodby in litt.; 29 birds, including one flock of 25, 19 September 1977, Safety Sound-Taylor Lagoon area, R. J. King pers. comm.; one, 3 October 1986, extralimitally at Kotzebue, Selawik NWR unpubl. notes).

Gadwall—*Anas strepera*

The Gadwall is a casual summer visitor on the Seward Peninsula. A pair was observed at Koyuk sometime between 25 and 30 May 1981 (D. A. Woodby in litt.) and at Safety Sound on 8 June 1982 (J. L. Dunn in litt.). Nearby extralimital records include a pair at Kotzebue from 27 May until at least 3 July 1982 (R. P. Schulmeister in litt.), an individual 32 km east of Selawik on 16 August 1986 (Selawik NWR unpubl. notes), a pair on the Inglutalik River delta on 28 July 1976 (Shields and Peyton 1977), and a female with seven approximately 1-week-old chicks about 6 km south of Stebbins on 16 July 1980 (D. A. Woodby in litt.). The Gadwall is an uncommon breeder in Southwestern Alaska (Kessel and Gibson 1978) and has been increasing in numbers in recent years in western Central Alaska and Western Alaska (U. S. Fish and Wildlife Service 1978-1987).

Eurasian Wigeon—*Anas penelope*

The Eurasian Wigeon is a rare migrant and summer visitor on the Seward Peninsula. A migrant male was present near Nome 20-22 May 1987 (W. S. Scott in litt.), one was confiscated from an Eskimo at Golovin on 26 May 1931 (USNM 365049), and another was at the Wales airport on 10 June 1977 (H. K. Springer in litt.). In summer, this wigeon has been identified only until late June (pair, 27 June 1971, pond along lower reaches of the Kuzitrin R, S. O. MacDonald and Kessel pers. obs.; male with a flock of 30 American Wigeons, 26 June 1973, Nugnugaluktuk River estuary, D. D. Gibson and Kessel pers. obs.; and two males, 26 June 1982, Safety Sound, J. L. Dunn in litt.). Whether it remains all summer and possibly breeds is not known; even if present, the hen would not be easily distinguishable from the American Wigeon after desertion by the drake. The only fall record is of two birds collected by R. W. Hendee on 5 August 1922 at King Island (Bailey 1925).

The Eurasian Wigeon is a common breeder in the Palearctic. Since the mid-1960s, increasing numbers have been wintering in western North America, especially in the Pacific Coast states; and Edgell (1984) believes that many of these are breeders from northeast Asia that cross over to the Pacific Flyway of North America to winter and then return to Asia in spring to breed. The presence of pairs of Eurasian Wigeon and of Eurasian X American Wigeon hybrids in North America suggest breeding on this continent, also (ibid.).

American Wigeon—*Anas americana*

A fairly common summer visitant and an uncommon breeder, the American Wigeon occurs widely across the Seward Peninsula. It is rare west of about 166⁰ W, although almost every year a few spring migrants get as far west as Wales between mid-May (one, 18 May 1978, Tin City, Flock and Hubbard 1979) and mid-June (two pairs, 11 June 1981, Wales, T. G. Tobish in litt.). It is somewhat more numerous and widespread in prairie drought years than otherwise. Breeding is largely confined to the Interior Lowlands and tributary drainages, although some nest at the base of the Peninsula at freshwater ponds along the lower reaches of the larger rivers (e.g., brood of eight small young on 20 July and four large young on 29 July 1949, Buckland R estuary, Alaska Game Commission 1949). I have seen broods at McCarthys Marsh, on the upper Burnt River, at Lava Lake, and in ponds along the Taylor Highway at the Pilgrim and Kuzitrin river bridges. All these sites were characterized by open, lacustrine waterbodies with peripheral sedge-grass wet meadows. A preference for protected ponds probably explains the near absence of wigeons during breeding at exposed coastal sites, such as Cape Espenberg and Cape Woolley, even when Wet Meadow is present.

While a few of Alaska's American Wigeons winter along the Pacific coastline of Alaska, especially in Southcoastal and Southeastern Alaska (Kessel and D. D. Gibson unpubl. data), most winter in Puget Sound, the Willamette River Valley of Oregon, and the Central Valley of California (Bellrose 1980). Returns from banded wigeons (Hansen 1960, McKnight 1962) indicate that most, if not all, birds from Selawik (and hence probably the Seward Peninsula) and from Minto Lakes, Yukon River flats, and Tetlin Lakes in Interior Alaska, migrate over interior routes, i.e., through southern Yukon Territory, then either through interior British Columbia or east of the Rocky Mountains to reach these wintering grounds. Some of those that migrate east of the Rockies continue to coastal southeastern United States (ibid.).

Spring migrants usually first reach the Seward Peninsula during the second week of May, about the same time as the Green-winged Teal (earliest, one, 4 May 1988, Deering, and pair, 9 May 1983, Nome, J. D. Walters unpubl. notes; but four, 2 May 1986, extralimitally at Kotzebue, Selawik NWR unpubl. notes). Migration peaks during the third week of May, with some movement continuing into June, especially in years of prairie drought.

American Wigeons breed as yearlings; some pair bonds are formed on the wintering grounds, but others, especially in yearlings, are not completed until the breeding grounds are reached (Palmer 1976). The hen selects an upland site for the nest, sometimes as far as 370 m from water (Bellrose 1980). Most nests from Interior Alaska and Selawik have been in mixed grass-sedge and woody vegetation and have been placed under a low, overhanging shrub (ANRS). Hence, although no nests have been reported, those in the Interior Lowlands of the Peninsula are probably in Dwarf Shrub Meadow and Low Shrub Thicket bordering the Wet Meadow and ponds where broods have been seen. Continent-wide clutch sizes from 179 nests averaged 8.5 eggs, although 19 nests in Alaska averaged only 7.3 eggs (Bellrose 1980); range 5-10 eggs (ANRS). Incubation lasts 23-25 days; the young are raised on local waters, with the hen staying with the chicks until they are full-grown or nearly so (Bellrose 1980). She passes her flightless period while with the brood (Palmer 1976). Wigeon young in Alaska fledge at about 37-44 days (Bellrose 1980).

Back-dating from observed downy broods indicates that sometimes egg-laying begins during the last week of May, with early hatching in late June (four "large downy chicks" [Class Ic = about 2 weeks?] and two broods of Class Ib chicks [= about 8 days], 5 July 1969, Pilgrim R ponds at Milepost 61.5 Taylor Highway, Kessel pers. obs.). Most egg-laying, however, apparently occurs during the first half of June, with hatching during the first half of July. The late hatchings are probably from renestings (e.g., two broods of Class Ia chicks, 17 July 1973, McCarthys Marsh, Kessel and D. D. Gibson unpubl. notes). A few paired birds are still present in late June (two pairs 22-24 June 1975 at Buckland; four pairs 26-28 June 1971 at the mouth of the Kuzitrin R in Imuruk Basin), indicating that renesting may still be possible through June. These chronologies would result in fledging beginning in the population in mid-August and continuing through the month (first fledging noted at Selawik on 10 August 1955, Shepherd 1955).

American Wigeons are largely vegetarians, feeding primarily on the stems and foliage of aquatic plants, especially the pondweed *Potamogeton filiformis* when it is available; some small invertebrates are consumed, especially by the young chicks (Palmer 1976). In Kotzebue Sound the birds also feed extensively on a green alga (W. R. Uhl pers. comm.). Wigeons usually feed in shallow water, taking items at or near the surface or by tipping up to stretch for items below. In deeper water, they often associate with other waterfowl, including swans, that feed on the bottom and cause plant material to break off or otherwise float to the surface where it becomes available to the wigeon. They also graze young shoots of grasses and sedges at pond edges and on adjacent slopes.

Most males desert the females during the first week of incubation, although some remain into the second week (Bellrose 1980). They usually repair to larger water-bodies or coastal estuaries, where they form flocks with other postbreeding or failed breeders. Flocks of 10-40 birds, mostly drakes, are common by the end of June (e.g., 24 June 1970, Serpentine R mouth; 26 and 27 June 1971, Lake Omiaktalik and the mouth of the Kuzitrin R; 26 and 27 June 1973, Nugnugaluktuk R estuary; and 25 and 26 June 1975, Buckland R estuary—all Kessel pers. obs.). As the drakes regain flight in early August, and later as young begin fledging in mid-August, there is a steady increase in the number of wigeons on protected estuaries and deltas, which then serve as staging areas (Nugnugaluktuk R estuary—300 birds on 2 August and 350 on 25 August 1981, Eldridge 1982; Buckland R estuary—350 on 26 August 1981, Eldridge 1982; Imuruk Basin—1300 in 1980-1981, Woodby and Divoky 1983; Safety Sound and Taylor Lagoon—520 between 26 and 31 August 1977, Drury et. al. 1981; Fish R delta-Golovnin Bay—700-800 in 1977 and in 1980-1981, Drury et al. 1981 and Woodby and Divoky 1983; Moses Point—1100 between 26 and 31 August 1977, Drury et al. 1981, and 3100 in 1980-1981, Woodby and Divoky 1983. Note: these fall staging numbers are all from prairie drought years).

While some drakes and failed breeders probably depart during August, the peak fall exodus occurs during the first half of September; they are uncommon after the third week of September (latest, 750 still present on the Fish R delta and another 200 in the wetlands between there and Koyuk, 1 October 1976, Drury et al. 1981).

Canvasback—*Aythya valisineria*

A rare migrant and summer visitant, the Canvasback is most numerous on the Peninsula in late May and during June, usually occurring as pairs, single males, or small flocks (earliest, two birds, 6 May 1981, Koyuk, and 20 birds, 8 May 1980, Golovnin Lagoon, Woodby and Divoky 1983). Numbers and flock sizes increase in years of prairie drought, e.g., 1977, 1980, and 1981 (25 on 15 June 1977 at Taylor Lagoon and 75, including 40% females, on 27 June 1977 at the mouth of the Flambeau R, J. O. Biderman in litt.; 100 on 7 June 1980 at Safety Sound, U. S. Fish and Wildlife Service 1978-1987, and 40 still there on 13 June 1980, Woodby and Divoky 1983; 42 on 28 May 1981 at Kiwalik Lagoon, Eldridge 1982; 80 on 7 June 1981 at Safety Sound, J. L. Dunn in litt.).

Canvasbacks are most frequent in the Coastal Lowland lagoons and river estuaries, but they also occur on Lacustrine Waters of the Interior Lowlands (e.g., observed spring and fall 1965-1967, Pilgrim R flats, R. R. Emmons pers. comm.). They have not been reported west of 166° W, only to Imuruk Basin (21 birds on 26 May 1980 and 17 on 3 June 1981, Woodby and Divoky 1983) and the mouth of Arctic River (male, 3 June 1976, Noble and Wright 1977).

No breeding has been reported from the Seward Peninsula, but a pair successfully raised a brood of five at Kotzebue in 1987 (Selawik NWR unpubl. notes) and the species is a casual breeder on the Yukon Delta (Kessel and Gibson 1978 and subsequent unpubl. data). The population on the Peninsula decreases sharply after June, perhaps the result of a pre-molt migration. The Nugnugaluktuk River estuary appears to be a molting site, however; 200 birds were there on 8 August 1981, with only 15 still remaining by 25 August (Eldridge 1982). Other specific fall records include six seen by W. H. Drury on 31 August 1977 at Taylor Lagoon (J. O. Biderman in litt.), a flock of 25 seen by R. R. Emmons (pers. comm.) during the 1965 hunting season (September) on the Pilgrim River flats, and 14 seen by R. J. King (pers. comm.) in the Safety Sound-Taylor Lagoon area on 19 September 1977.

Redhead—*Aythya americana*

A very rare migrant and summer visitant, and a casual breeder, the Redhead had not been recorded on the Seward Peninsula prior to the prairie drought year of 1977, and its subsequent occurrences have been limited to similar drought years or the year immediately thereafter. It has been recorded from mid-May to mid-September (earliest, 15 birds on 12 May 1981 during a coastline survey flight between Cape Espenberg and Kotzebue [Eldridge 1982], and two on 18 May 1981 at Moses Point [Woodby and Divoky 1983]; latest, seven, 10 September 1981, Golovnin Lagoon [Woodby and Divoky 1983], but extralimitally, an astonishing 160 birds, 16 September 1977, Selawik L [R. J. King pers. comm.]).

In 1977, ten Redheads were seen with wigeons on 20 May on the Kitluck River flats (J. M. Wright unpubl. notes), one was present on 6 June at Cape Espenberg (Schamel et al. 1979), and two were seen on 14 August by W. H. Drury during an aerial flight over Safety Sound (J. O. Biderman in litt.).

In 1980 and 1981, small numbers of Redheads were widespread along the Norton

Sound coastline, from Breving Lagoon (four on 7 July 1980) and Imuruk Basin (four on 3 June 1981) to Koyuk (Woodby and Divoky 1983); and a pair was seen on the lower Kuzitrin River during U. S. Fish and Wildlife Service aerial surveys on 8 June 1980 and 2 June 1981 (J. I. Hodges and B. Conant in litt.). A nest with seven eggs was found at Koyuk on 9 June 1980, and a brood of nine chicks, about 4 days old, was seen in this same area on 17 July 1980, probably from the same nest (D. A. Woodby in litt.)

In 1982, following the drought years of 1980 and 1981, two male Redheads were with Canvasbacks on Safety Sound on 26 June (J. L. Dunn in litt.) and 10 were with 75 Canvasbacks on a large inland lake north of Kwiniuk Inlet on 27 June (R. J. King pers. comm.).

The Redhead is an uncommon migrant and rare breeder in eastern Interior Alaska and becomes progressively less numerous westward (Kessel and Gibson 1978).

Ring-necked Duck—*Aythya collaris*

The Ring-necked Duck is a casual spring migrant on the Seward Peninsula, where it had not been recorded prior to 1978. On 10 June 1978, a male was observed on the Pilgrim River flats along the Taylor Highway (T. G. Tobish in litt.). Since then, this duck has been recorded twice during aerial waterfowl breeding population surveys (U. S. Fish and Wildlife Service 1978-1987, J. I. Hodges and B. Conant in litt.): a male, 6 June 1984, lower Kuzitrin River, and a pair, 13 June 1985, Nugnugaluktuk River.

The Ring-necked Duck is an uncommon migrant, rare summer visitant, and very rare breeder in eastern Interior Alaska; numbers decrease westward, and it becomes casual west of 153° W (Kessel and Gibson 1978).

Tufted Duck—*Aythya fuligula*

A Palearctic species, the Tufted Duck is a casual spring migrant along the Bering Sea coast of the Peninsula, where it was reported twice in 1975. A pair was in a small pond near the Nome airport on 17 June 1975 (W. C. Russell in litt.), and a male was in a small pond near Wales on 11 June 1975 (P. G. DuMont unpubl. notes). The Tufted Duck occurs regularly in the western and central Aleutian Islands and is a casual spring migrant and summer visitant in the northern Bering Sea (Kessel and Gibson 1978).

Greater Scaup—*Aythya marila*

A common migrant and breeder, the Greater Scaup is widely distributed across the Peninsula. During the breeding season it is most numerous in the uplands, Interior Lowlands (including the Agiapuk River delta and the lower Kuzitrin River flats), and the lake-studded wetlands north of about 66° N, but it also breeds in the Coastal Lowlands, especially along the lower reaches and deltas of the major rivers that flow into coastal lagoons, e.g., Serpentine, Arctic, Flambeau, and Fish rivers.

This overall abundance distribution seems to reflect the availability of preferred habitats (see below). The total breeding population of the Peninsula is about 50,000 birds (King and Lensink 1971, U. S. Fish and Wildlife Service 1978-1987).

During the summer the Greater Scaup of the Peninsula are almost entirely birds of lacustrine fresh water, although some of the ponds they use on lower river deltas and near lagoon shorelines may be brackish. Scaup select medium to deep water-bodies that may vary in size from tiny ponds to large lakes but that contain open water and have Wet Meadow shorelines vegetated largely by sedges or grasses. Most postbreeding adults also use ponds and lakes for molting, although a few move to river estuaries, protected bays, and lagoons. Most scaup apparently move to coastal sites for premigratory staging, using especially the coastal lagoons and adjacent lakes.

Greater Scaup winter along both coastlines of the contiguous United States and along the Gulf of Mexico, and a number winter along the entire Pacific coastline of Alaska, including the Aleutian Islands (American Ornithologists' Union 1983). It seems likely that the scaup from the Peninsula may winter in any of these regions. Greater Scaup banded at Selawik (probably scaup from the same population as those in the Kotzebue Sound region of the Seward Peninsula) and at Minto Lakes in Interior Alaska have been recovered almost entirely from eastern United States and the Gulf of Mexico (Hansen 1960), whereas those from Takslesluk Lake on the Yukon Delta (King 1973) and from the Innoko River (Hansen 1960) have been found not only at these eastern points, but also along most of the North American Pacific Coast. Scaup from the Interior Lowlands of the Peninsula and the Norton Sound region could either move eastward through Interior Alaska with the Kotzebue Sound birds or could move down the coastline and join the Yukon Delta or Innoko birds.

The first spring migrants reach the Peninsula in mid-May (earliest, 11 May 1905, Imuruk Basin, Anthony 1906; 12 May 1982, 10 between Shishmaref and Cape Espenberg, 50 at Kiwalik Lagoon, and 10 at Buckland, Eldridge 1982). Movement continues through the first week of June, usually peaking between 19 and 30 May, depending on seasonal environmental conditions. Scaup have not been reported from the western tip of the Peninsula, at Wales, until June.

Greater Scaup, as other *Aythya*, are capable of breeding as yearlings (Palmer 1976), although the percentage that do so and are successful is unknown. Pair formation begins on the wintering grounds and continues during migration (Palmer 1976); most (except some yearlings?) are paired by the time they reach Alaska. Nesting begins a week to 10 days after the birds arrive. The nest is usually concealed in a clump of dried grass or sedge near the margin of a pond and consists of a depression lined with graminoid leaves and down. Clutch size in 81 nests at Great Slave Lake, Northwest Territories, averaged 8.5 eggs (D. L. Trauger and R. G. Bromley in Bellrose 1980); 16 clutches from the Seward Peninsula averaged 7.4 eggs (several sources, including 12 nests at Cape Espenberg in Schamel et al. 1979). Eggs are laid at the rate of one per day, and incubation begins with the laying of the last egg (Cramp 1980a). Incubation lasts about 25 days (Hildén 1964), and the chicks gain flight in 40-45 days (Cramp 1980a). The male stays with the female until mid-incubation (Hildén 1964). The female stays with the brood through most of the prefledging period, leaving to undergo molt when the chicks have reached Class IIc (Kessel pers. obs.).

Back-dating from brood observations indicates that some egg-laying may begin on the Peninsula during the last few days of May (brood of seven Class Ib chicks,

5 July 1969, Pilgrim R flats, and brood of four Class IIb chicks, 22 July 1973, extralimitally at Kotzebue, both Kessel unpubl. notes), but peak egg-laying in most years is during the second week of June. Renesting after failed attempts may continue through July; I collected a laying hen (UAM 974) with a soft-shelled egg in the oviduct and several discharged ovarian follicles on 29 July 1958 extralimitally near Selawik, but success of such a late clutch is unlikely. The peak of hatch occurs in mid-July, with a few broods continuing to hatch through the first week of August. Thus, fledging should begin in early broods by the end of the first week of August and almost all should be flying by the third week of September.

The diet of adult Greater Scaup consists about equally of vegetable and animal matter, especially aquatic insects, crustaceans, molluscs, and parts of aquatic plants (Palmer 1976). Food items are obtained primarily by diving. Newly hatched chicks feed predominantly on insects, picking some from the surface of the water, but they also dive for subsurface food soon after leaving the nest.

Postbreeding flocks of males begin to form by the fourth week of June (congregations by 23 June 1951 [Thayer 1951] and 23 June 1976 [Noble and Wright 1977] on lakes along lower Serpentine R; about 200, mostly males, 27 June 1973, Nugnugaluktuk R estuary, and 74 males, 29 June 1973, North Killeak L [Kessel and D. D. Gibson unpubl. notes]). Some males are flightless by early July (5 July 1976, Serpentine R, Noble and Wright 1977), but the heaviest molt in the male population is during the last half of July and early August. Premigratory aggregations begin forming in Coastal Lowlands by the second week of August. On 8 August 1981, there were 1900 scaup in the Nugnugaluktuk River estuary (Eldridge 1982)—probably a combination of molters and staging migrants, since only 200 remained there on 25 August 1981; flocks of 30-55 birds gathered in the Safety Sound-Taylor Lagoon area in mid-August 1975 and 1976 (Drury et al. 1981); and 250 scaup were in Kiwalik Lagoon on 26 August 1981 (Eldridge 1982).

With the addition of fledged juvenals and, later, the newly molted hens, numbers at staging sites build up during late August and early September, reaching a peak during the second week of September (1530 scaup on 10 September 1980 and over 1000 on 10 September 1981, Golovnin Lagoon, Woodby and Divoky 1983). Numbers drop rapidly after mid-September as birds depart on migration, although a few scaup, especially families of late broods, probably remain until freeze-up (latest reported, 103 scaup, 1 October 1976, aerial survey over the Moses Point wetlands, Drury et al. 1981; extralimitally, male, 28 October 1935, St. Lawrence I, Murie 1936).

Lesser Scaup—*Aythya affinis*

Probably a very rare spring migrant and early summer visitant, the Lesser Scaup has been recorded only a few times on the Peninsula. I had close views of a lone adult male on a small pond at about Milepost 15 Inmachuk River road on 22 June 1973. In the prairie drought year of 1977, a male was near the mouth of the Nome River on 8 June, one was at the Kuzitrin River near the Taylor Highway on 13 June, and a male and female were on the Fish River delta on 16 June (J. O. Biderman in litt.). Similarly, in the prairie drought year of 1981, four were reported from the Koyuk area between 25 and 30 May by D. A. Woodby (unpubl. notes), and about 60 Lesser Scaup, in a raft of diving ducks that included 300 Greater Scaup, 80 Canvasbacks, and 2 Redheads, were carefully examined by J. L. Dunn and others (in litt.) in Safety Sound on 7 June. In 1986 two males on a pond near Nome were closely compared to Greaters by D. E. Wolf (in litt.) on 7 June.

Lesser Scaup are common breeders in Interior Alaska; they become progressively less numerous westward, but are still fairly common as far west as McGrath and the Koyukuk River. In the Selawik-Kotzebue area, Lesser Scaup, mostly males, are rare spring migrants and summer visitants (Selawik NWR unpubl. notes). Males are rare postbreeding molters on the Yukon-Kuskokwim Delta (King 1973).

Common Eider—*Somateria mollissima*

The Common Eider is a common coastal migrant, a rare winter visitant, and a common breeder about the Seward Peninsula. During the summer it occurs in the Coastal Lowlands and in Nearshore and inner Inshore waters. The greatest density of breeding birds occurs at Cape Espenberg, where D. D. Gibson and I counted more than 500 birds, mostly females, 3-5 July 1973, and where on waterfowl study plots in 1976 and 1977, Schamel et al. (1979) found densities ranging from 5.0 to 13.0 nests/10 ha. One colony on a 0.33-ha island in a pond on Cape Espenberg in 1977 contained 322 Common Eider nests (Seguin 1981). This eider is also a common breeder in the Nugnugaluktuk River estuary and locally along the northwest coast of the Peninsula on the outer fringes of Lopp and Arctic lagoons. It also breeds in lesser numbers on the outer islands of the Buckland River estuary and along the Norton Sound coastline, including Safety Sound and the wetlands west of Koyuk Inlet. It is absent from the enclosed waters of Imuruk Basin, but nests in small numbers in the wetlands that stretch from the mouth of the Serpentine River to the mouth of the Arctic River, within Shishmaref Inlet. Overall, an estimated 4900 Common Eiders breed on the Seward Peninsula (King and Lensink 1971), and another 100,000 pass through the Bering Strait during migration. (This rough estimate is based on the number that breed in western Canada [Barry 1986], the number that occur in the Beaufort Sea and that pass Barrow spit [Thompson and Person 1963, Johnson 1971, Johnson and Richardson 1981], the number that nest along the northwest Chukchi Coast [Divoky 1978], the limited nesting range in northeast Siberia, and an unknown number of non-breeders summering in the Chukchi Sea.)

When onshore, Common Eiders on the Seward Peninsula are most frequently found in Wet Meadow and Salt Grass Meadow habitats and in *Elymus* Grass Meadow, never far from the shoreline of a pond, lagoon, or outer coastline. Within these habitats, factors offering protection from both mammalian and avian predators strongly influence nest site selection (Gorman 1974, Schamel 1977, Seguin 1981). Sites isolated by deep water have been shown to be more successful than more exposed sites (Seguin 1981), and nests are frequently placed near some concealing feature of the environment, such as a patch of *Elymus* or some driftwood or under available shrubbery. Colonies are often closely associated with nesting Glaucous Gulls, and Schamel (1977) found that eiders nesting between 50 and 100 m of a Glaucous Gull nest evidently benefited from the protection provided by the gulls in chasing off avian predators—although eider nests at other distances proved less successful. On the Seward Peninsula, colonies are commonly on small islands just inside lagoon inlets or inside mouths of estuaries, e.g., Lopp Lagoon, Safety Sound, and the Nugnugaluktuk and Buckland river estuaries. On one such island inside the "Second Inlet" of Lopp Lagoon on 9 July 1974, the nests of Common Eiders and Glaucous Gulls were so dense (eight eider nests and one gull nest within a 3-m radius) that I found three nests that contained a mix of eider and gull eggs. I was unable to determine which species was incubating these mixed clutches, although a four-egg "clutch" of two eider and two gull eggs was undoubtedly being incubated by an eider; the other "clutches" consisted of one and two eider eggs, respectively, and one gull egg each.

While a few individual Common Eiders may overwinter as far north as open leads in the sea ice permit (e.g., Point Hope, Gabrielson and Lincoln 1959) and as far south along the Pacific Coast as Washington and Oregon (American Ornithologists' Union 1983), most winter in the Bering Sea, where they often occur in mixed flocks with King Eiders. Here, they are widely distributed through the Aleutian Islands and, as ice conditions permit, northward in leads and polynyas of the sea ice, including at St. Lawrence Island ("considerable numbers," Fay 1961), on the south coast of the Chukotsk Peninsula ("comparatively regular," Portenko 1972), the Diomede Islands ("wintered, in 1912-13," Thayer and Bangs 1914; "flocks of thousands," Dement'ev and Gladkov 1952), and near Cape Woolley (present 23 November [yr?], Gabrielson and Lincoln 1959; present 15 February 1969, J. J. Burns unpubl. notes; "eider ducks" present 8 April 1984, Beltz School unpubl. notes).

It is not possible to distinguish the earliest spring migrants from overwintering birds, and the timing of the vanguard of the spring movement northward varies considerably with annual differences in ice conditions. However, the main movement at the Seward Peninsula begins in early May ("beginning to show up" on the Bonanza R flats, 24 April 1965, J. J. Burns unpubl. notes; first at Wales, 5 May 1922, Bailey 1943; first large flocks at Nome, 8 May 1969, J. J. Burns unpubl. notes), and it peaks, depending on weather, between about 20 May and mid-June (Bailey 1943, Flock and Hubbard 1979, Schamel et al. 1979, Eldridge 1982, D. R. Paulson in litt., M. L. Ward unpubl. notes). This extended passage is the result of some sex and age segregation, with adult males leading the migration, followed by some mated pairs, and then an increasing proportion of females and immature birds (Palmer 1976). While most birds migrate over water, apparently a few spring migrants sometimes fly directly over the western third of the Peninsula itself (D. Tevuk in Myres 1958).

The commencement of nesting is closely associated with the ice melt in the vicinity of nest sites (Fay and Cade 1959, Schamel 1977) and thus may vary annually by a week or more. Overall, most local breeders on the Peninsula have probably established themselves at their breeding sites by the first week of June. Males generally do not breed until 3 yr of age (Palmer 1976); females begin laying at 2-4 yr of age (26% in second year, 42% in third year in Scotland) and have an average adult life expectancy of 26 yr (Baillie and Milne 1982). First-time layers begin nesting about a week later than older females (Baillie and Milne 1982). The female selects the nest site (Cooch 1965, Milne 1974, Schamel 1977), often the same site or one nearby that she used the preceding year (Cooch 1965, Milne 1974). The nest consists of an earthen bowl lined with varying amounts of down, shed down which the female preens from her abdomen, usually beginning after the third egg is laid (Cooch 1965, Palmer 1976). At Cape Espenberg, egg-laying occurred from 10 June to about 11 July 1976 and from 4 June to 4 July 1977, with two nests in 1977 not receiving eggs until 27 and

29 July (Seguin 1981). Egg-laying was under way on the Fish River delta by 1 June 1981 (D. A. Woodby in litt.). Eggs are laid at 24-h intervals, with clutch size varying with the amount of body fat reserves of the female (Baillie and Milne 1982). Mean clutch size at Cape Espenberg ranged from 4.3 ± 1.2 eggs in 1976 to 4.8 ± 1.8 eggs in 1977 (range 1-9 eggs), except on a dense island plot in 1977, where the mean was 7.2 ± 3.1 eggs (Seguin 1981). On an island in Lopp Lagoon that had been "egged" by local villagers about a week earlier, clutch size in 37 nests that I tabulated on 4 July 1974 was 3.8 ± 1.8 eggs (range 1-7 eggs). Generally, clutch sizes of late nests and renestings and of females less than 7 yr old are smaller than early nestings and those of older birds (Milne 1974, Baillie and Milne 1982).

The attentiveness of the female increases during laying, and she usually stays on the nest after about the third egg (Cooch 1965, Baillie and Milne 1982), although actual incubation usually does not begin until the clutch is complete (Cramp 1980a). Incubation of the last-laid egg in 79 nests in Scotland averaged 25.9 days (Milne 1974) and in 57 nests in the St. Lawrence River estuary averaged 26.0 ± 1.4 days, with a range of 23-30 days (Guignion 1968). The female apparently fasts throughout incubation, leaving the nest only occasionally to obtain water (Milne 1974, Schamel 1977). Hatching at Cape Espenberg ranged from 10 to 26 July 1976 and 1 July to 3 August 1977, with one extremely late date of 29 August 1976 (Seguin 1981); it ranged from about 1 to 18 July 1981 on the Fish River delta (D. A. Woodby in litt.). All other Seward Peninsula observations of eggs and hatching fall within these dates.

After hatching, the female and chicks move immediately to the nearest water and then out into protected Inshore Waters along the coast, where they remain until fledging in September, at about 60-65 days of age (Palmer 1976). The female stays with her brood for varying lengths of time, depending in large part on her physical condition and whether or not her preferred food (molluscs) occurs where the chicks can obtain their diet of crustaceans (Gorman and Milne 1972).

Breeding males usually remain with their females until the beginning of incubation and then return to the seacoast, e.g., I watched flocks of 11-14 males along the outer coast of Lopp Lagoon on 2 and 4 July 1974, and J. M. Wright (unpubl. notes) watched about 20 males feeding off Cape Deceit on 5 July 1978. Nonbreeders remain at sea along ice edges as long as ice persists ("great flocks" between King I and St. Lawrence I, 27-28 June 1921, Bailey 1925; mixture of 2500-3000 Common and King eiders halfway between King I and the mainland, 18 June 1965, J. J. Burns unpubl. notes), and thereafter they apparently move inshore to coastal waters for the summer (Portenko 1972, King and Dau 1981).

Common Eiders feed almost entirely on animal matter, primarily on molluscs and on crustaceans, especially isopods and amphipods (Palmer 1976, Cramp 1980a). They feed by dipping near the water surface, by dabbling and tipping in shallow waters, and by diving to depths up to about 16 m (Palmer 1976).

Beginning in July, postbreeding males join the flocks of nonbreeders in Inshore Waters, most apparently molting in small groups along the coast. Along the Norton Sound coastline, Woodby and Divoky (1983) found non- and postbreeding eiders most common near exposed rocky outcrops, e.g., Cape Nome and Cape Woolley. Noble and Wright (1977) reported molting in Shishmaref Inlet, and Common Eiders undoubtedly molt also off the barrier strip along the northwest coast of the Seward Peninsula.

No extensive molt migration of postbreeding males has been recorded passing through the Bering Strait. Apparently the heavy passage of postbreeding males and failed breeders from the western Canadian Arctic and Beaufort Sea (Thompson and Person 1963, Johnson 1971) molts in coastal waters of the Chukchi Sea between Point Lay and Peard Bay (Bailey 1925; local residents of Barrow as quoted in Thompson and Person 1963 and Palmer 1976; Watson and Divoky 1972; Kessel, D. D. Gibson, and S. O. MacDonald pers. obs.; Lehnhausen and Quinlan 1981; D. R. Herter in litt.). Likewise, no concentrated movement through the Bering Strait during fall migration has been reported, perhaps because the movement is too extended and diffuse.

Locally on the Seward Peninsula, onshore breeding populations drop off rapidly between late July and early August (see Schamel et al. 1979), and Common Eiders become uncommon thereafter until postbreeding females and juvenals form migratory flocks along the coast during late September and October. On 27 October 1980 at least 760 "female-plumaged eiders, mostly Common," were distributed along the Norton Sound coast from Nome to Koyuk, mostly flocks of 40-100 birds but one of 250 (Woodby and Divoky 1983). This date corresponds to a similar observation of large flocks containing many young birds in the Chukchi Sea between Barrow and Wainwright 27-29 October 1921 (Bailey 1925).

Ice conditions determine the final fall departure dates, with all but a few winter residents having departed by mid- to late November.

This widespread eider exhibits considerable morphologic variation across its range. The form on the Seward Peninsula is the Beringian subspecies, *S. m. v-nigra*.

King Eider—*Somateria spectabilis*

The King Eider is an abundant migrant, uncommon summer and rare winter visitant, and a very rare breeder about the Seward Peninsula. The only confirmed breeding records have been from Cape Espenberg, where Schamel et al. (1979) found a nest, later abandoned, in 1976 and four nests in 1977, one of which was successful. Throughout the summer, however, singles and small groups of nonbreeders feed, loaf, and molt in Inshore Waters, especially off the Safety Sound-Cape Nome area, in the vicinity of Sledge Island and the adjacent mainland, and off the outer coast of Lopp Lagoon (Drury 1976b, Kessel pers. obs., Kessel and Gibson unpubl. data).

The King Eiders of western North America winter primarily in the Inshore Waters of the Alaska Peninsula, eastern Aleutian Islands, and the southern Bering Sea (Palmer 1976, King and Dau 1981), but some winter as far north as leads and polynyas in the sea ice occur (see localities listed above under Common Eider, where King Eiders usually far outnumber the Commons in winter). They begin their northward movement somewhat earlier than the Common Eiders, although early arrivals are difficult to distinguish from overwintering birds. In early seasons the first of the migration may be under way by early April (first seen 6 April 1922 at Wales, Bailey 1943; two flocks reported 7 April 1934 at Uelen, Chukotsk Peninsula, Portenko 1972; a major passage beginning 10 April 1915 past the mouth of Sinuk R, Hill 1923). In most years, the main push is apparently under way by the third week of April (several flocks, 20 April 1922, Wales, Bailey 1943; "lots of eiders," 20 April 1967, north side of King I, J. J. Burns unpubl. notes; thousands flew past Wales, about 21 April 1978, Flock and Hubbard 1979) and continues until mid-May. During this period, depending on weather, great strings of thousands of King Eiders follow the open leads through Bering Strait (Bailey 1943, Flock and Hubbard 1979) or may fly along the frozen coastline (Hill 1923) or even take shortcuts over land (across the Seward Peninsula from Imuruk Basin northward, D. Tevuk in Myres 1958; across the Chukotsk Peninsula, Portenko 1972). Nonbreeders continue to move into and through the waters of the Seward Peninsula through mid-June (2500-3000 male King and Common eiders between King I and the mainland, 18 June 1965, J. J. Burns unpubl. notes; flocks moving north past Wales in late June 1977, K. V. Hirsch and D. A. Woodby in litt.; last seen at Wales 18 June 1978, D. R. Paulson unpubl. notes). Altogether, over a million King Eiders probably pass through the Bering Strait during migration (Thompson and Person 1963, Johnson 1971, Portenko 1972).

Most postbreeding male and failed female King Eiders from western North America apparently migrate to the waters of the Chukchi Sea off northwest Alaska to molt (see above under Common Eider), and birds from Siberia apparently molt locally in bays and estuaries along the northern Siberian coastline (Portenko 1972). Thus, while summering nonbreeders may molt in the waters of the Seward Peninsula, Bering Strait, and elsewhere in the Bering Sea, the breeding populations from the Arctic do not move back through the Bering Strait until after the flight feathers have been replaced. These postbreeders apparently move back south through Bering Strait during September and October, but the movement is diffuse, both geographically and temporally, and no spectacular movements comparable to those of spring have been reported.

The main fall passage is over by the end of October (King Eiders prominent in hunter kills until about mid-October 1914, off Sledge I, Hall 1923; ceased being common at the end of October 1933 at Uelen, Chukotsk Peninsula, Portenko 1972) and, as with Common Eiders, all but a few winter residents have departed by mid- to late November.

Spectacled Eider—*Somateria fischeri*

A Beringian species of restricted distribution, the Spectacled Eider is an uncommon migrant and a rare local breeder and summer visitant about the Seward Peninsula. The only confirmed breeding localities are (1) the Salt Grass Meadow-Pond complex west of the mouth of the Arctic River at the edge of Shishmaref Inlet, where, while tramping the flats on the evening of 26 June 1970, I flushed three single females and two pairs and where J. M. Wright (unpubl. notes) found three nests 20-24 June 1977 in which clutches when completed contained 3-6 eggs, the first of which hatched on 7 July and (2) Cape Espenberg, where Schamel et al. (1979) found two nests each in 1976 and 1977, of which all but one in 1977 were successful. Judging from their persistent occurrence, they may also be rare breeders along the inner margins of Lopp and Arctic lagoons. D. A. Woodby (in litt.) saw them regularly during the summer of 1977 off the outer coast between "First" and "Second Inlet" of Lopp Lagoon and concluded that they were breeders, an adult male was seen on a tundra pond near Wales on 25 June 1979 by S. Hills (unpubl. notes), a few were seen about Wales by Bailey (1943) during July and early August 1922, two female-plumaged birds (juvenals?) were seen on a tundra pond near Wales on 7 September 1973 by D. D. Gibson and G. J. Divoky (unpubl. notes), and C. Ongtowasruk, a life-long resident of the area, told me that they nested "only rarely" in the region—although Bailey (1943) was told that they did not breed at Wales. Otherwise during the summer, only a few scattered individuals, including subadult and adult males and female-plumaged birds, occur about the coastline, mostly where washed with Strait waters, but sometimes in Norton Sound as far east as Safety Sound.

While occasional overwintering Spectacled Eiders have been reported from various sites throughout much of the Bering Sea, their main winter range has yet to be discovered (Dau and Kistchinski 1977). Recent evidence tends to confirm S. M. Uspenskii's suggestion (in Johnson et al. 1975), however, that they winter in the Gulf of Anadyr: (1) Migrants arrive at the Yukon-Kuskokwim Delta in spring from the northwest (Dau and Kistchinski 1977), (2) a mass migration was observed about 65 km south of St. Lawrence Island on 29 May 1973 (ibid.), and a similar movement was witnessed in this same general region on 17 May 1980 (R. H. Day unpubl. notes), in which "scattered flocks of high hundreds, low thousands," composed of more than 80% females, were flying due east toward the Yukon Delta, and (3) the earliest spring sightings have all occurred north of 63° N (see below). Wintering Spectacled Eiders are not limited by feeding behavior to shallow waters, since they feed on pelagic invertebrates (two mid-winter stomachs from the Pribilof Islands contained 90% amphipods [Preble and McAtee 1923]), which are abundant at the sea water-pack ice interface.

Annual spring arrival dates at the Seward Peninsula, as with the other species of eiders, is influenced by seasonal variations in ice conditions. The earliest evidence of movement over the years has been in late April-early May. Extralimitally, a male was collected on 23 April 1902 at Cape Chaplin, Chukotsk Peninsula (Portenko 1972), one was seen on 25 April 1978 off Gambell, northwest St. Lawrence Island (E. P. Knudtson in litt.), and the species was reported by residents of Wainwright at the end of April 1958 (Myres 1958). A male was collected at Wales on 2 May 1942 (Bailey 1943), another was shot near Little Diomede Island on 11 May 1958 (Kenyon and Brooks 1960), and here also on 11 May 1964 Spectacled Eiders were present in mixed flocks with King and Common eiders (J. J. Burns unpubl. notes). The main movement usually comes sometime between mid-May and the first week of June (main flight occurred mid-May 1934, extralimitally at Uelen, Chukotsk Peninsula, Portenko 1972; many moving 3 June 1922, Wales, Bailey 1943). Migration may continue through much of June, the later birds undoubtedly nonbreeders (75 at Wales, 10 June 1983, M. L. Ward unpubl. notes; a "flight" at Wales, 23 June 1922, Bailey 1943). Spectacled Eiders did not actually show up at their Seward Peninsula breeding sites until 31 May 1976 (Arctic R, Noble and Wright 1977) and 31 May 1977 (Cape Espenberg, Schamel et al. 1979).

While occasional nonbreeding individuals spend the summer in the Nearshore and Inshore waters of the Peninsula as they apparently do also along the Bering Sea coast of the Chukotsk Peninsula (Portenko 1972), the species does not become numerous again until September. Judging from the probable world population of 400,000-500,000 birds (Uspenskii 1972, Johnsgard 1978), 200,000 or more Spectacled Eiders must move south through the Bering Strait during the fall passage, but no conspicuous migratory movements have been recorded.

A flock of 420 "mottled-plumaged" birds was observed 24 km east of Cape Darby in Norton Sound on 11 September 1977 (Woodby and Divoky 1983), not far from where a similar "large flock" of Spectacled Eiders, almost entirely molting males, was seen extralimitally by Nelson (1883:100) 40 km west of Stuart Island, off St. Michael, on 15 September 1881. Also extralimitally along the south shore of St. Lawrence Island, a flock of 500-1000 molting males was observed on 18 September 1980 (Woodby and Divoky 1983).

The last Spectacled Eiders apparently leave the region in late October-early November (latest, adult males, 22 and 23 October 1934, extralimitally at Uelen, Chukotsk Peninsula; first-year male collected, 10 November 1946, Wales, Bailey 1948).

Steller's Eider—*Polysticta stelleri*

The Steller's Eider is an uncommon migrant, rare summer visitant, and possibly a very rare breeder on the Seward Peninsula. In all, of the world's estimated 500,000 Steller's Eiders (Uspenskii 1972), probably 350,000 migrate through the Bering Strait, but most apparently on the Siberian side. A few nonbreeders remain in the waters of the Peninsula during the summer, especially at Wales and along the Norton Sound coastline (Bailey 1943, Drury 1976b, D. A. Woodby and K. V. Hirsch unpubl. notes). The statement by Gabrielson and Lincoln (1959:213) that Steller's Eiders were "abundant in May and June 1951 at Mint River" appears to be an error, however, based on a questionable interpretation of an Alaska Game Commission report (1951) that stated in generic fashion that "King, Pacific, and Stellers eiders were abundant" on an aerial survey on 15 June 1951 between Mint River and Shishmaref. The only suggestion of breeding on the Seward Peninsula is a report of the Vega expedition taking three chicks at Port Clarence on 24 July 1879 that "still had the embryonal down over the growing feathers" (Portenko 1972:191).

This Beringian eider winters primarily in Nearshore and Inshore waters along both coasts of the western half of the Alaska Peninsula and east to Kodiak Island (Jones 1965, Forsell and Gould 1981, Gill et al. 1981); a smaller population winters along the Asiatic coastline, primarily from the Commander Islands south to the northern Kurile Islands (Palmer 1976). Except for a small population that nests on the Yukon Delta (Brandt 1943, Gabrielson and Lincoln 1959, Harris 1967, Yukon Delta NWR unpubl. data), essentially all breeders pass through the Bering Strait on migration to their breeding grounds along the coasts of the Arctic Ocean, primarily in eastern Siberia (Jones 1965).

Spring migrants begin to move through the Strait in mid-May (earliest, 12 May 1922, Wales, Bailey 1943; 13 May 1962, Wales, J. J. Burns unpubl. notes), with the main movement usually occurring during the last week of May and the first few days of June. Many immatures also move north through the Strait, especially during the latter phases of spring migration ("lots of males" between Sledge I and the mainland on 19 June 1965 [J. J. Burns unpubl. notes], and three adult males and 47 immatures at Cape Woolley on 25 June 1983 [R. and B. Mearns unpubl. notes]), although others remain throughout the summer in the Inshore Waters of the Bering Sea (Fay and Cade 1959, Portenko 1972, Gill et al. 1981, King and Dau 1981).

The southward movement after the breeding season can vary in timing by almost

3 months, depending on whether the migration takes place before or after the wing molt (Jones 1965). Thus, migration through the Bering Strait could occur any time between late July and early October. While a few birds may remain far north as late as mid-October (three still present at Barrow, 12 October 1977, G. E. Hall in litt.; one seen at Wainwright, 13 October 1921, Bailey 1925), most have passed through the Strait by that time (latest, extralimitally, 15 October [yr?], six juveniles shot at St. Michael, Nelson 1887; 6 November 1964, three shot, south side of St. Lawrence I, J. J. Burns unpubl. notes; 7 November 1935, male collected on St. Lawrence I, Murie 1936).

Harlequin Duck—*Histrionicus histrionicus*

The Harlequin Duck is an uncommon breeder on the mainland of the Seward Peninsula, where it is widely distributed along the clear, shallow, rapidly flowing creeks and rivers that drain the Southern and Northern uplands. Immediately before and after breeding, these birds flock and feed along the coastline, especially at the base of rocky headlands.

Harlequins winter commonly in the Aleutian Islands (Bellrose 1980) and as far north in sea ice polynyas as the Pribilof Islands (Preble and McAtee 1923) and St. Matthew Island (McRoy et al. 1971). Spring migrants begin arriving at the Seward Peninsula during the third week of May (earliest, 24 from the Solomon R to the mouth of the Nome R, including 15 at Cape Nome, 19 May 1983, and 2 at Deering, 19 May 1988, J. D. Walters unpubl. notes; pair, 20 May 1978, Wales, Flock and Hubbard 1979) and may still be arriving in seasonally late years until mid-June.

Breeding pairs move inland to nesting sites almost as soon as they arrive (male on Grand Central R, 24 May 1969, D. G. Roseneau unplub. notes), although pairs nesting along streams near the coast may remain at coastal sites for prenesting activities, including courtship, copulation, and feeding (Dzinbal 1982). Nests are usually located near water (95% within 5 m), most frequently along rocky shores or on alluvial islands of fast-moving creeks (Bengtson 1972a), but sometimes on the islands of alpine ponds (ANRS). The female selects the nest site, which usually has some overhead protection, such as shrubbery, debris, or an overhanging bank, and she builds a nest of graminoid materials lined with down (Bengtson 1972a, Palmer 1976). Eggs are laid at 1- or 2-day intervals, with clutches averaging about 6 eggs (77 clutches in Iceland averaged 5.7 eggs, range 3-9 eggs, Bengtson 1972a). Incubation lasts an average of 28 days (range 27-29 days), with the female leaving the nest only about once every 48 h during this period (Bengtson 1972a). She may go to the coast, if nearby, for feeding (Dzinbal 1982; also, three pairs in bay at Deering, 15 June 1985, J. D. Walters unpubl. notes). Some broods stay on the inland rivers until fledging, whereas others, especially those from nests near the coast, may swim and drift to the coast while still flightless. The young gain flight at about 55-56 days of age, and the female remains with the brood until then (Kuchel 1977).

The males stay with the females until incubation begins (ibid.) and then return to the coast, where they flock with other males and failed females. Such postbreeding flocks have been reported from Cape Mountain (29 males, 28 June 1979, S. Hills unpubl. notes), Cape Woolley (35 males and 2 females, 18 June 1983, R. and B. Mearns unpubl. notes), about Sledge Island (116 males and 4 females, 18-19 June 1975, Drury 1976b), and in the Topkok-Bluff area (55 males, 3 July 1975, and 35 males, 11 July 1975, Drury 1976b), as well as off Cape Nome (6-10 birds, including 29 June 1977 and 3 July 1966, Kessel pers. obs.).

Based on the above observations and chronologies, on the fact that I have seen males inland on creeks as late as early July (e.g., two males on the Nome R at Milepost 19 Taylor Highway on 21 June 1972; two males on the lower Inmachuk R on 21 June 1973, and a pair and two males on a dredge pond on the upper Inmachuk R on 22 June 1973; and two males and a female on Gold Run on 3 July 1967), and on the age of observed broods (7-10-day-old downy chicks, 5 August 1973, Hot Springs Ck, D. D. Gibson unpubl. notes; three-fourths-grown young, 9 September 1976, Solomon R, H. K. Springer in litt.), the following breeding schedule can be derived for the Seward Peninsula: egg-laying from the last week of May through the first week of July, but peaking the first 2 weeks of June; hatching from end of June to mid-August; and fledging from the second week of August to the third week of September or later.

Harlequin Ducks feed almost entirely on animal matter. When inland during the breeding season, they feed largely on aquatic invertebrates, with the smallest chicks taking food from the water's surface and from among shoreline vegetation; but they also take other items opportunistically, such as occasional small fish (Palmer 1976). When at the coast, they consume snails, mussels, echinoderms, and small crabs from rocky substrates, as well as free-swimming invertebrates, especially crustaceans, from among rock crevices and seaweeds; and at river mouths they may feed on drifting salmon roe (Palmer 1976, Dzinbal and Jarvis 1984).

Harlequins do not breed until they are at least 2 yr old (Palmer 1976), and immatures spend their summer in flocks in the waters about the islands and mainland coasts of the Bering Sea. While these immatures summer along the south coast of the Chukotsk Peninsula (Portenko 1972) and about St. Lawrence Island (Fay and Cade 1959), they do not appear to frequent the shorelines of the Seward Peninsula. In fact, after mid-July, even the flocks of postbreeders have left to molt elsewhere.

Fall migration is imperceptible, since the postbreeding males and failed females largely disappear by mid-July, and the movement of successful females and young to the coast is diffuse, both in terms of timing and of bird densities. Most of these birds have probably left the waters of the Seward Peninsula by the end of September (latest, six males flew past Deering on 26 September 1985, and two birds were still at Deering on 3 October 1987, J. D. Walters unpubl. notes; but extralimitally, one, Cape Thompson, Chukchi Sea, 6 November [yr?] Williamson et al. 1966).

Oldsquaw—*Clangula hyemalis*

Circumpolar in distribution, the Oldsquaw is a rare winter visitant and an abundant breeder on the Seward Peninsula, where, among waterfowl, it is second in numbers only to the Northern Pintail. Estimated population levels have fluctuated widely over the years, varying from fewer than 20,000 birds in 1957 to 128,000 in 1978; numbers have been in a sharp downtrend since 1978 (Figure 21). In the 10-yr period 1978-1987, the average estimated number of Oldsquaws on the Peninsula was

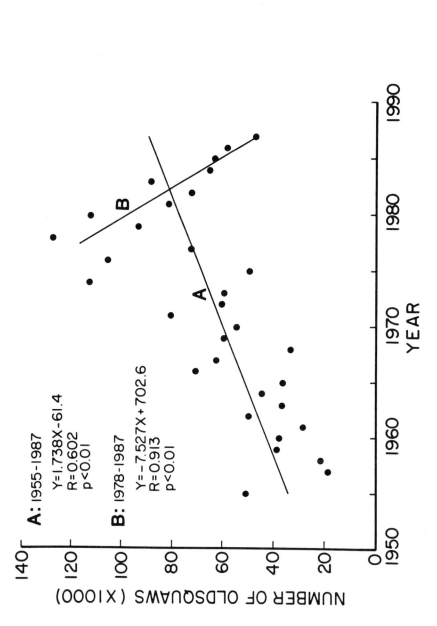

Figure 21. Estimated numbers of Oldsquaws on the Seward Peninsula 1955-1987. Data based on aerial samples of 72.5 km^2 (28 mi^2) of wetlands made during the U. S. Fish and Wildlife Service annual waterfowl breeding population surveys. The fitted regression lines show an overall population increase over the 32-year period but a decline since 1978 (courtesy J. I. Hodges, USFWS, Juneau, AK).

81,600 ± 25,000 (U. S. Fish and Wildlife Service 1978-1987). Oldsquaws are widely distributed throughout the Coastal and Interior lowlands, including Imuruk Basin, McCarthys Marsh, and the lower Serpentine and Arctic rivers, and throughout the Northern Uplands and Southern Uplands where lacustrine waters are present. They are most numerous at Cape Espenberg and in the Wales-Lopp Lagoon area. At Cape Espenberg, on a 25-ha Wet Meadow census plot, Schamel et al. (1979) found 8.4 nests/10 ha in 1976 and 12.8 nests/10 ha in 1977; these densities are high for the species, and other habitats supported considerably lower densities. Here, as well as in the Wales flats-Lopp Lagoon area and at McCarthys Marsh, according to my ground survey counts, Oldsquaws constitute 30% of the duck population. Along coastal Norton Sound in 1980-1981, they were only 4.1% of the duck population (Woodby and Divoky 1983).

While a few breeders on the Peninsula nest on coastal beaches, most move varying distances inland to breed along lagoon shores, in river estuaries, or about freshwater ponds and lakes. Breeding ponds are usually shallow and have considerable bottom sediment, which causes turbidity when disturbed by diving ducks or ducklings and may provide escape cover for the chicks (Alison 1976). After breeding, most adults and fledglings move to coastal ponds and lagoons or protected marine waters to molt, although a few molters may gather on some of the largest lakes, e.g., Imuruk Lake (J. J. Burns pers. comm.).

Oldsquaws winter commonly in the Aleutian Islands (Bellrose 1980) and in the southern Bering Sea into the front zone of the sea ice (Irving et al. 1970), and they occur regularly farther north in polynyas about the major islands (Nunivak I, 10 March 1968, J. J. Burns unpubl. notes, and 7-10 February 1977, C. P. Dau unpubl. notes; St. Matthew I, several rafts, 6-7 February 1970, McRoy et al. 1971; St. Lawrence I, estimated 500,000+, December through mid-April, Fay 1961). In the northern Bering Sea and about the Seward Peninsula, wintering varies with ice conditions, but Oldsquaws have been reported in leads in winter from Cape Nome (a few present in early December 1969, W. L. Foster in litt.), Cape Woolley (present on 15 February 1969, J. J. Burns unpubl. notes), King Island (fairly numerous on 7 February 1968, J. J. Burns unpubl. notes), and the Diomede Islands (present throughout the entire winter of 1912-1913, Thayer and Bangs 1914). They have not been reported wintering north of the Bering Strait.

Spring movement begins as soon as leads open in the sea ice, sometimes by late April, although the earliest migrants are difficult to separate from possible overwintering individuals (seen 17 April 1978 and two flocks present 29 April 1978, 3-4 km out on ice off Nome, G. Taxac and W. Noyakuk, respectively, Beltz School unpubl. notes; six shot on 24 April 1965, Bonanza River flats, J. J. Burns unpubl. notes; first seen 28 April 1922, Wales, Bailey 1943). These early dates agree with Fay's (1961) observations that overwintering flocks at St. Lawrence Island begin to disperse between the middle and end of April as the ice dissipates. On average, the main migration to and past the Seward Peninsula occurs from the second week of May through the first week of June.

Oldsquaws apparently do not breed until they are 2 yr old (Palmer 1976). Potential breeders pair on the wintering grounds (Alison 1975), with courtship and pairing in the Bering Sea occurring primarily during the last half of April (Preble and McAtee 1923, Fay and Cade 1959). Upon arrival at the Seward Peninsula, pairs move to their breeding territories as soon as open water is available. The female selects the nest site, which may be the same as or nearby that of the preceding year; she apparently does not scout for the actual site until she is imminently ready to lay the first egg (Alison 1975). Nests are placed in a variety of situations, including on peninsulas, islets, and islands in ponds and lagoons, in Wet Meadow or Dwarf Shrub Meadow tundra surrounding ponds, or on beaches; and the degree of concealment varies widely. Nests are seldom far from water. The average distance of mainland nests from water at Churchill, Manitoba, was 28.6 m (maximum 200 m), while those on islands and beaches were much closer (Evans 1970). The nest cup usually is lined with dried shrub leaves, in which the first eggs are buried after laying; down is added to cover the eggs as additional eggs are laid, especially between the third and fifth eggs (Alison 1975).

The mean clutch size in 29 nests at Cape Espenberg in 1976-1977 was 6.2 ± 0.2 eggs (Schamel et al. 1979). Eggs are laid at about 26-h intervals; incubation, which does not begin until the clutch is completed, lasts an average of 26 ± 0.8 days ($n = 106$ eggs; range 24-26 days, depending at least in part on the position of the egg in the nest)(Alison 1975). The female leaves the nest twice a day for maintainence activities. The male remains nearby into early incubation and then repairs to postbreeding molt localities. There is no evidence of renesting, but if a nesting attempt is unsuccessful, a new pair will frequently take over the territory and undertake nesting (ibid.), a succession that undoubtedly accounts for late clutches and broods on Seward Peninsula. Failed females may remain on their breeding ponds for several weeks to a month after nesting failures (ibid.).

As soon as the newly hatched chicks are dry, the female takes them to the nearest water, where they usually remain for their first 1.5 weeks. Thereafter, the female may lead them periodically to successively larger ponds (Alison 1976); most remain on ponds until they fledge at 35-40 days of age (Alison 1975). As in other sea ducks, some mixing and combining of broods occurs.

Back-dating from observed events indicates that egg-laying on the Seward Peninsula may begin by the end of the third week of May (brood about a week old on the Fish R delta, 22 June 1981, D. A. Woodby in litt.; earliest clutch extralimitally at St. Michael, five eggs, 18 May [yr?], Nelson 1887). Peak laying, based on back-dating from brood observations, must occur during the last week of May and the first week of June; and some laying continues through mid-June, as evidenced by the presence of eggs and newly hatched chicks as late at 17 July. In 1922, Bailey (1925) thought that nesting was only beginning at Wales by 4 July, which seems highly unlikely. Broods are common by the first week of July, and early broods should begin to fledge by the first of August, with the bulk having gained flight by the third week of August.

Oldsquaws feed almost entirely on animal matter obtained mainly from the substrate (epibenthos) of ponds, lagoons, and coastal waters. They are capable of diving to depths of over 60 m, and apparently commonly feed at depths of 30-50 m (Schorger 1947, Bellrose 1980). Data from the Bering (winter) and the Chukchi and Beaufort (summer) sea areas have shown a dietary preference for amphipod and mysid crustaceans, with lesser amounts of molluscs and other invertebrates and occasional small fish (Preble and McAtee 1923, Johnson 1984); while on breeding ponds, more aquatic insect material may be consumed, including caddis fly and chironomid larvae (Bergman et al. 1977). Food may also be taken at the edges and undersides of pans of sea ice (Bailey 1925, Johnson and Richardson 1981).

Postbreeding flocks of males become conspicuous after about 20 June. On the Serpentine River in 1951, flocks had reached "appreciable proportions" by 23 June and "very large congregations" were observed 27-29 June; there was a general exodus of males to the coast about 1 July (Thayer 1951). Similar large flocks of several hundred males were present on the Serpentine River 4 and 5 July 1976 (Noble and Wright 1977). Many flocks of 15-70 males were present along the coast between Bluff and Cripple River 22 June-1 July 1975 (Drury 1976b), and several flocks of 30-75 birds frequented the outer coast of Cape Espenberg 3-5 July 1973 (Kessel and D. D. Gibson unpubl. notes). Molting birds were common along the protected spits at Port Clarence and Breving Lagoon in July 1980 and 1981 (Woodby and Divoky 1983).

No conspicuous aggregations of nonbreeding (yearling) Oldsquaw have been reported about the Seward Peninsula.

Fall migration along the Chukchi Sea coast occurs throughout September, peaking during the last half of the month ("mass flight," 16-19 September 1878, Cape Schmidt, and "vast flight," 23 September 1933, Uelen, USSR, Portenko 1972; "biggest day," 19 September 1980, Icy Cape, Lehnhausen and Quinlan 1981; 2400 during a 3-hr shipboard transect, 25 September 1970, off Point Lay, Watson and Divoky 1972). In coastal Norton Sound, 600 Oldsquaw were counted on 22 September 1975 between Bluff and the inlet of Safety Sound (Drury 1976b). Oldsquaw are uncommon after the first of October and rare after mid-October ("small number," 18 October 1970, just north of Bering Strait, Watson and Divoky 1972; three, 19 October 1985, and twenty, 24 October 1987, off Cape Deceit, J. D. Walters unpubl. notes; twenty, 3 November 1985, open leads near Deering, J. Moto in J. D. Walters unpubl. notes). Because of some overwintering in Seward Peninsula waters, latest cited dates are extralimital: 6 November [yr?], Cape Thompson, Williamson et al. 1966; 9 December 1882, Barrow, Murdoch 1885.

Black Scoter—*Melanitta nigra*

The Black Scoter is a fairly common, widely distributed breeder on the Seward Peninsula. During the breeding season, it occurs about pond areas in the uplands but is most numerous where the Coastal Lowlands abut the uplands. It is rare or absent from such lowlands as Cape Espenberg and Lopp Lagoon, from coastal river estuaries, and from the outer (southern) fringes of the wetlands adjacent to the north edges of the waters of Imuruk Basin. It is fairly common, however, averaging about 11% of the duck population, in pond areas above the estuaries of such large rivers as the Buckland, Serpentine, Arctic, Kuzitrin, Flambeau, and Fish; on the Agiapuk-Kuzitrin river deltas in Imuruk Basin; and at some interior lowland sites, such as McCarthys Marsh, the Pilgrim-Kuzitrin river lowlands along the Taylor Highway, the flats along the Inmachuk River, and the flats just north of Killeak Lakes. Appropriate habitat is limited in the uplands, but in the Lava Lake-Agnes Lake-upper Noxapaga River area 7-10 July 1973, D. D. Gibson and I observed a mated pair and six individual females that undoubtedly were incubating birds. Birds not engaged in breeding activities utilize the coastal Inshore Waters around much of the Peninsula's coastline, their numbers varying with season and location.

This scoter winters commonly along the north side of the Alaska Peninsula (Gill et. al. 1981, R. H. Day pers. comm.), along the Aleutian Chain (Murie 1959), and in Southcoastal Alaska (Forsell and Gould 1981, Isleib and Kessel 1973). The first spring migrants usually arrive in Seward Peninsula waters during the third week of May (16 May [yr?], extralimitally at St. Michael, Nelson 1887; 19 May 1981, southern Kotzebue Sound, Eldridge 1982; 19 May 1983, Bonanza R bridge, J. D. Walters unpubl. notes), although on 6 May 1922 one was shot from a flock at Wales by Bailey (1943), and he reported that several others were seen with King Eiders on 8 May 1922. In most years the main movement occurs during the last week of May, but some movement continues as late as the second week of June.

As with other *Melanitta*, Black Scoters apparently do not breed until they are 2 yr old, some not until 3 yr (Palmer 1976, Cramp 1980a, Brown and Houston 1982). Nests are placed somewhat back from the pond edge, usually within 30 m and mostly between 3 and 10 m (Bengtson 1970). They consist of a depression lined with grass and down and are usually concealed in a large clump of grass or under low shrubs (Brandt 1943, Thayer 1951, Palmer 1976). Nests are difficult to find, and only three clutches have been reported from the Seward Peninsula, consisting of 9, 7, and 4 eggs (Bailey 1943, Thayer 1951). On the Yukon-Kuskokwim Delta, clutches in ten nests averaged 7.4 ± 1.1 eggs, range 6-9 eggs (Yukon Delta NWR unpubl. data). Eggs are probably laid at an average interval of about 1.5 days, as is the case with White-winged Scoters (Vermeer 1969, Brown and Brown 1981); incubation begins with the laying of the last egg (Cramp 1980a). The male leaves the female soon after the clutch is completed (Palmer 1976, Bengtson 1966). Incubation of one clutch on the Yukon-Kuskokwim Delta lasted at least 28 days (9-egg clutch found on 27 June 1967 hatched on 24 July) and another hatched at 28 days (last egg of a 9-egg clutch was laid on 9 July; 2 eggs were lost during incubation, but other eggs hatched on 30 July) (Yukon Delta NWR unpubl. data). Broods remain on their natal ponds until fledging, which occurs at 45-50 days of age (Cramp 1980a); the female may return to the sea for molting before the young have fledged (Palmer 1976).

Based on back-dating from brood observations, earliest egg-laying on the Seward Peninsula may begin during the first week of June (brood on the lower Serpentine R, 11 July 1951, Thayer 1951; and a brood in Norton Sound, 16 July 1981, Woodby and Divoky 1983), but in most years it does not begin until mid-June, with peak laying occurring during the last 10 days of the month. A high proportion of Black Scoters were still in pairs 22-26 June 1975 at Buckland and 25-29 June 1971 at Imuruk Basin, but by 7-10 July 1973 at Lava Lake and vicinity and 15-17 July 1973 at McCarthys Marsh, most of the population consisted only of females. At the Serpentine River, postbreeding males were gathering in large flocks by 27 June 1951 (Thayer 1951).

The peak of hatching should occur during the last week of July, which would mean that most broods would not fledge until the second week of September. Two four-chick broods on the lower Flambeau River on 4 September 1980 were estimated to be only 2 weeks old (D. A. Woodby in litt.) and thus would not have fledged until the first week of October. This late seasonal timing allows little margin for renesting attempts, although some does occur (Bengtson 1972b). Extralimitally at St. Michael, Nelson (1887) reported a clutch of fresh eggs on 3 August and a brood of downies on 9 September, but it is improbable that such late nestings could be successful.

Food of Black Scoters consists 90 + % of a wide variety of animal matter, mainly molluscs with significant amounts of crustaceans (Palmer 1976, Bellrose 1980).

After leaving the females in late June-early July, the postbreeding males gather in flocks—first locally, sometimes with male Oldsquaw and Greater Scaup (late June 1951, Serpentine R, Thayer 1951; 26 June 1971, Imuruk Basin, Kessel pers. obs.), and later on coastal Inshore Waters (flock of five, 6 July 1969, east of Cape Nome, Kessel pers. obs.; flocks of 5, 8, and 20 in late June 1975 between Sledge I and Cripple R and 20 on 3 July 1975 on the sea between the inlet of Safety Sound and Bonanza R, Drury 1976b). These birds soon leave the Seward Peninsula coastline for molting grounds, perhaps in the coastal waters off the Yukon-Kuskokwim Delta, where large flocks of Black Scoters, including nonbreeders, and other species of scoters, molt between Cape Romanzof and Cape Peirce (King and Dau 1981, Dau 1987).

From mid-July until fledglings from inland breeding ponds arrive, there are few Black Scoters in the coastal waters of the Peninsula. Numbers increase sharply in September (Woodby and Divoky 1983; also, 100+ on sea between Bonanza R and Bluff, 22 September 1975, Drury 1976b), but these depart quickly on fall migration (latest, eight, 19 October 1985, and a female, 24 October 1987, off Cape Deceit, J. D. Walters unpubl. notes).

Surf Scoter—_Melanitta perspicillata_

The Surf Scoter is an uncommon summer visitant and a rare breeder on the Seward Peninsula. It is locally common in the Kotzebue Sound region, where the breeding population and the flocks of non- and postbreeders appear to be an extension of the Interior Alaska population, which breeds in the Kobuk (Dean and Chesemore 1974) and Noatak river drainages (Manuwal 1974) and in the northeast quadrant of the Seward Peninsula. Based on my observations of single females at inland ponds in late June and July and on one brood observation (details below), the Surf Scoter breeds from the headwaters of the Burnt River, northeast of Imuruk Lake, through the uplands from there and Lava Lake into the Noxapaga River drainage and down at least to its junction with the Kuzitrin River; also in pond areas north and west of Killeak Lakes and probably in the Nugnugaluktuk River drainage. In the Lava Lake-Noxapaga River area, 6-9 July 1973, I recorded at least 12 single females, and on the evening of 10 July I watched a flock of 9 females fly over Lava Lake. Occasional pairs, small parties with a female, or single breeding-plumaged males have been observed in late June and July outside of this delineated area—in the upper estuary of Buckland River (Kessel and F. G. Scheider pers. obs.), at the mouths of the Serpentine and Arctic rivers (Noble and Wright 1977; also, Kessel pers. obs.), in the bay at the northwest edge of Imuruk Basin (Kessel and S. O. MacDonald pers. obs.)—but there has been no concrete evidence of breeding.

Flocks of Surf Scoters, mostly males, occur on the coastal waters of Kotzebue Sound throughout the summer, but it is not possible to distinguish between spring migrants, nonbreeders, and postbreeders; Grinnell (1900a) commented that it was the commonest scoter in the Kotzebue Sound region. Apparently resident flocks are present from late May (ten, Buckland R mouth, 28 May 1981, Eldridge 1982) through early September (200, Chamisso I, 13 August 1977, DeGange and Sowls 1978; flock of 20 males flew past Cape Espenberg, 8 September 1973, D. D. Gibson unpubl. notes).

F. G. Scheider and I saw small flocks in the Buckland River area 23-26 June 1975; Schamel et al. (1979) reported birds at Cape Espenberg 10-16 July 1976 (maximum, 90 on 12 July) and on 7 July 1977 (20 birds); D. D. Gibson (unpubl. notes) saw a flock of 19 males and one female flying past Cape Deceit on 29 July 1973; and several thousand molting males spent July 1949 at the mouth of Buckland River (Alaska Game Commission 1949). Surf Scoters are much less numerous elsewhere around the coastline; Woodby and Divoky (1983) reported that they constituted less than 1% of the ducks in coastal Norton Sound during summer 1980, having counted only about 175 birds.

Surf Scoters are common to abundant winter residents in Southcoastal and Southeastern Alaska, although a few also winter in the Aleutian Islands and along the south shores of the Alaska Peninsula (Kessel and D. D. Gibson unpubl. data). Circumstantial evidence suggests that the Seward Peninsula breeders, and perhaps most of the Kotzebue Sound birds, are from the Southcoastal-Southeastern wintering populations and that spring migrants fly overland between Southcoastal Alaska and Kotzebue Sound: Many migrant Surf Scoters have been seen apparently leaving Prince William Sound by flying inland directly over the mountain ranges (Isleib and Kessel 1973), and the earliest spring arrival dates reported from the Peninsula are from Kotzebue Sound and are in agreement with arrival dates at Fairbanks and Ambler (earliest, 19 May 1981, five birds counted during an aerial survey between Cape Espenberg and the Nugnugaluktuk R, Eldridge 1982; 19 May 1974, first seen extralimitally at Ambler, Kobuk R, D. K. Wik in litt.; first seen most years 12-19 May at Fairbanks, Kessel unpubl. data). It seems likely that the summering Surf Scoters in coastal Norton Sound include birds from the population that winters in Southwestern Alaska.

Nesting apparently begins soon after the migrants arrive. Based on intervals for egg-laying and incubation found in the other *Melanitta* species, i.e., laying rates of one egg about every 36 h and an incubation period of 28 days (above; also, Brown and Brown 1981), and based on back-dating from a brood of seven Class Ia chicks that D. D. Gibson and I saw in a pond south of Andesite Creek, 65°34' N, 164°01' W, on 8 July 1973 and from a brood of eight Class Ib chicks near the mouth of the Redstone River tributary of the Kobuk River, 67°09' N, 156°39' W, on 19 July 1963 (UAM 5368), egg-laying is underway by late May-early June. The last date I have seen mated pairs within known breeding areas is 28 June (1973 near North Killeak L), meaning that a few females may not have begun incubation by this date. Late June is also the time when male flocks begin increasing in inner Inshore Waters, apparently with the addition of postbreeding males.

Huge flocks of molting scoters, predominantly this species, molt in inshore coastal waters off the Yukon-Kuskokwim Delta from July through September (King and Dau 1981, Dau 1987); and, beginning in late June-early July, in the extralimital waters of Norton Sound between St. Michael and Stuart Island (Nelson 1887). On 23 August 1878, Nelson (1887:82) by kayak approached a tremendous flock that formed "a continuous band...about 10 miles in length and from one-half to three-fourths of a mile in width...." A similar flock was present in early September 1879 (ibid.). It is not known if Surf Scoters from Kotzebue Sound are included in these Bering Sea flocks.

The last Surf Scoters do not leave the Seward Peninsula until October (latest, five brown-plumaged Surf Scoters, probably juveniles, 6 October 1984, and 19 ducks believed to be Surf Scoters, 17 October 1984, off Deering, J. D. Walters unpubl. notes; last in mid-October 1878 and 1879 as ice formed along the coast, extralimitally near St. Michael, Nelson 1887).

White-winged Scoter—*Melanitta fusca*

The White-winged Scoter is an uncommon to rare spring migrant and summer visitant in the coastal Inshore Waters of the Seward Peninsula, where a few occur from time to time at more or less random locations around the entire coastline; and it is a locally common probable breeder in Imuruk Basin. The population in Imuruk Basin, a sizable one, is disjunct from the nearest known breeding sites at St. Michael (Nelson 1887) and in the Kobuk (Irving 1960) and Noatak (Manuwal 1974) river drainages. Between 25 and 28 June 1971, on the creeks, sloughs, bays, and ponds of the Agiapuk River delta at the north edge of Imuruk Basin and the lower reaches of the Kuzitrin River, S. O. MacDonald and I counted at least 250 White-winged Scoters, making them almost 50% more numerous than any other species of duck in this productive wetland. The fact that 46% were in pairs strongly suggests breeding. We saw three single females and several flocks of males, further suggesting, as with other species of scoters in late June, that males were deserting females that had begun incubation. The only other inland record of White-winged Scoters is of a group of three that D. D. Gibson and I watched fly down Andesite Creek, west of Lava Lake, on 7 July 1973.

This scoter winters uncommonly along the north side of the Alaska Peninsula (Gill et al. 1981), and it is common to abundant in the Aleutians and along the entire Pacific coastline of Alaska (Kessel and D. D. Gibson unpubl. data); the wintering grounds of the Imuruk Basin population are unknown. The White-winged Scoter is the last of the spring migrant waterfowl to arrive. Although most reported first sightings have been during the first week of June, extralimital dates suggest that earliest arrivals at the Peninsula are probably during the fourth week of May (16-24 May most years at Fairbanks, Kessel unpubl. data; 18 May 1924, Yukon-Kuskokwim Delta, Brandt 1943; 31 May [yr?], Cape Thompson, Williamson et al. 1966). The pattern of fall departures probably parallels the timing of the other species of scoters (latest, five, 1 October 1983, flying past Deering, J. D. Walters unpubl. notes; common, extralimitally along coast at St. Michael, late September until mid-October freeze-up, Nelson 1887).

Common Goldeneye—*Bucephala clangula*

An uncommon migrant and local breeder at the base of the Peninsula, the Common Goldeneye is a rare spring migrant and summer visitant farther west. It reaches Kotzebue Sound by mid-May (14 May 1981, 12 birds on Kauk R delta in southern Eschscholtz Bay; and 19 May 1981, 8 birds between Shishmaref and the mouth of the Nugnugaluktuk R, 34 on Kiwalik Lagoon, and 40 in the Buckland R estuary; all Eldridge 1982), although most spring observations beyond the base of the Peninsula have been of individuals or small groups during early June (e.g., female, 1 June

1929, collected at Wales, Bailey 1943; male, 6 June 1974, Cape Nome, and pair, 3 June 1976, Nome, H. K. Springer unpubl. notes; seen June 1976, King I, and one, 10 June 1977, between Topkok and Bonanza R, W. H. Drury fide J. O. Biderman in litt.; pair, 17 June 1971, lower Nome R, D. G. Roseneau unpubl. notes; male, 29 June 1980, Safety Sound, and subadult male, 13 June 1983, Wales, T. G. Tobish in litt.).

Common Goldeneyes breed in the forested southeast portions of the Peninsula, where, in 1973 along the Kwiniuk River, J. H. Lee (pers. comm.) first saw a female and brood on 27 July and then another three broods on 6 August. The occasional birds seen near Pilgrim Hot Springs (1964, fide K. Emmons pers. comm.) and in the Pilgrim-Kuzitrin area along the Taylor Highway (two, 24 June 1975, W. H. Drury pers. comm.) have probably worked their way inland up the Niukluk River drainage from this southeast population; they are probably only visitants, although the large cottonwoods at Pilgrim Hot Springs and at other sites along these rivers could provide adequate nesting sites.

Bufflehead—*Bucephala albeola*

The Bufflehead is a rare migrant and summer visitant on the Peninsula. I saw a female in the pond area along the Pilgrim River at Milepost 61.5 Taylor Highway on 5 July 1969; in 1974 at Cape Nome, H. K. Springer and A. Bernecker (unpubl. notes) saw three Buffleheads on 6 June and two on 10 June; and in 1981, four were reported from Koyuk by D. A. Woodby (unpubl. notes) 25-30 May. Hunters reportedly take occasional Buffleheads in fall (J. J. Burns pers. comm.).

Common Merganser—*Mergus merganser*

The Common Merganser appears to be a rare spring migrant on the Peninsula. It has been reported three times at Wales in recent years, flying along the coast: D. R. Paulson and M. Perrone viewed a flock of two males and three females at close range on 12 June 1978 (Paulson unpubl. notes), and T. G. Tobish (in litt.) reported a flock of two females and a male on 11 June 1981 and a lone female on 14 June 1983. Elsewhere, two males on 7 June 1986 were studied by D. W. Wolf (in litt.), one at the mouth of the Nome River and the other on the ice off the inlet of Safety Sound; and four birds were seen along the Norton Sound coastline between 12 and 19 June 1987 by M. W. Schwan and R. H. Armstrong (unpubl. notes).

The Seward Peninsula is in a hiatus between the northern extremities, of the breeding ranges of two subspecies of Common Merganser. *Mergus m. merganser* from Asia is a rare spring migrant through the western Aleutian Islands (Gibson 1981), and an adult male found dead on a beach at Punuk Islands, St. Lawrence Island, on 29 June 1979 was of this subspecies (F. H. Fay, photos identified by D. D. Gibson), so the migrants at Wales may have been this form, too. The more easterly birds appear to be the North American form, *M. m. americanus*, but clarification of the occurrence of the two subspecies on the Peninsula requires concrete documentation.

Red-breasted Merganser—*Mergus serrator*

A fairly common, widely distributed breeder, the Red-breasted Merganser nests throughout the uplands as well as the lowlands of the Peninsula, wherever ponds are present either near the flowing waters of creeks and rivers or near the coast. It is most numerous in the wetlands along the lower portions of the larger rivers, somewhat inland from the coast, e.g., the upper estuaries of the Buckland and Nugnugaluktuk rivers, Imuruk Basin and the lower channels of the Kuzitrin River, the Flambeau River flats, and the Fish River delta, although it is also numerous along such clear-flowing waters as the Inmachuk, Pilgrim, and Nome rivers. Only a few nest in the more exposed coastal wetlands, such as about Cape Espenberg or around Lopp Lagoon. Red-breasted Mergansers constituted 2.5% of the duck population in the Imuruk Basin area 25-28 June 1971 (21 counted, mostly pairs or single females, S. O. MacDonald and Kessel pers. obs.) and 4.5% of the duck population in the Buckland River estuary 23-26 June 1975 (44 birds counted, F. G. Scheider and Kessel pers. obs.). They made up 2.3% of the ducks in coastal Norton Sound in 1980 (Woodby and Divoky 1983). Some birds occur in the Nearshore and inner Inshore waters of the Peninsula coastline throughout the summer, being pre-, post-, or nonbreeders, depending on seasonal phenologies.

While only occasional birds winter in the Bering Sea (female, shot 16 December 1910, St. Paul I, Evermann 1913; female-plumaged bird, 8 February 1977, Nunivak I, C. P. Dau, Yukon Delta NWR unpubl. data), this merganser is a locally common winter visitant in the Aleutian Islands and along both sides of the Alaska Peninsula and is common in the Nearshore and Inshore waters of Southcoastal and Southeastern Alaska (Kessel and D. D. Gibson unpubl. data). The first spring migrants in early years could arrive at the Peninsula by the first week of May, judging from nearby extralimital dates (ibid.), but in most years first sightings are not until mid-May (8 birds, 13 May 1981, extralimitally along Selawik R, Eldridge 1982; about 30 birds, 14 May 1983, scattered about Cape Nome, J. D. Walters unpubl. notes). Movement continues to mid-June.

The chronologies of the events in the breeding cycle of the Red-breasted Merganser have been well summarized by Palmer (1976): The species first breeds when 2 yr old; North American clutches usually contain 7-10 eggs (average 9), laid at about 1.5-day intervals [although a brood of 13 chicks was near the Kuzitrin River bridge on 7 August 1969 (D. G. Roseneau unpubl. notes)]; incubation usually begins with clutch completion, and the basic duration is 29 days, although some eggs have taken as long as 35 days to hatch; and chicks remain in the nest for 12-24 h and are still downy at 4 weeks. Age at fledging is given by Cramp (1980a) as 60-65 days.

Using these statistics to back-date from observed events shows that some egg-laying on the Seward Peninsula begins during the first week of June (earliest, 5-day old chicks at Safety Sound on 19 July 1980 [D. A. Woodby in litt.] would mean that egg-laying began about 4 June), but it peaks during the second and third weeks of June. This timing is corroborated by the fact that while many inland birds are still paired 23-28 June, small postbreeding flocks have formed by early July. Thus, most hatching should occur between about 21 July and 7 August, with peak fledging not occurring until the last third of September and early October.

The main diet of Red-breasted Mergansers consists of small fishes and some crustaceans, with aquatic insects and small crustaceans being important to ducklings (Palmer 1976).

Breeding males leave their mates soon after incubation begins (Palmer 1976), first forming small groups on local waterbodies and then usually moving to coastal sites; failed females and some yearling nonbreeders are also constituents of these flocks (10 birds, 26 June 1970, Salmon L [W. J. Weiss and I. H. Black in litt.]; flock of 30 birds, 2 July 1974, flying along the coast off Lopp Lagoon barrier strip; 55 birds in small flocks of up to 18 birds, 5 July 1973, bay side of Cape Espenberg; flock of 11 female-plumaged birds, 15 July 1973, Imuruk L [all Kessel and D. D. Gibson unpubl. notes]; 42 birds during 29 August 1975 aerial transect, on coastal lagoons between Cape Douglas and Cape Woolley [Drury 1976b]).

It is not possible to distinguish groups of molting postbreeders from premigratory staging flocks, because of their broad overlap in Nearshore and inner Inshore waters during late summer and fall, but migration is apparently under way by September (30 birds on 7 September and a maximum of 170 on 8 September 1977 at Cape Espenberg after an absence of the species during the entire month of August [Schamel et al. 1979]).

With the late and extended breeding schedule of the Red-breasted Merganser, the successful fledging of late broods is dependent upon the time of freeze-up, and these fledglings must depart immediately. Hence, the last fall observations are closely correlated with freeze-up dates each year (latest, ten, 12 October 1985, off Cape Deceit, J. D. Walters unpubl. notes; one, 19 October 1970, Nome boat harbor, Watson and Divoky 1972; a female-plumaged bird, 14 November 1970, extralimitally at Kobuk, D. K. Wik in litt.).

Osprey—*Pandion haliaetus*

Primarily a bird of forested regions, the Osprey is a rare probable breeder on the Seward Peninsula, where it is largely restricted to the major drainages of the southeast quadrant of the Peninsula. While it has been reported beyond treeline near Solomon (one sitting in tall willows along the Solomon R and later flushed by a harassing Mew Gull, 19 June 1970, D. G. Roseneau and W. Walker pers. comm.) and Deering (one carrying a fish along Inmachuk R, 13 June 1988, R. Moto in J. D. Walters unpubl. notes), it has been reported most frequently from the Niukluk-Fish River drainage (one, 20 July 1966, below Council, R. L. Rausch and J. J. Burns pers. comm.; one, 4 July 1977, 6 km upriver from White Mountain, N. G. Tankersley in litt.; one, second week of June 1980, Fish R delta, D. A. Woodby unpubl. notes). In 1973, J. H. Lee reported it both from the Kwiniuk River (one 8 km upriver on 10 July and one, carrying a fish, 16 km upriver on 27 July) and the Tubutulik River (two or three [family?] flushed from a sandbar 29 km upriver on 12 August). There is no concrete evidence of breeding, but extralimitally on the Kobuk River delta, where the species was fairly common in 1885 (Townsend 1887) and 1899 (Grinnell 1900a), an active nest, apparently with young, was noted in a broken-topped spruce on 12 August 1898 (Grinnell 1900a).

Bald Eagle—*Haliaeetus leucocephalus*

The Bald Eagle is a rare summer visitant and perhaps a casual breeder on the Seward Peninsula, where occasional individuals straggle westward from their normal range in the forested valleys of Interior Alaska. An immature flew about the west end of Cape Mountain on 25 June 1972 (F. G. Scheider pers. comm.); there was an adult at Cape Nome on 27 June 1976 (H. K. Springer unpubl. notes); and another was at Milepost 28 Teller Highway on 30 August 1971 (Alaska Department of Fish and Game unpubl. notes). Hearsay from local residents suggests that an occasional pair may nest on the Peninsula, and in 1975, R. Nassuk of Koyuk told me that they have nested at Bald Head. Extralimitally, a nest was found in 1980 on an upper tributary of the Unalakleet River (Mindell 1983), which drains into the head of Norton Sound.

Northern Harrier—*Circus cyaneus*

An uncommon to rare migrant, summer visitant, and breeder, the Northern Harrier is most numerous in the Interior Lowlands of the Peninsula and in the uplands bordering Norton Sound and southern Kotzebue Sound. Individuals range throughout the Peninsula, however, to Breving Lagoon (one, first week of August 1980, D. A. Woodby unpubl. notes), Wales (one, 31 May 1964, Breckenridge and Cline 1967; one, 10 June 1983, M. L. Ward unpubl. notes), Ear Mountain (female-plumaged bird, 22 June 1974, Kessel pers. obs.), Arctic River (up to three individuals, 17 June 1967 and thereafter, Noble and Wright 1977), Kitluk River mouth (one each, 20 and 24 May 1977, J. M. Wright unpubl. notes), and Cape Espenberg (occasional visitants during summers 1976 and 1977, Schamel et al. 1979).

Two pairs nested near Bluff in 1977, fledging families of four and five young (Drury et al. 1978), and a nest with three eggs in a patch of low-height Dwarf Birch in Dwarf Shrub Meadow habitat was found on 24 June 1978 at Utica Creek, upper Inmachuk River, by J. M. Wright (unpubl. notes). In addition, circumstantial evidence, such as a female and two juvenals at the junction of Hot Springs Creek and Serpentine River 3-6 August 1973 (D. D. Gibson unpubl. notes) and persistent pairs elsewhere during June, suggests breeding in the Northern and Southern uplands and Interior Lowlands as far west as 165°30′ W.

An open-country bird, the harrier favors Dwarf Shrub Meadow habitat on the Peninsula, especially where this habitat abuts wetlands. It is most frequently seen coursing over expanses of this open tundra and hunting habitat "edges," especially wetland edges, for voles and small birds. At the Pilgrim River flats along the Taylor Highway on 7 July 1967, I watched a female persistently chasing Red-necked Phalaropes along the edges of a marshy pond.

Northern Harriers are rare winter visitants as far north as the North Pacific coastline in Southwestern and Southcoastal Alaska (Kessel and Gibson 1978). They usually arrive on the Peninsula early in May (earliest, one, 28 April 1971, Nome, Alaska Department of Fish and Game unpubl. notes; male, 30 April 1983, Nome, J. D. Walters unpubl. notes; and a female, 30 April 1983, extralimitally on the Choris Peninsula in Kotzebue Sound, S. Hills unpubl. notes). There is a small but conspicuous fall movement beginning in mid-August and peaking during the last week to 10 days of August.

Only a few, mostly "brown individuals" (juvenals or perhaps adult females), remain as late as the second week of September (latest, one, 17 September 1986, Deering, J. D. Walters unpubl. notes, and one, 21 September 1980, Safety Sound, D. A. Woodby unpubl. notes).

Sharp-shinned Hawk—*Accipiter striatus*

The Sharp-shinned Hawk is a casual fall migrant on the Seward Peninsula. A bird flew through Wales Village and then out to sea toward the Strait on 20 August 1977, and another was seen at Moses Point on 13 September 1980 (D. A. Woodby in litt.). This highly migratory raptor breeds widely throughout the forested regions of Alaska, including the taiga of Interior Alaska (Gabrielson and Lincoln 1959, Kessel and D. D. Gibson unpubl. data), and it is a rare migrant and probable breeder to the western extremity of the taiga in the lower Kobuk River valley (Grinnell 1900a, Kessel and D. D. Gibson unpubl. data) and probably to the head of Norton Sound.

Northern Goshawk—*Accipiter gentilis*

The Northern Goshawk is a rare migrant, summer visitant, and possible breeder on the Peninsula. One was flushed twice from tall willows near Nome on 9 May 1983 (J. D. Walters unpubl. notes); one was seen at Koyuk during the last week of May 1981, and a juvenal was seen at Moses Point 22-26 August 1980 (D. A. Woodby unpubl. notes); and two adults were observed in the spruce woods of the Fish-Niukluk River drainages during summers in the mid-1960s, one at Council and one at Aggie Creek, 24 km east of Council (J. J. Burns pers. comm.). In September 1881, at Elephant Point in Eschscholtz Bay, Nelson (1883) watched two goshawks as they emerged from a small alder patch and flew away. This accipiter is a widely distributed year-round resident and breeder throughout the forested regions of Alaska, being most numerous in the large river drainages of Interior Alaska (Gabrielson and Lincoln 1959, Kessel and D. D. Gibson unpubl. data). It occurs more regularly than its smaller cousin, the Sharp-shinned Hawk, at and just beyond the western extremities of the taiga (Kessel and D. D. Gibson unpubl. data).

Rough-legged Hawk—*Buteo lagopus*

A conspicuous but uncommon breeder, the Rough-legged Hawk is widely distributed across the Peninsula. It is the most numerous of the Peninsula raptors, although annual numbers fluctuate widely in response to prey availability, especially voles and lemmings. It occurs throughout both the Southern and Northern uplands and at many lowland sites where cliffs, bluffs, or tors are present. Around the periphery of the Peninsula, nesting sites include Cape Deceit (23 June and 29 July 1973, Kessel and D. D. Gibson pers. obs.; two pairs in 1984, J. D. Walters unpubl. notes), Devil Mountain (old stick nests in 1970 and 1971, D. G. Roseneau pers. comm.), Ear Mountain (defensive bird, 21 June 1974, Kessel pers. obs.), Sledge Island (pair,

8-12 June 1950, Cade 1952), Topkok Head (nest with two well-feathered young, 12 July 1969, D. G. Roseneau unpubl. notes), and Bluff (two pairs in 1975, Drury 1976b; pair in 1978, Ramsdell and Drury 1979; pair, 6 June 1983, R. and B. Mearns unpubl. notes). During annual surveys of large parts of the Peninsula between 1968 and 1972, counts of active nests on the Peninsula varied from 10 to 82 pairs (Swartz et al. 1975), and D. G. Roseneau (pers. comm.) estimates that in the high year of 1970 there were probably 100 breeding pairs on the Peninsula.

Rough-legged Hawks are open-country birds, occurring mainly in the tundra or alpine regions of the Peninsula. Primary nesting habitat is Cliffs and Block-fields, either Inland or Coastal, and includes coastal, riverine, or upland cliffs and tors. On 10 July 1973, D. D. Gibson and I came across a defensive pair using an unusual but homologous habitat—the fractured lava flow near Lava Lake. In addition, Peninsula pairs sometimes use such man-made structures as abandoned mining dredges and bridges for nest sites. One ground nest, which contained 5 eggs when found (including a runt egg), was placed on the shoulder of Teller Highway (D. G. Roseneau unpubl. notes), before as much vehicular traffic used the road as today.

Occasional individuals may overwinter as far north as Southcoastal Alaska (Isleib and Kessel 1973, MacIntosh 1986), but most rough-legs winter in southern Canada and in the northern and western United States (American Ornithologists' Union 1983). A nestling banded on 13 July 1970 along Kougarok Creek was recovered near Troy, Idaho, the following July; and an almost-fledged nestling banded on 26 July 1970 near Serpentine Hot Springs was recovered in southcentral Colorado, just east of the Rocky Mountains, on 25 November 1970 (W. Walker pers. comm.).

Rough-legged Hawks are early migrants, arriving at their northern breeding grounds while the landscape is still largely blanketed with snow. The Seward Peninsula birds apparently migrate through Interior Alaska, judging from timing and movements through the latter region (Kessel unpubl. data). Spring migrants usually arrive at the Peninsula in late April-early May (earliest, 17 April 1988, upper Inmachuk R, K. Kowalski in J. D. Walters unpubl. notes; 26 April 1980, Milepost 10 Teller Highway, D. Levinson, Beltz School unpubl. notes; two, 28 April 1971, about Milepost 18 Teller Highway, Alaska Department of Fish and Game unpubl. notes; but, extralimitally, one collected, 10 April 1876, St. Michael, Friedmann 1934, and first, 10 April 1943, Mountain Village, H. C. Kyllingstad in litt.).

Arrivals go immediately to their nesting areas, often choosing either the previous year's site or a nearby alternate. The nesting site is usually a horizontal platform on a ledge or at the top of a vertical cliff face or tor, with the nest placed on a rock or dirt substrate. The birds may build new nests or repair old ones, using sticks for the main body of the nest and lining the structure with finer vegetation. Egg-laying dates may vary widely among sites and among years, depending on when ledges become snow-free. On average, egg-laying on the Peninsula begins during the second week of May. At a nest near the Penny River, however, egg-laying must have begun about 23 April 1977 (fledged young, 4 July 1977, H. K. Springer pers. comm.), and laying may continue in the population through the end of the month (still three eggs, 1 July 1968, headwaters of Snake R, and two 10-day-old chicks, 18 July 1971, in nest along the East Fork of Solomon R, D. G. Roseneau unpubl. notes). Clutch size for nine 1968 Seward Peninsula nests reported by D. G. Roseneau (unpubl. notes) was 3.8 ± 1.2 eggs, range 2-6 eggs; clutch sizes tend to be smaller in years of low vole populations compared to years of rodent highs (Cramp 1980b). Incubation, which begins with the laying of the first or second egg, lasts 28-31 days, and is performed largely by the female (ibid.). The male provides food for the incubating female and only occasionally relieves her at the nest (ibid.). Concordant with this division of duties, the female begins her molt as soon as egg-laying is completed, whereas the male does not begin until later [about 10+ days?](Cade 1955, D. G. Roseneau unpubl. data).

Hatching on the Peninsula usually begins in early June and peaks in mid-June, but it may range from as early as the last week of May to as late as early July (see above). The male continues to do most of the hunting during the early nestling stage (Cramp 1980b). Most Peninsula young fledge between mid-July and early August, when they are 39-43 days of age (ibid.), although one brood fledged by 7 July 1977 and the 1971 East Fork chicks would not have fledged before 17-19 August (see above). Families remain in the general area of the nesting site for an additional 2 weeks before postbreeding dispersal begins. Dispersal becomes evident by mid-August (three juvenals hunting independently on the flats near Nome on 11 August 1968, and juvenals numerous along the Teller Highway by 13 August 1968, D. G. Roseneau unpubl. notes).

Voles and lemmings constitute the primary food of Rough-legged Hawks. This diet is supplemented by other small mammals, especially ground squirrels, and by birds, especially ptarmigan and young passerines (Springer 1975, Mindell 1983) and sometimes sea-cliff birds (Drury et al. 1978). Ptarmigan and other resident supranival prey are particularly important in early spring when migrant rough-legs arrive before much bare ground is exposed.

Fall departures from the Peninsula begin in late August, but the main exodus is during the first half of September (latest, one, 28 September 1967, Teller Highway, J. J. Burns unpubl. notes). It is likely that occasional birds remain into early October, judging from late occurrences in Northern and Interior Alaska (Kessel and D. D. Gibson unpubl. data).

After studying a large series of Rough-legged Hawks, Cade (1955) found no justification for recognizing any occurrence of the Siberian *kamtschatkensis* (= *pallidus*) in Alaska (contra Friedmann 1934, Bailey 1942, 1948), even though the population in Western Alaska shows some *kamtschatkensis* influence from probable contact during the Pleistocene.

Golden Eagle—*Aquila chrysaetos*

An uncommon breeder on the Seward Peninsula, the Golden Eagle is the least abundant of the three wide-ranging cliff-nesting raptors, being outnumbered by both the Rough-legged Hawk and the Gyrfalcon. It is widely distributed through the Northern Uplands and Southern Uplands and the foothills of the Highlands. Pairs nest in both Inland and Coastal Cliffs and Block-field habitats where cliff and tor sites face broad expanses of open landscape. Immatures hunt and soar over the entire Peninsula, from Wales and Ear Mountain eastward. Judging from accumulated observations over the years, there is a maximum breeding population during favorable years of 20-25 pairs on the Peninsula (Swartz et al. 1975, ANRS, Kessel unpubl. data).

The number of breeding pairs may vary up to 40% annually, however (Swartz et al. 1975).

Golden Eagles are migratory at the northern extremities of their breeding range, but some birds regularly winter as far north as Southcoastal Alaska (MacIntosh 1986, Kessel and D. D. Gibson unpubl. data) and at least some years in the Alaska Range (Kessel unpubl. data), and several recent occurrences farther north in Western Alaska indicate that they could be casual in winter on the Seward Peninsula, too (overwintering subadult in the eastern Igichak Hills, just north of Kotzebue Sound, seen 4 January, during February, and 4 March 1979, during the extreme Snowshoe Hare population high, W. R. Uhl pers. comm.; an adult male [UAM 5463] caught in a trap about 48 km southwest of Shungnak [66°15' N, 158° W] in January 1988, J. S. Dixon in litt.; and an adult about 50 km east of Chevak, Yukon Delta, 26 January 1986, B. J. McCaffery unpubl. notes). Golden Eagles move back to their summering grounds as early as weather permits (earliest, one, 27 March 1905, Imuruk Basin, Anthony 1906; but, extralimitally, one, 28 February 1988, Igichak Hills, Selawik NWR unpubl. notes, and an immature, 14 March 1974, Waring Mts, D. K. Wik in litt.).

Golden Eagles do not breed until they are 3 or 4 yr old, and they may live up to 25 yr (Cramp 1980b). On the Seward Peninsula, nest sites are on the ledges of cliffs and tors. There may be several alternate nest sites within the range used by a pair, sites among which the eagles may shift between years. Many of these nesting areas continue to be occupied over a number of years by a pair or successive replacements. Unused nests are frequently occupied by Rough-legged Hawks, Gyrfalcons, or Common Ravens. Nests, built of sticks and twigs broken from trees and shrubs and lined by finer vegetation (Bent 1937, Cramp 1980b), are refurbished each year. When a site is first used, the nest may be relatively small, but over the years accumulated materials result in some impressively large nests.

The typical clutch size on the Seward Peninsula, as elsewhere, is two eggs; sometimes only one egg is laid, but no three-egg clutches have been reported on the Peninsula. While there is variability in behavior among pairs, the female usually does most or all of the incubating, brooding, and direct feeding of the young; and the male brings food back to the vicinity of the nest for the female or for the female to feed to the young—although the female may leave the nest to hunt, also (Brown and Amadon 1968, Cramp 1980b). Incubation begins after the laying of the first egg, and there may be a 3-4-day interval between eggs, so hatching is asynchronous (ibid.). Incubation takes 43-45 days (R. S. Palmer in litt.). The young are brooded more or less continuously by the female for their first 2 weeks, but after 3 weeks the young are alone most of the day while both parents search for food. The first feathers begin showing through the chick down at 3+ weeks, and body feathering is essentially complete by 45-50 days (Brown and Amadon 1968). First flight may occur at 65-70 days of age (ibid., Ellis 1979), but may take a few days longer in Alaska (D. G. Roseneau pers. comm.). Young begin to feed directly on food items brought to the nest at 30-50 days of age, and the adults continue bringing food to the young for several weeks after they have fledged (ibid., Cramp 1980b). In roughly half of the nestings reported from the Seward Peninsula, only one chick has survived to fledging.

Using the above developmental periods and back-dating from aged nestlings and fledging dates show that egg-laying on the Peninsula may begin as early as the first week of April (chicks fledged at Bluff on 29 July 1976, Steele and Drury 1977; at least by 24 July 1977, Drury et al. 1978; and about 27 July 1978, Ramsdell and Drury 1979) and continues into early May. Most hatching occurs during the first half of June, but the Bluff nests (above) must have hatched during the third week of May. Fledging begins in late July (above) and probably continues until mid-August (one large "very well feathered" eaglet, 6 August 1979, Taylor Highway, R. and B. Mearns unpubl. notes). The young stay in the vicinity of the nesting area for about 2 weeks after fledging. In Scotland (Brown and Amadon 1968), the juvenals remain dependent on parental assistance for about 3 months after fledging, although I suspect this dependency is reduced to 2 months or less at the northern extremity of their range in Alaska, i.e., in the Brooks Range and on the Seward Peninsula.

Golden Eagles are opportunistic hunters, although they favor medium-sized prey and tend to favor mammals. Medium-sized mammals are few on the Peninsula, however, so avian prey is also important. The mammal prey on the Peninsula consists primarily of ground squirrels, although Tundra Hares are taken when available and in 1971 a pair of eagles on the upper Penny River took as many as five or six red foxes (D. G. Roseneau pers. comm.). Other frequent items include ptarmigan, especially Rock Ptarmigan, and ducks (D. G. Roseneau unpubl. notes; Kessel pers. obs.). Near sea cliffs, the eagles feed on seabirds and their carcasses (Drury et al. 1978, Springer and Roseneau 1978, E. C. Murphy pers. comm.), and they take other carrion when available.

Fall migration information from the Peninsula is unavailable, but judging from movements through Interior Alaska (Kessel unpubl. data), some birds, probably subadults and failed breeders, begin to leave the Peninsula by the second week of September, with the main exodus occurring before the end of the month. A few birds undoubtedly tarry into October.

American Kestrel—*Falco sparverius*

The American Kestrel is a casual migrant on the Seward Peninsula, where it occasionally strays from its normal range in the taiga of Interior Alaska. A male hovered above and sat on tussocks at the top of Cape Deceit on 3 May 1986, before flying farther westward along the coast (J. D. Walters unpubl. notes); a male was at Milepost 16 Glacier Highway on 30 May 1988 (T. H. Pogson pers. comm.); and a late straggler was perched on a pole in the small boat harbor at Nome on 19 October 1970 (G. J. Divoky and G. E. Watson pers. comm.). Extralimitally, there have been three recent migrants recorded at Kotzebue: a male on 7 May 1978 (D. P. Harrington in litt.), an individual on 6 May 1982, and another for a week in mid-August 1987 (Selawik, NWR unpubl. notes); and a pair nested unsuccessfully at the mouth of the Noatak River 29 May-28 June 1985 (three eggs in nest box, abandoned, W. R. Uhl pers. comm.).

Merlin—*Falco columbarius*

A rare migrant, especially in fall, and a rare probable breeder, the Merlin occurs regularly as far west as treeline on the Peninsula. No nesting has been reported, but it breeds in the Nulato Hills (pair nested in an isolated spruce grove on the Andreaf-sky R in 1985, B. J. McCaffery unpubl. notes), and an apparently territorial bird was seen in medium alder shrub at Milepost 62 Taylor Highway in late May and early June 1988 by R. E. Gill and J. M. Wright (pers. comm.). Additional breeding season observations include an adult female seen by D. G. Roseneau and W. Walker on the Teller Highway at Penny River on 30 June 1970 (Roseneau unpubl. notes), a female closely observed in flight at Nome by K. Kaufman (in litt.) on 14 June 1986, an adult bird that flew past F. G. Scheider and me on the hills above Koyuk on 3 July 1977, and two separate birds seen between Elim and Cape Darby by J. M. Wright (pers. comm.) during an aerial survey on 4 June 1988. Nelson (1883, 1887) reported receiving a Merlin skin that was brought aboard the Revenue Steamer *Corwin* while it was anchored near Sledge Island during the summer of 1881. Birds of open taiga and taiga-tundra ecotonal areas of Interior Alaska, Merlins typically nest in spruce trees, usually on old magpie (*Pica pica*) nests or "witches brooms," but they also nest on the ground (ANRS).

Most Merlin reports on the Peninsula have been during the last half of August and probably represent dispersing postbreeders and juvenals and birds beginning migration, e.g., single individuals in 1980 at Golovin 13-18 August, Moses Point 22-26 August, and Koyuk 26-28 August (D. A. Woodby unpubl. notes); one, Kwiktalik Mountains east of Golovnin Bay 24 August 1977 (N. G. Tankersley unpubl. notes); and in the vicinity of Deering, single birds on 19 August 1983 and 21, 27, and 29 August 1984 (J. D. Walters unpubl. notes); latest, one male collected 22 September and another 24 September 1913, Pilgrim Hot Springs (J. Koren unpubl. notes).

Peregrine Falcon—*Falco peregrinus*

The Peregrine Falcon is a rare migrant and breeder on the Peninsula, where it usually nests in association with colonies of seabirds in the Coastal Cliffs and Block-fields habitat. Judging from known nesting sites, probably three to five pairs nest on the Peninsula each year; although in early June 1988 birds were observed at at least nine probable nesting sites along the southern coastline between Koyuk and Wales (J. M. Wright pers. comm.).

Peregrines from tundra and taiga regions are highly migratory, the North American birds wintering from the temperate United States south to southern South America (American Ornithologists' Union 1957). They are probably present on the Seward Peninsula from mid-April to mid-October (extralimitally, 16 April 1975, Ambler, D. K. Wik in litt.; extreme dates 26 April through 19 October [yr?] at Cape Thompson, Chukchi Sea, Williamson et al. 1966), although most birds have left by mid-September.

The few available data on breeding chronologies indicate that egg-laying begins in mid-May and that the young fledge from late July to mid-August. This timing enables the fledged young to become independent of their parents before local avian prey decreases significantly and before they begin migration.

The diet of Peregrine Falcons consists primarily of small birds, especially shorebirds and passerines, but is supplemented by such larger birds as jaegers, small gulls, ducks, and ptarmigan (Cade 1960, D. G. Roseneau pers. comm.); some seabirds are taken by Seward Peninsula peregrines (A. M. Springer pers. comm.).

The Peninsula peregrines present inter- and intra-specific identification problems. Some gray-plumaged Gyrfalcons are strikingly peregrine-like in appearance and can be mistaken easily for them by the uninitiated or casual observer. A pair at Bluff was described by D. G. Roseneau (unpubl. notes) thusly: "Both adults were blue-grey with dark heads and clean white breasts with fine markings and very peregrine looking." Also, questions regarding the subspecific status on the Peninsula of this variable species remain unanswered. A male collected at Wales on 25 May 1939 was ascribed to the Asian form *F. p. calidus* (=*harterti*) by Hanna (1940b), but White (1968) found it identical to average *F. p. tundrius* that he described from the tundra regions of North America. The validity of the subspecies *tundrius* as separate from the North American *F. p. anatum* needs further examination, however, based on accumulating data by D. G. Roseneau and others (pers. comm.) showing the frequent occurrence of *tundrius*-colored juvenals in Alaska's taiga population and the clinal geographic trend of these occurrences.

Gyrfalcon—*Falco rusticolus*

A resident species, at least in years of adequate food supplies, the Gyrfalcon is an uncommon migrant and breeder and a rare winter resident and visitant on the Seward Peninsula. It is widely distributed across most of the Peninsula, in the cliff and block-field habitats of the foothills of the Highlands, the Northern and Southern uplands, including mainland coastal cliffs, and in the Interior Lowlands where cliffs, bluffs, or tors are present. The Gyrfalcon is the second most abundant breeding raptor on the Peninsula. Overall, however, based on my counts, it is only about half as numerous as the more abundant Rough-legged Hawk, but population levels are more stable. During annual surveys of large parts of the Peninsula between 1968 and 1972, counts varied from 34 to 49 pairs, but numbers dropped to 13 pairs in 1971, apparently because of unusually stressful winter and early spring weather conditions, which decimated ptarmigan populations, almost the sole food resource for the Gyrfalcons at that time of year; numbers were up to 36 pairs again by 1972 (Swartz et al. 1975). On average, D. G. Roseneau (pers. comm.) estimates that a total of about 70 pairs breed on the Peninsula. Few nonbreeders occur on the Peninsula during the summer; during 1968-1970 studies, Roseneau (1972) found only two pairs and four other individuals that were possible nonbreeders.

Little is known about the wintering Gyrfalcon population, but some birds are apparently winter visitants from other regions. Not only is there a conspicuous fall movement of birds in the region (see below), but during the winters of 1967-1968 and 1968-1969, J. J. Burns (unpubl. notes and pers. comm.) noted an increased number of white-plumaged birds, suggesting an influx of birds from Siberia where this color phase is more common. Local breeders constitute some of the wintering population, also. During 1970-1971 near Nome, a pair was observed at a site throughout the winter by R. E. Pegau, and at two other sites, fresh ptarmigan kills, mites, or tracks in fresh snow were found by W. Walker and D. G. Roseneau (pers. comm.). In northern Yukon Territory, Platt (1976) saw signs of activity in January and February 1975 at about half of the nesting cliffs of the region that had been used during previous breeding seasons. He found greater mid-winter site tenacity in males than females, although some pairs were together again at cliffs by February; all wintering birds observed were over 1 yr old.

Breeding activity in the resident pairs begins in late winter; scrape formation and copulation, early signs of pair formation, were observed in northern Yukon Territory by late March 1975 (Platt 1976). Nest sites on the Seward Peninsula are usually on ledges of steep-faced cliffs or tors (upland or coastal and including river bluffs) that are adjacent to expanses of open country. At times, pairs nest on dredges and other mining structures (White and Roseneau 1970); one pair nested in a depression at the top of a tor near Serpentine Hot Springs (D. G. Roseneau unpubl. notes); and a pair raised two young in an old raven nest in a large Balsam Poplar along the Pilgrim River in 1966 (R. Emmons pers. comm.; J. Bahnke in D. G. Roseneau unpubl. notes). Gyrfalcons are scrape-nesters, but on the Peninsula they usually make their scrapes on top of old stick nests constructed by Rough-legged Hawks, Golden Eagles, and Common Ravens (Roseneau 1972). Tenacity to nesting cliffs between years is low; of 34 active sites observed on the Peninsula in 1968, only 8 were reused by Gyrfalcons in 1969, and 77% of 107 nesting sites observed 1968-1970 were used only once by Gyrfalcons (Roseneau 1972).

Gyrfalcons, especially the females, probably begin breeding when 2 yr old (Roseneau pers. comm., Cramp 1980b), although Platt's (1977) captive birds did not begin breeding until their fourth year. Egg-laying in Platt's captive birds began when daylength reached 14.5 h; this daylength on the Seward Peninsula is reached on 12 April. Backdating from the earliest fledging dates recorded on the Peninsula (four young on 10 July 1969, D. G. Roseneau unpubl. notes, and four young that had been out of their nest for about a week on 14 July 1986 and thus had fledged by 7-8 July, W. R. Tilton pers. comm.) shows that under favorable conditions, egg-laying may begin this early on the Peninsula, too. More typically, however, egg-laying begins 20-26 April and peaks in the population during the last few days of April and the first few days of May. Laying in the population continues until about 15 May, rarely as late as 21-23 May. Renesting may occur in Gyrfalcons if eggs are lost early in incubation (Platt 1977), so the late clutches on the Peninsula could be the result of renesting or later nest initiations by first-time breeders.

Sixteen clutches on the Seward Peninsula in 1968-1969 (Roseneau unpubl. notes) averaged 3.6 ± 0.5 eggs, range 3-4. Eggs are laid at intervals of 48 h or less (P. J. Bente pers. comm.), with incubation usually beginning with the laying of the third egg (Platt 1977); hence, the last chick may hatch 1-2 days later than the rest of the brood. Incubation lasts 35 days (Platt 1977). It is performed largely by the female, with the contribution of the male varying among pairs and with the stage of the breeding cycle; most frequently, the male will sit on the eggs briefly while the female leaves to feed on the prey he has brought to her (Platt 1977, Bente 1981), although he may be somewhat more attentive during the last few days of incubation and the first few days after the young have hatched (Bente 1981). The male typically brings food to the nesting area throughout the incubation and nestling periods. The female stays close to the nest and broods the young more or less continuously until they are 6-10 days old, at which time she may begin to hunt for food, also (Platt 1977, Bente 1981). Fledging on the Seward Peninsula occurs at 48-50 days (D. G. Roseneau unpubl. notes). Thus, on the Seward Peninsula, most clutches hatch between the fourth week of May and the first week of June, and the young fledge from mid-July into early August—or as late as mid-August for late nestings.

The staple food of Gyrfalcons in northern Yukon Territory and in northern and western Alaska is ptarmigan (Cade 1960, White and Cade 1971, Roseneau 1972, Platt 1977), both Rock and Willow ptarmigan on the Seward Peninsula (Roseneau 1972). This diet is supplemented opportunistically in summer on the Peninsula with ground squirrels, Long-tailed Jaegers, shorebirds, passerines, waterfowl, Short-eared Owls, voles, and, in the case of sea-cliff nesters, seabirds (Roseneau 1972).

Young Gyrfalcons remain dependent on their parents for capturing prey for more than a month after fledging (two chicks that fledged 21-25 July 1968 were still in the area of their nest cliff on 24 August, doing some hunting but still receiving food from a parent [D. G. Roseneau unpubl. notes]); and families apparently remain together well into September and even October (Platt 1976, J. J. Burns in D. G. Roseneau unpubl. notes).

There is a movement of Gyrfalcons into and through the Seward Peninsula region from mid-August at least through September. At Little Diomede Island the passage was noted in late August and early September by S. W. Stoker (pers. comm.), where birds often stop to rest awhile and then fly off toward Wales; the movement was unusually large in 1974 and included several white birds. An eastward movement of up to three birds a day passed Cape Espenberg 18 August-12+ September 1976 and 23 August-21+ September 1977 (Schamel et al. 1979 [where reported as Goshawks], D. Schamel photo of juvenal Gyrfalcon). Six or eight "dark adults or immatures" visited Bluff in September 1975 (W. H. Drury in litt.). Juvenals, which do not winter in their northern natal regions (Platt 1976), predominate in this fall movement, but some adults (subadults?) are present, also. Other than being generally southward, the movement lacks consistent directional orientation; the above reports suggest a generally eastward movement on the Peninsula, but one nestling banded in the Nome River valley on 3 July 1972 was recovered from central Kamchatka, USSR, the following winter on 24 January 1973 (W. Walker pers. comm.). Some of these birds spend their winter on the islands and sea ice of the northern Bering Sea (winter along south coast St. Lawrence I [near polynyas], Fay and Cade 1959; Big Diomede I, 15 December 1912, Thayer and Bangs 1914; hunting Oldsquaws and murres off King I, 8-9 February 1968, J. J. Burns unpubl. notes).

Most Gyrfalcons on the Seward Peninsula are gray in color, although the plumage of individuals varies from a dark gray, with occasional dark-helmeted heads, to white. Of 55 adult birds examined for color in 1968, 12.7% were dark gray, 56.4% gray, 16.4% light gray, 5.4% straw (cream tone with gray bars), and 9.1% white (D. G. Roseneau unpubl. notes). Cade (1960) and Vaurie (1961) concurred that this highly polymorphic bird should be considered a monotypic species.

The largest falcon, the Gyrfalcon is a powerful bird. One attacked D. G. Roseneau's (unpubl. notes) survey plane as it passed a nest cliff on 26 June 1968; the bird had to climb at a 45° angle to catch up to the plane, which was flying 120 kph (75 mph), but it overtook the plane within 0.4 km.

Spruce Grouse—*Dendragapus canadensis*

The Spruce Grouse is probably an uncommon resident in the southeast quadrant of the Peninsula, the only region where its required habitat of coniferous forests is adequate. On 2 July 1972, H. E. Kingery (pers. comm.) saw a female along upper Hot Springs Trail northwest of Elim. Residents of both Koyuk and Elim report the occurrence of Spruce Grouse in the vicinity of their villages, and L. Daniels told me in 1972 of a brood of 9 chicks at Elim. Spruce Grouse apparently occur as far west on the Peninsula as the spruce forests around Council (J. J. Burns pers. comm.), and at least two strayed beyond spruce habitat to Deering in 1987—a female 2-7 October and an adult male on 8 October (J. D. Walters unpubl. notes).

Willow Ptarmigan—*Lagopus lagopus*

A fairly common resident, the Willow Ptarmigan fluctuates widely in abundance from year to year and locality to locality, varying from uncommon to common. It is widely distributed across the Peninsula, in the Northern and Southern uplands, the Interior Lowlands, and in the Coastal Lowlands where sufficient low shrub cover exists. In fact, its summer occurrence correlates closely with the presence of Low Shrub Thicket and extends as far north as Cape Espenberg and as far west as around Shishmaref Inlet, Ear Mountain (all Kessel pers. obs.), and the inland margin of Lopp Lagoon (Bailey 1943).

In winter, Willow Ptarmigan withdraw from the western portions of the Peninsula (west of about 166° W) and from the northern Coastal Lowlands. Here, shrubbery is low and restricted to wind-protected locations that become drifted with snow. The favored willow buds are thus unavailable as winter food. How far these birds move is unknown, but ptarmigan in varying numbers, in flocks up to several hundred birds, winter throughout the Interior Lowlands (Anthony 1906) and wherever willows are exposed in the Southern and Northern uplands. Numbers at exposed sites vary with the extent of snow cover and the severity of the winter. Birds were notably absent from the Peninsula after severe conditions in winter 1970-1971, including heavy snow, freezing rain, and high wind that formed a hard snow crust (Swartz et al. 1975). Some birds may have moved out of the affected region, but mortality was probably high, too, judging from the extremely low numbers seen during the following summer (Kessel pers. obs., D. G. Roseneau pers. comm.).

As soon as snow melt allows, Willow Ptarmigan again move back toward their breeding areas. Extralimitally at Bethel on the Yukon-Kuskokwim Delta, this movement was evident 13 March 1964, 2-6 April 1971, 12 April 1965, and 17-23 April 1963 (Yukon Delta NWR unpubl. data), although farther out on the Delta, it was not until 3 May 1924 that they arrived "in force" (Brandt 1943). On the Seward Peninsula, a loose flock of 2000 ptarmigan was present along the Flambeau River on 6 April 1968 (J. J. Burns unpubl. notes); whether this flock consisted solely of overwintering birds or had been supplemented by spring arrivals is unknown, although the latter appears likely. Breeding-plumaged males still in flocks were reported by Bailey (1943) on 25 May (12 birds) and 31 May 1922 (40 birds) at Wales, where few if any breed; and several flocks, undoubtedly migrants, were present on Little Diomede

Island on 31 May 1966 (J. J. Burns unpubl. notes). On the other hand, Willow Ptarmigan had established territories near Buckland by 15 April 1953 (J. W. Brooks unpubl. notes), and by 30 April 1978, males were conspicuous and displaying on the tundra extralimitally at Kotzebue (D. P. Harrington in litt.).

Willow Ptarmigan, which breed during their first year, are territorial and typically monogamous. The female joins a courting male on his territory, and the two remain largely confined to the territory until their brood leaves the nest. The nest is usually placed at the base of an overhanging shrub, either in moss or graminoid vegetation and often between sedge tussocks. It consists of a shallow depression, sometimes sparsely lined with dried grasses and other leaves. Clutch size in eight nests from the Peninsula (various sources) averaged 8.5 ± 1.9 eggs, range 6-11 eggs; nine additional egg sets reported by Bailey (1943) from the Lopp Lagoon area averaged 8 eggs. Extralimitally on the Yukon-Kuskokwim Delta, 26 clutches observed over the years averaged 9.8 ± 1.9 eggs, range 7-14 eggs, mostly 8-11 eggs (Yukon Delta NWR unpubl. data). Eggs are usually laid at daily intervals, and incubation begins with the laying of either the last or next-to-last egg; the female usually covers the eggs with litter when she leaves the nest prior to incubation (Jenkins et al. 1963). Incubation is performed entirely by the female, while the male guards the territory and the nest. Incubation lasts 20-25 days, but averages 22 days (Conover 1926, Jenkins et al. 1963).

The chicks leave the nest within 12 h of hatching. Both parents care for the young, a behavior unique among North American grouse (Weeden and Ellison 1968), although typically they are brooded only by the female. They are capable of flying when only 12-13 days old (Cramp 1980b), but they are not fully grown until 30-35 days of age and may not be entirely independent until a month after that (ibid.).

Early egg-laying begins 17-18 May extralimitally on the Yukon-Kuskokwim Delta (Yukon Delta NWR unpubl. data), and apparently at about the same time on the Seward Peninsula. The main egg-laying period on the Peninsula is during the last week of May and the first few days of June, but it may continue in the population as late as mid- to late June, depending on the season and locality (eight quarter-incubated eggs on 6 July 1922 at Mint R, Bailey 1943; brood of eight chicks hatched 9 July 1967, Milepost 70 Council Road, near Bear R, Kessel pers. obs.). Renesting after early nest failures has been reported (Jenkins et al. 1963). First hatching occurs about 15 June, and barely flying chicks have been reported as early as 26 June 1969 (D. G. Roseneau unpubl. notes). The main hatch in the population occurs during the last week of June and the first few days of July. Mortality rates are high in young ptarmigan, with only 20-35% surviving to 11 months of age (Weeden and Ellison 1968).

Willow Ptarmigan are essentially vegetarians, and, appropriately, willows predominate in their diet. Willow leaves and some buds and twigs are eaten in summer, but these are widely supplemented with leaves of blueberries and other deciduous plants and with available berries, including blueberries, crowberries, and cranberries (Roberts 1963, Weeden 1965c, 1969). Young chicks, as with other grouse, consume varying quantities of invertebrates during their first few weeks of life (Cramp 1980b). The most important food in winter is the buds and twigs of willows, which constitutes 90 + % of the diet at snow-covered localities (Roberts 1963, West and Meng 1966, Weeden 1969), including 96% in 43 crops collected near Nome (Weeden 1969).

Flocks begin to form again in early August, the first through the combining of family groups and probably failed breeders (400 + birds, including broods of half-grown young, 9 August 1915, junction of Sinuk R and Boulder Ck, Hill 1922; flocks, 12 August 1980, Safety Sound, D. A. Woodby unpubl. notes). Migration from the western and northern parts of the Peninsula has begun by the end of September (large flocks appeared in Imuruk Basin by 1 October 1904, Anthony 1906; flocks of up to 100 birds about Nome on 20 October 1965, J. J. Burns unpubl. notes). There is a partial segregation of sexes during the winter as a result of migration; the males tend to remain closer to the breeding grounds than the females, which may move from the tundra into taiga regions for the winter (Weeden 1964).

Ptarmigan are an important prey species for several predators of the Seward Peninsula, especially during winter when most bird species have migrated southward and when small mammals are either hibernating or protected by a mantle of snow. They are a primary food resource for Gyrfalcons throughout the year and a supplemental resource for Rough-legged Hawks, Golden Eagles, Peregrine Falcons, Snowy Owls, and both Arctic and Red foxes. Compared to other predators, Gyrfalcons and Golden Eagles elicit strong fright reactions in ptarmigan, causing them to either ''freeze'' or flee (White and Weeden 1966).

During the course of a year, adult ptarmigan wear three sets of plumages. They undergo a complete prebasic molt at the end of the breeding season in early summer, then a partial supplemental molt of body feathers that results in their white winter plumage, and finally another partial body molt (pre-alternate) into their spring breeding plumage.

Rock Ptarmigan—*Lagopus mutus*

The Rock Ptarmigan is an uncommon but widespread resident of the Seward Peninsula. It breeds throughout the Northern and Southern uplands and the foothills of the Highlands, where it favors Dwarf Shrub Mat habitats, usually with a vertical component of patchy low shrubs or boulder rubble. It occurs at almost any elevation where this habitat is present, along streambeds and associated draws, on hillsides, and on ridges or tops of coastal bluffs where saddles or boulders provide some protection from winds. A family was present on Sledge Island during summer 1975 (W. H. Drury in litt.). Numbers fluctuate widely from year to year. On 6 June 1968, in a year of high abundance, over 40 territorial males occupied a Dwarf Shrub Meadow slope on the east side of the Bluestone River (D. G. Roseneau pers. comm.). On average over the years, however, I found only 8-10 adults/day while hiking in appropriate habitat.

The Rock Ptarmigan, like its congener, apparently withdraws from the harshest habitats during the winter months (Bailey 1943), probably because its primary food plant, the Dwarf Birch (*Betula nana*), becomes covered with snow. It is nomadic in winter, with movements affected by weather, snow conditions, and food supply, but generally it remains closer to its breeding sites than the Willow Ptarmigan (Weeden 1964). Most winter observations on the Peninsula have not distinguished between species, but Rock Ptarmigan occur in many of the same areas as do Willow Ptarmigan as well as at less protected sites. Both species of ptarmigan scratch out shallow depressions in the snow for overnight roosting in winter, but the Rock Ptarmigan is less restricted to shrub patches for roosting (Roberts 1963, Weeden 1965c).

Few data are available from the Peninsula upon which to determine seasonal chronologies, but the timing of breeding activities appears closely similar to that of the Willow Ptarmigan. Males return to breeding areas and establish territories as soon as environmental conditions permit, conditions that may vary annually by 1 or 2 weeks. The females return shortly thereafter and select the best nesting areas, each pairing with the male holding the territory surrounding her chosen site (MacDonald 1970). Both sexes breed as yearlings (Weeden 1965a). Most pairing is monogamous, although there are instances of both polygyny and polyandry (Weeden 1964). The nest is a shallow depression, usually in mat-type vegetation, and may have some dried grasses and a few feathers in the cup; it may or may not be under or beside protective vegetation or boulders (Bailey 1926, Roberts 1963, Weeden 1965c).

Egg-laying on the Peninsula may begin as early as the third week of May, but it peaks during the last week of May and the first few days of June. The laying period in the population appears more synchronized than in the Willow Ptarmigan, possibly because of the harsh, more restrictive environment and the probably related occurrence of few renesting attempts (see Weeden 1965a). Usually 3-11 eggs are laid (Weeden and Ellison 1968). The mean clutch size in 101 nests in Interior Alaska from 1960 to 1964 was 7.0 eggs (Weeden 1965a), but the mean varied from 6.5 eggs in 1963 (ibid.) to 9.0 eggs in 1966 (Weeden and Theberge 1972). The eggs of a clutch are laid at 24-30-h intervals (Weeden and Ellison 1968), and the female covers the eggs with bits of nearby vegetation when she leaves the eggs during the laying period (MacDonald 1970). Incubation, performed entirely by the female, lasts for 20-22 days, averaging about 21 days (Weeden 1965c, Weeden and Ellison 1968, MacDonald 1970).

The male guards the territory and accompanies the incubating female when she feeds; most terminate these duties about the time of hatching, although a few may accompany broods for awhile (Weeden 1965c, MacDonald 1970). The chicks remain in the nest for 3-12 h after hatching, and, after leaving the nest, the female continues brooding them intermittently for several days, probably longer at night; they can fly weakly when only 10-11 days old (Weeden 1965c). Most hatching on the Peninsula occurs during the last third of June.

The most important food for the Rock Ptarmigan throughout Alaska is Dwarf Birch, the catkins and buds of which form 90 + % of the diet during winter (Roberts 1963, Weeden 1969, Moss 1973). When available, especially in summer and fall, this diet is supplemented by berries, leaves of a variety of plants, including *Dryas* and *Salix*, and invertebrates (Roberts 1963, Weeden 1969, Moss 1974).

After leaving their territories, the males shift away from the main brood-rearing areas for molting and feeding, and small flocks of these males and failed females form during late June and July (Weeden 1964). Females with broods move about to productive feeding sites during July and early August, after which families begin to group together; by late August, some of the adult males and failed females begin to join these flocks (Weeden 1964). Flocking peaks in late September, after which a partial sorting of sexes occurs as the females, both adults and juvenals, begin their fall shift to wintering areas (Weeden 1964), some apparently into shrubby openings in the taiga at the base of the Peninsula and beyond. Nelson (1887:135) reported that

> In autumn, toward the last of October and first of November, this bird unites with the common [Willow] Ptarmigan in great flocks, on the northern shore of Norton Sound, and migrates thence across the sound to Stuart's Island, thence reaching the mainland. The birds are frequently seen by the natives while they are passing Egg Island, on their way to the island just mentioned. They are said to commence their flight just before dark in the evening. . . . In April the birds return to the north, always traveling in the evening or night, as they do during their autumnal migrations.

Rock Ptarmigan receive heavy predation from the same predators as the Willow Ptarmigan. They also have the same three sets of annual plumages, but the timing of the spring molt in the males differs relative to the courtship period. The male Rock Ptarmigan courts and mates in its white winter plumage, whereas the male Willow Ptarmigan begins its pre-alternate molt in early May, attaining a chestnut-red plumage on its head, neck, and upper breast that contrasts with the white body. It courts and mates in this striking plumage and then gradually continues its pre-alternate molt into its summer plumage while the female is incubating.

American Coot—*Fulica americana*

A casual spring migrant, an American Coot was seen at the mouth of the Buckland River during a ground survey on 6 June 1981 (Eldridge 1982). This coot is a rare migrant and summer visitant in eastern Interior Alaska (Kessel and Gibson 1978).

Sandhill Crane—*Grus canadensis*

A locally common migrant and fairly common summer visitant and breeder, the Sandhill Crane is widely distributed throughout the wetlands of the Seward Peninsula. An average of 1580±860 cranes was estimated to summer annually on the Peninsula between 1957 and 1978 (calculated from Conant et al. 1985). Numbers increased sharply beginning in 1979, however, and the 1979-1987 average, even excluding the extremely high counts of 17,300 cranes in 1982 and 12,500 in 1986 was 5300±2700 birds (U. S. Fish and Wildlife Service 1978-1987). In addition, at least 20,000 cranes (Breckenridge and Cline 1967, Flock 1972) traverse southern portions of the Peninsula while migrating to and from breeding grounds in northeastern Siberia.

During summer cranes are somewhat more numerous in the Coastal Lowlands than in the uplands and Interior Lowlands, favoring well-vegetated coastal barrier strips (e.g., off Lopp Lagoon and at Cape Espenberg) and large river estuaries that open directly into coastal bays (e.g., Buckland and Nugnugaluktuk rivers). They are closely associated with a habitat complex of ponds and Wet Meadow, and both breeders and small flocks of nonbreeders frequent such wetlands throughout the summer. The river estuaries are also used extensively during premigratory staging and fall migration, although protected river deltas and wetlands on the inner side of lagoons are apparently preferred (e.g., Agiapuk and Kuzitrin river deltas in Imuruk Basin and Fish R delta). In view of the low vegetation profile of the crane's habitat, it is amazing how inconspicuous breeders can make themselves by squatting and walking on folded legs, humping their backs, and flattening stretched necks low over the ground!

The Sandhill Cranes of the Peninsula winter mostly in eastern New Mexico-western Texas and adjacent northern Mexico, and they migrate between there and the Peninsula via the Central Flyway east of the Rockies and through Interior Alaska (Kessel 1984, Tacha et al. 1984). Birds of the north side of the Peninsula apparently reach Kotzebue Sound via the Koyukuk lowlands and then move along the coastline, where they have been reported flying west in spring past Deering (J. D. Walters unpubl. notes). Those of the southern and interior portions of the Peninsula and those that migrate on to Siberia enter the Seward Peninsula region in the Norton Bay area (Kessel 1984).

The first spring migrants reach the Peninsula while the landscape is still largely frozen and snow-covered, in some years as early as the end of April (30 April 1986, Deering, J. D. Walters unpubl. notes; and extralimitally, 25 April 1978 and 28 April 1980, Ambler, D. K. Wik; 27 April 1980, Old Chevak, Yukon Delta, C. M. Boise in litt.; 29 April 1944, Mountain Village, H. C. Kyllingstad in litt.). Most first arrivals over the years have been during the first few days of May, however (1 May 1978, 2 May 1980, 3 May 1981 and 1983, all vicinity of Nome, Beltz School unpubl. notes). Depending on weather conditions, which strongly influence the migratory movement, the peak of crane migration usually occurs between 6 and 14 May, although a major movement of 15,000-20,000 birds passed Wales (Breckenridge and Cline 1967) and Little Diomede Island (J. J. Burns in litt.) on 23 May 1964, an unusually late spring. Subadult nonbreeders may still be arriving in mid-June (flocks of up to 40 cranes flying north past Wales, 14-16 June 1976, D. D. Gibson unpubl. notes).

The Koyuk-Inglutalik wetlands at the head of Norton Bay appear to be a "traditional" overnight roosting area for migrant cranes in both spring and fall (Shields and Peyton 1979, Woodby and Divoky 1983). Other wetlands may also be used in spring from time to time, e.g., Fish River delta (Woodby and Divoky 1983), but it seems probable that birds leaving the Koyuk-Inglutalik roost in the morning usually fly nonstop either to their Seward Peninsula breeding grounds or to Siberia. Several bits of evidence suggest this pattern: (1) the distance from the head of Norton Bay to Siberia can be traversed by cranes in a single day's flight under favorable weather conditions (Kessel 1984), (2) Anthony (1906) wrote of a day-long passage of cranes that passed over Imuruk Basin on 10 May 1905, arriving from the east and heading toward Wales—i.e., they did not land, (3) the major spring flights past Wales do not begin until 12:00-13:00 h (Breckenridge and Cline 1967, Flock 1972)—about the time it would take cranes to fly the 400-km distance if they left the roost at 04:00 h, which they often do at this time of year (Kessel 1984), and (4) no other major spring roost sites have been reported.

The migratory pathways followed by the Siberian birds vary with weather conditions. Most migrants roughly follow the southern coastline of the Peninsula, but unknown numbers fly over the Norton Sound and Bering Strait ice pack (Flock 1972, Kessel 1984), and some fly as far inland as the north side of the Kigluaik Mountains (see Anthony 1906 above). Of these latter birds, some probably follow a straight path from Norton Bay, over the Darby Mountains and McCarthys Marsh and into the Pilgrim and Kuzitrin river drainages, and perhaps others move inland up the Fish and Niukluk river drainages. Fewer migrating cranes have been reported in spring than fall along the southern coastline (Shields and Peyton 1979, Woodby and Divoky 1983), probably because (1) migration is more rapid and concerted toward the end of spring migration than during fall staging and the beginning of fall migration, so less time is spent on the ground, (2) more birds in spring than fall bypass the Peninsula by flying out over the ice, (3) there are more staging and roosting localities on the Peninsula in fall (see below) than in spring, and (4) the summer's crop of young birds has been added to the fall population.

Local breeders, which are at least 3 yr old (Drewien 1974), are among the first birds to arrive, and nesting begins as soon as nest sites are free of snow. Nests typically are placed in sedge or grass meadows near water, although some are placed in drier upland sedge meadows. The nest is little more than a platform of flattened grass or sedge. Almost all clutches consist of two eggs (e.g., Brandt 1943, Schamel et al. 1979), with the second egg laid about 2 days after the first (Drewien 1974). Incubation begins with the laying of the first egg; both members of the pair participate, but only the female incubates at night (ibid.). The incubation period of an egg at Shishmaref Inlet was 28 days (Noble and Wright 1977). Although no evidence of renesting was noted by Boise (1977) on the Yukon Delta, cranes in Idaho will renest if eggs are lost during the first half of incubation (Drewien 1974); a clutch that hatched in Norton Sound on 19 July 1980 (Woodby and Divoky 1983) was probably from a renest.

On the Seward Peninsula, laying usually begins in mid-May and peaks in most years during the last 2 weeks of May (earliest, 7 and 11 May, back-calculated from clutches that hatched 4 and 8 June 1977 on the Inglutalik R, Shields and Peyton 1979). Hatching usually begins in the second week of June and continues through the month, with some late clutches not hatching until July (hatching 3 July 1973, Cape Espenberg, Kessel and D. D. Gibson unpubl. notes; hatched 19 July 1980, Norton Sound, see above). Families remain on their natal territories until fledging (Drewien 1974, Boise 1977). On the Yukon Delta, young may begin flying at 49 days of age, but are probably not capable of sustained flight for another 10 days or so (C. M. Boise pers. comm.); one chick still had not fledged at 60 days (Boise 1976). Thus, fledging on the Peninsula may begin in early August and is well under way by mid-August. The adults undergo their wing molt and flightlessness while on the breeding territory, regaining flight by the time the young fledge. Flightless birds are competent swimmers if they need to cross water to escape danger or reach feeding sites (Kessel pers. obs.).

Cranes are omnivorous. They feed on tundra berries, plant shoots, and roots, probing and digging with their heavy bills for the latter; and opportunistically they feed on a wide variety of adult insects and small vertebrates, including microtine rodents, nestling birds, and fish (Nelson 1883, Walkinshaw 1949, Boise 1977), and sometimes on carrion (stranded Walrus [*Odobenus rosmarus*] carcasses, late July-early August 1986, Cape Espenberg, D. M. Hopkins pers. comm.).

Premigratory flocks begin to form in early August, the first apparently of failed breeders and coalesced flocks of nonbreeders (first cranes gathered between 3 and 10 August 1948 at Lava Lake, D. M. Hopkins in litt; apparent southward movement by 5 August 1976, Shishmaref Inlet, Noble and Wright 1977); and families begin to aggregate almost as soon as the young fledge. There was an exodus of flocks from Lava Lake about 10 August 1948 (D. M. Hopkins in litt.), and on 13-14 August 1965, J. J. Burns (unpubl. notes) watched five flocks, each of 8-12 cranes, move eastward past the lower Nome River flats. These early movements are probably of local birds shifting to coastal sites for premigratory staging. Movement becomes increasingly evident after mid-August, with the early departure of non- and failed breeders. Bean (1882) reported cranes crossing the Bering Strait at the Diomede islands as early as 18 August 1880, and migration along the coast at the Akulik-Inglutalik River delta began on 19 August 1976, when flocks of 6-12 birds passed along the coast (Shields and Peyton 1977). The main passage of fall migrants does not usually begin until the last of August, however, and it continues through the first 3 weeks of September, usually peaking about 15-19 September (peaked 15 September 1949 at Council, D. M. Hopkins in litt.; peaked at 16,000 birds on 16 September 1977 at Koyuk-Inglutalik wetlands, Shields and Peyton 1979; peaked at 4500-5000 birds flying along the coast "several miles out over the sea" on 19 September 1975, Drury 1976b). This mid-September peak is the result of a combination of the major passage of breeders from Siberia with the exodus of successful local families from the Seward Peninsula. The latest reported dates for the Peninsula have been 7 October 1985 (flock of five, flying high 6 km south of Deering, headed eastward, J. D. Walters unpubl. notes) and 8 October 1966 (two flocks flying with five Tundra Swans over the mainland hills north of Sledge I, J. J. Burns unpubl. notes).

A number of Peninsula wetlands are used in fall as staging or overnight roosting sites, the most used being on the southern portions of the Peninsula because of their position on the route of the Siberian migrants: Imuruk Basin (about 6700 cranes, 5 September 1981, Woodby and Divoky 1983), the Fish River delta (2400 on northwest slope of Golovnin Bay, 19 September 1977, R. J. King pers. comm.; about 3000 birds, 6 September 1980, Woodby and Divoky 1983), and the Koyuk-Inglutalik wetlands (16,000 cranes, 16 September 1977, Shields and Peyton 1979; about 3000 cranes, 6 September 1980, Woodby and Divoky 1983).

Migrant pathways in fall, as in spring, may be either coastal or inland north of the Kigluaik Mountains, depending on weather conditions, especially prevailing winds. Birds roosting in Imuruk Basin, as well as local families from the interior of the Peninsula, apparently move along the Kuzitrin drainage, then southeastward over the lowlands between the Kigluaik and Bendeleben mountains and down the Niukluk River to about Council, and then head directly toward the Koyuk-Inglutalik wetlands (an "enormous passage" passed Council 14-16 September 1949, circled to gain altitude at Council, and then headed off in a generally easterly direction [D. M. Hopkins in litt. and pers. comm.]). Other interior birds, especially those from the upper Kuzitrin River basin, probably move either directly eastward to the Koyukuk River drainage or perhaps down the Koyuk River drainage to the Koyuk-Inglutalik wetlands. Most cranes summering on the coastal wetlands of the northwestern portions of the Peninsula probably work their way eastward along the southern shore of Kotzebue Sound to the Koyukuk River and thence through Interior Alaska.

Black-bellied Plover—*Pluvialis squatarola*

The Black-bellied Plover is a rare migrant and summer visitant and a locally uncommon breeder on the Peninsula, where it is essentially restricted to the outer coastal fringes of the Coastal Lowlands. A small breeding population occupies the Cape Woolley-Woolley Lagoon area and the base of Point Spencer spit, and occasional individuals or small groups of migrants or nonbreeders frequent various wetland sites around the periphery of the Peninsula between May and September. Dry habitats are selected for nesting, usually in Dwarf Shrub Meadow, either on raised sites on the flats or on upland slopes above the coastal wetlands (Brandt 1943, Kessel et al. 1964, but contra Gabrielson and Lincoln 1959). At Woolley, breeding Black-bellied Plovers occur between about 5 and 7 km along the north-south spur road between Milepost 40 Teller Highway to the inner edge of the Woolley flats, an area of rocky dwarf shrub and dry sedge. After breeding, families move to damper sedge-grass sites for feeding and cover. Nonbreeders and staging migrants feed primarily on tidal flats.

Alaska's Black-bellied Plovers winter along the east coastline of the Pacific Ocean, from southern British Columbia to Chile; they are primarily coastal migrants, although most Bering Sea birds apparently cut overland across the Alaska Peninsula (American Ornithologists' Union 1983). The first spring migrants arrive on the Yukon Delta during the first week of May (earliest, 29 April 1980, C. M. Boise in litt.; 4 May 1986, B. J. McCaffery unpubl. notes; 5 May [yr?], Gabrielson and Lincoln 1959) and probably arrive on the Seward Peninsula a few days later. Stragglers, apparently non-breeders, are still moving in late May-early June (one each, 26 and 28 May and 9 June 1983, Wales, M. L. Ward unpubl. notes; two pairs, 3 June 1985, Nome R mouth, J. L. Dunn in litt.; one, 12 June 1977, Wales, D. A. Woodby and K. V. Hirsch unpubl. notes).

Nesting territories are occupied almost as soon as the birds arrive, judging from the seasonal chronologies outlined below. Almost all clutches consist of four eggs, laid at approximately 36-h intervals (Hussell and Page 1976). The male stands guard at the nest during egg-laying and sometimes sits on the incomplete clutch (ibid.). After clutch completion, incubation is shared by both parents; it lasts 26.5-27.0 days

(Holmes and Black 1973, Mayfield 1973, Hussell and Page 1976, contra Brandt 1943). The young stay at the nest until the last-hatched chick is dry; brooding by the parents continues for at least several days after the chicks leave the nest (Hussell and Page 1976). The female deserts the family when the chicks are about 12 days old (ibid.). Fledging occurs at about 23 days (ibid.), the male staying with the chicks until then (Parmelee et al. 1967, Hussell and Page 1976).

Back-dating from observations of various-aged young shows that egg-laying begins during the third week of May (earliest, about 17 May, based on the last of four chicks hatching 17 June 1983, R. and B. Mearns unpubl. notes, a brood still in the nest on 18 June 1988, P. G. Connors pers. comm., and 10-12 "winter plumage" juvenals that flew along coast, 16 July 1977, Kitluck R, J. M. Wright unpubl. notes), with most clutches initiated during the last third of May. Hatching peaks during the last third of June, and most young should fledge during the third week of July.

Food of Black-bellied Plovers consists of a variety of invertebrates. Mostly insects and terrestrial invertebrates are consumed by birds while in their dry breeding habitats, but when at damper sedge-grass sites and on tidal flats, they take other available items, including crustaceans, molluscs, and polychaete worms (Cramp 1983).

Because of the small population on the Seward Penisula and the resultant absence of sizable flocks, distinguishing between summer visitants and early fall migrants is not feasible. Some fall migration is apparently already under way in the population by the end of June, however, judging from the fact that thousands of adults pass through the Yukon Delta from late June to early August, and even larger numbers of juvenals from early August through mid-September (Gill and Handel 1981). Few individuals remain on the Seward Peninsula after mid-September (latest, one, 21 September 1983, standing in snow along Inmachuk R at Deering; one each on 22 and 24 September and one on 4 October 1985, Deering; all J. D. Walters unpubl. notes).

Lesser Golden-Plover—*Pluvialis dominica*

Golden-plovers are common, widespread breeders and uncommon summer visitants on the Peninsula. They are most numerous in the Northern and Southern uplands and are relatively rare during breeding in the Coastal and Interior lowlands. Overall, these plovers are the seventh most common shorebird of the region (Table 5), although their conspicuousness makes them seem relatively more abundant. Along the 400-km length of the southern highway system, I counted a total of only 80 golden-plovers in 1967 and 71 in 1977. During nesting, they show a preference for Dwarf Shrub Mat habitat or the drier portions of Dwarf Shrub Meadow. They nest on dry knolls and ridges in the lower uplands, such as inland from Woolley Lagoon, Nome, and Solomon, to the slopes and ridges of the higher hills. They are often the only bird on the high, wind-swept ridges of the mountain foothills. After the young hatch, families move to damper nearby sites for feeding, including Wet Meadow and moist Dwarf Shrub Meadow habitats. A few nonbreeders, probably first-year birds, remain in the Coastal Lowlands during June and probably July (14 mottled-plumaged birds, 26 June 1971, Imuruk Basin; nine, five in "poor" plumage, 26-27 June 1973, Nugnugaluktuk R estuary; individuals and small groups totaling at least 25 birds,

25-26 June 1975, Buckland R estuary; all Kessel pers. obs.). A flock of 13 golden-plovers on 16 June 1984 atop Cape Deceit (J. D. Walters unpubl. notes) were probably nonbreeding yearlings, also. Postbreeders and migrants forage both on dwarf shrub tundra and on tidal mudflats and muddy margins of sloughs and lagoons (Kessel and D. D. Gibson pers. obs., Connors 1978, Woodby and Divoky 1983).

Two forms of golden-plovers breed on the Peninsula (see below), and they winter in different geographic areas. *Pluvialis d. dominica* winters in South America and in spring migrates northward mostly through Central America and the interior of North America, reaching the Seward Peninsula via Interior Alaska; *P. d. fulva* winters in southern Asia and on islands in the central and southern Pacific Ocean and pro-bably migrates north along both coasts as well as transoceanically over the North Pacific to reach the Aleutians and Bering Sea and eventually the Seward Peninsula (American Ornithologists' Union 1983). Spring migrants, apparently of both forms, arrive at the Peninsula in mid-May (earliest, one, 9 May 1981, Golovin, D. A. Woodby in litt.; one, 10 May 1972, Penny R, Alaska Department of Fish and Game unpubl. notes; seen, 14 May 1984, Milepost 4.5 Teller Highway, N. Levinson, Beltz School unpubl. notes). Movement continues throughout May, the later birds undoubtedly being nonbreeders.

Apparently some first-year birds are capable of breeding, although many may re-main on their wintering ranges and not breed until their second year (Connors 1983, Johnson and Johnson 1983). Most pairing evidently occurs on the breeding grounds (Parmelee et al. 1967). The nest consists of a shallow depression, usually surround-ed by mat vegetation and often containing bits of lichens, dead leaves, etc. The most frequent clutch size is four eggs, but sometimes only three are laid. Eggs are pro-bably laid at 36-h intervals, as in the Black-bellied Plover. Some incubation, which is shared by both parents, may begin before the last egg is laid (Parmelee et al. 1967, Cramp 1983). Incubation lasts 26 days (Parmelee et al. 1967). The young may re-main in or near the nest for about 24 h and thereafter are accompanied by both parents, apparently until fledging, which occurs at about 22 days of age (ibid.).

Applying these chronologies to observed events on the Seward Peninsula indicates that most egg-laying occurs during the last week of May and the first few days of June, and peak hatching occurs in late June and early July (two 10-11-day-old chicks, UAM 3129, on 3 July 1969 at Crete Ck would have hatched about 23 June; a 1-2-day-old chick at Willis Ck would have hatched 25 June 1977; both Kessel pers. obs.). That some laying begins earlier is illustrated by an almost fully grown juvenal, still accompanied by an adult, that I saw on 10 July 1967 along the East Fork of the Solomon River; the laying of the clutch from which this chick hatched would have begun during the second week of May. Peak fledging should occur during the last 2 weeks of July (flock of 14 juvenals, 22 July 1973, feeding in dwarf shrub tundra along the shore of Kuzitrin L, D. D. Gibson unpubl. notes), although late broods, including those from any renesting attempts, may not fledge until early August.

Golden-plovers feed mainly on insects while on the breeding grounds but oppor-tunistically take other invertebrates as available, such as at damp or muddy foraging sites; they regularly consume tundra berries in spring and fall (Bent 1929).

Adults disappear from the breeding grounds soon after the young fledge (Parmelee et al. 1967). They apparently depart immediately on migration, since Johnson and Johnson (1983) reported that most *fulva* adults and first-year birds return to Hawaii during August, a few by early August and many by mid-August. Most plovers were gone from the Serpentine Hot Springs area by 4 August 1973 (D. D. Gibson unpubl. notes), and adults disappeared from the southern Seward Peninsula about 10-20 August 1975 (Drury 1976b). Flocks of young golden-plovers begin gathering in the lowlands in August (4 August 1977 and 17 August 1976, Cape Espenberg, Schamel et al. 1979). They become increasingly numerous at Coastal Lowland sites during August, peaking in the last few days of August and the first few days of September. An influx of migrant juvenals occurs in late August-early September (peaked at an estimated 13,800 plovers, mostly juvenal *fulva*, in late August 1977 and 1978 along the barrier strip off Shishmaref Inlet, Connors and Connors 1985; 12 birds/10 ha in early September at Woolley Lagoon, Woodby and Divoky 1983), and the main exodus is over by mid-September (latest, three, 23 September 1975, Safety Sound inlet, Drury 1976b; several, 1 October 1899, Nome, Grinnell 1909b).

Connors (1983) found no evidence of intergradation or of interbreeding of *fulva* and *dominica* in areas of sympatry, and he has recommended that they be recognized as full species, the Pacific Golden-Plover and the American Golden-Plover, respectively. Until Connors' study, field observers had failed to distinguish between the two forms, which are strikingly similar, both morphologically and ecologically. In the Nome area in 1985 and 1986, however, J. L. Dunn (in litt.) noted that the pairs on the flats near the coast were *fulva*, while those on the hills were *dominica*; he found no mixed pairs.

Mongolian Plover—*Charadrius mongolus*

A bird of central and northeast Asia, the Mongolian Plover is a very rare spring migrant and a possible casual breeder on the Seward Peninsula. Records of spring migrants include a female collected from the sandy shoreline of Lopp Lagoon on 11 June 1922 by A. M. Bailey and a male collected near Wales on 4 June 1945 by D. Tevuk (Bailey 1948); a bird seen near Nome on 8 June 1977 by H. K. Springer (Kessel and Gibson 1978); and one seen at Safety Sound on 29 May 1979 by P. J. Baicich and O. K. Scott (in litt.). A pair in an extensive basin at 275-m elevation on Brooks Mountain, at the headwaters of Lost River, was observed attempting copulation on 26 June 1973 (R. J. Gordon in litt.), suggesting possible breeding.

Common Ringed Plover—*Charadrius hiaticula*

The Common Ringed Plover is a casual spring migrant on the Peninsula: one was heard by D. R. Paulson (unpubl. notes) near Wales on 4 June 1978 and a male with no brood patch was collected by him on 21 June 1978 (UAM 4091), and one was observed by K. J. Zimmer (in litt.) at the Nome River mouth on 13 June 1988. This plover is an ecological Palearctic counterpart of the Nearctic Semipalmated Plover and is a very rare spring migrant on islands of the Bering Sea (Kessel and D. D. Gibson unpubl. data); it has bred on St. Lawrence Island (Sealy et al. 1971).

Semipalmated Plover—*Charadrius semipalmatus*

An uncommon but widespread breeder on the Peninsula, the Semipalmated Plover is primarily a bird of the Northern and Southern uplands; it also occurs, however, along gravel-bedded rivers that transect lowlands. The species is largely absent along coastal barrier strips and beaches, e.g., Cape Espenberg, outer side of Lopp Lagoon, and Safety Sound, although a hatching clutch was found 1 July 1977 behind a beach bank between the Kitluk River and Cape Espenberg in vegetation killed by storm tides (J. M. Wright unpubl. notes). It is also largely absent from most of the major river estuaries, e.g., Buckland, Nugnugaluktuk, and Koyuk rivers, and from Imuruk Basin. The habitat of the Semipalmated Plover on the Peninsula is almost exclusively flat gravel-sand alluvial bars or lake shores, although during migration a few may feed along tide-bathed coastal beaches and mudflats.

The western populations of Semipalmated Plovers winter primarily in Pacific coastal areas from central California to central Chile (American Ornithologists' Union 1983). Migration in spring is probably up the Pacific Coast, although many birds move inland after reaching Southcoastal Alaska. The first spring migrants arrive at the Seward Peninsula in mid-May (earliest, 13 May 1970 and 17 May 1969, Wales, Flock and Hubbard 1979; 14 May 1975, Wales, D. K. Wik in litt.; 16 May 1988, Deering, and 17 May 1983, Nome, J. D. Walters unpubl. notes; but, extralimitally, as early as 8 May [yr?], Mountain Village, Gabrielson and Lincoln 1959; 8 May 1984, Bethel, K. Kertell in litt.; 9 May 1978, Ambler, D. K. Wik in litt.).

Nests are usually placed on a well-drained, gravel or coarse sand surface, sometimes 15-30 m from water. The nest consists of a shallow scrape, sometimes scantily lined with bits of vegetation, especially small dried leaves. The usual clutch is 4 eggs; the mean size of 32 clutches in Central, Western, and western Northern Alaska, was 3.9 ± 0.3 eggs, range 3-4 eggs (data from various sources, including ANRS and Kessel and D. D. Gibson unpubl. data). Eggs are laid daily, and, judging from hatching patterns, incubation may begin with either the third or fourth egg. Both sexes share in incubation, the length of which is somewhat variable, lasting 23-25 days (Sutton and Parmelee 1955a, Jehl and Hussell 1966, Parmelee et al. 1967).

Some egg-laying on the Seward Peninsula may begin during the fourth week of May, since egg-laying for a clutch that hatched on 18 June 1978 along the Inmachuk River (J. M. Wright unpubl. notes) must have begun on 23 May. Peak laying is usually during the first week of June, however; and peak hatching is in early July, with a few broods not hatching until mid-July. Young leave the nest as soon as the last-hatched chick is dry, and families usually remain in the general vicinity of the hatching site until fledging. Both parents attend the young, apparently until fledging (Sutton and Parmelee 1955a, Parmelee et al. 1967), which occurs between 23 and 31 days (Sutton and Parmelee 1955a), probably about 25-27 days. Thus, many of the young of the Seward Peninsula should be fledged by the end of July and most by early August.

The diet of these plovers consists almost entirely of small invertebrates, including aquatic insects, crustaceans, and various small worms (Palmer 1967), the specific composition differing between the marine and upland habitats.

Little is known about fall movements on the Seward Peninsula, but non- and failed breeders, and perhaps adults from early successful broods, probably depart before the end of July. Gill and Handel (1981) reported that adult Semipalmated Plovers move south along the Bering Sea coast in July and the juvenals from early August to mid-September. On the Seward Peninsula, however, many adults probably do not leave until late July-early August. The species is rare after mid-August (latest, two, 1 September 1985, Deering, J. D. Walters unpubl. notes; one, sometime between 6 and 10 September 1980, Fish R delta, D. A. Woodby unpubl. notes).

Killdeer—*Charadrius vociferus*

As in other parts of Western Alaska (Kessel and Gibson 1978), the Killdeer is a casual spring migrant and summer visitant on the Seward Peninsula. The species was seen at Safety Sound during field work on 23-25 May and one was seen there again on 23 June 1981 (D. A. Woodby in litt.). A bird was seen at Wales on 7 June 1983 and had been heard there previously on 28 May and 4 June 1983 (M. L. Ward in litt.).

Eurasian Dotterel—*Charadrius morinellus*

A Palearctic plover, the Dotterel is a very rare summer visitant and breeder on the Seward Peninsula, occurring on the western half of the Peninsula, primarily in alpine habitats. Over the years, it has been recorded most consistently at Cape Mountain, including 15 and 19 June 1929 (two collected by A. Nagozruk, Bailey 1930), 6 June 1931 (female collected by D. Tevuk, Bailey 1943, 1948), 24 June 1972 (two pairs, female collected, Kessel and Gibson 1978), 13 June 1976 (one flew inland from Bering Strait to Cape Mt, D. D. Gibson unpubl. notes), and summer 1977 (two seen flying overhead by J. and L. Erckmann, K. V. Hirsch and D. A. Woodby in litt.). Other localities have included Ear Mountain (one flew past, 21 June 1974, Kessel pers. obs.), King Island (female collected, 23 July 1897, Stone 1900), Brooks Mountain (two pairs, 26 June 1973, R. J. Gordon in litt.), Sledge Island (pair collected, 14 June 1950, Cade 1952), and the ridge east of Milepost 25 Taylor Highway (pair, 21 June 1972, F. G. Scheider and Kessel pers. obs.; one, 22 July 1972, J. Piatt in litt.; pair, 10 June 1974, D. D. Gibson and others pers. comm.).

Evidence for breeding is circumstantial. An ovum of the female collected on 24 June 1972 on Cape Mountain (UAM 3291) was 21 mm in diameter, indicating laying. The two pairs on Brooks Mountain, which were in the same alpine basin as the Mongolian Plover on 26 June 1973, were both observed "creeping silently away between hummocks, head and tail down" (R. J. Gordon in litt.), suggesting nesting. And the 3-yr tenure of paired birds at the Taylor Highway site between 1972 and 1974 is indicative of breeders returning to prior years' territories.

[Greater Yellowlegs—*Tringa melanoleuca*]

The Greater Yellowlegs may be rare, at least at the base of the Seward Peninsula, but none has been unequivocally identified. The Greater Yellowlegs is a rare spring and fall migrant in coastal areas as far north as the Yukon Delta (Gill and Handel

1981, Yukon Delta NWR unpubl. notes), and it is apparently regular in small numbers in the Kotzebue-Selawik area of Kotzebue Sound (Selawik NWR unpubl. notes).

Lesser Yellowlegs—*Tringa flavipes*

A rare summer visitant and probable breeder, the Lesser Yellowlegs is probably present on the Peninsula from early May ("yellowlegs," 7 May 1976, Deering, J. D. Walters; Lesser Yellowlegs, 14 May 1983, near Nome, H. K. Springer pers. comm.) to mid-September (two, during 10-16 September 1980 visit, Moses Point, D. A. Woodby unpubl. notes). The birds represent a peripheral extension of the Interior Alaska population and occur primarily in the southeastern portions of the Peninsula, where forest and tall shrub habitats are juxtaposed with freshwater wetlands. (Members of this Interior population also reach Kotzebue Sound at the deltas of the Kobuk and Noatak rivers, Selawik NWR unpubl. notes.) There is a small population in the Norton Bay area, as far west as the Kwiniuk River (one, 12 June 1973, 8 km up river, and four, 29 July 1973, 16 km up river, with a total of 20-25 birds during summer 1973, mostly after 1 August, all J. H. Lee pers. comm.) and Moses Point (1-2 individuals recorded June, July, and September 1980, D. A. Woodby unpubl. notes), and also along the lower Fish River (three, White Mountain, 13 August 1980, and one each in the Golovin-Fish R delta area on 13 and 23 May and 7 June 1981, D. A. Woodby in litt.; "yellowlegs," 35 km up river, 20 July 1966, R. L. Rausch pers. comm.). Since 1978, a few apparently breeding pairs have established themselves as far west as Nome (Drury et al. 1981, H. K. Springer pers. comm., D. A. Woodby in litt., J. D. Walters unpubl. notes, others).

Elsewhere on the Peninsula, the Lesser Yellowlegs is casual (remains found, 1970, in Gyrfalcon nest about 8 km north of Serpentine Hot Springs on ledge overlooking flats between the North and Middle forks of the upper Serpentine R, D. G. Roseneau pers. comm.; one, 5 June 1978, Wales, D. R. Paulson unpubl. notes; and one, first week of July 1980, Breving Lagoon, D. A. Woodby in litt.).

In addition to the observations of uncertainly identified "yellowlegs" cited above, one was seen on 28 May 1978 on the upper Inmachuk River, and another on 25 July 1977 along the coast at the mouth of the Kitluk River (J. M. Wright unpubl. notes); one flew past Deering on 22 August 1985 (J. D. Walters unpubl. notes); and one was at Wales on 29 May 1983 (M. L. Ward in litt.).

The Seward Peninsula is at the periphery of the range of both the interior Lesser Yellowlegs and the coastal Greater Yellowlegs, so all yellowlegs in the region should be examined carefully for accurate identification.

Wood Sandpiper—*Tringa glareola*

The Palearctic Wood Sandpiper is a very rare spring migrant and casual summer visitant on the Peninsula, primarily along the Bering Strait coastline. Occurrences include one at Cape Woolley on 7 June 1974 by H. K. Springer and A. Bernecker and one at Safety Sound on 18 July 1976 by J. C. Wingfield (Kessel and Gibson 1978), and several at Wales—at least three, two in song, on 13-14 June 1976 by D. D. Gibson (unpubl. notes), one on 10 July 1978 by W. J. Erckmann and S. Hills (D. R. Paulson unpubl. notes), one on 4 June 1979 by S. Hills (unpubl. notes and photo), and one on 27 May 1987 by R. Eastman and P. J. Baicich (in litt.).

The Wood Sandpiper is a fairly common spring migrant and rare fall migrant in the western and central Aleutian Islands, where it has bred, and a rare to very rare migrant and casual summer visitor elsewhere in the Bering Sea region (Kessel and Gibson 1978, subsequent unpubl. data).

Solitary Sandpiper—*Tringa solitaria*

The Solitary Sandpiper is probably a very rare summer visitant and breeder on the Seward Peninsula. Only a few birds have been reported, representing a peripheral extension of the Interior Alaska population, which reaches the Noatak and Kobuk rivers and the lower Yukon River as a rare summer visitant and breeder (Kessel and Gibson 1978). Reported observations on the Peninsula include one seen along the Kuzitrin River near the Taylor Highway by W. H. Drury on 12 or 13 June 1977 (J. O. Biderman in litt.); birds just west of Nome and at the Penny River in 1978 (H. K. Springer pers. comm.); near Nome on 14 May 1983 (H. K. Springer pers. comm.) and on 27 May 1985 (R. L. Scher in litt.); one at Safety Sound inlet on 24 May 1981, one at Golovin on 20 May 1981, and at least one apparently territorial bird about 3 km east of White Mountain on 8 June 1980 and 28 June 1981 (D. A. Woodby in litt.).

Wandering Tattler—*Heteroscelus incanus*

The Wandering Tattler, a Beringian bird, is an uncommon breeder on the Peninsula. It is widespread and conspicuous throughout the nonforested portions of the uplands, but is much more abundant in the Southern Uplands than in the Northern Uplands, where it is rare. Along a 10-km stretch of the East Fork of the Solomon River 10-11 July 1967, I found a pair of tattlers every 0.8 km; and, along Glacier Road on 13 July 1967, a pair was resident on almost every tributary stream flowing toward the Snake River that crossed the road. There were significantly fewer birds in these areas and along Fox River in 1977 than in 1967, possibly because flash floods, according to H. K. Springer (pers. comm.), destroyed most nests during the preceding breeding season. In 1975, W. H. Drury (1976b) estimated 8-10 birds in the creeks that crossed the 116-km Teller Highway and 10-15 birds along the southern 100 km of the Taylor Highway. In the Northern Uplands, a few pairs breed along the Inmachuk River and in the Serpentine Hot Springs area, and possibly sometimes at Cape Mountain-Lopp Lagoon (Kessel and D. D. Gibson unpubl. data).

This abundance pattern is undoubtedly due in large part to habitat availability. Breeding birds occur primarily in boulder-strewn, gravelly alluvium along creeks that are bordered in part by shrubbery, usually of medium or tall height—a habitat enhanced by the Pleistocene glacial morainal deposits in the Southern Uplands. Gravel shorelines of lakes (e.g., Salmon Lake) or lagoons (e.g., Lopp Lagoon) are used occasionally, but probably mostly as feeding sites by breeders from nearby creeks; and in fall, a few migrants feed along coastal beaches (Breving Lagoon, 2-7 August 1980, D. A. Woodby unpubl. notes; Cape Nome and Topkok, mid-August 1924, Conover 1926; near Bluff, 16 September 1975, Drury 1976b). Adults may wade belly-deep in creek waters to feed (Kessel pers. obs.), and both downies and adults swim readily (Dixon 1933, Weeden 1965b).

Wandering Tattlers winter primarily along the Pacific Coast from southern California through Mexico and on Pacific islands, including the Hawaiian and Philippine islands and those of the southwest Pacific (American Ornithologists' Union 1983). Spring migrants arrive almost simultaneously along the entire Pacific coastline of Alaska in late April or early May (Kessel and Gibson 1978), but they do not reach their Bering Sea breeding grounds until mid-May or later (earliest, 14 May 1943, extralimitally at Mountain Village, H. C. Kyllingstad in litt.; 19 May 1983, Solomon R, J. D. Walters unpubl. notes; 22 May 1905, southern slopes of Kigluaik Mts, Anthony 1906; 24 May 1978, Inmachuk R, J. M. Wright unpubl. notes).

Little is known about the tattler's breeding biology or chronologies on the Seward Peninsula. The only concrete evidence of breeding consists of a 1-2-day-old chick (UAM 3075) that I collected on 10 July 1967 on the East Fork of the Solomon River, two large (115 mm tall) downies with an adult on 20 July 1973 along the Inmachuk River seen by D. D. Gibson (unpubl. notes), and a nest of four eggs on 7 July 1987 on mine tailings along Humboldt Creek ($65°50'$ N, $164°25'$ W) found by R. V. Harris (pers. comm.), where he had also noted a nest with eggs during the last week of June 1986. In Interior Alaska, however, tattlers do not begin to lay until 1-1.5 weeks after arrival in spring (Weeden 1965b), which may average several days later than on the Seward Peninsula. Nests are placed on a gravel surface, sometimes up to 90 m from water, and vary considerably in complexity; the usual clutch is four eggs (O. J. Murie 1924; A. Murie 1946; Weeden 1965b; G. and V. Staender, ANRS). Incubation lasts 23-25 days, including 3 days between pipping and hatching (Weeden 1965b). Most reported clutches from Interior Alaska have hatched during the last third of June, although some may not hatch until mid-July (15 July 1966, Brooks Range, G. and V. Staender, ANRS; 20 July 1932, Alaska Range, Dixon 1933). The young leave the nest within a day of hatching (Weeden 1965b) and are attended by both parents, at least for the first week or two; they apparently remain in their natal areas with at least one parent until fledging. Fledging age is unknown, but is probably about 4 weeks, judging from the fact that 20-day young have only about 30 mm primaries (Dixon 1933) but that the birds on Weeden's (1959) study area disappeared during the last week of July.

Food consists of invertebrates, primarily insects, which are obtained in part by probing about stones both under water and along shorelines; other insects are caught in flight or otherwise taken opportunistically from various substrate surfaces (Dixon 1933, Kessel pers. obs.).

Fall migration is under way by mid-July (Kessel and Gibson 1978); the earliest birds are adults, probably failed breeders. The main exodus is during August, after the young have fledged (latest, one, 14 September 1986, Deering, J. D. Walters unpubl. notes, and one, 16 September 1975, on stony beach west of Bluff, Drury 1976b).

Gray-tailed Tattler—*Heteroscelus brevipes*

The Gray-tailed Tattler is a casual spring migrant on the Seward Peninsula. One was closely observed on 15 June 1977 and was seen again, with a second, banded bird, on 16 June in the Nome River estuary by L. G. Balch, C. T. Clark, G. B. Rosenband, and others (in litt.). Another was carefully examined and heard uttering its diagnostic call at the mouth of the Nome River on 16 June 1986 (K. Kaufman in litt.). This Siberian tattler of western Beringia is a rare migrant on the islands of the Bering Sea (Kessel and Gibson 1978).

Spotted Sandpiper—*Actitis macularia*

The Spotted Sandpiper is an uncommon breeder on the Peninsula. Overall, it is about half as numerous as the Wandering Tattler, and it is more restricted in distribution. As an extension of the population from the forested regions of Interior Alaska, the species is most common in the southeastern portions of the Peninsula, including in the Fish, Niukluk, and Kuzitrin river drainages. The apparent western edge of the breeding range extends from the Inmachuk River (Kessel and D. D. Gibson pers. obs., J. W. Wright unpubl. notes) southwest into the headwaters of the Kuzitrin River (defensive adult, upper Noxapaga R at Goose Ck, 12 July 1973, D. D. Gibson pers. comm.), down the drainages to at least as far west as somewhere between the Taylor Highway and Pilgrim Hot Springs (five birds, including a pair, during 18-km trip down Pilgrim R, 6 July 1971, Kessel and S. O. MacDonald pers. obs.), and, along Norton Sound drainages, at least as far west as the Penny River (one, 25 June 1977, Kessel pers. obs.). In addition, three migrants were reported from near Shishmaref Village on 1 June 1976 by Noble and Wright (1977).

Seward Peninsula birds are found almost exclusively in a habitat of riverine Alluvia, the major exception being the migrants mentioned above that were on the sandy Shishmaref barrier strip. Characteristically, they occur along rivers with enough flow, at least seasonally, to maintain bare alluvial habitat, but which also have backwaters or pools of quiet water.

While occasional Spotted Sandpipers may winter as far north as Southcoastal Alaska (Kessel and Gibson 1978), most western birds winter from southwestern British Columbia to middle South America (American Ornithologists' Union 1983). Spring migrants, depending on the year, usually reach Fairbanks, Alaska, between 8 and 18 May, and probably arrive a few days later on the Peninsula (earliest, 16 May 1988, J. D. Walters unpubl. notes, and 23 May 1978, J. M. Wright unpubl. notes, both along the Inmachuk R).

Several types of mating systems have been noted in Spotted Sandpipers, varying from monogamy to serial polyandry—a female with two or more sequential but overlapping mates (Hays 1973). Due to the low numbers and densities on the Seward Peninsula, most matings are probably monogamous. Males and females arrive at about the same time, and, in temperate North America, egg-laying begins within a week of arrival (Hays 1973); but in Interior Alaska, egg-laying appears to be delayed for about 2 weeks (Kessel unpubl. data, ANRS).

The adults search together for a nest site, but the male does most of the nest construction (Maxson and Oring 1980). The nest consists of a scrape in a sand or gravel substrate, lined with small pieces of dried plant materials; it is usually placed in the open, but may be at least partially hidden under a small shrub, rock, or debris. Eggs are laid at 1-day intervals until the usual clutch of four eggs is completed (ANRS). Most incubation is done by the male; it begins sporadically during laying and becomes steady with the third or fourth egg (Maxson and Oring 1980). Females of monogamous matings contribute some to the incubation effort, but in polyandrous situations, the female leaves the first male as soon as she finds another male within her territory with which to mate (Hays 1973, Oring and Knudson 1973). Incubation normally lasts 20 days; the young leave the nest soon after hatching and are cared for by the male until they fledge (Hays 1973), which occurs at 13-16 days of age (Palmer 1967). The young remain in the vicinity of their hatching sites throughout the summer (Hays 1973).

There are few nesting data from the Seward Peninsula upon which to base local breeding chronologies (four clutches, 1-6 July 1978, one of which began hatching on 5 July, upper Inmachuk R, J. M. Wright unpubl. notes; adult with large downy, 30 July 1973, upper Inmachuk R, D. D. Gibson unpubl. notes). Generally, however, timing appears to be about a week to 10 days later than in Interior Alaska, where peak egg-laying occurs during the first week of June and peak hatching during the fourth week of June, with some hatching continuing into the second week of July (Kessel unpubl. data, ANRS). Thus, some young could fledge by the second week of July in the Interior, but probably not until the last week of July or the first week of August on the Seward Peninsula (two fledglings extralimitally on the middle Noatak R, 7 August 1973, Manuwal 1974).

Spotted Sandpipers are opportunistic foragers, consuming a variety of terrestrial and aquatic arthropods, especially such insects as chironomids and mayflies (Maxson and Oring 1980).

The first birds to leave the breeding grounds are the adult females, and, judging from movements in Interior Alaska (Kessel unpubl. data), fall departures from the Peninsula are well under way by early August. Most of the population is gone by the fourth week of August, but a few late-hatched birds probably remain until early September (latest recorded, male collected 29 August 1900, near Dexter, about 13 km Taylor Highway, McGregor 1902).

Terek Sandpiper—*Xenus cinereus*

An Old World taxon, the Terek Sandpiper is casual on the Peninsula. An individual feeding with other sandpipers at Safety Sound on 29 June 1987 was carefully viewed by F. Mueller, A. Bernecker, and C. Veyzlaff (Mueller in litt.). The species is a rare migrant in the western Aleutian Islands and a very rare migrant and casual summer visitant on the other islands and coasts of the Bering Sea (Kessel and Gibson 1978, subsequent unpubl. data).

Upland Sandpiper—*Bartramia longicauda*

Casual on the Seward Peninsula, the only record is a dead, largely desiccated juvenal Upland Sandpiper (UAM 5293) that was found at Wales in early June 1983 by B. S. Basham and J. M. Langham, apparently having died the preceding fall. The species is a regular breeder in the Brooks Range as far west as the headwaters of the Noatak River (Kessel and Gibson 1978) and probably the Selawik Hills (pair in distractive behavior, 30 June 1986, Selawik NWR unpubl. notes).

Whimbrel—*Numenius phaeopus*

The Whimbrel is a fairly common breeder on the Peninsula. It is widely distributed throughout both the Northern Uplands and Southern Uplands, where it favors Dwarf Shrub Meadow habitat, especially where tussocks and hummocks are present. After the breeding season, many birds move to the Coastal Lowlands, forming flocks of up to 100 birds that also use Dwarf Shrub Mat and Wet Meadow habitats of coastal barrier strips and lagoons. In addition, some fall migrants use tidal mudflats (Gill and Handel 1981), such as those at lagoon inlets and at the mouths of river estuaries.

Western populations of the Whimbrel winter locally along the Pacific Coast from central California to southern Chile (American Ornithologists' Union 1957). They move northward along the outer Pacific Coast of Southeastern and Southcoastal Alaska during spring migration, with some apparently taking a more direct trans-Gulf route (Isleib and Kessel 1973, Kessel and D. D. Gibson unpubl. data); many then move inland to reach their breeding grounds (Kessel and D. D. Gibson unpubl. data). While in some years a few birds probably arrive at the Seward Peninsula as early as the first week of May, judging from extralimital records (4 May 1976, Ambler, D. K. Wik in litt.; 5 May 1980, Yukon-Kuskokwim Delta, C. M. Boise in litt.; 6 May 1986, St. Marys, B. J. McCaffery unpubl. notes), in most years they arrive during the second week of May (earliest, two, 10 May 1983, Nome, and one, 11 May 1988, Deering, J. D. Walters unpubl. notes; female collected, 11 May 1913, Solomon, J. Koren unpubl. notes). Migration peaks in the third week of May, but may continue through May and into early June (migratory flocks 27-31 May and 6-10 June 1981, Fish R delta, D. A. Woodby unpubl. notes).

Whimbrels, which live to be 11+ yr old, are monogamous over a period of at least several years, and return to the same territory—but not the same nest site—each year; they apparently first breed at 3 yr of age (Skeel 1983). The nest is usually on a tussock or hummock (Grinnell 1900a; Skeel 1983), characteristically within 1 m of a shrub and often on the leeward side of the nest tussock/hummock or a shrub (Skeel 1983). The usual clutch is four eggs (Grinnell 1900a, ANRS). Incubation, which begins with the laying of either the third or fourth egg, is shared by both parents (Skeel 1976) and varies from 22-26+ days (Jehl and Hussell 1966, Skeel 1976). Both parents care for the young for at least the first week; families remain on the territory for awhile, but then move to other feeding areas; the fledging period is 35-40 days (Cramp 1983).

Applying these data to observed events, egg-laying on the Seward Peninsula probably begins in late May (a nearly hatched clutch of eggs, 17 June 1899, Kobuk R delta, Grinnell 1900a; females with 10-12 mm ova collected, 23 and 25 May 1951,

Anaktuvuk Pass area, Brooks Range, Irving 1960); it peaks during the first third of June, but may continue through the third week of June (nest with two fresh eggs, 20 June 1899, Kobuk R delta, Grinnell 1900a)—the latter probably renestings. Hatching would then occur during the last half of June into mid-July and fledging from the last week of July through about 24 August. The few egg and brood dates from the Seward Peninsula corroborate these dates, as does a nearly fledged juvenal collected on 30 July 1898 at Cape Blossom by Grinnell (1900a).

During the breeding season Whimbrels feed almost equally on invertebrates, especially insects, and tundra berries, the proportions varying with temporal availability. Invertebrates are taken at or near the surface of various substrates (Cramp 1983); berries of the previous year are consumed early in the season, and they become a favored item when fresh ones become available later in the summer. Birds feeding in intertidal areas take a wide variety of crustaceans, molluscs, annelids, etc., mostly by superficial probing along the waterline (ibid.).

Small postbreeding flocks begin forming in late June, probably composed of failed breeders; most remain in tundra habitats, but tend to move into lowlands and toward the coasts (e.g., lowlands northeast of North Killeak L, Cape Espenberg, Safety Sound barrier strip, all Kessel pers. obs.; Imuruk Basin, Woodby and Divoky 1983). Flocks in the Coastal Lowlands increase progressively in number and size during July, and they become increasingly obvious during late July and August with the fledging of young birds. Fall staging peaks 10-26 August, although some migration is already under way by that time. Most of the population has left the Peninsula by the end of August or the first few days of September (latest, one, 7 September 1977, Cape Espenberg, Schamel et al. 1979; ten, 11 September 1977, extralimitally at the Akulik-Inglutalik R delta, Shields and Peyton 1979).

The pale-backed Siberian form of the Whimbrel, *N. p. variegatus*, is probably a casual migrant in the Bering Strait area of the Peninsula. One was seen on Cape Mountain on 30 May 1978 by W. J. Erckmann (D. R. Paulson unpubl. notes), and this form is a rare migrant on the islands of the Bering Sea (Gibson 1981).

Bristle-thighed Curlew—*Numenius tahitiensis*

The Bristle-thighed Curlew is an uncommon breeder on the Seward Peninsula. It apparently nests only in the Northern Uplands, where it is widespread, at least west of about 164°30' W. A Beringian sandpiper, it has an extremely restricted distribution, breeding only in the mesic alpine uplands of the ridges of the Nulato Hills and across the northern half of the Seward Peninsula. Postbreeding birds move immediately to nearby Coastal Lowlands, e.g., on the Peninsula to Cape Espenberg and the Lopp Lagoon barrier strip.

This shorebird favors a Dwarf Shrub habitat, both in the uplands during breeding, where it nests in hummocky, mesic areas of dwarf shrub, and later along the coastal barrier strips. During breeding it is often closely associated with two other large sandpipers, the Whimbrel and the Bar-tailed Godwit. On average, it nests at more arid sites and hence slightly higher on slopes than the other two species, but a number of times I have had all three species flying about me as I intruded into one or another's territory. Under these circumstances, they act as a mixed community, responding to each other's vocalizations.

Bristle-thighed Curlews winter on the islands of the central and southwestern Pacific Ocean (American Ornithologists' Union 1983) and fly a direct oceanic route to their Alaska breeding grounds. They usually arrive in the vicinity of their breeding grounds in mid-May, although in some years they may arrive in early May (earliest, two, 13 May 1981, Golovin, D. A. Woodby in litt.; but extralimitally on the Yukon-Kuskokwim Delta, four, 5 May 1980, C. M. Boise in litt.; 9 May 1947 and 10 May 1944, Mountain Village, H. C. Kyllingstad in Gabrielson and Lincoln 1959.)

Little is known about the breeding biology of the Bristle-thighed Curlew, because its nesting grounds were not discovered until 1948 (Kyllingstad 1948, Allen and Kyllingstad 1949). The nest is little more than a depression in tundra vegetation, often placed near a small hummock (Allen and Kyllingstad 1949). Ten completed clutches from the southern Nulato Hills, including eight in 1987, all contained four eggs (ibid., B. J. McCaffery pers. comm.). Incubation is shared by both parents (Allen and Kyllingstad 1949), and both parents care for the chicks at least until they are over 3 weeks old (B. J. McCaffery pers. comm). Based on the few data available, the timing of the Bristle-thighed Curlew's breeding cycle appears closely similar to that of the Whimbrels of the region. A clutch of four eggs near Mountain Village hatched on 17 June 1948 (Kyllingstad 1948), indicating that egg-laying began about 22 May—assuming an incubation period similar to that of the Whimbrel. Four nests in the southern Nulato Hills had completed clutches when found 27 May-15 June 1987, and the latest clutch found was initiated on 8-9 June 1987 (B. J. McCaffery pers. comm.); this last clutch, if successful, would not have hatched until about 5-7 July. A chick (UAM 3627) collected on the Seward Peninsula on 10 July 1977 by H. K. Springer was of an age to have hatched around 26 June. Fledging age is unknown, but again appears similar to that of the Whimbrel. An ''immature'' was sketched by O. J. Murie on 5 August 1924 at Hooper Bay (Gabrielson and Lincoln 1959), where they do not breed; and young of the year arrived on the Yukon-Kuskokwim Delta by about 10 August 1970 (P. G. Mickelson, Yukon Delta NWR unpubl. data). Thus, fledging apparently begins by late July.

Food items taken on the breeding grounds are probably similar to those taken by Whimbrels, i.e., invertebrates, especially insects, and tundra berries. A spring migrant was observed feeding on crowberries and cranberries on 30 May 1984 on the Yukon-Kuskokwim Delta (K. Kertell in litt.), where they have also been observed feeding on ripening berries in fall (Gabrielson and Lincoln 1959).

Postbreeding birds on the Seward Peninsula begin gathering in the Coastal Lowlands by late June (three, 22 June 1970, Safety Sound barrier strip, J. and M. Piatt in litt.; one, 30 June 1976, and three, 3 July 1973, Cape Espenberg, Schamel et al. 1979 and Kessel and D. D. Gibson unpubl. data, respectively; one on 3 July and eleven on 12 July 1974, outer barrier strip of Lopp Lagoon, Kessel pers. obs.). No data on fall staging on the Peninsula are available, but the peak of fall departures apparently occurs in mid-August and most are gone by the fourth week of the month (latest, juvenal male, 1 September 1911, Safety Sound, A. C. Bent, USNM 2339810; and, extralimitally, one seen, 10 September 1980, Yukon-Kuskokwim Delta, R. E. Gill in litt.).

Far Eastern Curlew—*Numenius madagascariensis*

A Far Eastern Curlew on the southern shore of Lopp Lagoon on 10 June 1975 was viewed carefully at rest and in flight by P. G. Dumont (in litt.). This shorebird from eastern Asia may be a casual spring migrant in Western Alaska (Kessel and Gibson 1978).

Black-tailed Godwit—*Limosa limosa*

A casual spring migrant, the Black-tailed Godwit has been recorded twice on the Seward Peninsula. A specimen (MCZ 309227) was collected at "Diomede Island" on 22 May 1907 by A. H. Dunham; and a bird was observed and photographed at Golovin on 21 May 1981 by S. W. Allison and D. A. Woodby (in litt., photo). This Palearctic species is a casual spring migrant in the western and central Aleutian Islands and on the Bering Sea islands (Kessel and Gibson 1978).

Hudsonian Godwit—*Limosa haemastica*

The Hudsonian Godwit is an uncommon summer visitant and possibly a rare breeder on the Seward Peninsula, where it is present from mid-May through August (earliest, one, 12 May 1981, Golovin, D. A. Woodby in litt., but three, 5 May 1986, extralimitally at St. Marys, B. J. McCaffrey unpubl. notes; latest, fifteen, 27 August 1977, extralimitally on the Akulik-Inglutalik R delta, Shields and Peyton 1979). It occurs primarily at the base of the Peninsula, especially in the wetlands of the Buckland River estuary and around Norton Bay (see details in Kessel and Gibson 1978; also, thirty, 23 July 1980, Moses Point area, D. A. Woodby in litt.) but also as far west as the Fish River delta (D. A. Woodby in litt.). Farther west, this godwit is a very rare visitant, usually in late summer (a juvenal, Inmachuk R estuary, 28-29 July 1973, D. D. Gibson unpubl. notes; three, Cape Espenberg, 17 August 1976, Schamel et al. 1979; three, Arctic R, 24 July 1976, and two, Serpentine R, 25 July 1976, Noble and Wright 1977; one to two, Wales flats, 21 and 22 August 1977, D. A. Woodby in litt.; one, extralimitally at Plover Bay, Siberia, June [late 1860s], F. Bischoff, NMNH 58727; two adults with a flock of Bar-tailed Godwits, about 16 km south of Point Spencer, 6 July 1980, and an adult, Agiapuk R delta in Imuruk Basin, 28 June 1980, D. A. Woodby in litt.; a pair, Nome, 27 May 1985, R. L. Scher in litt.). Mostly, these birds utilize wet meadows and tidal flats while on the Seward Peninsula.

There is no concrete evidence of breeding on the Peninsula, and Shields and Peyton (1977) found no evidence of breeding in the Koyuk-Inglutalik wetlands, even though they observed birds along the shorelines throughout June 1976 (Kessel and Gibson 1978). Fledged juvenals have been reported from the Inmachuk River estuary (see above) and the Fish River delta (four, 3 August 1981, D. A. Woodby in litt.), but, even though the dates of late July and early August indicate recent fledging, it is not known whence they came.

Breeding chronologies of the Hudsonian Godwit are similar to those of the Whimbrel (see Hagar 1966), so the dates of occurrence on the Peninsula—mostly mid-June or later—suggest that most of these godwits are postbreeders or migrants or possibly nonbreeders. The estuarian habitat utilized by these birds is also indicative of non- or postbreeding birds. It is likely that most come from breeding grounds east of Kotzebue Sound (Baldwin Peninsula, Kessel and Gibson 1978; valley of the Kobuk R, McLenegan 1889; Selawik Hills, pairs emitting alarm calls, 27-30 June 1986 and 28 June 1987, Selawik NWR unpubl. notes) and east of Norton Sound, perhaps as far inland as the Koyukuk River wetlands (M. F. Smith pers. comm.).

Bar-tailed Godwit—*Limosa lapponica*

A Palearctic species, the Bar-tailed Godwit is a common summer visitant and fairly common breeder on the Seward Peninsula, where it is the most numerous of the large *Numenius/Limosa* sandpipers. Breeders are widespread throughout both the Southern Uplands and Northern Uplands west of treeline, where their preferred habitat is mesic Dwarf Shrub Meadow on low, gently rolling slopes above nearby pockets or valley bottoms of wetter habitats, such as Wet Meadow and margins of lacustrine and fluviatile waters. These slopes often have hummocky vegetation and often are shared with breeding Whimbrels. Breeders are rare in the flat, wetter lowlands, although some nest on mesic sites along the inner sides of coastal lagoons or basins (Lopp Lagoon, Bailey 1948; Safety Sound-Solomon Flats and Imuruk Basin, Kessel pers. obs.), in the flats along lower river courses (Shishmaref and Arctic rivers, Noble and Wright 1977), and at McCarthys Marsh (Kessel pers. obs.). Throughout the summer non- and postbreeders aggregate in flocks of up to 200+ birds at protected Coastal Lowlands, especially river estuaries and where rivers form deltas in lagoons e.g., Buckland and Nugnugaluktuk river estuaries, mouths of Serpentine and Arctic rivers, mud flats at the northeast end of Lopp Lagoon and the mouth of Kuzitrin River in Imuruk Basin, the drained lagoon east of mouth of Sinuk River, and the mud flats at Safety Sound and at the head of Norton Bay.

The Seward Peninsula population of Bar-tailed Godwits winters in the southwest Pacific and flies a transoceanic migration route between there and its Alaska breeding grounds (American Ornithologists' Union 1957, DeLong and Thompson 1968). It usually arrives in mid-May (earliest, one, 11 May 1980, Nome, D. A. Woodby in litt.; but extralimitally, one on 29 April 1980 and common by 5 May 1980, Yukon-Kuskokwim Delta, C. M. Boise in litt., and a male [DMNH 21923] collected on 3 May and a female [DMNH 21924] on 5 May 1939 at Wainwright by A. J. Allen). Migrants continue to arrive throughout May, with the late birds apparently being nonbreeders.

Age at first breeding is 2 yr (Cramp 1983). The nest is a simple depression with variable amounts of vegetative lining; it is placed on a dry site, often on a raised hummock and hidden by grasses (Brandt 1943). The usual clutch size is 4 eggs; the mean size of 40 Alaska clutches was 3.9 ± 0.4 eggs, with 36 clutches containing 4 eggs (data from Brandt 1943, Bailey 1948, Yukon Delta NWR unpubl. notes, Kessel and D. D. Gibson unpubl. data). Incubation, which begins with the laying of the last egg, takes 20-21 days (Cramp 1983). Both parents contribute to incubation and care of young (ibid.). Shortly after hatching, the parents lead the chicks to nearby wetlands for feeding, where they remain until fledging. Age at fledging is unknown, but appears to be about 30 days, based on some observed mid-July fledging dates (see below).

Applying the above chronologies to observed events shows that early egg-laying has begun by the fourth week of May (earliest, extralimitally on the Yukon-Kuskokwim Delta, 19 May 1969, based on a clutch that hatched 13-14 June, P. G. Mickelson, Yukon Delta NWR unpubl. notes; 20 May 1960, first egg of clutch, R. G. B. Brown, ANRS; 23 May 1970, based on eggs pipping 16 June, P. G. Mickelson, Yukon Delta NWR unpubl. notes; 24 May 1924, first egg of clutch, Brandt 1943). Peak laying occurs during the first half of June, however, and some, perhaps for renestings, may continue through June (clutch of four eggs still not hatched 23 July 1929, Lopp Lagoon, Bailey 1943). Thus, while early clutches may hatch by mid-June (above; also, two eggs of a four-egg clutch hatched 14 June 1960, the others 15 June, Yukon-Kuskokwim Delta, R. G. B. Brown, ANRS), most eggs hatch during the last week of June and the first week of July. I collected a 40.2-gram completely downy chick (UAM 3076), probably about 5 days old, on 7 July 1967, at Milepost 57 Taylor Highway; saw a brood of three approximately 2-week-old chicks on 12 July 1967 on the flats below Solomon; and saw a chick of similar age at McCarthys Marsh on 17 July 1973. First fledging occurs in mid-July ("parents with nearly fledged young...in mid-July," Norton Sound wetlands, Woodby and Divoky 1983:159; "three well grown young...that were still somewhat unsteady on the wing," 17 July 1946, St. Michael, Gabrielson and Lincoln 1959:405; two "immatures" collected, 23 July 1924, Hooper Bay, Brandt 1943).

The diet of Bar-tailed Godwits on their breeding grounds consists mostly of insects, although annelid worms, some seeds, and probably berries are consumed when available; when feeding on coastal mud flats, other invertebrates, such as molluscs and crustaceans are taken, often in belly-deep water (Cramp 1983).

It is not possible to distinguish failed and postbreeders, or even breeders from nearby territories, from the flocks of summer visitants that utilize the Seward Peninsula lagoon and estuarian mudflats and wet meadows throughout the summer. Successful breeders and newly fledged juvenals begin to augment these coastal populations in late July and early August and numbers peak during the third week of August. At this time, Woodby and Divoky (1983) reported primary use of "wet tundra" and some utilization of coastal barrier strips; they also reported relatively high concentrations ("100's") of birds at Moses Point and Koyuk.

Fall migration is under way by mid-August (see Shields and Peyton 1979), and most godwits have left the Peninsula by the end of August or the first few days of September (latest, "uncommon," 9 September 1980, Fish R delta, D. A. Woodby unpubl. notes; 35 birds, 12 September 1977, extralimitally on Akulik-Inglutalik R delta, Shields and Peyton 1979). Large concentrations and later departures of Bar-tailed Godwits from the Yukon-Kuskokwim Delta (Gill and Handel 1981; Yukon Delta NWR unpubl. data) and the Alaska Peninsula (Gill et al. 1981) suggest that many birds from farther north, such as those from the Seward Peninsula, move coastally to these staging areas before starting their southern transoceanic migration.

The North American breeding form of this Old World sandpiper is the Beringian subspecies *L. l. baueri*.

Ruddy Turnstone—*Arenaria interpres*

An uncommon breeder on the Seward Peninsula, the Ruddy Turnstone nests only west of about 164º W. Here it occurs in two distinctly different physiographic situations. It breeds on sandy coastal barrier strips, such as at Cape Espenberg, Sarichef Island, Lopp Lagoon, Breving Lagoon, Point Spencer spit, and Safety Sound; and, in the uplands, it breeds along the drainages of major gravel-bedded rivers, e.g., Nuluk, American, Sinuk, Penny, Nome, and Solomon rivers. In these latter situations, it is most common along the stony edges of rivers and creeks that cut through mesic tundra, and here I have found numbers up to 2.5-6.0 birds/km. A few pairs occur inland at more xeric sites, such as the pair with several 2-3-day-old chicks that I found in Dwarf Shrub Mat at Milepost 14 Teller Highway, above Penny River, and the individuals that were along the road and at a gravel pit inland at Milepost 47 Taylor Highway in both 1967 and 1977. The birds of the uplands favor situations with exposed rock or gravelly substrates, and they often use a rock for an elevated territorial perch. The birds on the barrier strips feed either at the edges of sandy pond margins or on nearby tidal flats and beaches, whereas the birds of the uplands usually feed along the alluvia and shorelines of fluviatile waters, but sometimes also along the shorelines of ponds and lakes.

The Seward Peninsula population of Ruddy Turnstones probably winters in the islands of the southwest Pacific Ocean, along with other Bering Sea turnstones (see below). They move northward in spring along the coast and through the islands of the western Pacific (Thompson 1974), usually arriving in the northeastern Bering Sea in mid-May (earliest, one, 12 May 1981, Golovin, and one, 14 May 1980, Safety Sound, D. A. Woodby in litt.; but extralimitally on the Yukon-Kuskokwim Delta, nine birds, 5 May 1980 and common by 14 May, C. M. Boise in litt., and first seen, 12 May 1969 and 13 May 1972 and 1973, Yukon Delta NWR unpubl. notes). Movement on the Seward Peninsula continues through May, the late birds probably being first-time breeders.

Turnstones do not breed until their second year, with most immatures remaining on their wintering grounds (Thompson 1974). The mating system is monogamous, with the pair highly territorial until the young are hatched. The nest is placed on a xeric site, either on bare sand or gravel or on prostrate mat-type vegetation. The nest is a depression, formed by the twisting of the female as she lays the eggs (Nettleship 1973), and it is lined with bits of leaves and lichens (ibid., Sauer and Urban 1964). Eggs are usually laid at the rate of one a day (Nettleship 1973, Cramp 1983). The usual clutch is four eggs; 24 of 26 clutches reported for the Seward Peninsula (Bailey 1943, Schamel et al. 1979, R. and B. Mearns in litt.), Yukon-Kuskokwim Delta (Brandt 1943, K. Kertell in litt.), and St. Lawrence Island (Fay and Cade 1959, Sauer and Urban 1964) contained four eggs. Incubation apparently begins sometime between the laying of the third and fourth egg, with the last chick often hatching about half a day after the rest of the clutch. Incubation takes 21.5-22 days (Parmelee and MacDonald 1960, Parmelee et al. 1967); it is performed primarily by the female, with irregular participation by the male (Cramp 1983). After hatching, however, the male is more solicitous of the chicks than the female; and, depending on food supply, the female may leave the family sometime during chick rearing (Cramp 1983). The male usually remains with the chicks until they fledge at about 19-20 days of age (Parmelee and MacDonald 1960, Nettleship 1973).

On the Seward Peninsula, some egg-laying begins by the third week of May (egg-laying for two clutches that hatched along the Nome R on 13 June 1983 [R. and B. Mearns in litt.] must have started on 19 May; and the clutch from which I saw a flying juvenal along the Nome R on 9 July 1969 must have been laid by 21-23 May). The main laying period is from the last few days of May through the first 10-12 days of June, resulting in a hatching peak during the fourth week of June and the first week of July. With these chronologies, most young should fledge during the last half of July.

Diet during the breeding season consists primarily of insects, including adults, pupae, and larvae; when these are not readily available, however, Ruddy Turnstones are opportunistic feeders, taking seeds and spiders in spring and berries in fall and scavenging about animal carcasses and garbage dumps (Nettleship 1973, Cramp 1983). Along the coast, breeders and postbreeders feed on a large variety of invertebrates, especially insects, crustaceans, and molluscs (Cramp 1983). Turnstones characteristically use a flipping action of their bill to overturn stones and tufts of soil to obtain concealed prey, but they also probe into sand and mud and search cracks, crevices, and seaweeds for food items.

Failed breeders return to the Coastal Lowlands almost immediately, some as early as late June. Families of successful breeders move from xeric habitats to more moist ones at creek or pond margins, or to nearby protected coastal shorelines. Inland chicks move to the coast upon fledging, so coastal populations build up gradually during July.

Some birds have begun the first leg of their fall migration by the first week of July, beginning to arrive about then at staging sites on islands of the Bering Sea south of their breeding range (Kessel and D. D. Gibson unpubl. data). Numbers on the Seward Peninsula drop off sharply after the third week of July, and only a few stragglers are left by mid-August (latest, one, 3 September 1977, Cape Espenberg, Schamel et al. 1979; but extralimitally, a specimen, 21 September 1927, Barrow, Gabrielson and Lincoln 1959).

The islands of the central and southern Bering Sea, including St. Matthew, Nunivak, and Pribilof islands, are used for fall staging (Thompson 1974, Kessel and D. D. Gibson unpubl. data), with the first birds to arrive apparently failed breeders; most young do not arrive until August, and they predominate by the third week of August (Thompson 1974). Staging also occurs on the north coastline of the Alaska Peninsula (Gill et al. 1981) and in the Aleutian Islands (Gibson 1981). From these fall staging sites, migration proceeds in a direct transoceanic flight to wintering grounds on the islands of the southwest Pacific Ocean (Thompson 1974).

Black Turnstone—*Arenaria melanocephala*

The only congener of the circumpolar Ruddy Turnstone, the Beringian Black Turnstone is a fairly common breeder on the Seward Peninsula. It is restricted to the Coastal Lowlands and, especially during breeding, primarily to the northern coastline from Lopp Lagoon to the Buckland River estuary. Here its favored habitat is Salt Grass Meadow, although some use is made of short Wet Meadow, such as that adjoining estuarian or delta ponds and drainages. Greatest breeding densities are at relatively protected sites, e.g., alluvial mouths of creeks and rivers where they drain into such lagoons as Lopp Lagoon and Shishmaref Inlet; middle and lower river estuaries, such as the Buckland and Nugnugaluktuk rivers; and protected bays, such as inner Espenberg Bay, south of Cape Espenberg. The lack of appropriate habitat seems to limit this turnstone as a breeder along the southern coastline, although it apparently breeds at Breving Lagoon (reported as "locally fairly common," 1-7 July 1980, D. A. Woodby unpubl. notes) and sometimes in Imuruk Basin, where it was "fairly common," estimated 100+ birds, 26 June-1 July 1980 (Woodby and Divoky 1983, D. A. Woodby unpubl. notes) and where a day-old chick was seen on 29 June 1980 (D. A. Woodby in litt.), but where S. O. MacDonald and I never sighted the species 25-29 June 1971. Migrants and postbreeders are rare to uncommon along the Norton Sound coastline.

Black Turnstones are rare winter visitants as far north as Southcoastal and Southeastern Alaska (Kessel and D. D. Gibson unpubl. data). Spring movement appears to be largely coastal until the birds cross over the base of the Alaska Peninsula, apparently via the Iliamna Lake lowlands. They fly directly across Norton Sound as they migrate northward, judging from the small number of migrants in coastal

Norton Sound. Spring migrants usually reach their breeding grounds during the second week of May, although in early seasons they may arrive during the first week (earliest, five, 10 May 1981, Golovin, and two, 12 May 1980, Nome [D. A. Woodby in litt.], and five, 12 May 1988, Deering [J. D. Walters unpubl. notes]; but, extralimitally on the Yukon-Kuskokwim Delta, arrived 1 May 1979 and 5 May 1978 and peaked 10-11 May each year [Handel 1982]; five birds, 4 May 1980 and common by 6 May [C. M. Boise in litt.]; and arrived 6 May 1974 and 1975 and common by 10 May each year [M. R. Petersen in Handel 1982]). Birds continue to arrive through the first week of June, but June arrivals are probably nonbreeding yearlings.

As with the Ruddy Turnstone, Black Turnstones probably do not breed until 2 yr of age, with most immatures remaining along the coasts south of the breeding range. Individuals that have bred show a strong fidelity to their territories of the preceding year, often resulting in a re-pairing of birds in subsequent seasons (Handel 1982, Gill et al. 1983). Nests are normally placed on a grass or sedge mat, usually close to water, especially small ponds (Brandt 1943, Holmes and Black 1973); sites may be entirely open or concealed by tall vegetation (Handel 1982). Nests are well-lined depressions (Handel 1982 contra Brandt 1943). Clutch size in 46 nests from the Yukon Delta and Seward Peninsula (various sources, including Brandt 1943, Yukon Delta NWR unpubl. data, ANRS) averaged 3.7 ± 0.6 eggs, with 76% containing the maximum complement of 4 eggs; 88% of 44 clutches on one of Handel's (1982) study plots also contained 4 eggs. A female takes 5-6 days to complete her 4-egg clutch (Handel 1982). Incubation, which may begin intermittently before the last egg is laid, lasts 22-24 days, mean 22.7 days (ibid.); one clutch was reported by Brandt (1943) to have taken 21 days to hatch. Fledging begins at 23 days of age, although sustained flight may not occur until 28-30 days (Handel 1982). Both sexes share in incubation and in the early care of the young. Families usually remain on their territories until fledging; the male stays with the chicks at least until then, but the female, on average, leaves about a week before the chicks fledge (ibid.).

Applying these temporal parameters to observed events, it appears that the overall nesting period in the population is more condensed than in Ruddy Turnstones. The Black Turnstones tend to arrive a few days earlier in spring, but egg-laying does not begin until later, i.e., not until the last week of May; and it is highly synchronized, with the peak lasting only about 5-7 days (Brandt 1943, Handel 1982, ANRS). In most years, hatching begins about 17 June and peaks during the next week. However, in early seasons, hatching may occur up to about a week earlier (Gill and Handel 1981). Fledging usually begins during the second week of July, and most young have fledged by mid-July (adult with three fledglings, 23 July 1977, Kitluk R, J. M. Wright unpubl. notes; well-fledged young, 15-22 July 1946, Yukon R Delta, Gabrielson and Lincoln 1959; but brood of two not-yet-fledged chicks, 16 July 1986, Deering, J. D. Walters unpubl. notes).

Black Turnstones are surface feeders, consuming insects and seeds while on the breeding grounds (C. M. Handel pers. comm.). These are taken opportunistically, wherever available, e.g., from plant surfaces, from beach windrows, and from pond margins and intertidal mudflats.

A few apparent nonbreeders feed along the coastal mudflats throughout June, and they are joined by failed breeders as they leave their territories during June. In early July these populations are augmented by off-duty parents and departing successful females (Handel 1982) and subsequently by fledged families in mid-July (flocking on mudbars in Shishmaref Inlet by 11 July 1976, with a noticeable drop in numbers by 26 July [Noble and Wright 1977]). The young begin migrating by late July and continue to depart throughout August. They are rare by 26-30 August (latest, one collected, 2 September 1880, Elephant Point, Eschscholtz Bay, Bailey 1948; three seen, 5 September 1973, Espenberg Bay, D. D. Gibson and G. J. Divoky unpubl. notes).

The small number of Black Turnstones in northern and eastern coastal Norton Sound in fall (Shields and Peyton 1977, 1979; D. A. Woodby unpubl. notes) suggests that the Seward Peninsula birds migrate over Norton Sound again, perhaps to stage on the tidal mudflats of the Yukon-Kuskokwim Delta. From there, judging from abundances reported from various sites (Kessel and D. D. Gibson unpubl. data), many retrace their spring route down the coast. The fact that numbers in Southcoastal Alaska are somewhat lower than in spring, however, suggests the possibility of some transoceanic movement across the Gulf of Alaska; this hypothesis is corroborated by the substantial fall passage of Black Turnstones at Middleton Island (D. D. Gibson unpubl. notes).

Surfbird—*Aphriza virgata*

The Surfbird is a rare migrant, summer visitant, and breeder on the Seward Peninsula, but locally it is an uncommon to fairly common breeder in the dry Dwarf Shrub Mat of alpine ridges and domes of the western Southern Uplands. East of the Nome River above Milepost 23 Taylor Highway, a bird incubating three eggs was found on 16 June 1977 (L. G. Balch, C. T. Clark, and G. B. Rosenband in litt.); a territorial pair was seen above Milepost 26 on 9 June 1978 (T. G. Tobish in litt.); a flock of 10 birds was observed in this same area on 11 June 1983, and two pairs and a single were found above Milepost 27-29 on 13 June 1983 (R. and B. Mearns in litt.). At both Milepost 41 Teller Highway and at Milepost 56-57 Council Road, in the upper Horton Creek drainage, Surfbirds were in full courtship displays during the first half of June 1988 (P. G. Connors pers. comm.). Nonbreeders, postbreeders, and fall migrants use Coastal Lowlands, including river estuaries and lagoons and outer coastal shorelines. On the Peninsula, they occur almost entirely along the Norton Sound coastline, although occasional postbreeders or migrants have been reported farther west (two, Breving Lagoon, 1 August 1980, D. A. Woodby in litt.) and in Kotzebue Sound (three collected, beach of Chamisso Island, 28 July 1946, Gabrielson and Lincoln 1959).

Surfbirds are present on the Peninsula between mid-May (earliest, pair, 15 May 1983, atop Anvil Mt north of Nome, J. D. Walters unpubl. notes) and early September (latest, single birds three times, September 1975, Drury 1976b). The first arrivals in spring, the breeders, fly directly to their alpine breeding sites. Beginning in late May-early June, a few nonbreeders arrive at coastal sites, where they may remain much of the summer (e.g., five birds, 29 May 1984, and two, 2 June 1982, vicinity of Nome, J. L. Dunn in litt.; up to 15 birds, 6-10 June 1974, Safety Sound, Kessel and Gibson 1978). While still few, coastal numbers increase gradually during June and July with the addition of failed and postbreeders. Fledged families move to the coast after mid-July (two juvenals, 22 July, and two adults and four juvenals, 23-24 July 1983, Bluff,

R. H. Day and E. C. Murphy pers. comm). The late summer and fall Surfbirds of the northern Norton Sound coastline are probably local Seward Peninsula birds, whereas those along Kotzebue Sound are more likely from mainland populations that breed in highlands to the north and northeast.

Accumulating data show that this alpine shorebird is a sparsely distributed breeder in many of the rolling highlands of Interior and Western Alaska, including the Nulato Hills east of Norton Sound, the Waring Mountains, Selawik Hills, and the western end of the Brooks Range (Kessel and Gibson 1978 and subsequent unpubl. data), and this small population on the Seward Peninsula further extends this pattern.

Great Knot—*Calidris tenuirostris*

A Beringian species from east Asia, the Great Knot is a casual spring migrant on the Seward Peninsula, where it has been reported five times—once from Cape Mountain (adult male collected, 28 May 1922, Bailey 1943), three times from the mouth of the Nome River (one, 8 June 1973, Kessel and Gibson 1978; one, 9 June 1980, R. W. Stallcup in litt.; and one, 29 May 1984, J. L. Dunn in litt.), and once from Safety Sound (one, 15 and 18 June 1987, M. W. Schwan and R. H. Armstrong unpubl. notes, photo). This species breeds in northeastern Siberia and is a casual spring migrant in the western and central Aleutian Islands and on the Bering Sea coasts and islands (Kessel and Gibson 1978).

Red Knot—*Calidris canutus*

The Red Knot is an uncommon breeder and fall migrant on the Peninsula. During breeding it is widely dispersed along most of the length of the Northern Uplands, where it nests on the high, exposed domes and ridges in open Dwarf Shrub Mat habitat: One or two territorial pairs occur annually on Needle Mountain near Wales (25 June 1972 and 30 June 1974, Kessel pers. obs.; regularly reported subsequent years); a pair was present on a high bench above Lost River in the York Mountains on 26 June 1973 (R. J. Gordon in litt.); at Ear Mountain, I counted five birds while hiking the alpine ridges on 21 June 1974 and flushed one from a nest with three eggs on 22 June 1974; on the windblown slopes at the headwaters of the Nuluk River, I counted a total of eight birds, including a group of four subadults (three in predominately gray, basic plumage, the other with more red feathers) on 27 June 1974; on a bald limestone dome above Portage Creek off American River, I watched a pair with four chicks only a day or two old (UAM 2766) on 27 June 1974; and on a shrub mat ridge at the headwaters of Hannum Creek (64°54′ N, 163°20′ W), I found a solicitous pair, probably with young, on 5 July 1971. A few also breed in the western portion of the Southern Uplands (nest with one egg, hills inland from Cape Woolley/Cape Rodney, 23 and 27 June 1983, R. and B. Mearns unpubl. notes, and nest with four eggs, terrace above Milepost 42 Teller Highway, 13 June 1988, T. H. Pogson pers. comm.; also, single bird, ridge top between Milepost 15-16 Teller Highway, 18 June 1968, D. G. Roseneau and W. R. Tilton pers. comm.; several, along road between Milepost 33-37 Teller Highway during snow storm on 13 June 1987,

M. W. Schwan and R. H. Armstrong unpubl. notes; birds in full "song" and aerial displays, Milepost 41 Teller Highway, 3 and 13 June 1988, P. G. Connors pers. comm.; and two birds seen, "high ridge near Nome," 9 June 1971, D. L. Johnson and R. L. Ake in litt.).

Red Knots winter along the Pacific coastline from southern California to the southern tip of South America, especially in the South Temperate Zone (American Ornithologists' Union 1983), and the Seward Peninsula birds are probably included in these wintering populations (but see below). Approximately 100,000 spring migrants, including about 30% in less than full alternate plumage (10% still mostly basic plumage), stage on the Copper River Delta in Southcoastal Alaska (M. E. Isleib pers. comm.) in mid-May each year. They depart on a direct west-northwest heading (Isleib and Kessel 1973), apparently flying nonstop to another, perhaps less regular, staging area on the coastal fringe of the Yukon-Kuskokwim Delta (Kessel and Gibson 1978, Gill and Handel 1981; also, about 125,000 present on 21 May 1980, flats at mouth of Kashunuk R, R. E. Gill in litt.). This population is undoubtedly the source of the Seward Peninsula breeders and those found farther north along the Chukchi Sea coast of Alaska, but most of the birds apparently continue their migration to northeast Siberia, probably constituting the bulk of the Red Knots that breed on the southern half of Wrangel Island (see Portenko 1972). Earliest arrivals recorded on the Bering Sea coast were in 1980, an early season, when the first bird was sighted on 8 May and small flocks were common on the Yukon-Kuskokwim Delta 15-19 May (C. M. Boise in litt.). Arrival times on the Seward Peninsula depend primarily on the arrival time of the body of this Pacific Coast population in Alaska, although few first arrival dates have been recorded (earliest, 18 May 1976, Shishmaref Inlet, Noble and Wright 1977); movement may continue through mid-June (20 alternate-plumaged birds on 6 June and 12 on 9 June 1974, Safety Sound, H. K. Springer and A. Bernecker unpubl. notes; 4 on 12-14 June 1987, Nome R mouth, and about 12 on 18 June 1987, Safety Sound, mostly in alternate plumage, M. W. Schwan and R. H. Armstrong unpubl. notes).

Other than the breeding data cited above, nothing is known of the breeding chronologies of the Red Knot on the Peninsula. Using data from the Canadian Arctic for back-dating (5 days for laying a typical clutch of four eggs [Nettleship 1974] and 22 days for incubation [Nettleship 1968]) shows that egg-laying for the chicks I found on 27 June 1974 must have begun about 1 June. A fledging period of about 18 days (Parmelee and MacDonald 1960) would have brought these same chicks to flight by mid-July. On average, I suspect that the nesting cycle begins about a week earlier than this brood indicates, since adult birds are already returning to the shorelines by late June (Gill and Handel 1981, Yukon-Kuskokwim Delta where they do not breed; groups of 12 and 3 Red Knots, 18 June 1983, Woolley Lagoon, R. and B. Mearns unpubl. notes; 8-10 birds, 20 June 1975, east of mouth of Sinuk R, Drury 1976b; 4 birds, 30 June 1977, on flats in Safety Sound, Kessel pers. obs.). What proportion of these early returnees are successful females that have left their broods, however, or are failed or nonbreeders, is unknown. In fact, the 18-20 June birds in the Cape Woolley-Sinuk River area (above) could have been off-duty breeders from the Cape Woolley/Cape Rodney highlands feeding off-territory (see Parmelee and MacDonald 1960, Nettleship 1974, Cramp 1983).

Red Knots feed primarily on invertebrates when available, but in the Canadian High

Arctic they consume considerable plant material (e.g., *Carex* achenes, *Equisetum* stems, seeds, new shoots), especially early in the season (Parmelee and MacDonald 1960, Nettleship 1974). Specific food items depend upon availability in the knot's widely divergent summer habitats. Various insects, including adult dipterans and beetles, predominate in the diet at xeric breeding sites; larvae of aquatic dipteran flies and caddis flies may be taken along creeks and pond margins; and molluscs, crustaceans, and marine worms are consumed at coastal sites (ibid., Portenko 1972, Connors 1978, Harrington 1982).

Juvenals begin to show up at coastal sites by late July (Connors 1978, Gill and Handel 1981), and migration is well under way by early August. Migration peaks in mid-August, but continues through the month (Connors 1978, Schamel et al. 1979, Shields and Peyton 1979), with the later birds being juvenals (latest, one, 2 September 1977, Wales, D. A. Woodby and K. V. Hirsch unpubl. notes).

With fall migration more protracted than in spring, no huge concentrations at restricted staging sites have been reported. The coastal mud flats of the central portion of the Yukon-Kuskokwim Delta, however, including Angyoyaravak Bay at the mouth of the Kashunuk River, host up to several thousand Red Knots from mid-July through August (Gill and Handel 1981; M. H. Dick, Yukon Delta NWR unpubl. data). Elsewhere, the Red Knot is known only as a rare fall migrant along the coasts of Southcoastal and Southeastern Alaska (Kessel and Gibson 1978) and along the Asian coastline (Dement'ev and Gladkov 1951).

Evidence suggests that at least some Siberian birds return to migrate down the North American coastline: (1) The number of late summer and fall birds staging on the Yukon-Kuskokwim Delta appears to exceed by several fold the probable breeding population of knots in northwestern Alaska, and (2) the timing of their peak numbers at the western tip of the Seward Peninsula at Wales in 1977 (26 July-12 August, Connors 1978:Fig.12; including flocks of 20-40 birds 6-11 August, D. A. Woodby and K. V. Hirsch unpubl. notes) fits their known departure patterns from Wrangel Island (birds leave "...at the end of July and not later than the first few days of August," Portenko 1972:351). The timing of the fall migrants at other sites on the Seward Peninsula are about the same, however, mostly late July and the first half of August (coastal Norton Sound, Woodby and Divoky 1983; Norton Bay, Shields and Peyton 1979), and it is not possible even to hypothesize the source of these birds, i.e., local, Alaska Chukchi Sea coast, or Siberia.

There are four relatively discrete populations of this circumpolar sandpiper in the world, comprising two currently recognized subspecies, *C. c. canutus* and *C. c. rufus* (Cramp 1983). The Wrangel Island-western Alaska population has been recognized by some authors as a third subspecies, *C. c. rogersi* —most recently by Portenko (1972), after examining an extensive series of specimens from Wrangel Island.

Sanderling—*Calidris alba*

The Sanderling is a rare spring migrant, very rare summer visitant, and uncommon fall migrant, primarily along the outer beaches of the Peninsula. It winters in small numbers along the entire Pacific coastline of Alaska, including the Aleutian Islands, and it is a very rare breeder in Northern Alaska (Kessel and Gibson 1978);

the majority of Sanderlings, however, winter along coastlines from temperate zones in the Northern Hemisphere south along the continental coastlines of the Southern Hemisphere, and most breed in the High Arctic of Canada and Greenland (Parmelee 1970, American Ornithologists' Union 1983).

The few spring migrants on the Seward Peninsula appear to be late stragglers, possibly nonbreeders (three birds, 26 and 27 May 1977, Cape Espenberg, Schamel et al. 1979; up to two birds, 29 May and 2 June 1984, up to four, 27-28 May, and one, 31 May-3 June 1986, and one, 31 May 1988, feeding at water's edge at Deering, J. D. Walters unpubl. notes; four birds, 5 June 1984, and five, 5 June 1985, Safety Sound, J. L. Dunn in litt.; and one, 12 June 1987, Nome, K. J. Zimmer in litt.). The summer visitants, in reality, may be the vanguard of adult returnees from farther north (nine birds on 16 July 1977 and "uncommon" on 26 and 28 July 1977, Wales, D. A. Woodby and K. V. Hirsch unpubl. notes; one, 25 July 1970, Safety Sound, Kessel and Gibson 1978; one on 25 July and two on 27 July 1977, Cape Espenberg, Schamel et al. 1979). The main fall passage begins 10-11 August, however, and continues for about a month. During this period, all around the Peninsula's coastline, flocks of up to 35-40 birds forage on zooplankton washed up along the ocean shoreline (Schamel et al. 1979, D. A. Woodby and K. V. Hirsch unpubl. notes). Numbers decrease after about 7-10 September, but movement continues throughout most of the month (latest, ten birds, 24 September 1977, Cape Espenberg, Schamel et al. 1979).

Semipalmated Sandpiper—*Calidris pusilla*

An abundant breeder, the Semipalmated Sandpiper is the second most common sandpiper of the Peninsula, being outnumbered only by the Western Sandpiper (Table 5). It is most abundant and widely distributed in the Coastal Lowlands, although a few occur near major inland waterbodies (e.g., 13 individuals, 2 in flight display, riverbars and benches at headwaters of Nuluk R at $65°41'$ N, $166°20'$ W, 28 June 1974; 11+ birds, open sedge-low shrub patch at rivulet discharge into North Killeak L, 30 June 1973; 3 juvenals, Noxapaga R alluvia near junction with the Kuzitrin R, 12 July 1973; total of 45 birds, including adults with fledging broods, Noxapaga R-Lava L-Imuruk L-headwaters Burnt R region, 6-15 July 1973; single bird, possibly a migrant, McCarthys Marsh, 17 July 1973; 2 adults and 3 juvenals, shoreline of Kuzitrin L, 22 July 1973; all Kessel and D. D. Gibson unpubl. notes). In the Coastal Lowlands, it is most abundant in lower river estuaries (e.g, Buckland, Nugnugaluktuk, and Koyuk rivers), in the outer fringes of deltas of rivers that enter lagoons (e.g., Serpentine-Arctic R deltas, those of streams entering Lopp Lagoon, the Agiapuk R delta in Imuruk Basin, Fish R delta, and the Moses Point area), and along sparsely vegetated, sandy barrier strips (e.g., Cape Espenberg and Safety Sound barrier strip). Sample breeding densities include 6.0-8.8 pairs/10 ha at Cape Espenberg (Schamel et al. 1979); 6.6 pairs/10 ha in Dwarf Shrub Meadow at edge of Arctic River delta (Wright 1979); an extrapolated 10.1-14.8 birds/10 ha at Imuruk Basin, Fish River delta, and Moses Point, and 26.8 birds/10 ha at Koyuk (Woodby and Divoky 1983); and 6.1-8.5 pairs/10 ha extralimitally on the Akulik-Inglutalik River delta (Shields and Peyton 1979). Populations in the Buckland and Nugnugaluktuk river estuaries are also high (Kessel pers. obs.), but density figures are unavailable. At the favored estuarian and lagoonal wetlands, Semipalmated Sandpipers often constitute 50% or more of all breeding shorebirds. Preferred habitat seems to require some nearby exposed mineral soil, usually silty or sandy, and water, either marine or fresh and either lacustrine or fluviatile. Where these features are found near Dwarf Shrub Meadows, the populations are highest.

Alaska's Semipalmated Sandpipers apparently winter primarily in Central America and northwestern South America (Spaans 1979); and, while the species is an uncommon migrant along the coasts of Southeastern and Southcoastal Alaska (Kessel and D. D. Gibson unpubl. data), most of the Alaska population migrates both spring and fall through the Great Plains region of interior North America (Martinez 1974, Harrington and Morrison 1979, Spaans 1979; also, individuals banded at Cape Espenberg on 27 and 29 June 1977 were recovered, respectively, at Gibara, Cuba, on 19 September 1977 and at Cheyenne Bottoms, Kansas, on 26 July 1980, G. C. West in litt.), with Seward Peninsula breeders traversing Central Alaska. The first spring migrants usually arrive on the Peninsula during the second week of May (earliest, flock of 50, 8 May 1981, Golovin, and one bird, 12 May 1980, Nome, D. A. Woodby in litt.; two, 10 May 1987, and one, 12 May 1988, Deering, J. D. Walters unpubl. notes; 11 May 1978, extralimitally at Kotzebue, D. P. Harrington in litt.; 12 May 1970, Wales, Flock and Hubbard 1979). Movement usually peaks during the last third of May.

Breeding behavior in Semipalmated Sandpipers has been studied at Barrow, Alaska, by Ashkenazie and Safriel (1979). The males establish territories soon after arrival. A day or two after pair formation, the male makes depressions in the vegetation and "presents" them to the female, who eventually chooses one and adds some lining to the depression while sitting in it and tossing bits of nearby vegetation over her back. Four to 6 days elapse between pair formation and the first egg; eggs are laid at the rate of one per day. Some incubation may begin during egg-laying, mainly by the male. Continuous incubation begins about 8 h before the last egg is laid and then is shared almost equally by both sexes. Incubation takes 20 days.

Maximum clutch size is 4 eggs, with the size of 171 clutches from the Seward Peninsula and Norton Sound averaging 3.7 eggs (data from Noble and Wright 1977, Schamel et al. 1979, Shields and Peyton 1979, Woodby and Divoky 1983, R. and B. Mearns unpubl. notes, J. M. Wright unpubl. notes). Egg-laying begins during the last few days of May (earliest, estimated 18 May 1981, an early year, peaked 27 May, coastal Norton Sound, Woodby and Divoky 1983), usually peaks during the first week of June, but continues to mid-June. Early clutches usually begin hatching in mid-June (17 June 1976 and 1977, Akulik-Inglutalik R delta, Shields and Peyton 1979; peaked 16 June 1981 [earliest, estimated 9 June], coastal Norton Sound, Woodby and Divoky 1983), but most clutches hatch during the last few days of June and the first week of July. Renesting may occur, and Schamel et al. (1979) recorded instances of nest initiation as late as 22 and 25 June 1976 at Cape Espenberg and a late hatch on 18 July 1976.

The brood usually remains on the territory and is cared for by both parents for the first few days, being brooded at night by the male (Ashkenazie and Safriel 1979). The male drives the female away 2-8 days after hatching and takes the chicks to wet habitats for feeding (ibid.), e.g., Wet Meadow and pond, creek, and lagoon shorelines. The male usually remains with the family until fledging, which occurs about 16 days after hatching (ibid.). Fledging in most years on the Seward Peninsula begins during the first week of July and peaks in mid-July.

The summer diet of Norton Sound Semipalmated Sandpipers consists primarily of larval insects, especially midges, flies, and beetles (Woodby and Divoky 1983).

The adult birds apparently leave on migration as soon as their breeding duties are completed, the females in late June and early July and the males during the first half of July, since there is no evidence of local staging. Juvenals, however, congregate and feed along muddy shorelines preparatory to migration, and they dominate at such littoral sites by the end of the first week of July (Connors 1978). The peak of the fall exodus of juvenals occurs during the last few days of July and the first few days of August, with numbers dropping precipitously after 3-4 August (see Connors 1978, Schamel et al. 1979, Shields and Peyton 1979) (latest, three birds, including at least one juvenal, sometime between 13 and 18 August 1980, Fish R delta, D. A. Woodby in litt.; 25 birds, 18 August 1977, extralimitally on Akulik-Inglutalik R delta, Shields and Peyton 1979).

Western Sandpiper—*Calidris mauri*

An abundant breeder and common fall migrant, the Western Sandpiper is the most numerous shorebird of the Peninsula and one of the three most abundant of all species of small birds—the others being two passerines, redpolls and longspurs (Tables 5 and 7). It is widely distributed throughout both the uplands and lowlands during the breeding season, nesting in the Dwarf Shrub Meadow habitat that is so extensive on the Peninsula. It is most numerous where this habitat occurs near wetlands, but it also occurs up to the drier alpine tundras and even into shrub patches that reach into mesic tundra areas along rivulets and hillside draws (Table 10). It is one of the few birds that occurs on the more exposed slopes and ridges of Dwarf Shrub Mat (Table 11), where it may go to feed on relatively calm days. This species does much of its feeding off-territory during nesting and has been seen traveling at least 2 km to wet areas for feeding (Holmes 1971a). At sites where Dwarf Shrub Meadow exists near wetlands having exposed mineral soils, Western Sandpiper territories are often intermixed with those of the Semipalmated Sandpiper. No density figures are available from the uplands, but sample densities of Western Sandpipers at coastal lowland sites include 6 pairs/10 ha at Cape Espenberg (Schamel et al. 1979); 3.4 pairs/10 ha at the mouth of Arctic River in Dwarf Shrub Meadow and 5.9 pairs/10 ha in Dwarf Shrub Meadow-Wet Meadow mosaic (Wright 1979); 10.0 nests/10 ha at Wales (Erckmann 1981); and an extrapolated 18.3 birds/10 ha at the base of Point Spencer spit, 7.6/10 ha at Safety Sound, and 1.7/10 ha at the Fish River delta (Woodby and Divoky 1983). Densities in the Buckland River estuary area appear higher than at any of the above sites, though specific figures are unavailable, and the species is also numerous in the vicinity of the Nugnugaluktuk River estuary (Kessel pers. obs.). An estimated 300 pairs were present in a 13-16-km stretch of upland Dwarf Shrub Meadow along the Council Road between Nome and Cape Nome in 1975 (Drury 1976b). Generally, Western Sandpipers are outnumbered by Semipalmated Sandpipers in the Coastal Lowlands.

Western Sandpipers winter along the coasts of California and North Carolina south along both coasts and through the West Indies to northern South America (American Ornithologists' Union 1983). Migrants move along the coasts of Southeastern and

Southcoastal Alaska in both spring and fall (Gabrielson and Lincoln 1959; Gill 1978, 1979; Schamel et al. 1979; Senner et al. 1981). They arrive on their breeding grounds with the appearance of snow-free patches of tundra (Holmes 1972), an event that may vary by a week or two among years. On average, they tend to arrive a few days earlier than the Semipalmated Sandpipers. In early years the species may arrive during the first week of May (earliest, 50 birds, 7 May 1981, Golovin, D. A. Woodby in litt.; four, 8 May 1987, Deering, and at least three, 10 May 1983, Nome and vicinity, J. D. Walters unpubl. notes; but, extralimitally, 3 May 1980 and 5 May 1976, Yukon-Kuskokwim Delta, C. M. Boise in Yukon Delta NWR unpubl. notes and in litt.). Usually, however, it arrives during the second week of May, with the peak influx occurring within a few days thereafter. Local numbers continue to increase until about 22-25 May.

The males are the first to arrive, with the females coming a few days later (Holmes 1973). The male establishes a territory, and the female comes to the territory for pairing (Holmes 1972). Pair bonds are monogamous, and nest site fidelity by both males and females is high in consecutive years (some even using the same nest cup), resulting in re-pairing by some individuals (Holmes 1971a). The nest is usually concealed beside some dwarf woody shrub and placed among dried graminoid leaves; and the nest cup usually contains small, dried leaves as part of the lining (Kessel et al. 1964, Holmes 1971a). Egg-laying begins within a few days after pairing, with the egg-laying rate averaging one per day; the normal clutch is 4 eggs, with smaller clutches occurring later in the season, probably from renestings (Holmes 1972). The average clutch size in 134 nests from the Seward Peninsula and around Norton Sound was 3.5 eggs (data from Noble and Wright 1977, Schamel et al. 1979, Shields and Peyton 1979, Woodby and Divoky 1983, and unpubl. data from ANRS, R. and B. Mearns, J. M. Wright, and Kessel), which is smaller than the mean of 3.9 eggs found in 215 clutches on the Yukon Delta by Holmes (1972). Incubation takes an average of 21 days, range 20-22 days (Conover 1926, Holmes 1972). Both parents incubate, the female usually from late afternoon to mid-morning, and the male the remainder of the day; the male's share increases during the incubation period (Holmes 1971a, Erckmann 1981). Hatching occurs over a 24-h period, and the young are usually accompanied by both parents when they leave the nest; however, the female is less solicitous than the male and leaves the family at varied times during chick-rearing (Holmes 1971a, 1972; Erckmann 1981; Gill and Handel 1981). The male stays with the chicks until fledging, which begins at about 18 days (Holmes 1972, D. Schamel in litt.).

Egg-laying on the Seward Peninsula usually begins fairly synchronously during the last week of May, peaking during the last few days of May and the first few days of June. It may begin 7-10 days sooner in early seasons, however (e.g., 17 May 1981, peaking 27 May, Woodby and Divoky 1983; 17 May 1983, back-dating from a hatching clutch at Solomon, see below). Laying for renests may continue as late as 22-25 June. Hatching peaks in mid-June in early years, but not until 22-26 June most years (earliest hatch, 8 June 1981, Woodby and Divoky 1983; 10 June 1983, Solomon, R. and B. Mearns unpubl. notes); and most fledging occurs during the first half of July, usually peaking around 7-10 July, although young from late broods may not gain flight until the end of July or even early August. Generally, the nesting phenologies of the Western Sandpiper are a few days earlier than those of the Semipalmateds, but because of slightly longer incubation and fledging periods, the young of the two species gain flight about the same time.

The summer diet of this sandpiper consists largely of larval and pupal insects, mostly flies, midges, and beetles; but other larval and adult insects and other invertebrates are taken opportunistically (Holmes 1972, Woodby and Divoky 1983).

A population shift toward wetlands begins as early as the last third of June. Some failed breeders leave their territories and move to tidal flats and coastal Salt Grass and Wet meadows; and young chicks are taken to nearby wetlands for feeding, either coastally or to pond, lake, or creek margins. By early July, large flocks begin to form on coastal mudflats, apparently augmented by postbreeding females (e.g., 1000+ "peeps," 65% Westerns, 3 July 1974, north end of Lopp Lagoon, Kessel pers. obs.; flocks of 50-220, vicinity Bonanza R mouth, 3 July 1975, Drury 1976b). Numbers continue to increase during the first half of July as families fledge and move to the coast, although by then some adults have already left on migration (some arrive back in California by early to mid-July [Holmes 1972]). After fledging, adults and juvenals form separate flocks (ibid.). Most adults have departed by mid-July, although a few, probably late breeders, may remain to the end of the month (Connors and Connors 1985, Woodby and Divoky 1983). The juvenals continue to feed at coastal littoral sites for several more weeks, building to peak numbers in late July-early August (Connors and Connors 1985, Schamel et al. 1979). As with Semipalmated Sandpipers, local populations decrease sharply during the first few days of August (ibid.). However, a major movement of Western Sandpipers passed through the head of Norton Bay 12-30 August 1977 (Shields and Peyton 1979), apparently migrants from farther north along the Chukchi Sea coast; and a few migrants continue moving through during September (latest, two, 10 September 1983, Inmachuk R, J. D. Walters unpubl. notes; 100 birds, 12 September 1977, Akulik-Inglutalik R delta, Shields and Peyton 1979; but 175 "peeps," 22 September 1975, mouth of Bonanza R [Drury 1976b unpubl. notes] and 6 "peeps," 24 September 1984, Deering [J. D. Walters unpubl. notes] were probably this species, too).

Rufous-necked Stint—*Calidris ruficollis*

Primarily a Siberian breeder, the Beringian Rufous-necked Stint is a rare migrant and breeder on the Seward Peninsula. The center of its North American distribution is at Wales, where, over the years, one to four individuals have been reported in a season and eight nests have been recorded (Ford 1934; Hanna 1940a; Bailey 1943, 1948; Kessel and D. D. Gibson unpubl. data). From the Wales area they apparently breed along the Chukchi Sea coast to at least Shishmaref Inlet (a highly plumaged male with enlarged but somewhat regressed gonads [UAM 3116, testes 7.5 x 4.6 mm and 5.5 x 4.5 mm], 24 June 1970, fed on a mud flat with a of flock 150 Western and Semipalmated sandpipers, southeast of Cape Lowenstern ["Seven-mile Point"]; and two individuals, 4 July 1972, 1 km farther east, J. Piatt in litt.) and coastally along Norton Sound to Safety Sound (pair hovering over tundra, 22 June 1973, Breving Lagoon, R. J. Gordon in litt.; pair with three just-hatched chicks, 21 June 1968, on tundra at about 20-m elevation along Sonora Ck, 24 km northwest of Nome, D. G. Roseneau and W. R. Tilton unpubl. notes; pair with at least two young [unaged],

10 July 1908, Nome, Thayer 1909; adult with brood, 23 June 1968, Safety Sound, M. Kessel pers. comm.; plus several sightings of 1-5 individuals 1972-1986 at the mouth of the Nome R and at Safety Sound, Kessel and D. D. Gibson unpubl. data). The only interior record has been of an apparent postbreeder that fed at a seepage at Serpentine Hot Springs on 22 July 1968 (D. G. Roseneau and W. R. Tilton unpubl. notes).

Little is known about the seasonal chronologies of this peep on the Peninsula. The earliest spring observation is of one on 28 May 1979 at the mouth of the Nome River (P. J. Baicich and O. K. Scott in litt.). Egg dates have ranged from 14 June 1945 (four eggs, Wales, Bailey 1948) to 30 June 1974 (four eggs, Cape Mountain at about 150-m elevation on moss hummock in hummocky creek draw with scattered large rocks, Kessel pers. obs.). All reported clutches have been of four eggs, and all nests have contained dried willow leaves. The earliest reported chick date is 21 June 1968 (see above). The latest fall report is of one on 31 July 1977 at Wales (D. A. Woodby and K. V. Hirsch unpubl. notes), but, extralimitally, a specimen was taken on 12 August 1931 at Point Hope (MVZ 60464, Kessel and Gibson 1978).

Temminck's Stint—*Calidris temminckii*

A lone Temminck's Stint in the marshy area of Village Creek at Wales on 13 June 1975 was well-observed by P. G. Dumont (in litt.). This Palearctic species is a rare spring migrant on the islands of the Bering Sea (Kessel and Gibson 1978 and subsequent unpubl. data).

[Long-toed Stint—*Calidris subminuta*]

Two "peeps" in the lower Village Creek marsh at Wales on 13 June 1975 were identified by P. G. Dumont (in litt.) as Long-toed Stints, but the descriptions are equivocal. This stint is a very rare spring migrant on the islands of the Bering Sea (Kessel and Gibson 1978).

Least Sandpiper—*Calidris minutilla*

A rare breeder, the Least Sandpiper is at the western fringe of its breeding range on the Seward Peninsula. It breeds regularly at Koyuk (pair behaving as with young, 1 July 1975, Kessel and F. G. Scheider pers. obs.; breeding birds banded and nests seen, first week of June 1976, Shields and Peyton 1977; two seen, 25-30 May 1981, D. A. Woodby unpubl. notes) and probably at Moses Point (two, 25-29 June 1980 and seen, 24 July 1980, D. A. Woodby unpubl. notes) and in the Niukluk and Fox river drainages (three, including a defensive pair, Niukluk R at Council, and a territorial bird at a gravel pit at Milepost 71 Council Road near Bear R, both Kessel pers. obs.). It also breeds in eastern Kotzebue Sound (peeping chicks not seen, but distractive adult approached within 3 m, 22 June 1975, Buckland, Kessel pers. obs.; and, extralimitally, nest with 3 eggs, 24 June 1967, Kotzebue, H. K. Springer in litt.).

Farther west its occurrence is more erratic. Two birds were near the dredge pond at the eastern edge of Nome on 13 June 1970 (R. C. Smith in litt.), and one was along the Teller Highway west of Nome on 7 June 1974 (H. K. Springer and A. Bernecker unpubl. notes).

In most years spring migrants probably arrive during the second week of May, judging from dates at Fairbanks and Ambler (Kessel and D. D. Gibson unpubl. data). Some postbreeding movement of adults, probably failed breeders, is visible at coastal sites by late June (Yukon-Kuskokwim Delta, Gill and Handel 1981), but on the Akulik-Inglutalik River delta, migration was not evident until 4 August 1977 and peaked 22 August 1977, "when hundreds...migrated through" (Shields and Peyton 1977:20).

Baird's Sandpiper—*Calidris bairdii*

The Baird's Sandpiper is an uncommon but widespread breeder on the Peninsula, extending across much of the Southern Uplands and Northern Uplands, at least west of about 162° W. It is most numerous in the Wales area, from where Bailey (1943) enumerated 23 egg sets that had been collected for museums and where, in 38 man-h of hiking 22-28 June 1972 about Cape Mountain, F. G. Scheider and I counted 32 individuals.

As in Central Alaska, the Baird's Sandpiper on the Seward Peninsula favors alpine habitats, nesting on slopes and terraces up to elevations of 300-400 m. It usually chooses sites where small patches of Wet Meadow or Grass Meadow are juxtaposed with Dwarf Shrub Mat.

This "peep," one of North America's longer-distance migrants, winters primarily from west central South America south through Chile and Argentina to Tierra del Fuego (American Ornithologists' Union 1983). Its main migration pathway is through the central plains of the United States and interior Canada (ibid., Jehl 1979), with the Seward Peninsula birds thus passing through Interior Alaska. In autumn, at least, most Baird's Sandpipers fly in two long nonstop flights to reach their wintering grounds, stopping only in a staging area in southern Canada-northern United States to rebuild energy reserves before resuming their trip to South America (Jehl 1979).

In some years, early spring migrants arrive by the second week of May (earliest, 12 May 1970, Wales, Flock and Hubbard 1979; also, extralimitally, 12 May [yr?], Mountain Village, Gabrielson and Lincoln 1959), but mostly they do not arrive until the third week and continue arriving through the end of the month. On average, the Baird's Sandpiper arrives a few days later than the Semipalmated Sandpiper.

Back-dating from observed events (see below) indicates that egg-laying begins on the Peninsula by at least 2-4 June—probably by late May in years of early snow melt. Clutch size is almost invariably four eggs (Drury 1961b, Parmelee et al. 1967). Both members of the pair share in incubation (ibid.), which lasts 19.5-21 days (Drury 1961b, Parmelee et al. 1967, Norton 1972). Both also attend the young for the first 5-7 days after hatching, when the female leaves; the male remains with the brood until close to the time of fledging, which occurs when the chicks are about 20 days old (Parmelee et al. 1967).

Few details of nests or broods have been reported from the Peninsula. A nest with eggs was found on 15 June 1922 by Bailey (1943). I collected a female (UAM 3117) with a brood of at least two 1-day-old chicks (UAM 3119, 3120) in the York Mountains near Lost River on 28 June 1970; and a pair with two downy "runners" was found in the hills southeast of Woolley Lagoon by R. and B. Mearns on 27 June 1983. These two broods should have fledged by about 16-18 July.

Baird's Sandpipers feed primarily on surface-active prey, especially insects (Drury 1961b, Holmes and Pitelka 1968). They frequently obtain insects from the surfaces of snow and melting pond ice (Kessel pers. obs.).

Postbreeding Baird's Sandpipers, compared to the other "peeps," make little use of coastal mud flats. When the adult females leave their broods in early July, they apparently begin their fall migration immediately (see Jehl 1979). The families remain near their natal areas, although they may shift to nearby pond, lake, and creek margins (or coastal sites if nearby), where most remain until migration—most adult males until mid- to late July and the juvenals into August (e.g., up to four, along beach edge of Kuzitrin L, 21-27 July 1973; two groups each of three birds, probably families, along Inmachuk R alluvia, 30 July 1973; one, alluvial river bar near Serpentine Hot Springs, 4 August 1973; all D. D. Gibson unpubl. notes). A few non- or postbreeders use coastal habitats, as do some juvenal migrants. Occasional birds frequented Cape Espenberg 18 June-11 August 1976 and 12 June-19 August 1977 (Schamel et al. 1979). D. A. Woodby (unpubl. notes) in 1980 reported four birds seen at Moses Point on 23 July, and others there on 24, 25, and 27 August; up to three at Port Clarence on 2-3 August; two adults and four juvenals at Safety Sound on 12 August; and an individual at Golovin between 13 and 18 August. And a passage of 5-10 birds used the mudflats off the Akulik-Inglutalik River delta 10-15 August 1977 (Shields and Peyton 1979).

Fall migration is protracted, as indicated above. Failed breeders probably begin to leave before the end of June, the successful females by early July; most adult males have left by mid-August and most juvenals by the end of August (latest, one, 4 September 1977, Wales, D. A. Woodby and K. V. Hirsch unpubl. notes; one, "early September" 1975, Bluff, Drury 1976b; last seen, 27 September 1980, Safety Sound, D. A. Woodby in litt.).

Pectoral Sandpiper—*Calidris melanotos*

The Pectoral Sandpiper is a common migrant, uncommon summer visitant, and rare breeder on the Seward Peninsula. It occurs most frequently in the Coastal Lowlands, especially at Cape Espenberg and about Lopp Lagoon, where in some years it is a locally uncommon breeder, and along river valleys draining directly into the Coastal Lowlands, including Livingston Creek and the Snake River. A few breeders also are scattered widely through the interior of the Peninsula (e.g., site-tenacious adult(s) with or behaving as if with young: headwaters Hannum Ck, 5 July 1971 [female, UAM 3179], Kessel and S. O. MacDonald pers. obs.; headwaters of Burnt R, 13 July 1973, Kessel and D. D. Gibson pers. obs.; pond edge along Andesite Ck, 7 July 1973, Kessel and D. D. Gibson pers. obs; junction of Hot Springs Ck and Serpentine R, 5 July 1971, S. O. MacDonald pers. comm.; headwaters of Nuluk R, 28 June 1974, Kessel pers. obs.); and probable breeders have been reported on the tops of some of the offshore islands, such as King (Bailey 1926) and Sledge (Cade 1952).

On the Peninsula, this sandpiper is associated almost entirely with Wet Meadow habitat, although a few fall migrants may also utilize nearby mudflats.

This large "peep" winters mainly in the southern third of South America and migrates mostly through the interior of northern South America, Middle America, and North America (American Ornithologists' Union 1983) to reach its northern breeding grounds; thus, those breeding on the Seward Peninsula arrive via Interior Alaska. Spring arrivals, as well as breeding times and breeding abundances, are strongly influenced by the persistence of snow cover (Pitelka 1959). In early years, the first birds arrive at the Peninsula by mid-May (earliest, four, 11 May 1980, Nome, and one, 12 May 1981, Golovin, D. A. Woodby in litt.; but, extralimitally, 4 May [yr?] at Bethel, Gabrielson and Lincoln 1959, and 9 May 1985, Kotzebue, Selawik NWR unpubl. notes), but in other years not until about 20-22 May. Migrants continue arriving through May, with some, perhaps nonbreeders, still arriving as late as the first days of June.

Birds arrive on the breeding grounds in near breeding condition, so mating begins only a few days after the birds arrive on their territories (Pitelka 1959). Mating is promiscuous, with females visiting the territories of males for copulation (Pitelka et al. 1974) and then usually nesting outside the male's territory (Pitelka 1959). Only the female incubates the eggs and cares for the young, with most of the males leaving the breeding grounds before clutches hatch (ibid.). Clutch size is almost invariably four eggs (Brandt 1943, Pitelka 1959). Incubation appears to be 23 days, at least Conover (1926) found an early season nest of four eggs that hatched 23 days after it was found; Conover also estimated a 30-day fledging period, but 23-25 days seems more likely in view of some barely fledged young that D. D. Gibson and I found on the upper Burnt River on 13 July 1973.

Based on observed events, Pectoral Sandpiper breeding chronologies on the Seward Peninsula are about 2 weeks earlier than at Barrow, Alaska (cf. Pitelka 1959), and are similar to those on the Yukon-Kuskokwim Delta (cf. Conover 1926, Brandt 1943, Gabrielson and Lincoln 1959). Early egg-laying begins about 24 May, but probably does not peak in most years until the first few days of June (earliest, eggs, 23 May [yr?], extralimitally at Takotna Forks, Gabrielson and Lincoln 1959; four eggs, 27 May 1984, extralimitally at Old Chevak, Yukon-Kuskokwim Delta, K. Kertell in litt.). Nesting may be delayed for a week or more in years of late snow cover, and, once begun in the population, may extend over a 30-day period (Pitelka 1959). In most years on the Peninsula, however, incubation in most of the population apparently starts about 27 May-4 June; and, with 23 days of incubation, hatching would begin 20-27 June (clutch hatching 21 June 1921, near Nome, Bailey 1926, and first young on 21 June 1924, Hooper Bay, Yukon-Kuskokwim Delta, Conover 1926). With this schedule, a fledging period of 23-25 days would have made the Burnt River fledging date (above) of 13 July 1973 possible. With late broods, fledging may not occur until mid-August or later.

The summer diet of Pectoral Sandpipers is insectivorous, consisting largely of dipteran, primarily tipulids, and chironomid larvae (Holmes and Pitelka 1968).

Small flocks of Pectoral Sandpipers are present throughout the summer, but their composition varies seasonally. Flocks in late May and first half of June are either migrants or nonbreeders; postbreeding males and failed females may congregate in small numbers during the last half of June; and successful females begin leaving their fledged broods about mid-July. Non- and failed breeders leave the Peninsula early, and, as the respective sexes of successful breeders complete their duties, they apparently depart immediately on their southward migration (Pitelka 1959), moving back through Interior Alaska and interior North America. The juvenals tend to move coastally to littoral or vegetated supralittoral areas for feeding prior to migration (Gill and Handel 1981, Woodby and Divoky 1983). Premigratory staging birds and migrants peak at these sites during the last half of August and the first few days of September (80 + in flocks at Sarichef I, 13-15 August 1973, D. D. Gibson unpubl. notes.; 160-400 birds, Cape Espenberg, 16-17 August 1976, with numbers of 50 or more occurring more or less regularly 11-29 August 1976, Schamel et al. 1979; migrants passed through the Akulik-Inglutalik R delta at the head of Norton Sound, 22-30 August 1977, Shields and Peyton 1978; peak numbers in Norton Sound occurred 25 August-9 September 1980 and 1981, Woodby and Divoky 1983). Small numbers of juvenals remain almost every year through mid-September (latest, one, 23 September 1975, Safety Sound, Drury 1976b).

Sharp-tailed Sandpiper—*Calidris acuminata*

A Siberian breeder, the Sharp-tailed Sandpiper is an uncommon fall migrant and a casual spring migrant on the Peninsula. The only confirmed spring record is one seen in Wet Meadow habitat near the Nome airport on 7 June 1977 by H. K. Springer (in litt.). In fall, while moving from their natal areas to wintering grounds in the islands of the southwest Pacific Ocean and Australia (American Ornithologists' Union 1983), some juvenals migrate along Alaska coastlines of the Chukchi and Bering seas and the Bering Sea islands (Kessel and Gibson 1978). On the Seward Peninsula, where they utilize Wet Meadows, and to a minor degree tidal flats, in the Coastal Lowlands, they are present primarily during the last week of August (earliest, 2 August 1980, Woolley Lagoon, D. A. Woodby in litt.) and the first two weeks of September (latest, specimen, 16 September 1910, Nome, Gabrielson and Lincoln 1959; but, extralimitally, ten birds, 18 September 1977, Akulik-Inglutalik R delta, Shields and Peyton 1979; one, 2 October 1987, Kotzebue, Selawik NWR unpubl. notes). Numbers usually peak during the first 10 days of September, when locally, they may become fairly common for brief periods (40 birds, 2 September 1977, Wales, D. A. Woodby and K. V. Hirsch unpubl. notes; 45 birds, 31 August 1976, Cape Espenberg, Schamel et al. 1979; "100's," estimated 6-10 September 1980, Safety Sound and Fish R delta, Woodby and Divoky 1983, D. A. Woodby unpubl. notes; maximum of 116 birds, 1 September 1978, extralimitally at Akulik-Inglutalik R delta, Shields and Peyton 1979).

Rock Sandpiper—*Calidris ptilocnemis*

A Beringian species, the Rock Sandpiper is an uncommon breeder on the Seward Peninsula. It reaches the northern extremity of its North American range on the Peninsula, where it breeds in the alpine tundras of the coastal mountains of the Bering Strait region, from Ear Mountain and Cape Mountain to the Kigluaiks. It is most numerous as a breeder on Cape Mountain, where it is fairly common (reported variously in A. M. Bailey's publications [1926, 1943, 1948] as "abundant," "common," or "fairly common" in 1922; 24 birds counted and one clutch of four eggs found during a 17-km circuit on the mountain by F. G. Scheider and me on 24 June 1972; and 17 birds and two four-egg clutches on a similar 14-km hike that I made on 30 June 1974). The species is an uncommon but widespread breeder in the Southern Uplands west of about 165° W, where I have found it at various sites along the Teller Highway, including along the lower slopes of the Kigluaik Mountains at Crete and Wesley creeks and where it has been reported at the ridge crest at Milepost 63, south of Teller (pair, 10 June 1975, Drury 1976b) and at Woolley Lagoon (one or two birds, 18 June 1983, R. and B. Mearns unpubl. notes; two adults with at least three chicks, 4 July 1976, H. K. Springer unpubl. notes). On the Peninsula, the Rock Sandpiper usually nests within 15 km of the coast, but it is 28 km inland at Ear Mountain, where I saw three separate birds near the top of the 700-m mountain on 21 June 1974, and about 43 km inland in the mountains along the east side of the Nome River, where I in 1972 and 1977 and R. and B. Mearns in 1983 found one to nine apparent breeders on 350-400-m-high Dwarf Shrub Mat and fellfield tundra between Mileposts 25 and 29 of the Taylor Highway.

The Seward Peninsula Rock Sandpipers winter along the coasts of Southeastern Alaska south to Oregon and northern California (Vaurie 1965) and apparently also in Southcoastal Alaska (Conover 1944, Isleib and Kessel 1973, MacIntosh 1986). They migrate coastally, sometimes arriving at the Yukon-Kuskokwim Delta by late April (earliest, flock of 350 birds, 24 April 1979, mouth of Kashunuk R, R. E. Gill in litt.), but they have not been reported from the Seward Peninsula until mid-May (earliest, seen, 18 May 1978, Cape Mountain, Flock and Hubbard 1979); migrants continue to arrive through May.

Few data are available from the Peninsula upon which to determine seasonal chronologies. On the basis of "numerous sets [of eggs] in the Museum, Academy, and Hanna collections," Bailey (1943:95) stated that "it is apparent that the average clutch is completed by the middle of June." The fact, however, that he found eggs "well-incubated" by 25 June 1922, and that chicks are hatching on the Yukon-Kuskokwim Delta by the third week of June (chicks still in nest, 19 June 1964, Kessel et al. 1964; adult with chick, 18 June 1984, K. Kertell in litt.) leads me to believe that egg-laying in the Peninsula population begins by the first week of June and probably continues for about 2 weeks. The 4 July 1976 brood (above) and two young "just able to fly" on 28 July 1922 at Lopp Lagoon (Bailey 1943) also indicate that nesting begins by early June.

The two nests I found on Cape Mountain on 30 June 1974 consisted of fairly deep cups, with the bottoms lined with lichens and dried willow leaves. Both were placed on dry sites in damp draws on the mountain, one close to a small rivulet. Both sexes participate in incubation (Bailey 1943), and both attend the chicks, at least early in their development (both parents with 4 July 1976 brood, above). Neither the incubation period nor the fledging period have been determined for the Rock Sandpiper, but 22 days each is probably a fair approximation.

After breeding, Rock Sandpipers move to littoral areas, especially tidal flats, for feeding and molting. The first adults return to the Yukon-Kuskokwim Delta flats in early July [non- and failed breeders?], with the juvenals beginning to arrive in late July and early August (Gill and Handel 1981). The shift to littoral areas on the Seward

Peninsula becomes noticeable in early August (Connors 1978, D. A. Woodby unpubl. notes), with the fledging of the young. On 12 August 1980, all of a dozen birds seen by D. A. Woodby and others (unpubl. notes) at Safety Sound appeared to be juvenals. As with other *Calidris*, the adults apparently leave by the time the young have fledged, perhaps with those from the Seward Peninsula moving to the Yukon-Kuskokwim Delta for molt and premigratory staging (see Gill and Handel 1981). Some juvenals remain on the Seward Peninsula well into September (latest, three to five birds, 16 September 1975, cobble beach at Tonok, Drury 1976b; one dead for 2-3 days found 27 September 1980, Safety Sound, D. A. Woodby in litt.; juvenal collected, 27 September 1933, extralimitally at Uelen, Chukotsk Peninsula, Portenko 1972).

Currently, there are four recognized subspecies of this Beringian sandpiper, all with breeding ranges about the Bering Sea. The form inhabiting the Seward and Chukotsk peninsulas is *C.p. tschuktschorum* (Conover 1944), although a male collected by A. M. Bailey at Wales on 8 June 1922 has been identified as *C. p. quarta* (DMNH 8962, Bailey 1943, Conover 1944), the resident race of the Commander Islands.

Dunlin—*Calidris alpina*

A common migrant and breeder, the Dunlin is the fifth most abundant shorebird on the Seward Peninsula (Table 5). It occurs in the Coastal Lowlands around the entire perimeter of the Peninsula, where it is associated primarily with wet meadows and tidal flats. During nesting it is present in greatest densities where Wet Meadow habitat is interspersed with drier sites of Dwarf Shrub Meadow, where nests are placed—e.g., hummocks and ridges within Wet Meadow and, to a lesser extent, on the lower slopes of hillsides adjacent to wetlands). The tundra flats at Wales and the barrier strip off Lopp Lagoon appear to have the highest breeding densities; here, in 52 man-h of hiking 22-28 June 1972, 325 Dunlins were enumerated (Kessel pers. obs.), and during censuses in 1977, there were about 8 birds/10 ha (Connors 1978). In 1980 Woodby and Divoky (1983) found 6.9 birds/10 ha at the base of the Point Spencer spit, 5.0 birds/10 ha at Koyuk, 4.8 birds/10 ha at Woolley Lagoon, 3.6 birds/10 ha at the Fish River delta, and 2.8 or fewer birds/10 ha at Safety Sound, Breving Lagoon, and Moses Point. At Cape Espenberg, Schamel et al. (1979) found fewer than 2 nests/10 ha. Postbreeders forage to varying degrees on tidal flats.

The Western Alaska populations of Dunlin winter along the Pacific Coast of North America (see below), some as far north as Southcoastal Alaska (Isleib and Kessel 1973, Gill 1979, MacIntosh 1986). The northward passage of Dunlins appears to be coastal, with the delta system of the Copper-Bering rivers in Southcoastal Alaska functioning as a major spring staging area during the first 3 weeks of May (Isleib and Kessel 1973, Isleib 1979, Senner et al. 1981). From there, they move westward, apparently overflying the base of the Alaska Peninsula between Kamishak and Kvichak bays (rare in May and August, Brooks R, Katmai National Monument, D. D. Gibson unpubl. notes) and thence to their breeding areas along the Bering Sea coast. In early seasons they begin arriving at the Yukon-Kuskokwim Delta as early as the first few days of May (C. M. Boise in litt., C. M. Handel in litt.) and probably a few days later on the Seward Peninsula (earliest, twenty, 7 May 1980, Nome, and two, 8 May 1981, Golovin, D. A. Woodby in litt.). Arrival times generally coincide with the availability of patches of snow-free tundra (Holmes 1971b), with arrivals at the Seward Peninsula peaking during the third week of May. Migration continues through May, the later birds perhaps first-time breeders or Asiatic Dunlins moving to Northern Alaska (e.g., flock of 150-200 birds, 3 June 1977, mouth of Kitluk R, J. M. Wright unpubl. notes).

Returning Dunlins exhibit strong site tenacity, coming back to the same breeding area year after year (Holmes 1970, Schamel et al. 1979). While some individuals may be capable of breeding in their first year, most apparently do not do so until their second (Holmes 1966, Norton 1972). Dunlins are monogamous and territorial, with most breeding activities confined to the territory, although some pairs may leave territories late in incubation to feed at nearby favored sites with other Dunlins (Holmes 1970). Nests are placed on a dry, often raised site, usually in a clump of relatively tall sedges or grasses; they are made of graminoid leaves and usually have small leaves of shrubs covering the bottom of the cup (Kessel pers. obs.). Most clutches contain 4 eggs; in fact, clutches from 51 Seward Peninsula nests averaged 3.9 eggs (Schamel et al. 1979, J. M. Wright unpubl. notes, D. A. Woodby in litt., Kessel and D. D. Gibson unpubl. data). Both parents incubate, with male attentiveness increasing during incubation (Holmes 1966); incubation lasts 21.5-23 days (Norton 1972, Erckmann 1981). Both sexes care for the chicks while they are young, but the females desert the family at varying times during the prefledging period (Holmes 1966). Time to first flight ranges between 21 and 26 days, occurring when the young are about three-fourths adult size (ibid.).

On the Seward Peninsula, egg-laying in the population begins as early as 16-19 May (back-dating from "fairly large young" found 23 and 25 June 1968 at Safety Sound and the mouth of the Sinuk R, respectively [Kessel unpubl. notes], and from "barely flying" chicks by 3 July 1981 at the Fish R delta and flying young on 5 July 1980 at Breving Lagoon [D. A. Woodby in litt.]) and continues through May, usually peaking during the last week of the month. At Cape Espenberg in 1976 and 1977, however, Schamel et al. (1979) reported nest initiation not beginning until the first week of June and continuing until mid-June or later. Late clutches at any locality are probably replacements from earlier nesting failures (Holmes 1966, 1971b) or laying by first-year birds (Norton 1972). Thus, while some broods may hatch during the second week of June, most hatch from mid-June through the first week of July. Fledging begins in early broods during the first week of July (above), and most chicks have fledged by the first of August.

Territories break down after hatching, and families move onto nearby wetlands, feeding about pond margins in Wet Meadow. At fledging, a general shift occurs toward coastal habitats—lagoonal wet meadows and shorelines, river estuaries, and sometimes tidal flats—with adults and juvenals usually forming separate flocks (Holmes 1966, Woodby and Divoky 1983).

Summer food of the Dunlin consists primarily of insect larvae. Chironomids predominate in the diets of Yukon Delta and Seward Peninsula birds (Holmes 1970, Woodby and Divoky 1983), but opportunistically they consume other readily available invertebrates, e.g., tipulid and beetle larvae and adults (ibid.) and, when on tidal mud flats, isopods, small molluscs, and other marine organisms (ibid., Schamel et al. 1979).

Dunlins undergo a complete molt prior to fall migration (Holmes 1971b). Some molting occurs on the Seward Peninsula (e.g., 33 birds, some in full alternate plumage and others molting, 13-14 August 1973, Sarichef I, D. D. Gibson unpubl. notes), but most go elsewhere to molt. Local breeders disappeared 20 July 1976 from the Akulik-Inglutalik River delta (Shields and Peyton 1977), and Woodby and Divoky (1983) reported that numbers of local breeders began decreasing in July 1980 and 1981—adults by mid-July and juvenals apparently in early August—before a major molt could occur. Where they go for molting and premigratory fattening is unknown, perhaps to the biologically productive Yukon-Kuskokwim Delta.

Large numbers of migrants arrive at Seward Peninsula wetlands rather abruptly during the last week of August (1200 birds, 19 and 22 August 1976, Cape Espenberg, Schamel et al. 1979; "very large number" of migrants, 22-24 August 1976, and 10,000-20,000 birds, 25-30 August 1977, extralimitally on the Akulik-Inglutalik R delta, Shields and Peyton 1977, 1979; highest littoral densities, 27-30 August 1977, Wales, Connors 1978), and numbers remain high through mid-September at such sites as Safety Sound and Moses Point (Woodby and Divoky 1983). This major August-September passage appears to be of Dunlins from Alaska's North Slope (see below). A few may still be straggling through in late September-early October (latest, one, 7 October 1983, and twelve, 9 and 10 October 1985, Deering, J. D. Walters unpubl. notes).

Fall migration patterns of Alaska's Bering Sea Dunlins have been studied by R. E. Gill, but are still poorly known. Populations from the Alaska Peninsula apparently depart en mass under favorable weather conditions and fly directly across the North Pacific to British Columbia and the northwestern United States and thence move south to wintering grounds primarily in the San Francisco Bay area of California (Gill 1979, pers. comm.). Yukon-Kuskokwim Delta birds may also fly over ocean expanses, but apparently after staging on the Copper-Bering River Delta (ibid.); they winter farther north, mostly in southern British Columbia and northern Washington (C. M. Handel in litt.). Perhaps the Seward Peninsula birds winter still farther north, accounting for the wintering populations in Southeastern and Southcoastal Alaska.

Two races of the Dunlin occur on the Seward Peninsula. The breeding form is *C. a. pacifica* (MacLean and Holmes 1971, UAM 2768-2774). During migration, however, the form from northern Alaska, *C. a. sakhalina* (MacLean and Holmes 1971; but *C. a. arcticola* by Browning 1977) that winters along the Pacific Coast of Asia, moves through the Peninsula's Coastal Lowlands. Migrants collected 28-30 May 1977 and 2-3 June 1976 at Wales and Cape Espenberg proved to be this subspecies (Senner et al. 1981). The late August influx of migrants to the Peninsula (see above) complements known departure dates from Barrow, Alaska (Holmes 1966), and several tens of thousands of this form begin staging in August on the Yukon-Kuskokwim Delta with *pacifica* (Gill and Handel 1981).

Curlew Sandpiper—*Calidris ferruginea*

A Siberian breeder, the Curlew Sandpiper is probably casual on the Seward Peninsula, where a single bird, with a Western and a Semipalmated sandpiper, fed at the edge of ice chunks 40 m out in Espenberg Bay on 22 June 1976 (D. L. Schamel in litt.). It is a casual migrant in western Alaska and a very rare breeder at Barrow in Northern Alaska (Kessel and Gibson 1978).

Stilt Sandpiper—*Calidris himantopus*

The Stilt Sandpiper is a casual, perhaps very rare, spring migrant on the Seward Peninsula, where it has been recorded at the Nome River mouth (one, 8 June 1975, by G. E. Hall and R. A. MacIntosh, Kessel and Gibson 1978), Wales (male, 12 June 1947, by D. Tevuk, Bailey 1948; one, 12 June 1979, S. Hills unpubl. notes), and Deering (one each, 6 June 1984, 29 May 1985, and 5 and 9 June 1988, Deering, J. D. Walters unpubl. notes). Normally this sandpiper migrates northward through central North America to breeding grounds in northern Canada and northern Alaska (American Ornithologists' Union 1983), but it is a very rare spring migrant in eastern Central Alaska during the same time span as on the Seward Peninsula, i.e., from late May to mid-June (Kessel and Gibson 1978).

Buff-breasted Sandpiper—*Tryngites subruficollis*

The Buff-breasted Sandpiper is a very rare spring and fall migrant on the Seward Peninsula. Spring records from the Peninsula include two birds at Nome on 5 June 1974 (Kessel and Gibson 1978), one at Koyuk on 28 May 1981 (D. A. Woodby in litt.), one at Ear Mountain, 17 June 1987 (R. V. Harris unpubl. notes), and a small group at Cape Woolley "courting and copulating into early summer" 1978 (H. K. Springer pers. comm.). The only fall records are of two birds on the Fish River delta 3 or 5 August 1981 (D. A. Woodby in litt.) and two juvenals at Kividlo on the barrier strip 17 km southwest of the Kitluk River mouth on 3 August 1987 (S. A. Steinacher unpubl. notes).

The pattern of occurrences of migrants in Western and Southwestern Alaska (Kessel and Gibson 1978 and subsequent data) and on Pacific islands and along the coasts of the Pacific Ocean (American Ornithologists' Union 1983) suggest the presence of a western population of Buff-breasted Sandpipers, distinct from the one that migrates spring and fall through interior North America and breeds regularly as far west as the eastern North Slope of Alaska (Kessel and Gibson 1978). A population breeds on Wrangel Island (Dorogoi 1983) and possibly elsewhere in the Siberian Arctic ("rather common...they were evidently on their breeding ground...," 1 August 1881, Cape Vankarem, Nelson 1883, 1887:120) and is the probable source of the Pacific population.

Ruff—*Philomachus pugnax*

A very rare migrant along the Chukchi Sea coast of the Seward Peninsula, the Ruff has been recorded from Wales (female, 4 June 1983, M. L. Ward unpubl. notes; one, 21 and 22 August 1977, D. A. Woodby in litt.); Shishmaref Inlet (male courting two females, 12 June 1976, Arctic R delta, Noble and Wright 1977; juvenal female, 14 August 1973, feeding with two Pectoral Sandpipers, Shishmaref, D. D. Gibson, UAM 2556); and on the flats about a kilometer south of Deering (female, 9 July 1986, J. D. Walters unpubl. notes). The behavior in Alaska of this Old World lekking species, including the 1976 courting party at the Arctic River, suggests that occasional breeding may occur (Kessel and Gibson 1978).

Long-billed Dowitcher—*Limnodromus scolopaceus*

The Long-billed Dowitcher is a fairly common spring migrant and breeder and a locally common fall migrant on the Seward Peninsula. It is widely, though patchily, distributed, occurring predominantly in the Coastal Lowlands. In the interior of the Peninsula, however, I have seen individuals and pairs of suspected breeders in the wetlands at the west end of Salmon Lake (three birds, 6 July 1967), at a sedge-bordered pond along the Kuzitrin River near the junction of the Noxapaga River (one, 12 July 1973), in a sedge draw at the headwaters of the Nuluk River (three separate individuals, 28 June 1974), in wet *Carex* and marshy areas of McCarthys Marsh (pair, plus twenty-five birds, including a flock of nineteen, 17 July 1973), and in the wetlands bordering the headwaters of the Burnt River (three pairs, ten individuals, a flock of ten, and a large, half-grown chick, 13 July 1973).

The patchy distribution appears related to environmental features. Densities are greatest where there are extensive flats studded with freshwater ponds and wet meadows, e.g., the Safety Sound area, Wales-Lopp Lagoon wetlands, lower Shishmaref and Arctic river wetlands, Cape Espenberg, mouth of the Buckland River estuary. Even then, recorded breeding densities have been fewer than 0.5 pairs/10 ha (Schamel et al. 1979, Woodby and Divoky 1983). On the flats near Wales, in 18 man-h of walking on 26 June 1972, F. G. Scheider, H. E. Kingery, and I counted a total of 51 dowitchers. There has been no evidence of breeding in the Norton Bay area, and few, if any, breed on the Fish River delta.

During summer, Long-billed Dowitchers are almost entirely birds of the Wet Meadow habitat about freshwater ponds and lagoons, but postbreeders and migrants, especially juvenals (Pitelka 1950), use saltwater littoral areas to some extent, including mud flats (Connors 1978; Woodby and Divoky 1983); I have also noted a tendency in summer for Seward Peninsula dowitchers to feed on Salt Grass Meadow.

Most dowitchers from the Peninsula probably winter in the southwestern United States and western Mexico and migrate northward primarily west of the Rocky Mountains, judging from Pitelka (1950) and the American Ornithologists' Union (1983). Spring migrants move both coastally through Southcoastal Alaska (apparently then cutting across the base of the Alaska Peninsula to the Bering Sea coast) and through Interior Alaska, the latter probably being the source of the dowitchers of the Seward Peninsula and northwestern Alaska (Kessel and D. D. Gibson unpubl. data). The first spring migrants may arrive on the Peninsula by mid-May (earliest, 12 May 1988, Deering, J. D. Walters unpubl. notes, and 14 May 1980, Safety Sound, Woodby and Divoky 1983), but the main influx usually occurs during the third week of May; migratory movement continues through May.

The egg-laying period in the population lasts for about 2 weeks, beginning during the first or second week of June, depending on the season (earliest, 4 eggs on 2 June 1978, Cape Espenberg, D. Schamel unpubl. notes). Nests are in Wet Meadow habitat, often on or at the edge of a raised tussock or mossy hummock, either near the edge of or surrounded by water (Conover 1926, J. M. Wright unpubl. notes, D. Schamel unpubl. notes). The nest is a fairly deep cup, lined with some sedge but often damp at the bottom (Conover 1926, Brandt 1943, J. M. Wright unpubl. notes). Clutch size in 35 Seward Peninsula nests averaged 3.9 ± 0.3 eggs, range 3-4 (data from S. Hills unpubl. notes, D. Schamel unpubl. notes, J. M. Wright unpubl. notes). According to Conover (1926), Brandt (1943), and A. A. Kistchinski (in Johnsgard 1981), both sexes incubate, the female more during early incubation and the male increasingly so as incubation progresses, and the female reportedly deserts the male about the time the chicks hatch, leaving the care of the chicks to the male. Incubation lasts 21-22 days (Conover 1926, Erckmann 1981), so the earliest clutches on the Peninsula should hatch by late June; most have hatched by mid-July. The fledging period is unknown, but a "practically fully fledged" juvenal was collected on 29 July 1924 on the Yukon Delta by Conover (1926:306).

Food consists of a variety of aquatic invertebrates, including midge and cranefly larvae, and some seeds (Johnsgard 1981). Feeding is primarily by probing soft substrates, often in belly-deep water.

Some flocks develop again as early as late June (flock of 30 flew along the Nugnugaluktuk R estuary, 26 June 1973, Kessel and D. D. Gibson unpubl. notes), although the main postbreeding flocking does not become conspicuous until the second week of July, when flocks that probably contain both failed breeders and successful females form (flock of 12 birds, 10 July 1974, south end of Lopp Lagoon, Kessel pers. obs.; 30-40 birds, 9-10 July 1977, Cape Espenberg, Schamel et al. 1979; many flocks of 20-50 birds, 11 July 1976 and thereafter, along lower Arctic R, Noble and Wright 1977).

Fall migration of adults is under way by the end of July (small flocks moved through head of Norton Bay 28 July-6 August 1976, Shields and Peyton 1977; migratory flocks at Moses Point 23-25 July 1980, D. A. Woodby unpubl. notes). They have mostly left by mid-August (Woodby and Divoky 1983), about which time the juvenals begin moving southward. Migration of juvenals peaks about 7-10 September (Shields and Peyton 1979, Woodby and Divoky 1983), but continues through the month (latest, 12 birds, 27 September 1980, Safety Sound, D. A. Woodby unpubl. notes).

Common Snipe—*Gallinago gallinago*

Ubiquitous and fairly common, the Common Snipe is widely and evenly distributed as a breeder across the Peninsula, in the freshwater wetlands throughout the Coastal and Interior lowlands and the Northern and Southern uplands. It is rare, however, on coastal barrier strips, such as those between Wales and Cape Espenberg. In coastal Norton Sound, overall densities in 1980-1981 were 0.08/10 ha (Woodby and Divoky 1983). Occurrence on the Peninsula is closely associated with Wet Meadow habitat, especially that which contains some low shrubs. The Common Snipe is largely restricted to habitats underlain with organic soils (Tuck 1972), which may explain its scarcity on barrier strips as well as its absence from littoral areas.

Although most of Alaska's snipe probably winter from Southeastern Alaska to western Washington and Oregon (ibid.), the species is a rare winter resident as far north as Southcoastal Alaska, especially in mild winters (Isleib and Kessel 1973, Erikson et al. 1983, MacIntosh 1986, Anchorage Audubon Christmas Bird Counts 1984-86). While it is possible in early years that a few spring migrants arrive on the Peninsula by the first week of May, they usually do not arrive until the second week (earliest, one, 8 May 1986, Deering, J. D. Walters unpubl. notes; but, extralimitally, 30 April 1986, St. Marys, B. J. McCaffery unpubl. notes; 4 May 1978, Ambler, D. K. Wik in litt.; 5 May 1978, Kotzebue, D. P. Harrington in litt.; 7 May 1951, Selawik, R. Skin, Alaska Game Commission 1951). Migrants continue to arrive over the next 2-3 weeks. The males arrive 10-14 days before the females, and yearlings apparently arrive later and breed later than the adults (Tuck 1972).

The males go directly to their breeding wetlands, where they establish territories and perform their conspicuous winnowing courtship flight. Activities intensify with the arrival of the females, and some promiscuity occurs (ibid.). Territory requirements include shelter for the breeding pair, a nest site, feeding areas (although some off-territory feeding occurs), a loitering spot for the male, and escape cover for the female; the arenas for the courtship flights are not restricted to this nesting territory (ibid.). The female selects the nest site within the male's territory, sometimes making four or five scrapes before choosing her final site; she then remains several days at that scrape, adding grasses and leaves before laying the first egg (ibid.). The nest site is a relatively dry site within the Wet Meadow habitat, often in a clump of sedge or grass or at the base of a shrub (ibid., ANRS).

Eggs are laid daily until the clutch is completed. Twelve completed clutches reported from the Seward Peninsula each contained four eggs (varied sources, including Bailey 1925 and 1948, ANRS), but some three-egg clutches have been reported elsewhere, especially later in the season, and are probably laid by yearlings (Tuck 1972). There has been no confirmation of renesting by a female if the first clutch is destroyed, although deserted territories are quickly assumed by new occupants (ibid.). Incubation, which may begin before the laying of the last egg, takes an average of 19 days (Jehl and Hussell 1966, Tuck 1972) and is performed entirely by the female (Tuck 1972). At hatching, however, the male becomes a solicitous parent, usually taking charge of the first hatched chicks, while the female cares for the later ones (ibid.). Young may begin to fly by 17-18 days of age, but cannot undertake sustained flight until 20 days old (ibid.).

Applying these chronologies to observed events shows that egg-laying on the

Seward Peninsula begins in late May (egg-laying for a clutch that hatched on 19 June 1966 [ANRS] and for a fledged young that I saw near Nome on 8 July 1971 must have begun by 29 May, and laying for a barely fledged young at Safety Sound on 4 July 1970 [D. G. Roseneau unpubl. notes] probably began 25-26 May) and continues in the population for at least 3 weeks (winnowing, which ceases when the male begins attending the newly hatched chicks, is infrequent after the first week of July; also, a clutch of four eggs was still being incubated on 8 July 1973 near Lava Lake [Kessel and D. D. Gibson unpubl. notes]). Thus, some young do not fledge until the end of July or even later.

Food of the snipe, obtained by probing into soft organic substrates, consists mainly of insects, especially larval craneflies and waterbeetles, and varying amounts of crustaceans, worms, and molluscs (Tuck 1972, Senner and Mickelson 1979). Grit, seeds, and undigested chitin and shell fragments are regurgitated as pellets (Tuck 1972).

The adults begin their molt while attending their chicks, the males beginning about 2 weeks earlier than the females (ibid.). After the young fledge, the molting adults remain solitary, while the juvenals tend to aggregate (ibid.)—although only small groups of fewer than ten birds have been reported from the Peninsula. Migration is under way by early August (groups of two to seven snipe migrated through eastern Norton Bay, 1-10 August 1976, Shields and Peyton 1977). There is some evidence from Newfoundland (Tuck 1972), where loose flocks of up to 300 migrants occur, that the young precede the adults in migration and that the adult females migrate ahead of the males. On the Seward Peninsula, snipe remain uncommon until the second week of September (D. A. Woodby unpubl. notes). Numbers drop rapidly thereafter, although it is likely that stragglers remain to the end of September (latest reported, one, 17 September 1975, Drury 1976b; extralimitally, 18 September 1973, Ambler, D. K. Wik in litt., and 5 October 1966, Yukon-Kuskokwim Delta, J. Geerdts, Yukon Delta NWR unpubl. data).

Red-necked Phalarope—*Phalaropus lobatus*

An abundant and widespread breeder, the Red-necked Phalarope is the third most numerous shorebird of the Seward Peninsula, being outnumbered only by the Western and Semipalmated sandpipers (Table 5). It occurs throughout the Coastal and Interior lowlands and the Southern and Northern uplands, favoring small lacustrine waterbodies surrounded by Wet Meadow habitat. Coastal birds sometimes use littoral areas, especially tidal mudflats, but apparently not as much as in other parts of Western and Northern Alaska (Connors 1978, Schamel et al. 1979, Woodby and Divoky 1983). Breeding season densities have been recorded at 14.9 birds/10 ha at Moses Point, 13.4/10 ha at Koyuk, 10.2/10 ha in Imuruk Basin, and 7.0/10 ha on the Fish River delta (Woodby and Divoky 1983). Censuses in Wet Meadow habitat have yielded 10 nests/10 ha at Cape Espenberg (Schamel et al. 1979) and 8.5 nests/10 ha on the lower Arctic River (Wright 1979). In addition to the above localities, I have found this phalarope especially numerous in the Buckland River estuary, the Wales-Lopp Lagoon area, and at McCarthys Marsh—all areas with substantial amounts of preferred habitat.

Red-necked Phalaropes winter at sea at southern latitudes, feeding at upwellings and convergences, often far from land. Seward Peninsula birds apparently winter in the South Pacific, but it is not known whether they winter with most of the North American birds in the Humboldt Current off the coast of Peru or with those from the northeast Asian population in the East Indies (see Cramp 1983).

Spring arrivals in Western Alaska are heavily dependent on seasonal thaw patterns, with populations apparently remaining at sea until local onshore breeding sites have thawed sufficiently. In environmentally late seasons, large rafts have been seen in the open leads of Norton Sound (H. K. Springer in Gill and Handel 1981), but in most years, arriving migrants go directly to their breeding areas. The first migrants usually arrive during the second week of May (earliest, one, 8 May 1980, Nome, and four, 8 May 1981, Golovin, D. A. Woodby in litt.; extralimitally, 7 May 1978, Kotzebue, D. P. Harrington in litt., and 8 May 1977, Akulik-Inglutalik R delta, Shields and Peyton 1979), although they arrive somewhat later at Wales and along the Chukchi Sea coast of the Peninsula (earliest, 18 May 1976, mouth of Arctic R [Noble and Wright 1977]; but often not until 27-29 May at Wales [Bailey 1943, Breckenridge and Cline 1967, Flock and Hubbard 1979, M. L. Ward unpubl. notes]). Females tend to return before the males (Tinbergen 1935, Cramp 1983, Reynolds et al. 1986), and experienced breeders return and begin breeding before the yearlings (Hildén and Vuolanto 1972).

All species of phalaropes exhibit a sex-role reversal during nesting, with the male assuming the duties of caring for the eggs and young (Erckmann 1981, Reynolds 1987); correspondingly, the female is more brightly plumaged and larger and more aggressive than the male (Reynolds 1987). Red-necked Phalaropes breed as yearlings (Hildén and Vuolanto 1972). Pairing may be either monogamous or, sometimes, serially polyandrous, with the female laying a second clutch if a second male is available (Hildén and Vuolanto 1972, Reynolds 1987). There is no evidence of territorialism (ibid.). A short, low aerial "ceremonial" or advertising flight by the female was described by Tinbergen (1935) but was not observed in a 5-yr study reported by Reynolds (1987). After making a number of nest scrapes, variously assisted by the male, the female makes the final site selection (Tinbergen 1935, O. Hildén in Cramp 1983). Nests on the Seward Peninsula are almost exclusively in Wet Meadow habitat, usually placed in a relatively dry spot on the top or side of a moss or sedge hummock and often concealed by overhanging blades of surrounding sedge. They consist of a depression lined with varying amounts of nearby vegetation. The male, with the female in attendance, usually builds the nest (Reynolds 1987). Copulation occurs while the pair is on the water. The usual clutch is 4 eggs; the mean size of 101 clutches from the Seward Peninsula was 3.8 eggs (calculated from Noble and Wright 1977, Schamel et al. 1979, J. M. Wright unpubl. notes, Kessel unpubl. data). Eggs are usually laid daily until the clutch is completed (mean interval for 11 eggs in Finland was 26.5 h, Hildén and Vuolanto 1972), and shortly thereafter the pair bond dissolves. The male may begin to cover the eggs intermittently as soon as the first egg is laid, but hatching is synchronous (ibid.), so effective egg-warming apparently does not occur until between the laying of the third and fourth eggs. Incubation in 30 clutches at Cape Espenberg lasted an average of 21.4 ± 2.6 days, range 17-29 days (D. Schamel in litt.) and in 4 clutches at Wales lasted 18.5 days, range 17-21 days (Erckmann 1981), with incubation shorter as the season progresses (Hildén and Vuolanto 1972, Reynolds 1987). The young remain in the nest 3-6 h, or overnight if hatching occurs in the afternoon; thereafter, the attending male may brood them off and on for 4-5 days, but then becomes progressively less solicitous and deserts the brood before they are 2 weeks old (Hildén and Vuolanto 1972, Erckmann 1981). Fledging occurs at 20-21 days (Reynolds 1987, D. Schamel in litt.).

Egg-laying usually begins by late May (28 May 1978, upper Inmachuk R, J. M. Wright unpubl. notes; 30 May 1977, extralimitally on Akulik-Inglutalik R delta, Shields and Peyton 1979), although farther west it may begin 7-10 days later (e.g., nest initiation at Cape Espenberg did not begin until 6 June 1977 and 11 June 1976 [Schamel et al. 1979], although an early nest at Wales contained four fresh eggs on 21 May 1981 [D. A. Woodby in litt.]). Laying in the population continues for 3-4 weeks. Thus, chicks from early layings should be hatching 21-22 June (earliest reported, 24 June 1977, Akulik-Inglutalik R delta, Shields and Peyton 1979), and the first chicks should fledge 11-12 July. Two late clutches at Cape Espenberg in 1976 did not hatch until 24 July (Schamel et al. 1979), which means that any chicks would not have fledged until mid-August.

The diet of the Red-necked Phalarope consists primarily of small insects and their larvae, especially midge larvae, but also may include small crustaceans and molluscs, seeds, and even tiny fish (Cramp 1983; Woodby and Divoky 1983); nereid polychaetes are important items for phalaropes at sea (Sanger 1986). The birds take food items from any available surface—water, soil, emergent vegetation, flotsam, etc.—while walking, wading, or swimming. They also stretch for subsurface items in water, sometimes even up-ending to reach them, and will grab at flying insects.

Adult females flock together and leave the breeding grounds in late June and early July, a period during which Woodby and Divoky (1983) reported large aggregations of females feeding on tundra ponds, and Shields and Peyton (1979) noted a significant local movement, which peaked at 400+ females/day on 7 July 1977, through the Akulik-Inglutalik delta region. Some males begin their body molt while caring for the brood; they may leave the chicks up to a week before they fledge. As the young begin fledging, they, and some adult males, form flocks of 100-200 on tundra ponds (Noble and Wright 1977, Woodby and Divoky 1983). Young remain in their natal areas for about a month after hatching (Shields and Peyton 1979, Reynolds 1987). Onshore numbers drop rapidly after July, with most birds gone from the Norton Sound wetlands by early August (Woodby and Divoky 1983) and from Cape Espenberg by 7-12 August (Schamel et al. 1979). There is apparently no major premigratory staging on the Seward Peninsula, as there is at Stebbins (Woodby and Divoky 1983) and on the Yukon Delta (Gill and Handel 1981).

Small numbers remain onshore through the first week of September (latest, one, 21 September 1980, Safety Sound, D. A. Woodby unpubl. notes), but they are apparently still offshore through September, since up to 250 birds were sighted off the Chukchi coast of Cape Espenberg 21-24 September 1977 after a passing storm apparently forced them shoreward (Schamel et al. 1979).

Red Phalarope—*Phalaropus fulicaria*

A common, locally abundant, migrant and breeder, the Red Phalarope on the Seward Peninsula is largely restricted to the coastlines that are washed by Bering Shelf Offshore Waters. It breeds mainly in the Coastal Lowlands from Wales to Cape

Espenberg, including in the fringe of wetlands in Shishmaref Inlet at the mouths of the Serpentine and Arctic rivers; a few also have been reported breeding at Breving Lagoon (Woodby and Divoky 1983). During migration it may be locally common as far into Norton Sound as Safety Sound, but it is rare along the coastlines of inner Norton Sound and southern Kotzebue Sound. Twice birds have been reported inland in Wet Meadow habitat along the Kuzitrin River at about Milepost 69 Taylor Highway (three, 5 June 1969, D. G. Roseneau and P. Wright unpubl. notes; pair, June 1975, Drury 1976b), but whether these were breeders or spring migrants is unknown. Densities in Wet Meadow habitat at Cape Espenberg have been reported at 6.4-7.2 nests/10 ha, whereas densities on the tundra flats near Wales were calculated at about 8.8 birds/10 ha (Connors and Connors 1985:Fig. 14B). While onshore, Red Phalaropes are seldom far from salt water, favoring areas of flat, fairly extensive wetlands. I have found them most numerous in the Wet Meadow-Pond habitat complex; a few also breed in Salt Grass Meadow, such as that at the mouth of Arctic River, where, on 26 June 1970, I counted 20 individuals during a 2-h walk across the flats and where a nest with four eggs was found on 24 June 1977 by J. M. Wright (unpubl. notes).

Except when breeding, Red Phalaropes are oceanic birds. The main wintering concentrations in the Pacific, which undoubtedly include the Seward Peninsula birds, are in the plankton-rich upwellings along the outer fringes of the Humboldt Current off western South America, especially off Chile (Cramp 1983). They are oceanic migrants, apparently moving primarily through the eastern Pacific (ibid.). With remarkable consistency, the first arrive in the northern Bering and southern Chukchi seas between 25 and 29 May (earliest, two males and two females, 25 May 1983, Wales, M. L. Ward unpubl. notes). Numbers increase quickly (e.g., at Wales, first seen 27 May 1964 and arrived in "large numbers" 28 May [Breckenridge and Cline 1967]; and eight birds, most of them females, seen 28 May 1979, but 400 seen at inshore ice leads the next day [S. Hills unpubl. notes]) and usually peak sometime during the first week of June, when many thousands are moving northward off the western coasts of the Peninsula; the passage continues to mid-June (100 on 17 June 1987, Safety Sound, M. W. Schwan and R. H. Armstrong unpubl. notes). On average, there is a tendency for females to slightly precede males in migration, although they sometimes arrive together at onshore breeding sites (Cramp 1983).

Pairing occurs either immediately upon arrival onshore or perhaps sometimes on marine waters just before birds come ashore (Cramp 1983). Red Phalarope breeding behavior includes a reversal of sex roles, wherein the female performs the "circle" aerial courtship display (Ridley 1980) and is the more aggressive member of the pair and the male incubates the eggs and cares for the chicks. First-year birds are capable of breeding (Schamel and Tracy 1977). Mating may be monogamous or serially polyandrous, with the pair bond varying from a few days to 2 weeks (ibid., Ridley 1980). Neither sex exhibits territorialism (Mayfield 1979, Schamel and Tracy 1987). Members of the pair search together for a nest site, one joining its mate when it begins a scrape and often sharing in the scraping activity; but only the male adds linings and forms the cavities (Mayfield 1979, Ridley 1980). The female chooses the final nest site by laying her first egg, after which the male rapidly adds lining from surrounding blades of sedges or grass and other small leaves (Mayfield 1979). Nests are usually in moist habitats, but often on a raised ridge, hummock, or tussock that provides a relatively dry site; they are often concealed by overhanging sedges, grasses, or low shrubs. Sites may be some distance from open water; on Bathurst Island, Canada, nests ranged from 5 to 200 m from water, averaging 67 m (Mayfield 1979).

Copulation in Red Phalaropes is almost always on land or in standing-depth water (Kistchinski 1975, Mayfield 1979, Ridley 1980). The usual clutch is 4 eggs; 78 clutches at Cape Espenberg averaged 3.7±0.7 eggs (range 1-4 eggs)(Schamel and Tracy 1987), and 25 of 26 clutches on the north coast of the Chukotsk Peninsula in 1970 contained 4 eggs (Kistchinski 1975). Small clutches may occur more frequently in phenologically late years (ibid.). Eggs are laid at approximately 24-h intervals, with the period decreasing slightly as laying progresses (Mayfield 1979). The male begins sitting on the eggs briefly as soon as the first one is laid, but apparently does not begin effective incubation until just before the last egg is deposited, because hatching is essentially synchronous (Mayfield 1979, Schamel and Tracy 1977). The length of incubation varies with the attentiveness of the males, being shortest in later nests and at higher latitudes (Schamel and Tracy 1987). At Cape Espenberg, the mean incubation at seven nests was 20.1±2.7 days, with a range of 17-24 days (ibid.); whereas at Wales, the mean at six nests was 22.5 days, with a range of 21-26 days (Erckmann 1981). The male removes the broken shells from the nest as the eggs hatch, and the young remain in the nest until they are dry (Mayfield 1979). The male then leads the brood to the vegetated fringes of nearby ponds for feeding, remaining relatively attentive to the chicks for about 5 days (ibid.). The male leaves the brood at varying times, anywhere from an average of 4.8 days (Erckmann 1981) to fledging (Cramp 1983). The young fledge at about 20-21 days (D. Schamel in litt.).

On the Seward Peninsula, egg-laying begins about a week after the phalaropes arrive onshore. At Cape Espenberg, the first eggs were laid on 6 June 1976 and 1977; the first young were noted on 29 June 1977 but not until 2 July 1976 (Schamel et al. 1979:Fig. 91). Egg-laying may continue in the population for almost a month, especially in early seasons (Schamel and Tracy 1987). Thus, fledging should begin in the third week of July and continue through mid- to late August.

Food items consist primarily of invertebrates, although some plant materials, especially seeds, may be taken (Cramp 1983). The range of diet is wide and includes larval and adult dipteran flies, beetles, molluscs, crustaceans, annelids, etc. (ibid.). Food is taken from substrate surfaces, or, in the case of females, just below the surface (Ridley 1980), and some flying insects are snatched from the air. Food is obtained while the birds are swimming, wading, and walking.

Adult Red Phalaropes return to sea soon after completing their breeding duties, the departure of females occurring about the time of hatching in the population, i.e., in late June and early July, and the successful males beginning to leave about mid-July, shortly before the first young begin fledging. The young birds apparently leave for the sea soon after fledging, also, with onshore numbers on the Peninsula dropping sharply about 17-24 July (Connors 1978, Schamel et al. 1979, D. A. Woodby and K. V. Hirsch unpubl. notes). The movement of juvenals directly to Offshore Waters is in striking contrast to their massive post-fledging movements to littoral areas in Northern Alaska (Connors et al. 1979). Red Phalaropes remain rare on the Peninsula until mid-September (17 juveniles, 11 September 1977, Wales, D. A. Woodby and K. V. Hirsch unpubl. notes; one each, 15 and 16 September 1977, Cape Espenberg, Schamel et al. 1979; ''a few,'' mid-September 1975, in surf at Bluff, Drury 1976b), but apparently continue to migrate through the Strait at least until mid-October (latest, one, 18 October 1970, Bering Strait, Watson and Divoky 1972; but, extralimitally, 22 October [yr?], Cape Thompson, Chukchi Sea, Williamson et al. 1966).

Pomarine Jaeger—*Stercorarius pomarinus*

The Pomarine Jaeger is a common migrant, an uncommon summer visitant, and a very rare breeder on the Seward Peninsula, where it occurs primarily in Offshore and Inshore waters and in the Coastal Lowlands. Occasionally it gets farther inland, such as an apparent pair that S. O. MacDonald and I watched flying in the vicinity of Harris Dome on 1 July 1971.

This species is primarily pelagic in winter, with the Alaska population apparently wintering mainly in the tropical waters of the Pacific Ocean (American Ornithologists' Union 1983, Cramp 1983). It migrates, often in large flocks, both coastally and over open seas, and it may be found along leads and polynyas in the sea ice in the Bering and Chukchi seas during spring migration. The earliest migrants arrive in mid-May (two, 14 May 1978, extralimitally at Kotzebue, D. P. Harrington in litt.; first seen, 16 May 1976, Shishmaref, Noble and Wright 1977). The spring movement peaks during the last few days of May and the first few days of June (Flock and Hubbard 1979, Woodby and Divoky 1983), but a few birds continue to move northward through the third week of June.

The Seward Peninsula is south of the main breeding range of the Pomarine Jaeger, although it has been known to breed as far south as the Yukon-Kuskokwim Delta (Brandt 1943). A nest, in which the eggs hatched about 4 July, was found at the mouth of Arctic River in 1976 (Noble and Wright 1977); and Pomarines probably bred in the region in 1967, when J. J. Burns (pers. comm.) reported them as being more numerous over the tundra than they had been any year since he arrived in 1961.

The preferred food of Pomarine Jaegers during the summer is voles and lemmings, primarily *Microtus oeconomus* and *Lemmus sibiricus*, but when these arvicolines are unavailable, they feed opportunistically on a variety of other animal foods, including small birds, carrion, fish, and some insects and marine invertebrates (Maher 1974). Breeding on the Seward Peninsula apparently occurs only in years when populations of arvicoline rodents are unusually high (see Brandt 1943, Pitelka et al. 1955b, Maher 1974).

In years when food resources on the northern breeding grounds are insufficient to support breeding, a major exodus of non- or failed breeders occurs in late June and early July (Maher 1974, Johnson et al. 1975, Lehnhausen and Quinlan 1981). But in years of successful breeding, departures from the breeding grounds do not begin until the second week of August at Barrow, and all birds have left their territories there by the first week of September (Pitelka et al. 1955b). The fall movement past Icy Cape in the Chukchi Sea in 1980 occurred mainly between 24 August and 15 September (Lehnhausen and Quinlan 1981).

Few fall migrants are seen about the shores of Norton Sound, indicating that the movement is primarily through the offshore waters. Over 100 adults were counted moving southwest between King and St. Lawrence islands 15-21 August 1986 (R. R. Veit in litt.). Peak fall migration probably occurs between late August and mid-September (latest, one, 18 October 1970, Bering Strait, Watson and Divoky 1972).

Pomarine Jaegers have both a light and dark color morph. Off Lopp Lagoon between 2 and 10 July 1974, five of 40 birds (12.5%) I saw were dark morphs.

Parasitic Jaeger—*Stercorarius parasiticus*

In the region as a whole, the Parasitic Jaeger is a fairly common breeder. It is most numerous, even common, in the Coastal Lowlands of the tundra portions of the Peninsula and somewhat less numerous in the Interior Lowlands (except Imuruk Basin) and in the Northern and Southern uplands. I found the greatest breeding season numbers (60+ individuals/3-day count) in the Buckland River estuary and at Cape Espenberg, and the second greatest numbers (30+/3-day counts) in the Shishmaref Inlet area, about the flats and barrier strip off Lopp Lagoon, and in Imuruk Basin. At Cape Espenberg during a 3-year study, 1976-1978, Schamel et al. (1979) estimated that 18-20 pairs nested each year and reported an unusually high density of 8 nests/ 10 ha in both 1976 and 1977. Unlike Pomarine Jaegers, which are dependent upon cyclic highs in vole and lemming populations for successful breeding, numbers of breeding Parasitic Jaegers do not exhibit extreme annual fluctuations (Maher 1974, Bergman et al. 1977, Schamel et al. 1979). Results of banding some adults at Cape Espenberg indicated a better than 85% return to the Cape and an apparent high fidelity to breeding territories of the previous year (Schamel et al. 1979).

During the breeding season, the Parasitic Jaeger is a bird of open tundra habitats, foraging widely over many of these habitats and nesting in those most open, e.g., Wet Meadow, Dwarf Shrub Meadow, and Dwarf Shrub Mat. If vistas are adequate, it is not averse to some nearby low- or even medium-height shrubbery, frequent habitat components in the uplands.

Wintering primarily in offshore coastal waters of the temperate and tropical Pacific Ocean (American Ornithologists' Union 1983), this jaeger migrates in both Offshore and Inshore waters, usually singly or in small groups. The first spring migrants may arrive at the Seward Peninsula from early to mid-May (earliest, 7 May 1981, Golovin, D. A. Woodby in litt.; and, extralimitally, 4-9 May in four reported years, Yukon-Kuskokwim Delta, Yukon Delta NWR unpubl. data, and 16 May 1978, Kotzebue, D. P. Harrington in litt.). The main movement, including transients to more northern breeding grounds, occurs from the fourth week of May through the first week of June, however; and, at least in some years, significant movement may continue until at least mid-June.

Arriving breeders apparently occupy their territories almost as soon as they arrive and lay their eggs within another 7-10 days (Maher 1974, Martin and Barry 1978). Nests, which are little more than a slight depression in the soil, are placed on relatively dry sites, either on elevated sites in wet areas, such as on hummocks, tussocks, or other raised areas, or on dry upland sites. Most clutches from northwest Alaska consist of two eggs (five of six clutches in my Seward Peninsula records; 18 of 20 nests reported by Maher [1974]; all of seven nests reported by Bergman et al. [1977]), although a few consist of only a single egg. Incubation begins with the first egg and lasts for close to 26 days (Maher 1974). The downy young leave the nest within a few days, but remain on the territory until well after fledging (Martin and Barry 1978). They fledge at about 29-30 days of age, but show at least partial dependence on the parents for 2-3 weeks after fledging (Maher 1974). Both members of the pair share in incubation and care of the young (Parmelee et al. 1967, Martin and Barry 1978).

Based on these data, early breeders on the Seward Peninsula should be laying eggs at least by 20 May, with peak laying being from the fourth week of May to the first week of June. Most hatching would then occur during the last half of June and most fledging during the last half of July. A late nest at Wales, probably a renesting attempt, still had eggs, however, on 16 July 1936 (Bailey 1943). This breeding schedule agrees with the observations of Woodby and Divoky (1983), who reported that a few fledged jaegers [species?] were seen in mid-July 1980 and 1981 and that most had fledged by the end of July.

While on their breeding grounds, Parasitic Jaegers are primarily bird predators, especially preying on passerines and shorebirds (Maher 1974, Martin and Barry 1978). They feed opportunistically on a wide range of items, however, including voles and lemmings, especially when such populations are high; eggs from exposed nests of loons, waterfowl, and terns; young waterfowl and ptarmigan; small fish pirated from terns, small gulls, and loons; and, less frequently, insects, berries, and carrion (Maher 1974, Eisenhauer and Paniyak 1977, Martin and Barry 1978, Schamel et al. 1979, Kessel pers. obs.). After the young have hatched, pairs frequently hunt together in teams (Pruett-Jones 1980), a behavior I have witnessed several times, including an episode at Cape Espenberg in which a pair of Parasitic Jaegers attempted unsuccessfully to decoy both Willow Ptarmigan parents away from their brood simultaneously. In the fighting, one ptarmigan would pursue a jaeger up 6-10 m into the air, and then the second jaeger would fly after the attacking ptarmigan, causing it to retreat to the ground. While one ptarmigan was involved in the chase, the other either stood by, ready to protect the chicks, or attempted to distract the second jaeger.

While some non- or failed breeders have begun their southward migration by July (flock of eight flew south past Wales, 18 July 1978, D. R. Paulson in litt.), successful breeders do not begin their exodus until August. At Icy Cape in the Chukchi Sea, the main fall movement in 1980 was between 24 August and 6 September, with the last one seen on 18 September (Lehnhausen and Quinlan 1981). At the Cape Espenberg breeding site, numbers decreased over the last 3 weeks of August 1976 and 1977, leaving numbers much reduced by early September (Schamel et al. 1979). They become rare on the Peninsula after about 10-11 September (latest, 18 September 1977, Cape Espenberg, Schamel et al. 1979, and 27 September 1980, Safety Sound, D. A. Woodby unpubl. notes; but, extralimitally, 29 September [yr?], Cape Thompson, Williamson et al. 1966, and 30 September 1970, Chukchi Sea at about 70°20' N, Watson and Divoky 1972).

Parasitic Jaegers have both a light and dark color morph. On the northern portions of the Seward Peninsula, dark morphs make up about 10-17% of the population (Schamel et al. 1979, Kessel and D. D. Gibson unpubl. notes).

Long-tailed Jaeger—*Stercorarius longicaudus*

A common breeder, the Long-tailed Jaeger is dispersed widely over the entire Peninsula, except in forested habitats. It is most abundant, however, in the Southern Uplands and Northern Uplands, where I recorded apparently breeding individuals or pairs fairly evenly distributed at one per 1.6 km in appropriate habitats between Nome and Teller on 24 June 1971 and in the expanses of Dwarf Shrub Meadow between Mileposts 71 and 83 Taylor Highway on 8 July 1967 and again on 22 June 1977. It is relatively uncommon in the Coastal Lowlands compared to the Parasitic Jaeger, although where lowlands are adjacent to uplands, such as at Wales (but not out on the Lopp Lagoon flats and barrier strip) and Imuruk Basin, the Long-tailed Jaeger is more abundant than where uplands are more remote. Numbers of Long-tailed Jaegers show some annual variation, apparently in response to population levels of voles and lemmings. In 1970, for example, W. Walker and D. G. Roseneau (pers. comm.) reported that there were "lots more" Long-tails on the Peninsula in June than in 1969, but only about half as many as in 1968. Studies elsewhere (Maher 1974, Andersson 1976b) have shown that a core population of Long-tailed Jaegers tends to return each year to established territories, and in years of high vole or lemming populations, additional pairs, apparently younger birds, establish territories and breed.

As other jaegers on the Peninsula, the Long-tails during the breeding season forage over essentially all open tundra habitats. They nest in the drier tundras, however, especially in Dwarf Shrub Meadow and Dwarf Shrub Mat and especially where openings, slopes or banks, mounds, or ridges provide views of the surrounding landscape.

Long-tailed Jaegers are highly pelagic during the nonbreeding season, with the western North American populations wintering mostly at sea off South America from Ecuador to Chile and migrating to and from the Southern Hemisphere well offshore (American Ornithologists' Union 1983). The first spring migrants may arrive by early May (earliest, 9 May 1981, Golovin, D. A. Woodby in litt., and 10 May 1988, Deering, J. D. Walters unpubl. notes; extralimitally, 8 May [yr?], Mountain Village, Gabrielson and Lincoln 1959, and 4 May 1980, Old Chevak, Yukon-Kuskokwim Delta, C. M. Boise in litt.), but the main influx usually begins 12-14 May and continues through the rest of the month. A few migrants may still be moving through during early June (100+ birds on 8 June 1982, mostly at Safety Sound feeding on crowberries in groups of up to 15 individuals, J. L. Dunn in litt.).

Arriving breeders settle on their territories almost immediately and begin egg-laying within 1-2 weeks (Maher 1974). Nests consist merely of a depression in the substrate, often on a somewhat elevated site. The usual clutch is two eggs, the maximum size that this species is capable of incubating because of the manner in which it holds the egg between its foot and the corresponding brood patch (Andersson 1976a). A few clutches consist of only a single egg, a situation, according to Andersson (1976b), that occurs more frequently when vole and lemming populations are not high. In two-egg clutches, the laying interval is usually 2 days, with incubation beginning with the first egg (Maher 1974). Incubation for five eggs on Ellesmere Island averaged 24.2 days (range 23-25 days) (Maher 1970), and other researchers have reported eggs that hatched in 24-25 days (Parmalee et al. 1967, Maher 1974, Andersson 1976b). The young leave the nest within a few days after hatching; siblings separate, but remain on the territory, sometimes 200-300 m from the nest site, until after fledging (Andersson 1971, 1976b). The average fledging age is 25 days, but may vary from 22 to about 28 days, depending in part on the availability of food resources (Maher 1974, Andersson 1976b). Families remain on their territories for 1-2 weeks after the young have fledged (ibid.). Both parents share in incubation and care of the young (ibid.); unlike Parasitic Jaegers, the parent Long-tails hunt singly, with one remaining at the nest and leaving only when the other returns (Maher 1974). Some renesting after loss of clutches has been reported for this species (Maher 1970, Andersson 1976a).

Using the above data to back-date from observed events shows that some egg-laying on the Seward Peninsula begins as early as 25-27 May (one young and one pipping egg, 17 June 1970, head of Banner Ck, D. G. Roseneau and W. Walker, ANRS; a flying juvenal with a parent, 12 July 1967, Safety Sound barrier strip, Kessel pers. obs.); it continues until the third week of June, apparently peaking during the first two weeks of June. Thus, hatching dates would range from mid-June to mid-July and fledging dates from the second week of July into the second week of August (one-third-grown chick, extralimitally at Cape Blossom, south of Kotzebue, 30 July 1898, Grinnell 1900a).

When on land during the summer, Long-tailed Jaegers show a diet preference for voles and lemmings, but they also prey on small birds, especially passerines and juvenal shorebirds, and feed to varying degrees, especially in low rodent years, on insects, berries, and carrion (Maher 1974, Andersson 1976b). In years of high arvicoline abundance in northern Sweden, Andersson (1976b) reported that adult weight and egg volume in Long-tailed Jaegers were greater, chicks grew faster, and chick mortality was lower than in other years and that three-fourths of successful chick production in the population occurred in years of high arvicoline populations; few, if any, pairs successfully raised young during periods of low arvicoline densities.

Almost every year, flocks of non- or failed breeders form between about 21 June and the first week of July. Such flocks consistently loaf and feed along the west-facing foothills of the Kigluaik Mountains between Mileposts 36 and 40 Teller Highway, where I observed flocks of 18-35 birds in 1967, 1969, 1971, and 1977. I have seen smaller flocks less consistently between Mileposts 42 and 46 Taylor Highway and on the Safety Sound barrier strip. These flocks largely disappear by mid-July, the birds having moved back to ocean habitats. Successful breeders and their families begin to vacate their territories and leave for Offshore Waters by the first of August. They are still fairly common onshore in mid-August, but disappear rapidly thereafter; 50-75 adults were counted moving southwest over waters between King and St. Lawrence islands 15-21 August 1986, including a flock of 13 on 21 August off King Island (R. R. Veit in litt.). Long-tailed Jaegers are rare onshore after 1 September (latest, 12 birds, 4 September 1977, Cape Espenberg, Schamel et al. 1979; one, 8 September 1973, migrating southward along the beach near Wales, D. D. Gibson unpubl. notes).

Common Black-headed Gull—*Larus ridibundus*

A very rare spring migrant and summer visitor from Siberia, the Common Black-headed Gull has been recorded on the Seward Peninsula six times in recent years: one, 5 June 1976, Safety Sound, and one, 8 June 1977, Nome River mouth (Kessel and Gibson 1978); one immature, 29 May 1979, Nome (R. W. Stallcup in litt.); a second-year bird, 11 July 1985, Koyana Creek near Bluff (M. P. Harris and E. C. Murphy pers. comm.), one, 21 July 1987, Nome River mouth (W. E. Rodstrom in litt.), and one, 14 June 1988, Nome River mouth (K. J. Zimmer in litt.). A sighting by Bailey (1943:102) on 29 May 1922 of "a single individual winging over the ice pack of Bering Strait, well offshore from the Cape" was probably of a Black-headed Gull, although it was reported as a Bonaparte's Gull.

Bonaparte's Gull—*Larus philadelphia*

Primarily a taiga bird, the Bonaparte's Gull is an uncommon breeder in the spruce woodlands of the southeast quadrant of the Peninsula, where it occurs about lacustrine waters along river drainages and tributaries as far west as the Fish and lower Niukluk rivers. It has been seen by all visitors to this latter area (16-19 July 1966, R. A. Rausch and J. J. Burns unpubl. notes; 15-16 July 1973, Kessel and D. D. Gibson unpubl notes; 4 July 1977, N. G. Tankersley in litt.; 14-15 July 1980 and 27-31 May 1981, D. A. Woodby unpubl. notes). Beyond the limit of spruce, it is a rare spring migrant and summer visitant (one, Topkok Head, 4 June 1983, R. and B. Mearns unpubl. notes; one, near Safety Sound inlet, 9 July 1969, Kessel pers. obs.; one, Nome, 12 June 1975, Drury 1976b; seven, briefly at the mouth of the Nome R, 15 June 1986, K. Kaufman in litt.; seen, Teller, 24 July 1946, Gabrielson and Lincoln 1959; one, Wales, 7-9 June 1983, M. L. Ward unpubl. notes; two with Sabine's Gulls and Arctic Terns, 4 June 1984, and one, 29 May and two 30 May 1986, the latter with Sabine's Gulls, all Deering, J. D. Walters unpubl. notes; one with Sabine's Gulls, Arctic R, 3 June 1976, Noble and Wright 1977). Reports by Grinnell (1900a:11) of "several...over a pond near the coast" at the northeast end of Lopp Lagoon on 28 June 1898 and "quite a number" near Cape Lowenstern, Shishmaref Inlet, on 1 July 1898 were more likely of Sabine's Gulls, which he did not report for this area. A similar error was made by Thayer (1951).

Spring migrants probably arrive during the second week of May (arrival dates extralimitally at Ambler, Kobuk R, ranged from 5 to 12 May between 1975 and 1980, D. K. Wik in litt.). Aside from the regular presence of birds in breeding habitat during July, the only breeding evidence is of an adult followed by three begging fledglings that D. D. Gibson and I watched at McCarthys Marsh on 15 July 1973.

Mew Gull—*Larus canus*

Primarily an inland species, the Mew Gull is a common breeder and summer visitant throughout the Interior Lowlands, about upland ponds, lakes, and rivers, and in the Coastal Lowlands at protected locations, such as river estuaries and river deltas surrounded by lagoon systems. Here it nests in Wet Meadow habitat along the margins and on islets of lakes, ponds, and sloughs. It is rare during the breeding season on the wetlands of exposed barrier strips (e.g., Wales and Cape Espenberg), although up to 100 birds (mostly non- or failed breeders?) may gather to loaf and feed at lagoon inlets and on mud and sand flats at the mouths of the major rivers. Some of these latter birds also fly and forage along the open coastline of Norton and Kotzebue sounds. Abundance of Mew Gulls increases along the coast, especially at inlets and river mouths, from mid-July into August, as first the failed breeders and then successful families leave their inland nesting areas.

Mew Gulls winter along the sea coasts as far north as Prince William Sound (Isleib and Kessel 1973), the Aleutian Islands (Byrd et al. 1974), and the north shore of the Alaska Peninsula (Gill et al. 1981). They migrate overland as well as coastally, and, in some years, may arrive at the Seward Peninsula as early as the first week of May (earliest, one, 7 May 1986, two, 8 May 1988 and 10 May 1987, Deering, and three, 10 May 1983, Nome, J. D. Walters, unpubl. notes; but, extralimitally, one, 1 May 1986, St. Marys, B. J. McCaffery unpubl. notes; two, 7 May 1978, Kotzebue, D. P. Harrington in litt.; present when observers arrived, 8 May 1977, Akulik-Inglutalik R delta, Shields and Peyton 1979). Migration may continue into early June (first recorded, 30 May 1969, Wales, Flock and Hubbard 1979; "fairly numerous," 28 and 29 May 1922, Wales, and "in migration," 3 June 1922, Little Diomede I, Bailey 1925:102).

Little is known about the breeding biology of this subspecies of Mew Gull (*L. c. brachyrhynchus*). Its nest on the Seward Peninsula is a depression in the ground, often on a slightly raised site. Egg-laying occurs during late May and early June, as soon as spring thaw exposes nesting sites. Clutches consist of one to three eggs, with at least 76% in Alaska being three eggs (ANRS). Eggs are laid at approximately 2-day intervals (Barth 1955). Incubation for 37 eggs at Anchorage, Alaska, averaged 24.3 ± 1.4 days, range 23-28 days (C. I. Adamson in litt.). The young leave the nest 3-5 days after hatching and hide along nearby vegetated shorelines, where they are vigorously guarded by their parents. Fledging begins at 25 days (C. I. Adamson in litt.). Chicks at various stages of growth are common on the Peninsula throughout July, with first fledglings reported for nearby areas at the end of July (27 July 1956, Selawik, Hudson 1957; 2 August 1976, Akulik-Inglutalik R delta, Shields and Peyton 1979).

The Mew Gull's basic diet, whether inland or along the coast, consists of many kinds of invertebrates, both terrestrial and aquatic, and small fishes; many other items are taken opportunistically, however, e.g., young birds and arvicolines, tundra berries, carrion, and garbage (Cramp 1983). Food items are picked from any substrate while the bird is walking or swimming, by dipping into water when flying or swimming, by pirating from other birds, and by scavenging from vertebrate carcasses.

Southward movement is under way at least by mid-August, and few birds are in evidence after early September (latest, "immature," 12 September 1984, Inmachuk R, J. D. Walters unpubl. notes; "immature," 13 September 1980, and adult, 21 September 1980, Safety Sound, D. A. Woodby unpubl. notes).

Herring Gull—*Larus argentatus*

An uncommon migrant and summer visitant along the coastlines, the Herring Gull has been recorded around almost the entire periphery of the Peninsula, but least commonly along the southern Kotzebue Sound coast (one at Igloo Point, 24 June 1975, Kessel and F. G. Scheider pers. obs.). Between 4 and 7 June 1976, 30+ adults, apparently nonbreeders, moved inland in a northeast direction from the Koyuk River (Shields and Peyton 1977). The only evidence of breeding is a report of a mixed Herring Gull-Glaucous Gull pair that produced young at Bluff in 1977 (Drury et al. 1978).

Some Herring Gulls of two subspecies (see below) winter as far north as the Pacific coasts of Southwestern (Aleutian Is—Sutton and Wilson 1946, Byrd et al. 1974) and Southcoastal Alaska (Kodiak Archipelago—MacIntosh 1986; North Gulf Coast-Prince William Sound—Isleib and Kessel 1973). Based on dates of observations in adjacent regions, spring migrants probably arrive at the Seward Peninsula in early May (earliest, extralimitally at St. Lawrence I [*vegae*], a few, 1 May 1954, R. A. Ryder unpubl. notes, and present, 7 May 1964, Thompson 1967; at St. Marys [probably *smithsonianus*], one, 30 April 1986, B. J. McCaffery unpubl. notes; and at Ambler [*smithsonianus*], first seen, 13 May 1972, D. K. Wik in litt.).

While a few birds, both adults and immatures, frequent the Coastal Lowlands throughout the summer, numbers, especially of juvenals and subadults, increase somewhat in late August and September. They were still "fairly common, mostly juvenals" at Safety Sound on 21 September 1980, but only one remained on 27 September 1980 (D. A. Woodby unpubl. notes). A few individuals remain into October (latest, six, 18 October 1970, Bering Strait, Watson and Divoky 1972; and extralimitally, adult and immature on 17 October and two adults on 19 October 1960, Cape Thompson, Swartz 1966).

Complicating our sketchy knowledge of the phenology and ecology of this gull in the region is the presence of two subspecies (Bailey 1948, subsequent obs.). The Peninsula is an overlap zone of the range peripheries (nonbreeders) of the dark-backed, cliff-nesting *L. a. vegae* from northeastern Siberia and the lighter-colored flat-land-nesting *L. a. smithsonianus* from Central and Southcoastal Alaska. The Herring Gull of the mixed breeding pair at Bluff in 1977 was identified by Drury as *vegae* (Patten 1980).

Thayer's Gull—*Larus thayeri*

The Thayer's Gull is a casual fall migrant along the coasts of the Seward Peninsula. An adult (USNM 536464) was collected near Nome in September 1970, and another specimen (USNM 78786) was collected extralimitally at St. Michael on 6 October 1878 by E. W. Nelson.

This gull breeds in the Canadian arctic islands (American Ornithologists' Union 1983) and apparently migrates overland to its primary wintering grounds along the Pacific Coast of North America (Isleib and Kessel 1973, MacIntosh 1986, American Ornithologists' Union 1983). It is an uncommon fall migrant, however, as far west in the Beaufort Sea as Barrow (Bailey 1948, Gabrielson and Lincoln 1959, Kessel and D. D. Gibson unpubl. data).

Several spring sightings from the Bering Sea and Kotzebue Sound regions have been reported, including reasonable descriptions of adults from Kotzebue (18 May 1985 and 4 May 1986, T. J. Doyle in litt.), St. Marys (13 May 1985, B. J. McCaffery unpubl.

notes), and St. Lawrence Island (4 June 1978, A. H. Rider in litt.); but the chances of confusing this gull with possible *Larus* hybrids are so great that spring occurrences must remain hypothetical until specimens are obtained.

Slaty-backed Gull—*Larus schistisagus*

The Slaty-backed Gull, a Beringian species, is an uncommon migrant and rare summer visitant to the coasts of the Seward Peninsula, where it has been recorded from outer Kotzebue Sound (one subadult at Cape Espenberg, 4 July 1973, Kessel and D. D. Gibson unpubl. notes) to Rocky Point (one showing territorialism in 1977, Drury et al. 1978) and off St. Michael (8 September 1915, Hersey 1917).

This gull winters commonly at the edge of the sea ice in the southern Bering Sea (G. E. Hall unpubl. notes, G. J. Divoky in litt., R. H. Day in litt.); and some birds follow the retreating sea-ice front zone northward, reaching the Seward Peninsula in mid- to late May (four adults, 16 May 1963, Wales, Kessel and Gibson 1978; 22 May 1964, near Nome, S. B. Young unpubl. notes; five adults, 26 May 1963, Fairway Rock, and one, 28 May 1976, off Wales, Kessel and Gibson 1978; one, 27 May 1979, Wales, S. Hills unpubl. notes; one adult, 28 May 1979, Nome R mouth, and one adult and at least three subadults, 28 and 29 May 1987, Wales P. J. Baicich in litt.). From then until September, adults and immatures frequent the coastlines, inlets, and river estuaries in small numbers. Most observations have been of one to three birds, but on a windy 29 June 1977, I counted four third-year and several second-year Slaty-backed Gulls with a large group of other gulls at the mouth of the Nome River, and T. G. Tobish (in litt.) saw at least 11 birds there on 15 June 1983 and 39+ on 9 July 1984.

September records are few, but there were at least five adults at Bluff on 7 September 1976, at least three immatures at Wales 9-11 September 1973 (Kessel and Gibson 1978), five adults near Nome on 11 September 1985 (R. H. Day unpubl. notes), and two females collected off Nome on 19 September and another on 21 September 1913 (J. Koren unpubl. notes).

Glaucous-winged Gull—*Larus glaucescens*

The Beringian Glaucous-winged Gull is a rare spring migrant and summer visitant and uncommon fall visitant along the coast and in Offshore Waters of the Seward Peninsula. It is an abundant resident in the southern Bering Sea but is replaced as a breeder in the northern Bering Sea by its ecological counterpart, the Holarctic Glaucous Gull. Glaucous-winged Gulls winter as far north in the Bering Sea as the sea-ice front zone (Irving et al. 1970, G. E. Hall unpubl. notes, G. J. Divoky in litt., Divoky 1977, Gould et al. 1982), and a few nonbreeders move northward with the sea-ice front in spring. Nelson (1887:53) stated that they arrived at St. Michael "early in May with *barrovianus* [=Glaucous Gull] and remain until the end of October," and Bailey (1925) reported seeing "a few" at Wales during a blow on 18 May 1922. Later, however, because of subsequent problems of identifying specimens collected along the Chukchi Sea coast and a general lack of information about the status of this species in the region, Bailey (1943) worried about his own sight identification.

A few birds, both adults and immatures and mostly singles, frequent the coastlines throughout June and July (Drury 1976b, Shields and Peyton 1977, P. W. Sykes in litt., D. A. Woodby unpubl. notes, Kessel pers obs.). Fifteen first-year gulls, apparently of this species (''large, solid black bills''), were at Wales, however, on 27 July 1975 (P. G. Connors and R. S. Greenberg in litt.). Also at Wales, D. R. Paulson (unpubl. notes) saw one to two first-year Glaucous-winged Gulls regularly between 26 May and 22 June 1978 (when he departed) and he was able to examine a dead bird. He also saw birds he thought might be Glaucous X Glaucous-winged hybrids or Glaucous X Herring hybrids.

Numbers, especially of immatures, increase during August and September, especially along the south coast from Wales into Norton Sound, where Woodby and Divoky (1983) reported them frequenting salmon spawning areas. They were reported as ''common'' at Wales 6-11 September 1977 and ''fairly common'' at Safety Sound on 13 September 1980 (D. A. Woodby unpubl. notes), and at least three adults and two second-year birds were observed with Glaucous Gulls along the outer beach near Wales on 7 and 8 September 1973 (D. D. Gibson unpubl. notes). The latest report has been of two birds on 27 September 1980 at Safety Sound (D. A. Woodby unpubl. notes), but a few undoubtedly remain until freeze-up in October.

Glaucous Gull—*Larus hyperboreus*

An abundant migrant and summer visitant and a common breeder and very rare winter visitant, the Glaucous Gull occurs at most of the wetlands of the Peninsula, nesting throughout the Interior and Coastal lowlands and about the lakes and major rivers in the uplands, as well as at coastal cliffs, and loafing and feeding along the coastal beaches, lagoons, and estuaries.

Glaucous Gulls regularly winter as far north as the southern Bering Sea, where numbers are present within the ice front zone (about 5 birds/km² in March-April 1976, Divoky 1977); a few overwinter as far north as open water is available, such as the polynyas at St. Lawrence Island (Fay and Cade 1959, Johnson 1976, Searing 1977) and open leads off Point Hope in the southern Chukchi Sea (Swartz 1966). They are one of the earliest migrants to arrive in the spring, the earliest arriving during the third week of April (15 April 1967 at Nome dump, J. J. Burns unpubl. notes; 19 April 1960 at Point Hope, Swartz 1966; 20 April 1922 at Wales, Bailey 1925; 22 April 1978 at Wales, Flock and Hubbard 1979). In most years they have arrived at the Seward Peninsula by the first week of May and are fairly common by mid-May; migratory movement continues into June (Woodby and Divoky 1983).

Pairs may nest singly, as is often the case at cliffs and along upland rivers, or in either loose or compact colonies, especially in river estuaries, on islands in lakes, and at wetlands on low-lying coastal spits and peninsulas. Nests at coastal cliffs are usually at or near the tops of cliffs or offshore rock stacks, either on grassy slopes immediately above the cliffs or on narrow projections or promontories at the tops of the cliffs. Away from cliffs, nests are most frequently surrounded by water—on islets in small ponds, islands in large lakes, alluvial islands in river estuaries, and commonly on tussocks, hummocks, or alluvial bars off the tips of small peninsulas—

out of easy reach of mammalian predators. Nests are constructed of available plant materials, and on some substrates may be large and bulky with a relatively deep cup. The greatest number of breeders at a Seward Peninsula sea cliff is at Rocky Point, where Drury et al. (1981) reported 55-75 pairs. On low-lying Cape Espenberg, Schamel et al. (1979) estimated 250 nests in 1976 and 300-350 in 1977, giving an unusually high density of 1.1-1.6 nests/10 ha.

Breeding schedules may vary as much as 2 weeks in response to spring weather conditions (Schamel et al. 1979, Springer et al. 1985a). In early seasons, egg-laying begins in late May (first egg on 21 May 1976 at Shishmaref Inlet, Noble and Wright 1977; peak laying, 20-28 May 1978 at Cape Espenberg, Schamel et al. 1979, and 27 May 1980 and 1981 in Norton Sound, Woodby and Divoky 1983). Clutch size usually varies from one to three eggs, with three being the most common (Swartz 1966, Steele and Drury 1977, Schamel et al. 1979); one four-egg and one five-egg clutch were reported from Cape Thompson in 1960 (Swartz 1966). Incubation lasts 22-28 days, averaging 26.6 ± 1.0 days (Strang 1976); so, while most hatching occurs in late June or early July, some may occur as early as mid-June (16 June 1960 and 1961 at Cape Thompson, Swartz 1966; eggs in "late stages of incubation" on 7 June 1953 at Little Diomede I, Kenyon and Brooks 1960; 4+-week-old chicks on 13 July 1975 at Topkok, Drury 1976a). Duration of the prefledging period may vary from 40 to 63 days, the wide range probably due to nutritional regimes (Schamel et al. 1979). At Cape Thompson, young capable of flight have been observed by the third week of July (Springer et al. 1985a), but the earliest reports from the Seward Peninsula have been 30 July (Woodby and Divoky 1983) and 1 August (Steele and Drury 1977, Ramsdell and Drury 1979). Most fledging on the Seward Peninsula does not occur until the second week of August and continues into early September (Steele and Drury 1977, Drury et al. 1978, Schamel et al. 1979), whereas most birds at Cape Thompson have fledged by 15-20 August (Swartz 1966, Springer et al. 1985a). Glaucous Gulls will renest after 8-14 days if eggs are lost early in incubation (Swartz 1966, Schamel et al. 1979), a fact taken into account by Eskimo egg gatherers. Two 10-day-old chicks at Safety Sound on 12 August 1980 (D. A. Woodby unpubl. notes) were probably from a renest and would not have fledged until mid-September, if at all.

Away from nesting locations during summer, Glaucous Gulls gather commonly along the coast, especially at or near the mouths of the larger rivers and at lagoon inlets; and transient groups form along the coast wherever such food as carrion (e.g., beached sea mammal carcasses and spent salmon) or garbage becomes available. Many, if not most, of the individuals in these coastal flocks appear to be nonbreeders, even though they include adult as well as subadult birds. The number of gulls using the coastline increases gradually from late July through early September, largely as a result of an influx of birds from elsewhere; their numbers are supplemented by newly fledged young after mid-August (Swartz 1966, Springer et al. 1985a, Ramsdell and Drury 1979, Schamel et al. 1979). A group of over 1500 Glaucous Gulls loafed on the beaches near Rocky Point on 4 August 1978 (Ramsdell and Drury 1979), about 1000 were on the delta of the Nugnugaluktuk River on 5 August 1981 (Eldridge 1982), and some 1130 were recorded along the beaches at Cape Espenberg on 5 September 1973, 800 together on the spit at the tip (D. D. Gibson unpubl. notes).

Glaucous Gulls feed primarily in Nearshore and Inshore waters, being most abundant near breeding colonies, along beaches, and in estuaries. Swartz (1967), however, reported them frequently out to about 40 km from land; he found them only occasionally farther from shore, and Ramsdell and Drury (1979) seldom saw them over the open sea unless associated with whale "smudges" or with seals and walruses on ice pans. In diet, these gulls are opportunists and extreme generalists, feeding on a wide range of vertebrate and invertebrate materials as predators or scavengers, with varying emphases on birds and their eggs, fish and fish offal, carrion, marine invertebrates, marine mammal birthing remains, Eskimo butcher leftovers, and household garbage (Fay and Cade 1959, Schamel et al. 1979, Drury et al. 1981, Sanger 1986, Kessel pers. obs., others); they may also take berries from the tundra in the fall (Drury 1976a, Schamel et al. 1979).

Because of the influx of gulls into the region beginning in late July, the time of the beginning of the main fall migration is difficult to ascertain. During the third week of August 1975, Drury (1976a) observed an eastward movement of adults and subadults past Bluff, but the peak of migration, at least farther north between Wainwright and Cape Thompson, is in mid- to late September (16 September 1921 at Wainwright, Bailey 1925; late September 1959 at Cape Thompson, F. S. L. Williamson MS; 10-27 September 1960 at Cape Thompson, Swartz 1966). Adults apparently vacate the breeding colonies before all the young have left, and, from late September to 21 October 1960 at Cape Thompson, immatures outnumbered adults along the beaches of the region (Swartz 1966). All age groups were still present at Bluff when observers left on 11 October 1976 (Steele and Drury 1977), and numbers did not begin to dwindle at Deering until 19 October 1985 (J. D. Walters unpubl. notes); twelve birds, including six adults, were still present at Deering on 27 October 1984 (ibid.). Populations are apparently augmented in late September and October by northern migrants, and Woodby and Divoky (1983) estimated that numbers in Norton Sound may reach 20,000 birds at this time, mostly in the northeastern portions. On 27 October 1980, during an aerial coastal survey between Nome and Koyuk, densities were calculated at 37.6 gulls/km, with almost half the birds in Golovnin Bay (ibid.).

A few stragglers remain in the region into November (at Deering, one flew past on 1 November 1983, three "immatures" were at an overflow on Kotzebue Sound on 4 November 1984, three adults were present on 3 November 1985, and one immature remained until 13 November 1985, J. D. Walters unpubl. notes), and the "gulls" at the Sinuk River on 8 November 1966 (J. J. Burns unpubl. notes) were probably this species (latest, young bird collected 7 December 1912 by J. Koren, "Diomede Island," Thayer and Bangs 1914).

A mixed Glaucous Gull-Herring Gull pair nested and produced offspring at Bluff in 1977 (Drury et al. 1978).

Black-legged Kittiwake—*Rissa tridactyla*

A common migrant and breeder, the Black-legged Kittiwake is found in summer at most of the mainland and island coastal cliffs of the Peninsula. Bluff, averaging 7900 birds, is the largest mainland colony; and King Island (6000 birds) and Little Diomede Island (20,000 birds) host the largest offshore colonies of the Peninsula (Tables 8 and 15). During the breeding season, these kittiwakes tend to feed within 13-32 km of their colonies if small fish are available, although they will forage

Table 15.   Number of Black-legged Kittiwakes at Bluff, Seward Peninsula, 1975-1987, as determined from census counts made between 1 July and 20 August (E. C. Murphy unpubl. data).

Year	No. kittiwakes
1975	5930
1976	4718
1977	6932
1978	6648
1979	9020
1980	9915
1981	10,332
1982	7642
1983	10,138
1984	696
1985	9980
1986	no data
1987	12,459

45-60 km offshore if necessary (Ramsdell and Drury 1979, Drury et al. 1981, Springer et al. 1984)—even up to 100 km before the young hatch (Hunt et al. 1981a). Birds farther from shore are probably mostly immatures and nonbreeders (Swartz 1967). Most of the kittiwakes seen flying along the coast at this time of year are traveling between breeding cliffs and foraging sites.

Black-legged Kittiwakes winter in oceanic waters as far north as the southern Bering Sea and northern Pacific Ocean (Preble and McAtee 1923, Gabrielson and Lincoln 1959, Shuntov 1972, Hunt et al. 1981b). Spring migration begins in mid-March with the warming of the ocean waters (Shuntov 1972), and during March and April kittiwakes are found in the vicinity of the sea-ice front zone in the Bering Sea (Irving et al. 1970, Divoky 1977). They move northward with the melting of the sea ice, the timing of which may vary widely from year to year. Kittiwakes sometimes reach the waters of the Seward Peninsula by mid-May (11 May 1958 and 15 May 1953, Kenyon and Brooks 1960; 14 May 1973, C. A. Grauvogel unpubl. notes; 17 May 1922, Bailey 1943; all Bering Strait), but often not until late May. A major movement through the northern Bering Sea and along the western coastline of the Peninsula, undoubtedly birds headed for more northerly breeding grounds in the Chukchi Sea, occurs between late May and mid-June (500-1100 birds/h 27-28 May 1973 at Gambell, St. Lawrence I, Johnson 1976; "up to thousands/day" 30 May-3 June 1976 at Gambell, W. C. Russell et al. in litt.; migration peak 27 May to 3 + June 1978, with up to 830/h on 2 June, at Wales, Flock and Hubbard 1979; numerous 4-6 June 1976 past the mouth of Arctic R, Noble and Wright 1977; "great northward movement" on 16 June 1922 at Wales, Bailey 1943). Movement continues through June.

Birds may be present in the open waters of the region for some time before they begin to occupy nesting cliffs. Nesting activities may begin as early as late May (population "had settled" on cliffs, 27 May 1978, Bluff, Drury et al. 1981; 500 kittiwakes on cliffs and "already forming pairs," 29 May 1986, Cape Deceit, J. D. Walters unpubl. notes; birds plucked fleece lining from a gun case for nests, 30 May 1973, Little Diomede I, C. A. Grauvogel unpubl. notes), but the main period of nest-building and egg-laying usually does not begin until mid-June or later. Black-legged Kittiwakes usually nest on the sheer faces of high cliffs, placing their well-constructed nests of mud and graminoid vegetation on various types of small ledges across the cliff faces or in cracks and crevices. The earliest egg date reported for the region is 10 June (1902) from Little Diomede Island (Gabrielson and Lincoln 1959). Average clutch sizes at Bluff varied from 1.0 (1985) to 1.8 (1983) eggs during the 10-yr period 1976-1985 (E. C. Murphy et al. in prep.). Typically, clutches consist of 1 or 2 eggs (Swartz 1966, Hunt et al. 1978, E. C. Murphy et al. in prep.), but some 3-egg clutches are laid (Palmer 1899, Swartz 1966, E. C. Murphy et al. in prep.). Incubation averages 25-31 days (Swartz 1966, Hunt et al. 1978), and chicks begin to fly at an average of 43 (Hunt et al. 1978) or 44 days (Swartz 1966) after hatching.

Over a 5-yr period at Bluff, peak egg-laying varied from 14 June (1979) to 7 July (1977) (Drury et al. 1981), first hatching from 7 July (1979) to 22 July (1976) (E. C. Murphy et al. in prep.), peak hatching from 11 July (1979) to 2 August (1977) (Drury et al. 1981), and first fledging from 20 August (1979) to 7 September (1977) (ibid.). This wide annual variation in the breeding schedule parallels seasonal environmental conditions, especially spring atmospheric temperatures and the dates of breakup of the sea ice (E. C. Murphy et al. in prep.), which in turn determine the time of warming of Inshore Waters.

Kittiwakes obtain their food from the sea surface, to maximum depths of 0.5 m (Hunt et al. 1981a). Food consists primarily of small fishes, supplemented, especially when fish populations are low, with crustaceans and other invertebrates (Drury et al. 1981; Springer et al. 1984, 1987; E. C. Murphy et al. in prep.). Reproductive success in the region is heavily dependent upon the seasonal concentrations of forage fish near colonies, with "boom and bust" years correlated with the abundance or absence of these small fishes (E. C. Murphy et al. in prep.). Clutches are smaller, egg volume less, incubation periods longer, chick growth rates slower, and fledging success lower in years of poor forage fish populations (Drury et al. 1981; Springer et al. 1985a, b); and the abundance and size of forage fish, e.g., Sand Lance, in turn are strongly affected by water temperatures, both of them increasing in warm years and decreasing in cold years (Springer et al. 1984, 1987).

Kittiwakes gradually leave the breeding cliffs during September, with chicks remaining longer than adults (Swartz 1966, Steele and Drury 1977). As fledging proceeds, birds form flocks on the water below the cliffs and fly about offshore; these flocks, as well as some birds on the cliffs, remain until mid-October or later (Swartz 1966, Steele and Drury 1977). The latest record is extralimital: several immatures still near Gambell, St. Lawrence Island, on 10 November 1957 (Fay and Cade 1959).

Black-legged Kittiwakes show an affinity for fresh water during the summer. They flock to fresh waterbodies for bathing and preening (Fay and Cade 1959, Sauer and

Urban 1964, M. H. Dick and L. S. Dick MS), and on the Seward Peninsula they regularly gather on alluvia and beaches near the mouths of the major rivers and on lakes near the coast. Also, rainy weather stimulates nest-building activities, apparently associated with the moistening of the soil and corresponding facilitation of gathering of mud and vegetation for nest construction (Ramsdell and Drury 1979, M. H. Dick and L. S. Dick MS).

Ross' Gull—*Rhodostethia rosea*

A little known resident of the Arctic Ocean, the Ross' Gull is a casual migrant in the waters of the Peninsula. The main known breeding areas are in the Wet Meadow-Lacustrine Waters and Shorelines habitat complex along the north coast of Siberia, between the Kolyma River delta and the Taymyr Peninsula (Blomqvist and Elander 1981), although a few small colonies have recently been reported in the North American Arctic—Canadian High Arctic, Hudson Bay, and Greenland (Bledsoe and Sibley 1985). Most Ross' Gulls apparently winter along leads in the Arctic Ocean (Blomqvist and Elander 1981, Bledsoe and Sibley 1985), but the species is a rare to casual migrant and winter visitant in the Bering Sea between late September and late June (Kessel and Gibson 1978). Movement into the Bering Sea appears to be via river drainages across extreme northeastern Siberia. The species passes "more or less regularly" along the Anadyr River during migration (Dement'ev and Gladkov 1951), and it is unknown to the Eskimos of the Bering Strait (Bailey 1925) and has been reported only once in recent years by visitors to the region (see below).

Two subadults have been reported from the north coast of Norton Sound, one at the Nome harbor and breakwater from 6 to 9 June 1974 (Kessel and Gibson 1978) and one at Safety Sound on 1 July 1978 (G. Tolman pers. comm.); a bird flew past Little Diomede Island during a sudden change of weather on 7 June 1987 (S. A. Steinacher pers. comm.); and a juvenile specimen was taken extralimitally near St. Michael, southern Norton Sound, on 10 October 1879 (Nelson 1887). In September 1983, apparently abnormal environmental conditions brought migrant Ross' Gulls into southern Kotzebue Sound. Five flew along the beach at Deering on 25 September, two were present there the next morning, and another was seen 1 km inland from Deering on 28 September (J. D. Walters unpubl. notes). These birds were undoubtedly part of the same movement that brought birds inland to the lower Koyukuk River and to near McGrath, 22-25 September 1983 (Osborne and Osborne 1986; UAM 4886, 4887).

Pelagic individuals feed primarily on juvenile Arctic Cod (*Boreogadus saida*) and invertebrates, especially amphipods, obtained by surface-seizing and by surface-plunging (Divoky 1976).

Sabine's Gull—*Xema sabini*

A fairly common breeder in the Coastal Lowlands of the Seward Peninsula, the Sabine's Gull occurs from the Buckland River estuary, around most of the periphery of the Peninsula, to the mouth of the Koyuk River. Greatest numbers occur along the northern coast, where I have counts of 86 birds in the Buckland River estuary, 23-26 June 1975; 44 on Cape Espenberg, 3-5 July 1973; and 150 about Shishmaref Inlet, especially about the mouths of the Serpentine and Arctic rivers, 23-26 June 1970. In a 25-ha Wet Meadow study plot on Cape Espenberg, Schamel et al. (1979) found nesting densities of 4.4 and 5.6 nests/10ha in 1976 and 1977, respectively.

During the breeding season, Sabine's Gulls occur primarily in Wet Meadow habitat about ponds, where they frequently nest on islands and peninsulas or on nearby tussocks and hummocks, or in Salt Grass Meadow, where they nest on the open flats. They seldom occur far from the brackish waters of estuaries or tidal sloughs.

Alaska's Sabine's Gulls winter in the oceanic waters of the Humboldt Current in the South Pacific (Blomqvist and Elander 1981). They return to their breeding grounds in the southern Bering Sea by early May (Yukon Delta NWR unpubl. data) and have been recorded in southern Norton Sound as early as the second week of May (6 May 1981, Woodby and Divoky 1983; 7 May 1851, Adams 1878; 10 May 1878, Nelson 1887), but usually they do not reach the Seward Peninsula until the second half of May. First reported Peninsula sightings in spring have been 17 May 1976 (Shishmaref Inlet, Noble and Wright 1977), 18 May 1981 (Koyuk, Moses Point, and Fish R delta, Woodby and Divoky 1983), and 21 May 1983 (Wales, M. L. Ward unpubl. notes). Migration may continue to mid-June (Bailey 1925).

These gulls usually nest in small, loose colonies. The nest is a slight scrape or depression, either on bare ground or a tussock, usually scantily lined with graminoid leaves. The breeding schedule varies with seasonal environmental conditions. Initiation of individual clutches began at Cape Espenberg between 5 and 16 June 1977, but not until 11-25 June 1976 (Schamel et al. 1979). Other reports of egg-laying dates along the north coast reveal similar timing. Clutch size varies from 1 to 3 eggs. Mean clutch size at Cape Espenberg was 2.0 eggs for 11 nests in 1976 and 2.7 eggs for 14 nests in 1977 (ibid.). Incubation lasts for 21.5-22.5 days (Parmelee et al. 1967). Hatching at Cape Espenberg occurred 27 June-8 July 1977 and 2-16 July 1976 (Schamel et al. 1979). Unlike most gulls, the chicks leave the nest almost immediately after hatching and conceal themselves along vegetated shorelines (Parmelee et al. 1967, Brown et al. 1967). Young are able to fly at 20 days of age (Schamel et al. 1979).

Food during the breeding season consists primarily of small fish and invertebrates (Day 1980, Divoky 1984); birds may prey heavily on dipteran insects during major emergences (Kessel et al. 1964, Brown et al. 1967). Feeding techniques include spinning and surface-seizing while sitting on pond surfaces, surface-plunging, running along shorelines, especially tidelines, and some scavenging (Brown et al. 1967, Kessel pers. obs.).

Shortly after fledging, adults and juvenals desert the breeding grounds for the coastlines and open sea. Numbers on the breeding grounds drop precipitously during the last few days of July, with few birds in evidence onshore after the first week of August (Schamel et al. 1979, Harris 1967). Juvenals from late nests, however, may remain until October. At St. Michael, Murdoch (1885:125) found that "In 1881 the young birds of the year...were quite abundant...till the end of October," but none was seen after 3 August in 1882. Nelson (1887) reported his latest sighting at St. Michael on 10 October 1879.

The main fall migratory movement occurs during September. Large flocks of 50-100 Sabine's Gulls moved past Icy Cape in the Chukchi Sea on 8 September 1921 (Bailey

1948), and small flocks were present on the Chukchi Sea between Barrow and Wainwright 23-24 September 1970 (Watson and Divoky 1972). In the southern Bering Sea, while movement is evident from August to October (Gould et al. 1982), most occurs in September (Hunt et al. 1981b); and the species is most abundant on the north side of the Alaska Peninsula in late September (Gill et al. 1981).

Ivory Gull—_Pagophila eburnea_

This high arctic gull is a fairly common migrant in the Chukchi and Bering seas, with individuals occurring in the Bering Sea from October through late June (Kessel and Gibson 1978). It nests on islands in the Arctic Ocean, primarily between 73° and 83° N (Blomqvist and Elander 1981, Thomas and MacDonald 1987) and is closely associated throughout the year with the sea-ice front zone. Its occurrence in the waters of the Seward Peninsula coincides with the annual advance and retreat of this ice zone, the exact dates of which vary from year to year.

Bailey (1925) recorded Ivory Gulls in the offshore leads of the Bering Strait between 1 May and 26 June 1922, with the main movement during the third week of May. Subsequent reports of spring migration have fallen within these dates and have confirmed late May as the migration peak. Seward Peninsula migrants have been recorded as far east as Cape Nome (two adults, 27 May 1984, J. L. Dunn in litt.) and Deering (one each, 10-13 May 1986 and 19-22 May 1985, J. D. Walters unpubl. notes). Dates of fall movement in the region have not been recorded but probably occur from late October to early December. It is likely that occasional birds remain about open leads and polynyas in the Strait region throughout the winter.

Ivory Gulls feed mainly on small fish, supplemented by invertebrates (Divoky 1976). They do some scavenging and are often seen in spring feeding on the remains of sea mammal kills left on the ice by hunters (Bailey 1943, others).

Common Tern—_Sterna hirundo_

An adult Common Tern was observed in flight and on a sandbar with 20+ Arctic Terns at the mouth of the Nome River on 12 June 1983; it was still present on 14 June (P. D. Vickery in litt.).

Only the northeastern Asiatic form of the Common Tern (_S. h. longipennis_) has been recorded in Alaska; it is a rare spring migrant and summer visitant in Southwestern Alaska (Kessel and Gibson 1978) and a very rare spring migrant in the northern Bering Sea (Kessel and D. D. Gibson unpubl. data).

Arctic Tern—_Sterna paradisaea_

An abundant, widely distributed breeder, the Arctic Tern occurs across most of the Peninsula during the breeding season. Never far from water, it breeds throughout the Coastal Lowlands and in the Interior Lowlands and uplands wherever lacustrine or fluviatile waters occur. It is most abundant where Wet Meadow-Pond complexes are present near coastal beaches, spits, and barrier strips, e.g., Safety Sound, Imuruk Basin-Port Clarence area, Lopp Lagoon barrier strip, Cape Espenberg, and the Buckland River estuary. Greatest numbers along the southern coast occur at Safety Sound (3.8 birds/km on transects in 1980 [Woodby and Divoky 1983]), and, on the northern coast, at Cape Espenberg (447 birds enumerated 3-5 July 1973, including a colony of about 40 pairs at the eastern tip of the Cape [Kessel and D. D. Gibson pers. obs.]; 10.8 nests/10 ha in 1976 and 13.2 nests/10 ha in 1977 in a Wet Meadow census plot [Schamel et al. 1979]).

When on land, Arctic Terns favor open, essentially flat terrain, often with no vegetation. Where vegetated, cover is of low height or very sparse. Typical habitats include Beaches and Tidal Flats, Alluvia, Salt Grass Meadow, and Wet Meadow. The coastal breeders forage primarily in Inshore Waters along the coast and often loaf, together with non-, failed, or postbreeders, on alluvial islands in river estuaries or on spits and islands adjacent to lagoon inlets.

Arctic Terns winter mainly in the sea-ice front zone of East Antarctica, from 150° E to 30° W (Salomonsen 1967), and the birds from Alaska and the western Canadian Arctic apparently migrate both inshore and offshore in the Pacific waters off North America (ibid., American Ornithologists' Union 1983, Kessel and D. D. Gibson unpubl. data). There are few observations of migrating birds in the Bering Sea or the Seward Peninsula area, although in spring they have been reported both coastally and offshore in the Bering Sea (migrating flocks of 20-25 birds moved north past Hooper Bay, Yukon-Kuskokwim Delta, on 24 May 1964, and they were "very common, especially out on pack-ice" on 27 May 1964 [H. K. Springer unpubl. notes]. During May 1980 and 1981, however, there was no indication of a coastal migration in Norton Sound [Woodby and Divoky 1983]. Divoky [1984:475] reported that "Shipboard observations in the Bering Sea in May have failed to find them in numbers").

The first spring migrants arrive along the Norton Sound coastline in mid-May (earliest, 12 May 1980, Norton Sound, Woodby and Divoky 1983; 13 May 1984, Cape Woolley, E. Muktoyuk, Beltz School unpubl. notes), and a few days later in Kotzebue Sound (12 May 1951, Selawik, Alaska Game Commission 1951; 16 May 1988, Deering, J. D. Walters unpubl. notes; 19 May 1987, Kotzebue, Selawik NWR unpubl. notes); but, in many years, first arrivals have not been reported at Wales or along the northwest coast until the last few days of May (Bailey 1943, Noble and Wright 1977, Flock and Hubbard 1979, Schamel et al. 1979, Kessel and D. D. Gibson unpubl. data). Peak arrivals occurred 21-27 May in 1980 and 1981 in coastal Norton Sound (Woodby and Divoky 1983), but not until 29 May-5 June 1986, 4-10 June 1984, and 4-12 June 1985 at Deering (J. D. Walters unpubl. notes).

Arctic Terns on the Peninsula usually nest in scattered pairs or in aggregates of a few pairs, but in the Coastal Lowlands they may also breed in colonies of up to about 50 pairs. Nests consist of little more than a slight indentation where the eggs are laid. Along coasts and rivers and about lakes with appropriate shorelines, nests are located on beaches and alluvia, often in the open but sometimes near a scrap of vegetation or driftwood. Where such substrates are unavailable, nests may be placed on vegetated islands or raised areas along the shorelines of various types of waterbodies, e.g., ridges, hummocks, and tussocks of Dwarf Shrub Mat or sedges and grasses.

Dates of egg-laying vary both annually and geographically. In coastal Norton Sound, egg-laying may begin during the last week of May (Shields and Peyton 1979, Woodby and Divoky 1983), but at Cape Espenberg in 1976 and 1977, egg-laying did not begin until 17 and 13 June, respectively (Schamel et al. 1979). Clutch initiation continues throughout June, with some renesting even commencing as late as the first week of July. Peak laying, however, occurred in coastal Norton Sound 30 May-6 June 1980 and 1981 (Woodby and Divoky 1983) and at Cape Espenberg about 15-22 June 1977 and 24-28 June 1976 (Schamel et al. 1979). The most frequent clutch size is 2 eggs (range 1-3 eggs), although it apparently varies with food availability. In coastal Norton Sound, 10 clutches from 1976 and 1977 averaged 1.9 eggs (Shields and Peyton 1979), and 15 clutches from 1980 and 1981 averaged 2.1 eggs (Woodby and Divoky 1983). At Cape Espenberg, 32 clutches in 1976 and 37 clutches in 1977 each averaged 1.9 eggs; there were no 3-egg clutches in 1976, only one in 1977, but they were "relatively common" in 1978 (Schamel et al. 1979).

The laying interval between the first and second egg varies from 1 to 4 days, and incubation may begin before the clutch is complete (Hawksley 1957). Incubation averages 22 days (usual range, 21-22 days), but any disturbances that keep adults from the nest, such as predator activity, can prolong the incubation period to at least 30-32 days (ibid., Boekelheide 1980). Chicks from Cape Espenberg were able to fly by 22-23 days of age, although one may have been only 19 days at first flight (Schamel et al. 1979). Families remained in the breeding area for about 2 weeks after the young had fledged (ibid.); young apparently become independent of their parents within a month after fledging (Boekelheide 1980). Thus, on the Seward Peninsula, the earliest chicks should hatch about 17 June and fledge about 8 July, whereas late broods will not fledge until mid-August or later.

During the summer, Arctic Terns feed on small fish and invertebrates, taken from inland waterbodies or from coastal Inshore Waters by plunging into the water head-first; some flying insects may also be taken (Schamel et al. 1979, Johnson and Richardson 1981, Woodby and Divoky 1983, Divoky 1984).

Postbreeding flocks in coastal Norton Sound begin to form in late July and early August, when flocks of up to 60 birds have been recorded, including family groups with some adults still feeding young (Woodby and Divoky 1983). Local birds had left the Akulik-Inglutalik River delta at the head of Norton Bay by 5 August 1976 (Shields and Peyton 1977), but numbers on the nearshore mudflats peaked on 19 August 1977 (Shields and Peyton 1979). Numbers on the wetlands of Cape Espenberg dropped off during the second week of August in both 1976 and 1977, with few birds left after about 23 August (Schamel et al. 1979). At Sarichef Island 13-15 August 1973, many of the 64 Arctic Terns along the beaches were fledglings that appeared to have been raised locally (D. D. Gibson unpubl. notes).

Thus, migration is under way by the second week of August. The bulk of the population has left by the end of the month, and the species is uncommon to rare by early September (latest, two alternate-plumaged adults and ten juvenals on 10 September 1973, Wales, D. D. Gibson and G. J. Divoky unpubl. notes; eight on 11 September and one on 14 September 1983, Deering, J. D. Walters unpubl. notes; two on 10 September 1977 and seven on 12 September 1976, Cape Espenberg, Schamel et al. 1979; and, extralimitally, last seen 2 October [yr?], Cape Thompson, Williamson et al. 1966).

Aleutian Tern—*Sterna aleutica*

A Beringian species, the Aleutian Tern is an uncommon breeder on the Seward Peninsula, nesting in the Coastal Lowlands, primarily along Norton Sound. It is locally fairly common at Safety Sound, where it was first discovered on 9 July 1969 when I observed 25 individuals loafing with about 35 Arctic Terns on an alluvial spit just inside the inlet of the Sound. Breeding was confirmed on 25 July 1970 when G. E. Hall (pers. comm.) found a colony of six pairs on the flats near Solomon and located two nests, each with one egg. Since that time a number of colonies have been found on islands in the Sound—from the mouth of Eldorado River in the west to the Bonanza River bridge in the east—the exact colony sites shifting somewhat from year to year. Numbers in Safety Sound were 160 adults in 1976, over 320 in 1977, 80 in 1978, and 480 in 1979 (H. K. Springer in Woodby and Divoky 1983).

Several other small colonies or probable colonies occur elsewhere around the outer coasts of the Peninsula. At the southwest end of Sarichef Island, there was a group of five Aleutian Terns (a sixth was dead from gunshot) on 13 August 1973, including one carrying food, probably to a fledgling; an empty nest cup was found, but no chicks (D. D. Gibson unpubl. notes). At Breving Lagoon on 3 July 1980, there were two groups of birds on apparent colony sites in *Elymus* on the inner side of the coastal barrier strip; one group consisted of six birds, the other of sixteen, but no nests or young were located (Woodby and Divoky 1983). About 30 birds present at Point Spencer in early June 1980 and 1981 (ibid.) were probably from a local colony. At the tip of the Moses Point barrier strip, there is a small colony, also. Birds from this colony apparently spend time on the outer beach where the Kwiniuk River cuts through the barrier strip between the Moses Point landing strip and the Moses Point fish camp, where D. G. Roseneau (unpubl. notes) watched at least twelve Aleutian Terns on 20 July 1969 and where I saw at least three on 30 June 1972 and was told by residents of the fish camp that they nested at the east tip of the barrier strip. Subsequently, a dozen or more Aleutian Terns were reported frequenting the landing strip beach during July 1973 (J. H. Lee pers. comm.), and Woodby and Divoky (1983) reported them in the vicinity of the barrier strip throughout the summers of 1980 and 1981. On Golovin spit, a colony of about 30 adults was found in June 1981 (Woodby and Divoky 1983). And F. G. Scheider and I watched five birds as they flew about the flats just upriver from the mouth of the Koyuk River on 2 July 1975, suggesting the possibility of a nearby colony.

During the breeding season Aleutian Terns use terrestrial habitats adjacent to the outer coastlines, where colonies are usually located on the inner sides of barrier strips or on islands or spits in lagoon systems or river estuaries behind outer barrier strips. Most colonies on the Peninsula have been in *Elymus* Grass Meadow, but the one on Golovin spit was on Dwarf Shrub Mat (Woodby and Divoky 1983), similar to the habitat described by Nelson (1887) for colonies near St. Michael.

The Aleutian Tern apparently winters at sea in the North Pacific (Vaurie 1965). The fact that it arrives onshore in the Gulf of Alaska about 2 weeks earlier in spring than in the Aleutian Islands (Kessel and Gibson 1978) suggests that it may winter in the North Pacific Drift System and arrive at Alaska sites via the Alaska-Aleutian Stream. After reaching the Aleutians, these terns apparently migrate through the off-shore waters of the Bering Sea to reach the Seward Peninsula, since there is no evidence of an onshore coastal migration anywhere in Alaska (Kessel and Gibson 1978).

The first migrants arrive in Norton Sound about a week later than in the Aleutians, and about a week later than the Arctic Tern. Woodby and Divoky (1983:186) stated that Aleutian Terns "first arrived on the breeding colonies from the open sea in late May and continued to arrive through early June," and at St. Michael, Nelson (1887) reported that they first arrived from 20 to 30 May, rarely earlier.

Egg-laying begins early in the second week of June and peaks in mid-June (Woodby and Divoky 1983), although some laying may continue for up to a month (nests still with eggs on 25 July 1969, above). There may be some renesting if first clutches are destroyed, judging from evidence provided by Holtán (1980), including destroyed nests within 1 m of occupied late-season nests and some clutches hatching later than the main hatch period and the fact that Nelson (1887) collected an unusually late egg at St. Michael on 1 September that contained a two-thirds-grown embryo.

The nest consists of nothing more than a suitable depression in short or matted vegetation. The commonest clutch size previously reported in Alaska has been 2 eggs (range 1-3 eggs) (Gabrielson and Lincoln 1959, Holtán 1980), but mean clutch size varies annually, probably in response to availability of food resources, and the number of 1-egg clutches appears to increase with latitude. On average over the years, two-thirds of the clutches at Safety Sound have consisted of a single egg (H. K. Springer pers. comm.), yet in 1980 and 1981 at a colony in Safety Sound and in 1981 at Golovin, 2-egg clutches predominated (average of 41 nests was 1.8 ± 0.4 eggs, D. A. Woodby in litt.). Farther north, along the southern Chukchi Sea coast in 1978, colonies at both Cape Krusenstern and at Tasaychek Lagoon had a predominance of 1-egg clutches (average of 64 nests was 1.4 ± 0.5 eggs, D. A. Woodby in litt.).

In 2-egg clutches, the laying interval between the eggs averages about 2 days, but may range up to 4 days, judging from the asynchrony of hatching reported by Holtán (1980). Incubation has been variously reported as averaging 22 days (Baird 1986) and 23 days (Holtán 1980), although Holtán (ibid.) reported at least one instance of only 20 days. Chicks stay in the vicinity of the nest for 2 or 3 days and then disappear into surrounding vegetation (Holtán 1980). They are capable of flight at about 25 days of age (range 25-31 days) (Holtán 1980, Baird 1986). Hatching on the Seward Peninsula began on 1 July in both 1980 and 1981 and peaked on 7 July, and fledging was first noted on 28 July with a peak about 4 August; most fledging was complete by 14 August and the birds disappeared from the colonies shortly thereafter (Woodby and Divoky 1983). Fledglings at the Copper River Delta also left the colony within a few days of fledging (Holtán 1980), but on Kodiak Island, Baird (1986) reported that they remained at the colony for 1 or 2 weeks after fledging.

During nesting, these terns usually forage in coastal waters, sometimes well offshore (seen 8-11 km offshore in Norton Sound in early July 1975, Drury 1976b), although they occasionally obtain insects from the surface of freshwater ponds (Holtán 1980, Woodby and Divoky 1983). Their diet consists mainly of crustaceans, especially the euphausiid *Thysanoessa*, and small fish (Baird and Moe 1978, Holtán 1980, Sanger 1986), which they obtain from the water surface by dipping.

Since families vacate colony areas soon after the young fledge, onshore populations begin to decline by early August. Substantial numbers may remain onshore until about 20 August (Drury 1976b, H. K. Springer in litt.; Kessel and D. D. Gibson unpubl. data), but most have departed by the end of the month. The species is rare after 1 September (latest, eight on 10 September 1977 at Cape Espenberg, Schamel et al. 1979; two on 11 September 1976 at Safety Sound and an adult on 19 September 1976 offshore 2 km from Nome, H. K. Springer in litt.).

Dovekie—*Alle alle*

Primarily a bird of the eastern High Arctic and North Atlantic Ocean, this alcid is a rare probable breeder at auklet colonies on islands of the Bering Strait (Kessel and Gibson 1978). Native residents have long been aware of the occasional occurrence of Dovekies in the region (Hanna 1961, Breckenridge 1966, Bédard 1966). More recently at Little Diomede Island, one was collected on 8 July 1948 (Hanna 1961), two on 16 June 1965 (Breckenridge 1966), one on 12 June 1968 (UAM 5384), one on 14 June 1975 (UAM 3399), and an adult male with enlarged testes on 17 June 1985 (UAM 5263). J. J. Burns (pers. comm.) reported seeing 15 birds there during June 1972, and S. W. Stoker (Kessel and Gibson 1978) reported that several pairs were present each year he worked there in the 1960s-early 1970s, including a pair resident at a burrow during May and June 1968. At King Island, a lone, alternate-plumaged adult was observed on 5 July 1976 by W. H. Drury and others (J. O. Biderman in litt.).

At St. Lawrence Island, where the bird occurs annually in small numbers (Kessel and Gibson 1978, subsequent unpubl. data), it has been recorded from 24 May (1965) to 9 September (1975) (Kessel and Gibson 1978). Dovekies winter in leads and polynyas of the Arctic Ocean (Kozlova 1957) and in the sea-ice front zone at the southern edge of the ice pack and farther south in the cold Atlantic currents (Cramp 1985). Because of early spring arrivals at St. Lawrence Island, Bédard (1966) hypothesized that the Bering Strait birds probably winter in the southern Bering Sea.

Common Murre—*Uria aalge* and Thick-billed Murre—*Uria lomvia*

Common Murres are abundant and Thick-billed Murres common breeders about the Seward Peninsula. They are common migrants and at least the Thick-billed is a rare winter visitant. Taken together, they are the second most abundant seabirds of the region, being exceeded in numbers only by the Least Auklet of the offshore islands (Table 8). While on land during the breeding season, murres usually occupy steep, rocky sea cliffs that have ledges or weathered pinnacles and other projections overlooking exposed coastal waters (Tuck 1961). Both species are found at most of the colonies of the Seward Peninsula (Table 8), often together on the same ledges. Common Murres are the dominant murre at most inshore colonies (Norton Sound and Kotzebue Sound), whereas Thick-bills predominate at the offshore colonies (Table 8). Historically, the proportion of the two murre species has fluctuated at colonies in the Bering Sea (Peterson and Fisher 1955, Fay and Cade 1959, Gabrielson and Lincoln 1959). A shift seems also to have occurred at murre colonies of the Seward Peninsula, with Common Murres increasing in recent years (compare Bailey 1948 with Paulson in litt. at Fairway Rock and with Drury et al. 1981 at Little Diomede Island, compare Grinnell 1900a with Swartz 1967 and Sowls et al. 1978 at Puffin and Chamisso islands, and see Table 8 for Sledge I). Swartz (1967) speculated that possibly Common Murres were spreading northward in correlation with long-term warming trends.

At Bluff, however, where most of the murres are Common Murres, numbers have dropped precipitously since 1975 (Table 16). This drop shows a strong correspondence with the decline in the per-effort success (catch per unit effort) of the Walleye Pollock (_Theragra chalcogramma_) commercial fisheries in the southeastern Bering Sea and suggests the possibility that competition for the reduced (limited) food resource has reduced overwintering survival of the Common Murres that breed on the Seward Peninsula (Murphy et al. 1986).

Most murres from the Seward Peninsula apparently winter primarily in the Bering Sea ice front zone, the continental shelf waters over the shelf break zone, and in southern Bristol Bay (A. M. Springer and D. G. Roseneau MS), although small numbers of Thick-bills may remain as far north as open leads and polynyas exist within the ice (Fay and Cade 1959, Swartz 1966). Near the Seward Peninsula, J. J. Burns (unpubl. notes) reported murres in leads around King Island on 5 February 1968 and found them in a lead near Cape Woolley on 15 February 1969. Birds leave their wintering grounds as the ice cover begins to dissipate in early April, and the first migrant murres usually arrive in the vicinity of the Seward Peninsula about mid-April (Fay and Cade 1959, Swartz 1966, Johnson 1976). The early migrants overfly large areas of pack ice, utilizing open water provided by leads and polynyas for resting and feeding (Divoky 1979). The main spring passage begins during the last few days of April and continues at least to mid-May (Bailey 1943, Kenyon and Brooks 1960, Johnson 1976). Some movement continues into June, the later birds being mostly subadults and nonbreeders (A. M. Springer and D. G. Roseneau MS).

Table 16.   Number of murres, mostly Common Murres, at Bluff, Seward Peninsula, 1975-1985, as determined from census counts (1975-1981, Springer et al. 1985a; 1982-1985, E. C. Murphy pers. comm.).

Year	No. murres
1975	69,900
1976	50,283
1977	37,675
1978	40,040
1979	34,976
1980	30,765
1981	28,910
1982	27,528
1983	29,308
1984	12,295
1985	35,693

Murre breeding schedules are strongly influenced by the dates of breakup of sea ice and snow melt at the cliffs and hence exhibit wide annual variation. Cliff occupancy may begin any time between late May and mid-June. Generally, Thick-billed Murres tend to occupy relatively narrow ledges, whereas Common Murres use wider ones and often occupy broad, flat platforms above the more vertical surfaces (Peterson and Fisher 1955, Drury and Steele 1977, Biderman and Drury 1978). The earliest reported egg date is of a Thick-billed Murre on 9 June (1950) at Sledge Island (Cade 1952). At Bluff, where most are Common Murres, between 1975 and 1979 the earliest egg was recorded on 12 June (1978); peak egg-laying occurred on 19 June 1978 but not until 15 July 1976 (Drury et al. 1981). After a variable incubation period of 30-35 days (Uspenskii 1956), eggs at Bluff begin hatching sometime during the second half of July (Murphy et al. 1986). Chicks remain on the ledges for about 21 days (Hunt et al. 1981b), and first departures from the Bluff cliffs over an 8-year period occurred between 29 July (1981) and 20 August (1977) (Murphy et al. 1986). Some hatching continues until late August, and Drury et al. (1978) reported two chicks, which failed to survive, that hatched during the first week of September 1977. Hatching was just beginning at Puffin and Chamisso islands on 11 August 1977 (DeGange and Sowls 1978). By mid-September, almost all murres have vacated the breeding colonies (Steele and Drury 1977, Drury et al. 1978). The departing chicks, some with down still remaining, jump from the cliffs and swim after adults out to sea (Gabrielson and Lincoln 1959, Tuck 1961). Murres remain on the waters of the region until freeze-up. They were still fairly common in the Bering Strait on 18 October 1970 (Watson and Divoky 1972).

Comparatively, the seasonal phenology of the Thick-billed Murre tends to be several days to a week ahead of the Common Murre (Cade 1952, Fay and Cade 1959, Swartz 1966, Drury and Steele 1977, Steele and Drury 1977).

A major difference between Common and Thick-billed murres, and one that enables them to exploit different habitats (Inshore Waters vs. Offshore Waters, respectively), is their food habits. Both species feed throughout the water column and take small, slender fish, especially gadids and Sand Lance in the northern Bering Sea and Chukchi Sea (Drury et al. 1981, Springer et al. 1984, 1987); but, while Common Murres use this food type almost exclusively when available, the more generalized diet of Thick-billed Murres also includes significant quantities of benthic invertebrates, especially crustaceans, and fishes, especially sculpins (ibid.). Thick-billed Murres tend to range farther from their nesting cliffs for feeding than Commons (Swartz 1967, Drury et al. 1981). In the Chukchi Sea, Swartz (1967) found that the greatest number of murres fed within about 65 km offshore of the breeding colonies, mostly within 50 km, and that beyond 8 km more than 90% were Thick-bills, compared to 60% at the cliffs. Common Murres from the breeding colonies at Bluff scatter southward for 40 km over Norton Sound for feeding and also gather to feed off the mouth of Golovnin Bay (40 km southeast) and the inlet of Safety Sound and Cape Nome (more than 50 km west) (Ramsdell and Drury 1979, Drury et al. 1981). Thick-bills nesting in Kotzebue Sound probably fly out to the vicinity of the main Chukchi Sea coastal currents for feeding.

Black Guillemot—*Cepphus grylle*

Black Guillemots are uncommon migrants in the Bering Strait, and they are probably rare winter and summer visitants and possibly rare breeders in the Seward Peninsula region. An almost circumpolar species (except western arctic Canada), their summer range overlaps that of the more southern, closely related, Pigeon Guillemot in the northern Bering Sea and southern Chukchi Sea. They occur sympatrically at Cape Serdtse Kamen on the Chukotsk Peninsula (Kozlova 1957) and at Cape Lisburne (Springer et al. 1985a) and Cape Thompson (Swartz 1966, Springer et al. 1985a), where they are known to breed; and they occur annually in small numbers during the summer as far south as St. Lawrence Island (Bédard 1966, Kessel and D. D. Gibson unpubl. data), where they probably also breed. No breeding has been reported in the Seward Peninsula region, but there are summer sightings, and observers should be alert for possible nesting on the islands of the Bering Strait. Summer records include an adult female in changing plumage taken near Teller on 1 August 1913 (Anderson 1915), a bird near Sledge Island in late July 1976 (J. O. Biderman in litt.), five on Fairway Rock on 11 July 1978 (D. R. Paulson unpubl. notes), and two alternate-plumaged birds at Wales on 14 June 1983 (T. G. Tobish in litt.).

In winter, the Black Guillemot is locally common as far south as the limit of sea ice advance in the southern Bering Sea, occurring in the open leads and polynyas within the ice (Kessel and Gibson 1978). During their winter cruises through the ice in the central and southern Bering Sea, G. E. Hall (unpubl. notes) and G. J. Divoky (in litt.) identified only this species of guillemot, and all specimens taken within the ice between November and April have been of this species. Specimens include a young male at St. Lawrence Island taken 23 November 1930 (Friedmann 1932) and two juvenile males (UAM 5369, 5370) taken there on 28 November 1929 (previously reported as Pigeon Guillemots by Fay and Cade 1959), four specimens taken at Wales between 28 April and 5 May 1922 (Bailey 1943), a female from 8 km southeast of Kivalina on 1 March 1961 (UAM 2361), two birds from leads off Point Hope in February 1960 (UAM 2363 and 2364) and 21 April 1960 (UAM 1262), and those reported from farther north by Bailey (1925), Gabrielson and Lincoln (1959), and others. Hence, it appears that November through April and possibly early May records within the sea ice are all Black Guillemots, including guillemots reported in the vicinity of Norton Sound in November (Nelson 1887) and at Little Diomede Island on 25 April 1953 (Kenyon and Brooks 1960).

Black Guillemots move northward out of the Bering Sea as the ice melts in the spring. Exact dates of the movement are unknown, but apparent migrants have been recorded from late April to early June. Migrants passed by Wales from 25 April to 29 May 1922 (Bailey 1943) and were still passing 22-29 May and "thereafter" in 1978 (Flock and Hubbard 1979, D. R. Paulson unpubl. notes). D. R. Paulson (unpubl. notes) found this species less common than the Pigeon Guillemot during migration, but not substantially so, and he was surprised to find it "so common in June." Farther south at Hooper Bay, an immature bird still in partial basic plumage was collected as late as 29 May 1964 (Springer 1966); and a bird seen off Cape Nome on 9 June 1974 (H. K. Springer and A. Bernecker unpubl. notes) was probably a migrant, as perhaps was one taken at St. Michael in "June" 1915 (Gabrielson and Lincoln 1959).

Dates of the fall movement are unknown, but doubtless coincide with the southward progression of fall freeze-up of the sea ice. Some birds remain off Point Barrow and at other northern points throughout the winter, wherever open leads develop (Bailey 1925, Gabrielson and Lincoln 1959, above specimens, others).

Pigeon Guillemot—*Cepphus columba*

The Pigeon Guillemot is uncommon about the Seward Peninsula; it is found at coastal cliffs on both the islands and mainland (Table 8), including the coastline of southern Kotzebue Sound (Sowls et al. 1978). The largest concentration is at King Island, probably because of the availability of suitable nesting sites (see Oakley 1981). Non-breeders usually make up 30-55% of local populations (Oakley 1981).

Pigeon Guillemots are fairly common winter visitants in the Aleutian Islands (Gabrielson and Lincoln 1959) and in the southern Bering Sea as far north as the Pribilof Islands (Preble and McAtee 1923). They appear to winter south of the sea ice edge, however, with most, if not all, April-November guillemot records within the sea ice being of Black Guillemots (see above).

Early spring arrival dates are uncertain, because of difficulties in distinguishing between the two species of guillemots and the fact that only in recent years have observers done so. Pigeon Guillemots, however, usually arrive about St. Lawrence Island during the third week of May (16 May 1976, Searing 1977; 17 May 1966, Sealy 1967; 19 May 1929, UAM 5381 and 5382, Fay and Cade 1959; 20 May 1973, Johnson 1976), and perhaps a few days later in the Bering Strait (1000 present [both species?], apparently an unusual concentration, on waters off shore ice south of Little Diomede I, 14 May 1973, C. A. Grauvogel unpubl. notes; two [species?] in narrow lead near Little Diomede I on 15 May 1958, and 20 during a day at sea on 20 May 1958, Kenyon and Brooks 1960; two at Wales on 23 May 1983, M. L. Ward unpubl. notes; first seen at Little Diomede I on 26 May 1977, Biderman and Drury 1978; three at Wales when observer arrived on 27 May 1979, S. Hills unpubl. notes; five at Wales on 29 May 1978 and regular thereafter, D. R. Paulson unpubl. notes; specimen from Wales taken 30 May 1929, Bailey 1943). Migration continues until mid-June (up to 5000 a day at Gambell 4-11 June 1976, P. W. Sykes in litt.; 36+ on open water around Teller on 10 June 1975, Drury 1976a; last past Wales on 21 June 1978, D. R. Paulson unpubl. notes), and they do not appear in numbers about colonies until the ice leaves the shoreline (Kenyon and Brooks 1960, Drury and Steele 1977).

In the Chukchi and northern Bering Sea region, Pigeon Guillemots nest in isolated pairs or small groups, laying eggs in crevices in rocky cliffs or among boulder rubble about cliff faces (Drury and Steele 1977, Biderman and Drury 1978, Springer and Roseneau 1978). Entrances to nest crevices are usually smaller than 30 x 30 cm (Oakley 1981).

Little is known of the breeding chronologies of Pigeon Guillemots about the Seward Peninsula. Egg-laying apparently occurs during the last third of June. The earliest recorded egg has been 3 July (1941) on Little Diomede Island (Bailey 1943), where none had been found by 25 June 1953 (Kenyon and Brooks 1960). Based on lengths of incubation and nestling periods and back-calculations from known fledglings, however, egg-laying must begin about 20 June. Pigeon Guillemots lay 1 or 2 eggs, usually 2, with a laying interval of about 3 days (Drent et al. 1964). In 15 nests at

St. Lawrence Island between 12 July and 6 August 1950, clutch size averaged 1.6 eggs (Fay and Cade 1959). Incubation, which does not become steady until after the second egg is laid, lasts 28-32 days, averaging 30 days (Drent et al. 1964). Hence, eggs should hatch in the northern Bering Sea in late July and early August. At St. Lawrence Island in 1950, none in the monitored nests had hatched by 6 August (Fay and Cade 1959), but adults at Cape Thompson were seen carrying food to a nest on 4 and 7 August 1961 (Swartz 1966).

The nestling period lasts an average of 35 days (range for 15 chicks at Mandarte Island, British Columbia, was 29-39 days) (Drent et al. 1964), and fledglings have been reported in the northern Bering Sea region by the end of August (grown young at the Diomedes on 27 August 1928, Jaques 1930; apparently flightless juvenal found dying on the beach at Bluff on 29 August 1977, Drury et al. 1978; first young seen at St. Lawrence I on 24 August 1976, but not numerous until 26 August, Searing 1977; fledged young numerous at St. Lawrence I on 31 August 1957, Fay and Cade 1959). Young are well-developed and potentially capable of flight when they leave the nest and are independent of their parents thereafter (Drent et al. 1964); however, young may be unable to take flight from water when they first leave the nest (Oakley 1981).

Pigeon Guillemots feed nearshore and inshore throughout the year (Kenyon 1961, Sowles et al. 1978, Hunt et al. 1981b, Oakley 1981), feeding by pursuit-diving primarily on small (less than 150 mm) epibenthic fishes and, opportunistically, on schooling fishes (e.g., Sand Lance) and, especially in winter, on crustaceans (Preble and McAtee 1923, Oakley 1981).

Departure dates from the region are unknown, partly because of apparent identification confusion with Black Guillemots. Pigeon Guillemots were last seen at Cape Thompson on 29 August 1960 and 28 August 1961 (Swartz 1966), which must have been close to fledging time for the chicks. None was positively identified between Point Barrow and Nome on a cruise between 22 September and 18 October 1970 (Watson and Divoky 1972), but they were apparently still present about the Diomedes on 6 September 1928 (Jaques 1930), and a juvenal female was collected at Nome on 13 September 1913 (J. Koren unpubl. notes). Thus, it appears that Pigeon Guillemots leave the Seward Peninsula during the first half of September, well before freeze-up. The latest record for the northern Bering Sea is a young bird collected on 11 October 1930 at Gambell, St. Lawrence Island (Friedmann 1932).

Marbled Murrelet—*Brachyramphus marmoratus*

The status in the Seward Peninsula region of this murrelet of the North Pacific coastlines is uncertain, although it appears to be a casual spring migrant, summer visitant, and breeder in the Bering Strait region. A pair of Marbled Murrelets and their egg were collected ''on rocky land above the Iron River about 70 miles north of Nome,'' on 10 June 1904 by A. H. Dunham (Bent 1919:143), apparently the Iron Creek of Orth (1967) at 65°33′ N, 165°17′ W, in the range south of Kougarok Mountain, a creek that drains into the American-Agiapuk river system and thence into Imuruk Basin (contra Day et al. 1983). Bent (ibid.) described the egg as '' 'massicot yellow'...covered with spots of 'bone brown' and 'deep quaker drab' '' and stated that ''it looks as if it might be correctly identified.'' This nesting was discounted by Gabrielson and Lincoln (1959) and Day et al. (1983), however, because it was far north of the usual breeding range. Color-calibrated photographs of the egg (UF 5384/UF 52400) were examined for me by L. F. Kiff (in litt.), and he identified it again as a Marbled Murrelet egg, finding the background color as described by Bent (ibid.). Such pale-yellow background coloration has been found only in Marbled Murrelet eggs, not in the otherwise similar eggs of the Kittlitz's Murrelet (Kiff 1981, Day et al. 1983).

Other nearby northern records of this murrelet include two observed and one collected at St. Lawrence Island on 29 July 1964 (Bédard 1966), three seen off the east end of St. Lawrence Island on 1 August 1986 (R. R. Veit in litt.), two females collected at Big Diomede Island on 19 May 1910 (Zoological Institute of the Academy of Science of USSR, Leningrad, Nos. 17481 and 17485), and the male of a pair shot in a lead near Idlidlya Island in Kolyuchin Bay on the north coast of the Chukotsk Peninsula on 29 June 1909 (Koren 1910). The Kolyuchin Bay specimen is the North American *B. m. marmoratus* (Kozlova 1957).

Kittlitz's Murrelet—*Brachyramphus brevirostris*

The Kittlitz's Murrelet, which nests at widely separate localities along Alaska's Bering and Chukchi sea coasts (Day et al. 1983), is a rare breeder in the mountains of the western half of the Seward Peninsula. It has been recorded in summer and during migration in the Bering Strait and as far east as Nome in Norton Sound (see below). It generally nests in isolated pairs high on mountain talus slopes, often more than 25 km from the coast and more often than not at the base of a rock on a north-facing exposure near the top of a ridge or mountain (Day et al. 1983).

At least some Kittlitz's Murrelets winter in the Aleutian Islands (Byrd et al. 1974), at the tip of the Alaska Peninsula (a bird at Cold Bay on 4 February 1972, G. V. Byrd in litt.), and in the southern Bering Sea (two small flocks in the sea-ice edge in Bristol Bay on 3 February 1970, G. E. Hall unpubl. notes). Since these birds exhibit a preference for ice-filled waters (Bailey 1948, Gabrielson and Lincoln 1959, Isleib and Kessel 1973, Watson and Divoky 1972), however, they might be expected to occur in leads in the sea ice farther north, also.

Early spring records include 15 April [1960?] at Cape Thompson (Williamson et al. 1966), 19 April 1980 in lead in pack ice off Point Hope (B. E. Lawhead pers. comm.), 22 April 1953 off Gambell, St. Lawrence Island (Fay and Cade 1959), and 28 April 1922 at Wales (Bailey 1925).

Nesting has been confirmed on Cape Mountain, where in 1922 Bailey (1943) found that Wales residents knew the species well and knew of its nesting there and where, subsequently, three nests have been reported, all by D. Tevuk (bird with brood patch collected with a "heavily incubated" egg on 19 July 1934 and an incubated egg collected on 29 June 1935 [Ford 1936]; male with brood patch collected with an egg on 16 June 1943 [Bailey 1948]). Another egg was found in the York Mountains on 21 June 1973 by R. J. Gordon (Day et al. 1983). The fact that a number of summer sightings have been reported along the coast between Nome and Cape Woolley suggests nesting in the Kigluaik Mountains also. These summer sightings include one 3-5 km off Nome on 14 June 1975 (P. G. Dumont in litt.); one near Sledge Island on 17 June and a pair on 20 June 1975 (Drury 1976a), and three more in 1976 (Steele and Drury 1977); two near Sledge Island on 28 June 1977 (H. K. Springer pers. comm.), and those of Ramsdell and Drury (1979), who reported seeing birds during summers 1976-1978 in an arc from about 16 km south of Sledge Island to the southwest and west to a point 16-24 km west of Cape Woolley.

In fall, it has been seen in small numbers as late as 18 October (1970) in the Bering Strait region (Watson and Divoky 1972).

Ancient Murrelet—*Synthliboramphus antiquus*

The status of the Ancient Murrelet in the waters of the Seward Peninsula is unclear, but it appears to be a very rare to rare fall visitant. A single bird was seen in the Chukchi Sea directly north of Bering Strait at 66°33' N, 169°38' W on 14 September 1976 (Gould et al. 1982), and, during a 16-22 September 1985 cruise, R. H. Day (pers. comm.) found about 100 Ancient Murrelets, most if not all adults, feeding along the front between Alaska Coastal Water and Bering Shelf Water off the mouth of Norton Sound and in Bering Strait just south of Little Diomede Island. On 22 September 1985 he counted groups of 9, 17, 11, and 15 birds flying north past Little Diomede Island into the Chukchi Sea, and later that day he saw groups of 2 and 7 adults on the waters between Diomede and Wales and a single adult 30 km west of Cape Woolley. Farther north off Cape Lisburne, at 68°54' N, 167°17' W, two were present on 26 August 1987 (M. W. Newcomer in litt.).

The Ancient Murrelet is a locally common to abundant breeder in the Aleutian Islands (Murie 1959, Gould et al. 1982, Nysewander et al. 1982, Byrd and Day 1986), and many birds disperse northward into the southern Bering Shelf region after the breeding season (Wahl 1978, Gould et al. 1982, R. A. MacIntosh in litt., R. H. Day pers. comm., R. R. Veit in litt.), especially during August and September. A few individuals have been reported previously from the vicinity of St. Lawrence Island (Sealy et al. 1971, Gould et al. 1982), but these are the first reports from the Bering Strait and Chukchi Sea.

Parakeet Auklet—*Cyclorrhynchus psittacula*

A common breeder on the offshore islands of the Bering Strait region, the Parakeet Auklet also occurs in small numbers at the inshore seabird colonies at Sledge Island and Bluff (Table 8). It breeds as far north as 66°57' N at Cape Serdtse Kamen, Chukotsk Peninsula (Kozlova 1957), but only to 65°45' N in Alaska (Little Diomede I); however, groups of birds have been seen in early July off the Seward Peninsula at Shishmaref Inlet (Grinnell 1900a) and at Cape Espenberg (flying flock of 12, 4 July 1973, D. D. Gibson unpubl. notes).

This auklet is primarily a scarp-face nester, using rock crevices in cliffs, shattered pinnacles, and rocky outcrops (Bédard 1969b); but about the Seward Peninsula, as elsewhere, it also nests in the crevices among beach boulders (Cade 1952) and in burrows dug into the vegetated mantle over old talus slopes (Drury and Steele 1977, Biderman and Drury 1978). It tends to be solitary, both when nesting and foraging, seldom forming aggregations of more than 50 birds (Gabrielson and Lincoln 1959, Bédard 1969b), although rafts of up to 200 birds have been recorded in May and June near Buldir Island in the Aleutians (M. A. Spindler MS), where some 4000-6000 breed (Byrd and Day 1986).

Based largely on negative evidence, Parakeet Auklets apparently winter on the oceanic waters of the North Pacific, but some winter in the the Aleutian Islands (Byrd et al. 1974) and Pribilof Islands (Preble and McAtee 1923, Divoky 1977). In most years, spring migrants reach the vicinity of St. Lawrence Island by mid-May (Fay and Cade 1959, Sealy and Bédard 1973, Johnson 1976, Searing 1977) and the Seward Peninsula by the fourth week of May (earliest in Bering Strait, 20 May 1958, Kenyon and Brooks 1960; 21 May 1978, Flock and Hubbard 1979; 22 May 1922, Bailey 1943; 22 May 1972, J. J. Burns unpubl. notes). Spring migrants continue to arrive at this northern terminus of their breeding range until about 10 June (birds continued to increase at Little Diomede colonies until 4 June 1958, Kenyon and Brooks 1960; they were not numerous at Little Diomede until 9 June 1977, Biderman and Drury 1978; they passed Wales at the rate of 1000/h on 28 May, 2000/h on 29 May, and 400/h on 10 June 1978, D. R. Paulson unpubl. notes).

These auklets may not settle on their nesting colonies for several days to a week after arrival. The first settled on cliffs at Little Diomede Island on 28 May 1966 (J. J. Burns unpubl. notes), on 29 May 1953 and 26 May 1958 (Kenyon and Brooks 1960), and on 30 May 1977 (Biderman and Drury 1978). Egg-laying does not begin for another 3 to 4 weeks after the birds have settled on the colony and may be further delayed by persistent snow cover (Sealy and Bédard 1973). Breeding phenology at the Seward Peninsula appears to be a week or more later than on St. Lawrence Island (cf. Sealy and Bédard 1973) and 2-3 weeks later than on the Pribilof Islands (cf. Preble and McAtee 1923, Hunt et al. 1978). While eggs were laid at St. Lawrence Island between 21 June and 7 July 1967 (Sealy and Bédard 1973), egg-laying at the Seward Peninsula apparently does not begin until early July. Egg-laying had not commenced at King Island on 27 June 1921 (Bailey 1925), at Fairway Rock on 25 June 1922 (Bailey 1948), nor at Little Diomede Island on 25 June 1953 (J. W. Brooks MS), but eggs were present at Little Diomede Island on 3 July 1941 (Bailey 1948) and on 9 July 1977 (Biderman and Drury 1978). The clutch consists of a single egg (Sealy and Bédard 1973).

Incubation lasts for 35-36 days (Sealy and Bédard 1973), so the first chicks about the Seward Peninsula should hatch during the second week of August. If hatching spans a week or 10 days, as on St. Lawrence Island (Sealy and Bédard 1973), some chicks would still be hatching during the end of the third week of August, a date corroborated by the occurrence of an egg on Sledge Island on 22 August 1910 (Gabrielson and Lincoln 1959). The nestling period ranges from 34 to 37 days (mean 35.3 days) (Sealy and Bédard 1973), so fledging should occur during the third and fourth weeks of September. The young fly from the nest site to water, landing some 500 m from shore, and are apparently independent of adults after fledging (ibid.).

Parakeet Auklets are primarily offshore feeders during the breeding season (Bédard 1969a, Leschner and Burrell 1977), but, relative to other auklets, are feeding generalists and thus able to nest at inshore as well as offshore colonies. They forage primarily by diving, feeding preferentially on macrozooplankton, especially euphausiids and amphipods, and, during the nestling period, calanoid copepods

(Bédard 1969a). They supplement this largely crustacean diet with significant amounts of other food, especially, in the northern Bering Sea, with cephalopods, polychaetes, and small fish (ibid.). As in other auklets, Parakeet Auklets transport food to their young in their gular pouches (ibid.).

Departure of the adults from the breeding grounds coincides with the fledging of the young (see Preble and McAtee 1923, Hunt et al. 1978); hence, departures in the southern Bering Sea precede those from the Seward Peninsula, which probably occur during the second half of September. Latest date for this species in the Seward Peninsula region is one sighted in the northern Bering Strait on 18 October 1970 (Watson and Divoky 1972). Other late dates include a young female collected at Barrow on 3 October 1932 (Bailey 1948) and three observed at sea northwest of Cape Lisburne on 9 October 1970 (Watson and Divoky 1972).

Least Auklet—_Aethia pusilla_

An abundant breeder, the Least Auklet, a Beringian endemic, is Alaska's most numerous colonial seabird (see Sowls et al. 1978). It is by far the most abundant seabird on the offshore islands of the Bering Strait, nesting by the many thousands on King Island, Fairway Rock, and Little Diomede Island (Table 8). While nesting within the region is restricted to these islands, scattered individuals have been reported from Norton Sound (6-8 individuals near Sledge I, 17-18 June 1975, and an "immature" near Bluff, 19 September 1975, Drury 1976a) and from the Chukchi Sea as far north as Barrow (Jaques 1930, Bailey 1948).

On the islands of the Bering Strait, this auklet nests in huge colonies in rocky talus (Kenyon and Brooks 1960, Drury and Steele 1977, Biderman and Drury 1978, others). It also uses rocky beach rubble and may nest in isolated pairs in small crevices in pinnacles and ridges and in cliff faces (Bédard 1969b). Densities are greatest in talus with rocks averaging less than 40 cm in diameter, a particle size smaller than that favored by the larger, often sympatric, Crested Auklet (ibid.); densities are also greater where talus is deeper (Searing 1977). Where Crested Auklets are present in areas of larger talus, the Least Auklet cannot successfully compete with its larger congener for the larger nesting crevices (Bédard 1969b).

Least Auklets have been recorded in numbers in winter in the Aleutian Islands (Gabrielson and Lincoln 1959, Murie 1959, Kenyon 1961) and the southern Bering Sea to the Pribilof Islands (Preble and McAtee 1923), probably in areas of strong upwelling, where deep water crustaceans are brought to within feeding range (Bédard 1969a). Spring migrants are often first recorded in the vicinity of their Bering Sea colonies simultaneously with the other two species of auklets, but there is an overall tendency for Least Auklet migration to be a few days later than that of Cresteds. Movement toward colonies in the southern Bering Sea may begin in early April (Preble and McAtee 1923), with birds generally reaching the vicinity of St. Lawrence Island in the third week of May (Searing 1977) and Bering Strait in the fourth week of May (offshore of Little Diomede I on 18 May 1953 and 23 May 1958 and on land 25 May 1953 and 26 May 1958 [Kenyon and Brooks 1960], 20 May and 1 June 1977, respectively [Biderman and Drury 1978], first seen 23 May 1972 [J. J. Burns unpubl. notes], none identified by 26 May 1973 but present by the thousands on 30 May

[C. A. Grauvogel unpubl. notes]; at Wales, a few seen in drift ice on 22 May 1922 [Bailey 1943], present by 27 May 1954 [R. A. Ryder unpubl. notes], none in flights of other auklets in late May 1978 [D. R. Paulson unpubl. notes]).

For St. Lawrence Island, Johnson (1976) commented that on 29 May 1973, while Crested Auklets were numerous, Least Auklets were ''still scarce''; and for Little Diomede on 30 May 1973, C. A. Grauvogel (unpubl. notes) commented that there were still four times as many Crested Auklets present as Leasts. Similarly, for Wales in 1978, D. R. Paulson (unpubl. notes) reported that while Least Auklets were not identified in the flights of larger auklets during late May, 1500 were counted flying along the coast on 10 June and 6000 on 15 June. It thus appears that the migration peak of Least Auklets is somewhat later than that of Crested Auklets and that migration continues into mid-June.

Least Auklets begin visiting the talus slopes within about a week of their arrival (Sealy 1968, others above), but egg-laying does not begin for about another 3 weeks. At St. Lawrence Island, both Sealy (1968) and Searing (1977) found this auklet laying a few days earlier than the Crested Auklet, with annual differences of 2 weeks between a seasonally early and late year; egg-laying continued for over a 2-3-week period (Sealy 1968).

There are few data on the breeding phenology of this auklet in the Bering Strait. Early dates recorded for the single-egg clutch are 1 July 1976 at King Island (Drury and Steele 1977), and, for Little Diomede Island, 12 June [yr?] (Bent 1919), 25 June 1953 (J. W. Brooks MS), 3 July 1941 (seven eggs collected, Bailey 1943), and 5 July 1977 (Biderman and Drury 1978). Chicks were heard under the rocks at Little Diomede Island on 30 July 1977, and 75-mm downies were found on 4 August 1977 (Biderman and Drury 1978), indicating that some laying began by 29-30 June 1977. Incubation in Least Auklets lasts 28-36 days, averaging 31.2 days, and the nestling period lasts 25-32 days, averaging 29.2 days (Sealy 1968). Thus, chicks could be expected to begin leaving their nests at least by the last week of August, well before the Crested Auklets, whose combined incubation and nestling period is almost 10 days longer.

Least Auklets are offshore feeders, but tend to forage closer than other auklets to their colonies (Murie 1959, Bédard 1969a, Searing 1977)—which occur only on islands with juxtaposed Offshore Waters or where currents cause advection of these waters over the Bering Shelf (Springer and Roseneau 1985). They feed almost entirely on small crustaceans, primarily the large *Calanus* copepods, but also take significant quantities of decapods and amphipods (Bédard 1969a, Searing 1977, Springer and Roseneau 1985).

As with other auklets, departure from the breeding grounds probably coincides with the time the young fly from the slopes, and thus would occur in late August and early September in the Bering Strait. The reduction of auklet numbers at the Diomedes between 27 August and 7 September 1928, commented on by Jaques (1930), was probably due largely to the postbreeding departures of Least Auklets. Few birds remain after mid-September (latest, female collected 7 October and male on 17 October 1913, Nome, J. Koren unpubl. notes).

Two unusual occurrences of this species in the Chukchi Sea region include an early spring record at Barrow on 1 April 1942 (Bailey 1948) and a mid-winter occurrence ''on a lake near Kotzebue Sound'' in January 1886 (Bent 1919).

Crested Auklet—*Aethia cristatella*

The Crested Auklet, a Beringian endemic, is an abundant breeder on the offshore islands of the Bering Strait, where many thousands nest on King Island, Fairway Rock, and Little Diomede Island (Table 8). Occasional sightings of one to three birds have been reported during the breeding season off Sledge Island and Bluff (Drury 1976a, Ramsdell and Drury 1979); none has been found nesting at these colonies, but an "immature" was seen near Bluff in early September 1975 (Drury 1976a). Scattered birds have also been recorded off the northwest coast as far as Cape Espenberg (Grinnell 1900a), probably birds associated with the Bering Strait colonies, and others stray even farther north in the Chukchi Sea (Bailey 1948, Swartz 1967).

In the Bering Strait region, the Crested Auklet nests almost exclusively in the interstices of rocky talus, a habitat it usually shares with its congener, the Least Auklet (Kenyon and Brooks 1960, Drury and Steele 1977, Biderman and Drury 1978, others). Where available, cliff crevices or beach boulder rubble may also be used (Murie 1959, Hunt et al. 1978, Sowls et al. 1978).

This auklet winters in numbers in the Aleutian Islands (Murie 1959, Byrd et al. 1974, G. J. Divoky in litt.) and in the southern Bering Sea to the Pribilof Islands (Preble and McAtee 1923). On average, it arrives on its breeding grounds a few days later than the Parakeet Auklet, usually arriving at St. Lawrence Island between 15 and 21 May (Fay and Cade 1959, Johnson 1976, Searing 1977) and a few days later in the Bering Strait region (offshore of Little Diomede I on 22 May 1953 and 20 May 1958 [Kenyon and Brooks 1960], 23 May 1966 and 24 May 1972 [J. J. Burns unpubl. notes], 23 May 1973 [C. A. Grauvogel unpubl. notes]; and near Fairway Rock on 23 May 1922 [Bailey 1943]). Most authors have reported dramatic increases in numbers within 3-5 days of first arrival, but Bailey (1948) commented that very few were present from 23 May 1922 until well into June. Migration continues at least into the first week of June; large flocks increased daily at Little Diomede Island at least until 3 June 1958 (Kenyon and Brooks 1960), and maximum numbers were seen off Wales on 6 June 1978 (D. R. Paulson unpubl. notes).

Crested Auklets begin to visit the talus slopes 4 to 9 days after arrival (Sealy 1968, Johnson 1976, Searing 1977), but do not begin laying their single-egg clutch for another month (Sealy 1968, Searing 1977). This species utilizes larger talus rubble than the Least Auklet (Bédard 1969b) and thus typically nests in areas of deeper talus (Searing 1977, Biderman and Drury 1978); hence, ice and snow may delay initiation of egg-laying beyond that of its congener (Searing 1977). Little is known of the Crested Auklet's breeding phenology in the Bering Strait region, although it appears similar to or a few days later than at St. Lawrence Island (cf. above references). Females collected on 24 June 1972 (J. J. Burns pers. comm.) and 4 July 1985 (S. A. Steinacher pers. comm.) at Little Diomede Island had hard-shelled eggs in their oviducts, and an egg was collected on Little Diomede Island on 30 June 1934 (Bailey 1943); but laying had not begun by 26 June 1953 (J. W. Brooks MS). Eskimo children gathered their first Crested Auklet egg of the season on 5 July 1977 and continued collecting them until 15 July, when "eyes" (embryos) were developing (Biderman and Drury 1978).

Incubation lasts for 34-37 days, averaging 35.6 days, and chicks remain in the nest for 30-35 days, averaging 33.5 days (Sealy 1968). Hence, hatching should begin about 1 August, and nest departures should begin during the first few days of September and continue until mid-September. Young fly directly from the nesting colonies to the sea several hundred meters offshore.

Crested Auklets are primarily offshore feeders (Murie 1959, Bédard 1969a), diving to obtain their planktonic crustacean prey. Calanoid copepods and euphausiids constitute over 90% of the diet in the northern Bering Sea (Bédard 1969a, Searing 1977).

Vacation of the colonies coincides with the departure of the chicks from their nest crevices (Sealy 1968), and Jaques (1930) noted a rapid decrease in auklet numbers (Crested or Least not indicated) about Little Diomede Island between 27 August and 7 September 1928. Few late fall records have been reported. A 10 September [yr?] date for Diomede Island is cited by Bent (1919); single individuals were seen along the Wales coastline on 9 and 10 September 1973 (D. D. Gibson unpubl. notes); and a juvenile was taken at sea off St. Michael in southeastern Norton Sound on 13 October 1879 (Nelson 1887). Farther north, 12 sightings, including one of over 100 birds swimming among ice cakes, were recorded 22-27 September 1970 between Point Barrow and Point Lay (Watson and Divoky 1972), and two specimens were taken at Barrow in the northern Chukchi Sea on 6 October 1932 (Bailey 1948).

Tufted Puffin—*Fratercula cirrhata*

Overall, Tufted Puffins are fairly common breeders about the Seward Peninsula, occurring at most of the coastal cliffs of the region. The vast majority, however, are concentrated on three offshore islands—Fairway Rock, King Island, and Little Diomede Island (Table 8); on Fairway Rock they greatly outnumber the Horned Puffin (D. R. Paulson unpubl. notes; Drury et al. 1981). On Sledge Island Tufted Puffins were reported as "slightly less common" than Horned Puffins in 1950 (Cade 1952:54), but during the latter 1970's, they made up less than 9% of the puffin population (Drury et al. 1981).

Most birds from the Bering and Chukchi seas disperse widely in winter over the oceanic waters of the North Pacific, although a few may remain as far north as the southern Bering Sea (Shuntov 1972), even to the Pribilof Islands (Preble and McAtee 1923). The earliest recorded arrival date in the northern Bering Sea is 17 May 1976 at St. Lawrence Island (Searing 1977), where they usually arrive between about 23 May and 4 June (Sealy 1973), depending on environmental conditions. First recorded arrivals at the Seward Peninsula average a few days later, from 26 May to 9 June (Little Diomede I, 26 May 1958 and 2 June 1953 [Kenyon and Brooks 1960], 31 May 1964, 2 June 1972, 9 June 1966 [J. J. Burns unpubl. notes], and 3 June 1987 [S. A. Steinacher pers. comm.]; King I, 28 May 1967 [J. J. Burns unpubl. notes]; Wales, 4 June 1978 [Flock and Hubbard 1979]; Cape Nome, 6 June 1974 [H. K. Springer and A. Bernecker, unpubl. notes]).

Breeding birds first land on the cliffs 1 to 2 weeks after arrival and may not take up continuous residency until egg-laying begins (Wehle 1980). Nest sites consist primarily of earthen burrows excavated along the tops of cliff edges, but this puffin also nests in cliff-face crevices (Swartz 1966, Sealy 1973) and among beach boulders (Sealy 1973, Drury and Steele 1977).

Little is known about the breeding schedule of Tufted Puffins in the northern Bering Sea, but their lengthy nesting period (see below) must make breeding success

problematical at these northern latitudes. It would seem that successful fledging might be limited to those sites and years when environmental conditions (especially timing of spring thaw at nest sites and fish availability for adults and nestlings) are close to ideal and limited to especially attentive parents. Sealy (1973) first observed adults carrying food to young on St. Lawrence Island on 2 August 1967, which means that egg-laying could have occurred by the third week of June; on 25 June 1922, however, Bailey (1943) reported that laying had not started on the Seward Peninsula offshore islands. Peak egg-laying extends for about 2 weeks (Wehle 1980), so the egg-laying period on the Seward Peninsula probably extends through the first half of July. It is unlikely, however, that eggs laid after the first week of July can successfully produce fledglings. Clutches consist of one egg and, while renesting occurs in Tufted Puffins (Wehle 1980), successful renesting at this latitude is unlikely because of the restricted season. Incubation lasts from 42 to 53 days (mean 46.5 days); the nestling period ranges from 38 to 59 days, depending largely on chick growth rates, which in turn depend on the quantity and quality of food received (Wehle 1980). As with other puffins, young Tufted Puffins are unable to fly when they leave the nest, but are apparently entirely independent of their parents once they leave the nest and swim out to sea (Amaral 1977).

Tufted Puffins are primarily offshore feeders, but, especially during the nestling period, they may feed inshore when food is abundant (Wehle 1980). The diet consists predominantly of small fish, although invertebrates (especially polychaete worms, squid, and octopus) are also eaten in significant quantities (Wehle 1980, Hunt et al. 1981a). As with Horned Puffins, the availability of Sand Lance or Capelin is a critical factor in the growth rates of nestlings (Wehle 1980).

Most immature birds remain on oceanic water through the summer (Shuntov 1972), but subadult birds come to colonies in July and partake in burrow excavation (Wehle 1980).

Numbers of Tufted Puffins in the northern Bering Sea decrease during the second half of September (Shuntov 1972). Given their long nesting period, approximately 85-90 days, this decrease coincides with the departure of the young from the colonies. Final departure dates from the Seward Peninsula are unknown. An influx of Tufted Puffins, probably migrants, occurred at Bluff on 12 September 1975, and numbers at the cliffs decreased markedly after 15 September; four adults were still at Topkok on 22 September 1975 (Drury 1976a). The last birds were seen farther north at Cape Thompson, Chukchi Sea, on 23 September 1961 and 25 September 1960 (Swartz 1966).

Horned Puffin—*Fratercula corniculata*

A common breeder in the region, the Horned Puffin is found at all of the coastal cliffs around both the mainland and islands. Horned Puffins typically nest in cracks and crevices in a rock substrate (Wehle 1980), and they occur about the Seward Peninsula wherever suitable rock cliff-faces are present. The largest concentrations, however, of over 10,000 birds each, occur on King, Little Diomede, and Puffin and Chamisso islands (Table 8); and on these islands, Horned Puffins also excavate earthen burrows for nest sites (Grinnell 1900a, Gabrielson and Lincoln 1959, Drury and Steele 1977, DeGrange and Sowles 1978). While Horned Puffins appear to prefer rock crevices for nesting, the availability of this habitat is limited; so, wherever they dig their own burrows into the soil, whether over old, vegetated talus slopes or otherwise, high densities may occur (Wehle 1980), and this phenomenon appears in part to explain the high population levels on the above Seward Peninsula islands.

Horned Puffins winter in the Aleutian Islands and in scattered numbers to the Pribilof Islands (Preble and McAtee 1923). The main spring migratory movement through the Bering Sea is during May, with birds usually reaching St. Lawrence Island between 15 and 28 May, although they arrived as early as 5 May in 1961 (Sealy 1973, Searing 1977). They apparently do not reach the waters of the Seward Peninsula until the end of May or early June (earliest, 29 May 1967, King I, and 1 June 1966, Little Diomede I, J. J. Burns unpubl. notes), and the passage continues until the third week of June (150 + near Teller on 10 June 1975, Drury 1976a; maximum numbers of 220 on 16 June 1978 moving northward past Wales, D. R. Paulson unpubl. notes; "a good many" migrating northward past Wales on 16 June 1922, Bailey 1943). Full breeding numbers were present on King Island by 10 June 1976 (Drury and Steele 1977), but none was yet present at Cape Deceit on 23 June 1973 (Kessel pers. obs.). Farther north at Cape Thompson, first arrivals were recorded on 6 June 1960 and 8 June 1961 (Swartz 1966).

Horned Puffins usually occupy their territories within a week of arrival in the vicinity of their colonies, but egg-laying may not begin for another 2 or 3 weeks (Wehle 1980). Although there is geographic and annual variability, the Horned Puffin's breeding season tends to begin a bit later than that of the Tufted Puffin, but it is shorter and more synchronized (Amaral 1977, Wehle 1980). The breeding schedule about the Seward Peninsula appears similar to that at St. Lawrence Island (cf. Sealy 1973), but earlier than at Cape Thompson (cf. Swartz 1966, Springer et al. 1985a).

The clutch consists of one egg (Sealy 1973, Wehle 1980), and re-laying will occur if the egg is lost early in the season (Swartz 1966, Wehle 1980). Peak egg-laying in this species extends for about 1 week (Wehle 1980). The earliest egg date reported for the region is 19 June 1978 (Ramsdell and Drury 1979), but egg-laying usually does not occur until late June or early July: egg-laying had not begun by 25 June 1953 at Little Diomede Island (Kenyon and Brooks 1960) nor by 25 June 1922 at Little Diomede

Island or Fairway Rock (Bailey 1943); first eggs were found on 9 July 1977 at Little Diomede Island (Biderman and Drury 1978) and on 1 July 1977 at Bluff (Drury et al. 1978); all 50 eggs collected on 9 July 1899 at Chamisso Island were still "fresh" (Grinnell 1900a); hatching dates in 1977 at Puffin-Chamisso Islands (see below) also indicate that eggs were laid during the first few days of July that year. Hatching dates in late July and the first few days of August (see below) indicate that some egg-laying occurs in late June in some years.

Incubation lasts from 38 to 43 days, averaging 39-41 days (Sealy 1969, Amaral 1977, Leschner and Burrell 1977), and in most years hatching occurs during the first third of August. Hatching had begun at Bluff by 27 July 1976, 28 July 1978, 31 July 1977, and 3 August 1975 (Steele and Drury 1977, Ramsdell and Drury 1979, Drury et al. 1978, and Drury 1976a, respectively); there were many chicks on Chamisso Island on 2 August 1914 (Hersey 1916), but hatching was just beginning there on 11-14 August 1977 (DeGange and Sowls 1978).

The nestling period ranges from 38 to 43 + days (Sealy 1973, Amaral 1977, Wehle 1980), depending largely on chick growth rates, which in turn depend on the quantity and quality of food received (Wehle 1980). Thus, the first chicks will leave their nests during the first week of September, while others may not leave until the end of the month. These dates are corroborated by observations of Drury (1976a), Steele and Drury (1977), and Ramsdell and Drury (1979). Young puffins are unable to fly when they leave the nest; they fall and flutter to the water below and swim immediately out to sea, apparently being entirely independent of their parents thereafter (Sealy 1973, Amaral 1977).

Horned Puffins are predominantly inshore feeders during the breeding season, usually concentrating their foraging within 1-2 km of shore (Sealy 1973, Wehle 1980). In Norton Sound, however, Ramsdell and Drury (1979) found moderate numbers out to 16 km offshore, and Swartz (1967:345) found them "far from shore" in the southern Chukchi Sea. Their diet is predominantly fish, which they obtain by diving and pursuit under water. They are somewhat more generalized feeders than Tufted Puffins, feeding on a greater variety of fish and supplementing their diet with significant quantities of squid, polychaete worms, and crustaceans (Wehle 1980). Chicks are fed fish almost entirely, and the availability of Sand Lance or Capelin is a critical factor in their growth rates (ibid.).

Subadult birds augment numbers at colonies by arriving during August and early September (Drury 1976a, Steele and Drury 1977), and numbers peaked at Bluff in mid-September 1975. At this time (12 September 1975), 3000 Horned Puffins were counted in an updraft in front of the cliffs (Drury 1976a). Numbers decrease rapidly after mid-September (Drury 1976a, Steele and Drury 1977), coinciding with the departure of the chicks. Some, however, remain at the cliffs at least until late September (40, including 4 young, on 27 September 1986, and 75 on 24 September 1984, but gone by 6 October 1984, Cape Deceit, J. D. Walters unpubl. notes), and there are a few October records in the waters of the Peninsula (latest, one, 18 October 1970, northern Bering Strait, Watson and Divoky 1972; two, 28 October 1984, flying east past Deering, J. D. Walters unpubl. notes).

Band-tailed Pigeon—*Columba fasciata*

Accidental on the Seward Peninsula, an adult female Band-tailed Pigeon (UAM 3137) was collected on 12 August 1969 at Milepost 8.3 Teller Highway by D. G. Roseneau. The bird had regressed ovules up to 3 mm in diameter and a brood patch, indicating that it had nested that season, although not necessarily on the Seward Peninsula.

This pigeon has been expanding its range in Alaska since 1961, when it was first recorded in Southeastern Alaska and where it is now an uncommon summer visitant and probable breeder (Kessel and Gibson 1978).

Mourning Dove—*Zenaida macroura*

The Mourning Dove is accidental on the Seward Peninsula. A partially decomposed carcass was found near Wales on 13 June 1965 by R. T. Wallen (Weeden and Johnson 1973). Since most occurrences of this dove in Alaska are of fall migrants or visitants (see Kessel and Gibson 1978) and since it is unlikely that a dying spring migrant at Wales would have decomposed significantly by 13 June, this bird probably died during fall 1964 and remained frozen over the winter.

Common Cuckoo—*Cuculus canorus*

The Old World Common Cuckoo is accidental on the Seward Peninsula. A dead bird (UAM 5470) was found at about Milepost 3 Taylor Highway on 13 June 1988 by D. E. Wolf; the bird had not been there the preceding day. This cuckoo is a casual or very rare spring migrant and summer visitant in the western and central Aleutian Islands (Kessel and Gibson 1978, subsequent data), and an adult female (UAM 3733) was taken on the Tutakoke River, Yukon-Kuskokwim Delta on 11 June 1979 (Gill and Handel 1980).

Oriental Cuckoo—*Cuculus saturatus*

The Oriental Cuckoo from Asia is accidental on the Seward Peninsula. A female was collected on 28 June 1946 near Wales by D. Tevuk (Hanna 1947, Bailey 1948). This record is one of only six in North America, all from the Bering Sea area (Kessel and Gibson 1978, subsequent unpubl. data).

Great Horned Owl—*Bubo virginianus*

A common bird of Central Alaska forests, the Great Horned Owl is at least an uncommon resident as far west on the Seward Peninsula as coniferous forests occur. Residents of Koyuk report its occurrence in that area. A pair 12 km up the Kwiniuk River and another 40 km up the Tubutulik River each had families of four fledglings on 6 August 1973 and 13 August 1973, respectively (J. H. Lee pers. comm.). Between Council on the Niukluk River and the lower reaches of the Fish River, 17-18 July 1966, J. J. Burns and R. L. Rausch (unpubl. notes) recorded three sightings, including a family of three fledglings on 18 July. Also, at least one bird was present at Bluff during summer 1975 (W. H. Drury in litt.). Beyond the forest, two were sitting in willows between the Kuzitrin River bridge and Bunker Hill on 2 and 3 March 1986 (D. R. Klein pers. comm.).

Snowy Owl—*Nyctea scandiaca*

A nomadic predator, the Snowy Owl varies from common to rare on the Seward Peninsula. It may occur during any month of the year and breeds in years when rodents are abundant. It is an open-country bird and may occur anywhere in the nonforested portions of the Peninsula, including on the major offshore islands and on the winter sea ice.

Throughout its Holarctic range, Snowy Owl breeding is closely associated with high vole or lemming populations (Watson 1957), and where this prey base is low, few if any owls occur. Hence, in such regions as the Seward Peninsula, population levels vary widely and breeding may occur in some years but not others. Observations on the Seward Peninsula indicate a preference for the uplands, especially the Dwarf Shrub Meadow habitat, where nests are placed on low promontories, such as tussocks or hummocks. Such sites are often snow-free earlier in the season than surrounding areas, and they provide a view of these surroundings for the nesting female. Nests in the lowlands about Igiak Bay and on vegetation atop boulders in the Askinuk Mountains on the Yukon-Kuskokwim Delta were reported by Murie (1929), and such locations are probably used occasionally on the Seward Peninsula as well.

Nesting densities vary with the density of available prey, with maximum recorded nest densities being about one territory per 2.5 km² and with nests sometimes within 1 km of each other (Watson 1957). No such densities have been recorded on the Seward Peninsula, but during the arvicoline high in 1967, I recorded 12 owls between Mileposts 1 and 31.5 Teller Highway during the first week of June.

Data have been recorded from only a few nests on the Peninsula, but nesting chronologies appear closely similar to those elsewhere on the North American tundras (Watson 1957). The earliest eggs are laid about 15 May (nest of 7 eggs found on 28 May 1976, H. K. Springer pers. comm.), but clutch initiations probably continue until early June. Eggs of a clutch are laid on alternate days, with incubation beginning with the laying of the first egg (Murie 1929, others). Clutch sizes also vary according to food supply (Watson 1957). Completed clutches in Alaska average 6.7-7.5 eggs (Pitelka et al. 1955b), although the mode is 8-9 eggs (Kessel and Gibson unpubl. data) and clutches of up to 11 and 15 eggs have been recorded (Murie 1929, Bailey 1948). Incubation, which is performed entirely by the female, usually takes 32-33 days (Murie 1929, Watson 1957, Parmelee et al. 1967), with the chicks hatching at 1-2-day intervals—longer between the later eggs in the clutch—in the same sequence as the eggs were laid (Watson 1957). The male brings food to the brooding female and defends the nest from predators (Parmelee et al. 1967, others).

Young begin hatching in mid-June on the Seward Peninsula, based (1) on a nest reported by Bailey (1926) that contained four small nestlings and three addled eggs on about 20 June 1921 and (2) on the 32-33-day incubation period. Most young stay in the nest 16-25 days and then scatter about on the surrounding tundra (Pitelka et al. 1955a, Watson 1957, Parmelee et al. 1967). In large clutches, some nestlings may leave the nest before the last eggs hatch. The female stays with the nest as long as any chicks remain, while the male takes over the feeding of the flightless young that have left the nest. Young begin flying short distances at about 30 days of age, but are unable to fly strongly until they are over 50 days old (Watson 1957, Parmelee et al. 1967). Thus, the first strongly flying young on the Seward Peninsula could be expected in early August.

Throughout the Holarctic, arvicolines, especially Brown Lemmings, are the main food of the Snowy Owl (Watson 1957), and owl population levels are closely correlated with lemming abundance (Brandt 1943, Pitelka et al. 1955b, Sutton and Parmelee 1956, Watson 1957, others). Other prey is utilized, however, especially when voles and lemmings are not readily available. Remains of five ground squirrels and four birds were found in 19 pellets from Cape Espenberg (Schamel et al. 1979), and in marshy areas of the Yukon-Kuskokwim Delta, Murie (1929) found extensive use of bird prey, including ducks, young geese, Mew Gulls, and ptarmigan. In winter at St. Lawrence Island, Fay and Cade (1959) found Snowy Owls preying almost entirely upon wintering waterfowl, especially Oldsquaw and King Eiders, ranging far out on the sea ice to open water where these ducks occurred. In southern Kotzebue Sound, an owl appeared to be hunting from an ice ridge 8 km from shore on 6 April 1984; a nearby pellet contained the undigested remains of a Collared Lemming (B. P. Kelly unpubl. notes).

Most owls have left the Peninsula by early winter, but if food is available, some stay throughout the winter. In 1969-1970 a few remained along the Teller Highway, where most sightings were between mid-January and the end of March and where three were seen at one time at Milepost 45 in early February (W. L. Foster in litt.). A specimen was collected on Big Diomede Island by J. Koren on 19 November 1912 (Thayer and Bangs 1914); a female was collected at Wales by D. Tevuk on 11 December 1946 (Bailey 1948); a bird was seen at Cape Woolley on 29 December 1968 and the Sinuk River on 23 January 1967 (J. J. Burns unpubl. notes); and one was seen several times near Deering during January 1984 (J. D. Walters unpubl. notes).

An illustration of the nomadic habits of this species comes from a family of nestlings banded near Cambridge Bay, southeast Victoria Island, Canada (69° N, 105° W) in July 1960 (Parmelee et al. 1967): One was recovered 80 km southwest of Ottawa, Ontario, on 19 October 1961; one on the west shore of James Bay, Ontario, on 8 May 1962; and one on Sakhalin Island, USSR, on 18 February 1962.

Northern Hawk-Owl—*Surnia ulula*

Although a resident of the open taiga woodlands of Interior Alaska, the Northern Hawk-Owl appears to be only a rare visitant on the Seward Peninsula. Two were recorded in the Imuruk Basin area on 7 March 1905 by Anthony (1906), and he reported a movement on the upper Nome River on 23 May 1905, stating (p. 184) that "at no time during the day were they absent from the landscape, and often five or six were seen at one time." A female was collected along the Nome River on 25 September 1913 by J. Koren (unpubl. notes). More recently, on 8 May 1978, a hawk-owl was seen near Nome by D. Levinson (Beltz School unpubl. notes), and between 22 and 26 August 1980, one was recorded near Moses Point (D. A. Woodby in litt.).

Short-eared Owl—*Asio flammeus*

The Short-eared Owl is an uncommon breeder and summer visitant on the Seward Peninsula, but like the Snowy Owl it is nomadic and may vary among years from rare to common. It is a diurnal, open-country owl and may occur anywhere in the nonforested portions of the Peninsula, including on the major offshore islands. During the breeding season it is found primarily in the Southern and Northern uplands and Interior Lowlands of the Peninsula, favoring the mesic Dwarf Shrub Meadow habitat.

This migratory owl is a rare winter visitant as far north as Southcoastal Alaska (Copper River Delta, Isleib and Kessel 1973; Kodiak I, MacIntosh 1986), but most birds winter farther south in North America (American Ornithologists' Union 1983).

Spring migrants may arrive on the Peninsula as early as the end of April (earliest, 27 April 1988, Deering, J. D. Walters unpubl. notes, and 29 April 1983, extralimitally on the Choris Peninsula, S. Hills unpubl. notes), but most spring arrivals are reported 10-15 May—a time when the landscape is still largely snow-covered. Birds may arrive in numbers, but will not remain unless voles or lemmings are available for food. Between 21 and 30 May 1971, D. G. Roseneau and W. Walker (pers. comm.) reported seeing 1-3 birds/20 km along the road system, but by 7-23 June numbers had dropped to 1 or fewer/160 km. Numbers were up to about 5 birds/20 km in the Interior Lowlands in July 1967 (Kessel pers. obs.) and June 1970 (D. G. Roseneau and W. Walker pers. comm.) and in the Southern Uplands in late June 1980 (T. G. Tobish in litt.), but there were only about 1.3 birds/20 km in the Southern Uplands in July 1967 (Kessel pers. obs.). In some years few if any birds are seen.

Short-eared Owls are ground nesters, usually concealing their nests in tall grass or sedge. A nest near Feather River was placed in the middle of a 1-m-diameter hummock of grasses that was still surrounded by snow when found on 27 May 1968 (D. G. Roseneau and W. R. Tilton pers. comm.). If local food is sufficient, nesting begins shortly after the birds arrive. A nest near Deering contained 3 eggs on 31 May and 5 on 3 June 1984 (J. D. Walters unpubl. notes), while the above Feather River nest was essentially complete on 27 May 1968, with a grass cup and some body feathers, but contained no eggs. A nest at the mouth of Arctic River, from which a bird was flushed on 14 May 1976, contained 1 egg (Noble and Wright 1977). Egg-laying in this nest corroborated the findings of Pitelka et al. (1955a) that laying intervals may vary from about 1 day to 4 days: On 15 May (13:15 h) the Arctic River nest contained 2 eggs; 17 May (15:30 h), 3 eggs; 18 May (11:30 h), 4 eggs; 19 May (11:45 h), 5 eggs; 21 May (16:05 h), 6 eggs; and 24 May (13:30 h), 7 eggs. Clutch sizes in 22 completed clutches at Barrow in 1953 ranged from 4 to 8 eggs, with an average of 6.3 and a mode of 7 eggs (Pitelka et al. 1955b). On the Yukon-Kuskokwim Delta in 1924, clutches ranged from 5 to 12 eggs, with a mode of 6 (Brandt 1943). Both data sets were obtained during high arvicoline populations, and therefore probably had larger clutches than in years of less abundant prey.

Incubation takes about 28-30 days at northern latitudes and is performed solely by the female (Pitelka et al. 1955a, b). Incubation apparently begins at various times during egg-laying (Brandt 1943), resulting in irregular hatching intervals and multiple-sized young in a brood.

Owlets stay in the nest for about 14 days at southern latitudes (Clark 1975). At Barrow, however, Pitelka et al. (1955a) had one nest in which all young were still in the nest at 21-31±1 days of age—although a chick from another nest was found 6 m from its nest when 16-17 days old. Both parents care for the young after they leave the nest, although only the female will brood them (Pitelka et al. 1955a). Fledging probably occurs 30-35 days after hatching (Witherby et al. [1943:333] indicated 24-27 days; Urner [1923:33] estimated 31-36 days). Thus, first flying young could be expected on the Seward Peninsula by the third week of July.

Food of the Short-eared Owl consists largely of arcivolines, but may include other small mammals, passerine birds, and shorebirds—the last primarily in coastal situations (Clark 1975). During the unusual high of Short-eared Owl nesting at Barrow in 1953, food was entirely Brown Lemmings (Pitelka et al. 1955b).

Most fall departures from the Seward Peninsula take place during September (latest, one shot on 28 October 1964 at Nome, after an unusually heavy fall passage, J. J. Burns pers. comm.; specimen, 23 November 1934, extralimitally at St. Lawrence I, Murie 1936).

Boreal Owl—*Aegolius funereus*

A bird of the closed mixed coniferous-deciduous forests of Interior Alaska, the Boreal Owl is probably a rare resident in the forests of the southeast quadrant of the Peninsula. In 1975, E. Kimatoak and H. Kavairlook told me it occurred in the Koyuk area; Kavairlook indicated that there had been "many a few years ago," but that they had died off and "there were none now." Such population fluctuations have also been noted in Interior Alaska (Kessel pers. obs.).

The Boreal Owl is a rare winter visitant beyond the forests. One was found roosting in an abandoned "igloo" on the Agiapuk River, northern Imuruk Basin, on 3 March 1905 by Anthony (1906), who also saw two or three other individuals that month in the willows along the lower Kuzitrin River. On 2 February 1970 a roosting bird was caught in an old building at Beltz School near Nome (W. L. Foster in litt.).

Hummingbirds—Trochilidae

Any species of hummingbird is accidental on the Seward Peninsula. A female-plumaged Ruby-throated Hummingbird (*Archilochus colubris*) was captured in a building at Nome on 13 August 1981 and was subsequently released without its tail feathers. These feathers (UAM 5106) were identified by R. C. Banks and M. R. Browning, NMNH (in litt.). An unidentified hummingbird was observed at Golovin in 1963 by L. Rasmussen (D. G. Roseneau pers. comm.).

Extralimitally, an adult male Rufous Hummingbird (*Selasphorus rufus*) was collected on Big Diomede Island on 10 June 1976 (Sorokin 1979), and a mummified adult male Ruby-throated Hummingbird was found among rocks on a beach near St. Michael, probably during summer 1925 (Swales 1926).

Belted Kingfisher—*Ceryle alcyon*

Belted Kingfishers, which breed throughout the forested interior of Alaska, are probably rare summer visitants and possible breeders in the forested southeast quadrant of the Seward Peninsula. They have been reported along the Tubutulik River, where one bird was seen by J. H. Lee (pers. comm.) about 70 km up the river on 13 August 1973 and another 15 km farther up the river on the following day, and along the Koyuk River, where H. Smith reported it as "common" between 29 June and 4 July 1982 (S. R. Robinson pers. comm.). Extralimitally, a pair of kingfishers was seen hunting in pools of the Inglutalik River at the head of Norton Bay on 19 August 1976 (Shields and Peyton 1977).

Eurasian Wryneck—*Jynx torquilla*

A dead male wryneck was found on the beach near Wales by D. Tevuk on 8 September 1945 (Bailey 1947, 1948) and is the only North American record of this aberrant woodpecker.

Downy Woodpecker—*Picoides pubescens*

The Downy Woodpecker may be a rare or uncommon resident in the forested portions of the Peninsula (fide local residents at Koyuk and Elim), but only two specific occurrences have been documented, both west of treeline. A "*Dryobates*, of the size of *pubescens*," seen among dwarf willows on the slopes south of Imuruk Basin on 27 March 1905 by Anthony (1906:182) was undoubtedly this species; and a mummified male (UAM 4985) was found in a cabin in the Nome River valley about 2 km west of Milepost 17 Taylor Highway on 1 June 1979 by D. G. Roseneau.

Northern Flicker—*Colaptes auratus*

A casual fall migrant on the Seward Peninsula, the Northern Flicker has been reported twice. A skin was obtained by Nelson (1887:160) from a native during the winter of 1880 "near Bering Strait," apparently from somewhere near the mouth of the Sinuk River; and a dead male was picked up by a villager in Teller in January 1982 (Nome Museum photo).

Olive-sided Flycatcher—*Contopus borealis*

The Olive-sided Flycatcher, an uncommon breeder in the scattered coniferous woodlands throughout Interior Alaska, may occur rarely at the base of the Seward Peninsula. Thus far, however, it has been reported only twice from the Peninsula: A single bird was observed flycatching from rocks at the base of Needle Mountain at Wales on 8 June 1977 by D. A. Woodby and K. V. Hirsch (pers. comm.), and one was observed as it perched and "hawked" for insects in Deering on 18 May 1987 by J. D. Walters (unpubl. notes).

Western Wood-Pewee—*Contopus sordidulus*

A casual spring migrant on the Seward Peninsula, a Western Wood-Pewee was observed feeding at the edge of a small pool adjacent to the inlet of Safety Sound by D. D. Gibson and others on 13 June 1973 (Gibson unpubl. notes).

Alder Flycatcher—*Empidonax alnorum*

While uncommon over the Seward Peninsula as a whole, the Alder Flycatcher is a fairly common probable breeder where appropriate habitat exists at the base of the Peninsula. In the vicinity of Buckland on 22, 24, and 26 June 1975, F. G. Scheider and I counted a total of 20 birds; and farther west, I found two singing males, one at Milepost 10 and one at Milepost 15.5 on the Inmachuk River road on 21 and 22 June 1974, respectively. Six singing males were recorded along the Inmachuk Road between Mileposts 2 and 13 on 18-20 June 1984 and two were at Utica Creek on 14 June 1985 (J. D. Walters unpubl. notes). Three Alder Flycatchers sang from dense willows in upper King Creek near Koyuk on 29 June 1975, and nine sang in the vicinity of Elim on 1 and 2 July 1972 (Kessel pers. obs.). Elim and the Inmachuk River are as far west as numbers and behavior indicate regular summer residency and breeding (although no nests have been reported), but scattered singing males have been recorded farther west: Safety Sound (one, 23 June 1968, W. A. Davis and M. M. Erickson pers. comm.; one, 15 June 1981, P. D. Vickery in litt.), Milepost 9 Teller Highway (one, 13 June 1981, P. D. Vickery in litt.), Pilgrim Hot Springs (one, 27 June 1988, T. H. Pogson pers. comm.), and North Killeak Lake (one, 30 June 1973, D. D. Gibson and Kessel pers. obs.). The favored habitat of this flycatcher is Tall Shrub Thicket that has a dense low shrub layer in the understory (Spindler and Kessel 1980), a habitat that is mainly riparian on the Seward Peninsula.

There is no information on migration dates for the Seward Peninsula, but based on data from Interior Alaska (Kessel unpubl. data), in most years the first spring migrants of this insectivorous species probably arrive between the last few days of May and the first few days of June, with populations building up over the next 10-12 days.

Nests are placed in crotches of shrubs, usually below 1 m. In Alaska, three to four eggs are laid over an equivalent number of days, and incubation lasts 13 to 14 days; nestlings remain in the nest for 12 days (ANRS). Thus, fledging should occur in mid-July.

The main fall exodus has probably occurred by mid-August, although stragglers may remain until the end of the month.

Say's Phoebe—*Sayornis saya*

An uncommon breeder on the Seward Peninsula, the Say's Phoebe occurs throughout most of the Peninsula, west to about 166°30′ W, where I have observed nests along the Bluestone River and on the cliffs of Tuksuk Channel at the west end of Imuruk Basin and where J. M. Wright (pers. comm.) saw birds at Cape Riley, southwest of Teller, on 15 July 1987. East of there, it occurs sparsely throughout the Southern and Northern uplands and in the Highlands, and it has been reported coastally at Bluff (W. H. Drury in litt.) and Cape Riley (above). Its primary nesting habitat is steep cliff faces, where it places its nest on ledges or in crevices under overhangs. It also uses analogous artificial habitats, such as the beams under the Bluestone River bridge at Milepost 58 Teller Highway, or abandoned buildings or mining dredges, as on the upper Inmachuk River and at Hannum Creek.

In Interior Alaska, the phoebe occurs from early May to mid-September (Kessel unpubl. data). The season may be a little shorter on the Seward Peninsula (earliest, one, 7 May 1988 and 16 May 1987, Deering, J. D. Walters unpubl. notes).

Little is known about the breeding biology of this flycatcher anywhere in its range. Varying amounts of data from 17 nests on the Seward Peninsula reveal egg dates that range from 29 May to 22 June, with four completed clutches containing 5 eggs and one with 4 eggs, and reveal nestling dates that range from 29 June (young less than 6 days old) to late July. In Interior Alaska (ANRS) eggs are usually laid on consecutive days and incubation often begins about halfway through egg-laying, so the young hatch over a period of 2 or 3 days. Incubation lasts about 18 days and the young remain in the nest for another 18 days, time periods that are each about 4 days longer than those cited by Bent (1942). A family of fledglings was reported on 28 July 1946 at Chamisso Island (Gabrielson and Lincoln 1959) and on 5 August 1979 at Milepost 30 Taylor Highway (R. and B. Mearns unpubl. notes).

Horned Lark—*Eremophila alpestris*

A Holarctic species, the Horned Lark is an uncommon breeder on the Seward Peninsula. During the breeding season, it is widely dispersed throughout the uplands and the foothills of the Highlands, wherever its preferred habitat of dry Dwarf Shrub Mat and fellfield occur—including at the brow of windblown coastal cliffs, such as Bluff, Topkok, and Cape Deceit.

Spring arrival dates vary from late April to early May, depending on spring weather conditions (earliest, 29 April 1988 and 5 May 1984 and 1985 at Deering and 4 May 1983 at Nome, J. D. Walters unpubl. notes; and 26 April 1943, H. C. Kyllingstad in litt., and 29 April 1985, B. J. McCaffery unpubl. notes, extralimitally in the southern Nulato Hills). Movement may continue into the third week of May.

Little is known about the breeding biology of the subspecies of Horned Lark that breeds in Alaska (*E. a. arcticola*). As elsewhere, the female scratches out a nest cavity in the ground and builds her nest in that cavity. Egg-laying on the Peninsula probably begins as early as the fourth week of May. Clutches in Alaska are usually four or five eggs (17 clutches averaged 4.4 ± 0.7 eggs, range 3-6, Kessel and Gibson unpubl. data), which is similar to other northern subspecies (Sutton and Parmelee 1955b, Drury 1961a) but about one egg larger than in more southern subspecies (Verbeek 1967, Cannings and Threlfall 1981). Studies of other subspecies give 11 to 12 days as the most frequent incubation period and a nestling period of only 9 to 10 days (Verbeek 1967, Cannings and Threlfall 1981). The female alone incubates the eggs and broods the young. The male defends the territory until the young leave the nest and helps feed the young from the time of hatching until they are independent (Cannings and Threlfall 1981).

Young leave the nest before they are able to fly, with their flight feathers only one-third to one-half grown and with almost no tail. They are not fully fledged until about 14 days of age, and they begin to become independent of their parents at 3 weeks (Cannings and Threlfall 1981). Thus, eggs on the Seward Peninsula should begin hatching during the second week of June (five small nestlings, 11 June 1983, north of Nome, R. and B. Mearns unpubl. notes); and the first young should be out of the nest by the end of the third week of June, although some nests may still contain young in the second week of July.

Nestlings are fed entirely on insects, whereas adults and juvenals feed additionally on berries and seeds (Verbeek 1967, Cannings and Threlfall 1981).

Postbreeding flocks begin to form in late July and become increasingly conspicuous during August. Some birds have departed by mid-August, although most movement probably occurs during September, with few birds left on the Peninsula by the end of September.

Purple Martin—*Progne subis*

Accidental on the Seward Peninsula, an adult female Purple Martin was collected by A. Nagozruk at Wales on 3 June 1929 (Bailey 1930, 1948). This swallow is casual in Alaska (Kessel and Gibson 1978).

Tree Swallow—*Tachycineta bicolor*

The Tree Swallow is an uncommon but widespread breeder on the Peninsula. It has been recorded breeding from Koyuk (Kessel pers. obs.) and Utica Creek (J. M. Wright unpubl. notes) to King Island (P. L. Drury pers. comm.). Most nest sites are in artificial habitats, such as bird boxes or openings in pipes or old buildings and mining dredges, but they also use natural cavities in mature Balsam Poplars.

Weather conditions strongly affect the spring arrival times of this early swallow, but first arrivals can be expected during the second week of May (earliest, three, 8 May 1985, Deering, J. D. Walters unpubl. notes; two "swallows," 9 May 1983, Nome, K. Murray, Beltz School unpubl. notes; and, extralimitally, one Tree Swallow on 6 May 1987 and more than fifty on 8 May 1982 at Kotzebue, Selawik NWR unpubl. notes). Tree Swallows continue to move through western Alaska throughout the month of May, with many "first arrival" dates being reported between 15 and 27 May. These late arriving birds may be first-time breeders searching for nest sites (see Kuerzi 1941, Chapman 1955).

Nest data upon which to base estimates of breeding chronologies in the region are unavailable. Elsewhere in the United States, the most frequent average clutch sizes are 5 or 6 eggs; incubation averages 14-15 days; and the nestling period averages 19-20 days (Stocek 1970). I have twice watched parents bringing food to young in cavities during the first week of July, and fledging at two nests on the Yukon-Kuskokwim Delta occurred on 19 July 1970 and 22 July 1972 (Yukon Delta NWR unpubl. data). Two pairs of adults with newly fledged young were noted on 5 August 1946 at Nome by I. N. Gabrielson (Gabrielson and Lincoln 1959).

Nestling food is entirely insects, but adults, unlike most other swallows, may use appreciable quantities of berries, seeds, and nonflying invertebrates (Bent 1942). These latter foods are consumed primarily under inclement environmental conditions and enable this species to arrive and survive on the Seward Peninsula earlier than other swallows.

In Western Alaska, most Tree Swallows have concluded nesting and departed by the end of July (Kessel and D. D. Gibson unpubl. data). Late records for the Seward Peninsula include a 6 August 1973 observation of an immature at Serpentine Hot Springs (D. D. Gibson unpubl. notes) and three birds recorded at Chamisso Island on 12 August 1977 (DeGange and Sowls 1978). In 1977, however, a group of twenty migrant Tree Swallows frequented Wales from 3 to 22 August, decreasing to three birds on 23 August; the last bird was seen on 3 September (D. A. Woodby and K. V. Hirsch unpubl. notes).

Violet-green Swallow—_Tachycineta thalassina_

Violet-green Swallows are probably rare spring migrants on the Seward Peninsula, but positive identifications have been reported only twice. Both observations were of single birds at Nome, one on 26 May 1968 by W. R. Tilton and D. G. Roseneau (unpubl. notes) and one on 10 June 1976 by H. K. Springer (pers. comm.).

Bank Swallow—_Riparia riparia_

An uncommon breeder on the Seward Peninsula, the Bank Swallow occurs primarily in the Interior Lowlands and the Southern and Northern uplands, where rivers cut through unconsolidated deposits and provide fresh-cut banks for nesting. Migrants have been reported as far west as Wales (two, 9 June, and one, 13 June 1978, D. R. Paulson unpubl. notes) and Breving Lagoon (two, sometime between 2 and 7 August 1980, D. A. Woodby unpubl. notes), but there appears to be little appropriate habitat for nesting west of about 166° W, and the amount of summer warmth west of there, in Young's (1971) floristic Zone 3, may be too little for successful breeding. It seems likely that the season for flying insects, upon which this species depends, is too short in Zone 3 and that cool burrow temperatures would require more energy for incubation and nestling development than this small swallow can provide.

Scattered pairs and small groups of Bank Swallows apparently nest along many of the rivers, and I have seen several larger colonies. There was a colony of 100 + birds in a bank along the Pilgrim River, downstream of the Taylor Highway, on 6 July 1971; 40 birds were flying about a colony on 25 June 1971 at the junction of the Agiapuk River and a creek locally called the "Toonu River," at the northwest edge of Imuruk Basin; there was a colony of about 40 birds between the Deering airstrip and Cape Deceit in 1973; and about 50 birds were present about the tailing piles at Milepost 15.5 Inmachuk River road on 23 June 1973. In addition to digging their nest cavities into river banks, Bank Swallows on the Seward Peninsula use road cuts and dredge tailings for nesting.

Most spring arrivals on the Peninsula probably occur between the last week of May and the first week of June (earliest, 29 May 1984 and 30 May 1988, Deering,

J. D. Walters unpubl. notes; but 22 May 1986, extralimitally at Noatak R delta, Selawik NWR unpubl. notes).

Almost nothing is known about their breeding chronologies on the Peninsula, but this swallow is present for scarcely 2 months, which is barely sufficient for its nesting cycle, from digging burrows and nest-building to strongly flying young. Clutch size in Interior Alaska is 4.1 ± 0.8 eggs (Hickman 1979); incubation lasts for 15 days, and young do not leave their burrows for the first time until they are 20-23 days old, and then may return to the burrow to roost and receive food from the parents until 28 days of age (Petersen 1955). On 29 July 1973 parents were still feeding nestlings at the Cape Deceit colony, and there was no evidence of reduced numbers up the Inmachuk River the next day (D. D. Gibson unpubl. notes). Extralimitally on the Kobuk River, a few young were still being fed in their burrows on 17 August 1898 (Grinnell 1900a).

The main fall exodus of Bank Swallows from western Alaska occurs during the first third of August, and few birds are seen after that time (latest, all extralimitally, seven on 18 August 1984, Kotzebue, J. D. Walters unpubl. notes; none after 19 August 1898, Kobuk R, Grinnell 1900a; two on 21 August 1986, 30 km east of Selawik, Selawik NWR unpubl. notes).

Cliff Swallow—*Hirundo pyrrhonota*

The Cliff Swallow is an uncommon breeder on the Peninsula east of an approximate northeast-southwest line connecting Grantley Harbor and Serpentine Hot Springs. Occasional spring migrants can be expected almost anywhere beyond the breeding range, as illustrated by recent records from Wales: two birds on 21 May 1969 (Flock and Hubbard 1979), two on 12 June 1976 (P. W. Sykes in litt.), two on 9 June 1978 (D. R. Paulson unpubl. notes), and one each on 28 May and 10 June 1983 (M. L. Ward unpubl. notes) and by the occurrence of a single bird flying near the mouth of the Serpentine River on 25 June 1970 (Kessel pers. obs.) and single birds on the Espenberg Peninsula 31 May and 3 and 7 June 1977 (Schamel et al. 1979). The dependency of Cliff Swallows on flying insects for food may prevent successful breeding west of 166° W. Locations of known Cliff Swallow colonies are given in Table 17.

Several habitat features are essential to nesting Cliff Swallows (Emlen 1954): (1) an open foraging area, (2) a vertical substrate with a protective overhang for nest attachment, and (3) a local mud source for nest construction. A wide entrance is required for nesting to occur inside barns or sheds (Samuel 1971). Substrates used for nesting colonies on the Seward Peninsula are listed in Table 17. In addition, a pair of Cliff Swallows was observed repeatedly entering with food and departing a sea cave on the west side of Cape Deceit on 29 July 1973 (D. D. Gibson unpubl. notes), and a small colony of 6+ nests was present on a 6-9-m sea cliff near Teller on 11 July 1947 (Hamilton 1948).

Because of these birds' dependence on flying insects for food, weather strongly influences their spring arrival dates on the Peninsula. On average, the Cliff Swallow's season on the Peninsula appears to be about 2 weeks longer than that of the Bank Swallow, with arrival dates at least a week earlier and departure dates about a week later than the Bank Swallow. Generally, the first spring migrants arrive during the

Table 17.   Location, size, and substrate of Cliff Swallow colonies on the Seward
Peninsula, Alaska, 1967-1977.

Location	No. nests	(year)	Substrate
Niukluk R, at and below Council	40	(1967)	riverine cliffs
	28* + 58*	(1977)	
Kuzitrin R bridge, Taylor Hwy	20	(1967)	bridge supports
	20	(1977)	
Pilgrim R bridge, Taylor Hwy	7*	(1977)	bridge supports
Jct. Taylor Hwy and Windy Ck	75-100 active	(1969) (1977)	riverine cliffs
Bluestone R	22*	(1969)	riverine cliffs
	6	(1973)	
	10+	(1977)	
Serpentine Hot Springs	25	(1969)	granite tors
	12-20	(1971)	
	16*	(1973)	
Pilgrim Hot Springs	52*	(1971)	inside abandoned barn
Inmachuk R, Milepost 15.5	50*	(1973)	under eaves of shed
Noxapaga R, between Andesite and Goose creeks	two small colonies	(1973)	riverine cliffs
Snake R bridge	10*	(1976)	bridge supports
NW edge Imuruk Basin (65°11′N 165°48′W)	15*	(1971)	shoreline limestone cliff

* Accurate counts; other numbers were estimates or partial counts

last third of May (earliest, one, 20 May 1982, extralimitally at Kotzebue, Selawik NWR
unpubl. notes; two, 21 May 1969, Wales, Flock and Hubbard 1979; and arrived
24 May 1978, upper Inmachuk R, J. M. Wright unpubl. notes).

Cliff Swallows build gourd-shaped nests of mud, with an entrance hole about
5 cm in diameter, which they line with grass. Nests of the preceding year may be
repaired or new ones built. The most frequent clutch size in North America is 3 or
4 eggs (Mayhew 1958, Samuel 1971), although earliest clutches, which are probably
laid by experienced breeders, may be 5 eggs (Myres 1957). Eggs are laid on consecutive
days, with intermittent incubation beginning after the first few eggs are laid and
becoming continuous with the laying of the next to last egg; incubation lasts for

15 days and young remain in the nest for 23-24 days (Samuel 1971), sometimes returning to the nest for 2 or 3 days before deserting permanently (Mayhew 1958). Both parents incubate and feed the nestlings and fledglings, and they remain together in the nest at night during the incubation and brooding periods (Samuel 1971). In all, from the beginning of nest building to strongly flying young, the breeding cycle may take almost 2 months.

Dates of nesting chronologies on the Seward Peninsula are few. In 1973 (Kessel and D. D. Gibson unpubl. notes) a colony on the Inmachuk was at the nest-repair/egg-laying stage on 22 June, with four nests checked containing 1, 2, 2, and 3 eggs. On 30 July, two nests in a nearby colony contained large, well-feathered young. Many nests in a colony at Serpentine Hot Springs fledged young on 6 August 1973 (ibid.), but birds from the Pilgrim River bridge colony at Milepost 60 Taylor Highway had disappeared by 31 July 1973 (N. G. Tankersly in litt.).

Fall departures occur soon after the young are fully fledged, which means that most Cliff Swallows will have left the Peninsula by mid-August (latest, two, 11 August 1984, Deering, J. D. Walters unpubl. notes).

Barn Swallow—*Hirundo rustica*

A very rare spring migrant and early summer visitant, the Barn Swallow has been reported only half a dozen times from the Peninsula. "They" were observed at Golovnin Bay on 28 June 1900 (McGregor 1902); one was seen flying over a sand spit of Sledge Island on 14 June 1950 (Cade 1952); one was seen along the Teller Highway in June 1975 and two on King Island on 11 June 1976 by W. H. Drury and party (J. O. Biderman in litt.); one flew about the outside and inside of my vehicle at Milepost 6 Teller Highway on 27 June 1977; one was closely observed at Wales on 18 June 1978 (D. R. Paulson unpubl. notes); another was seen at Golovin on 11 May 1981 (D. A. Woodby in litt.); and singles were seen at Wales on 28 May and 7 June 1983 (M. L. Ward unpubl. notes).

Since it is possible for any of three subspecies of Barn Swallows to occur on the Seward Peninsula (see Kessel and Gibson 1978), descriptive characteristics of all birds sighted should be carefully noted. Both the 1977 and 1978 observations cited above were of *H. r. erythrogaster*, the peach-breasted North American subspecies.

Common House-Martin—*Delichon urbica*

An Old World swallow, the Common House-Martin is accidental on the Seward Peninsula. A male was observed feeding over a dredge pond at Nome on 7 June 1974 and was collected the following day (UAM 3545, Hall and Cardiff 1978). It proved to be *D. u. lagopoda*.

Gray Jay—*Perisoreus canadensis*

Gray Jays are uncommon residents of the southeast portions of the Peninsula, as far west as forests extend. I have seen them consistently in the westernmost spruce woods at Milepost 68 Council Road, and I counted three adults and two juvenals in a 2.5-h hike along Fox River, downstream of the road, on 3 July 1977. Jays were fairly common about Elim in 1972, where H. E. Kingery and I, in 29 km of walking on 1 and 2 July, counted a total of twenty-five birds; half of these were juvenals, most still in family groups with adults. In winter, Gray Jays may wander beyond the forests: two fed on scraps at a cabin at Milepost 26 Inmachuk River road on 15 January 1984, and one was observed at about Milepost 3 in mid-February and again on 23 March 1986; and at Nome, N. Levinson reported one in late December 1985 (J. D. Walters unpubl. notes).

Jays frequent forests that contain substantial amounts of spruce (Spindler and Kessel 1980, Kessel MS), although during the nonbreeding season they may range into deciduous forests and tall shrubs. Nests are invariably built in spruce.

Almost nothing is known about breeding chronologies on the Seward Peninsula, but based on information from Interior Alaska (Dall and Bannister 1869, Brandt 1943, Kessel unpubl. data) and the lower Kobuk River (Grinnell 1900a), egg-laying on the Peninsula should be under way by the first week of April; the most frequent clutch size in Alaska is three or four eggs. Incubation, performed by the female, averages 20 days and the young leave the nest after 17-20 days, before they can fly well (Rutter 1969). Thus, young could leave their nests on the Peninsula by mid-May, although they remain inconspicuous for 2 or 3 weeks thereafter (Kessel pers. obs.), i.e., until early June.

Jays are omnivorous. They are largely insectivorous during the summer, but at other times of year, and even in summer, they will consume berries, seeds, carrion, and a variety of food scraps as may be available about human habitation.

Common Raven—*Corvus corax*

Although conspicuous, the raven is an uncommon resident on the Seward Peninsula. It is a widespread breeder in suitable habitat throughout most of the Peninsula, including on all the islands. Between 1968 and 1972, counts of breeding pairs made during aerial surveys of large parts of the Peninsula varied from 3 to 23, with the most usual number being about 15-20 pairs (Swartz et al. 1975). In addition, a number of nonbreeding subadults are present. Some birds probably leave the region in winter, but others congregate where food is available, such as about villages (45-50 birds frequented the Nome dump during the winters of 1969-1970 and 1970-1971, W. L. Foster pers. comm.; and 26-40 ravens were at the Deering dump during winters 1983-1985, J. D. Walters unpubl. notes).

Ravens on the Peninsula nest most commonly on cliffs, both inland and coastally, on tors, and on analogous artificial structures such as dredges and bridges. One pair nested on a dirt bank at Taylor (three young, early July 1985, D. L. Wetzel pers. comm.), and four times I have seen active tree nests: one in a 25-cm-dbh Balsam Poplar in a grove near the Pilgrim River bridge at Milepost 60 Taylor Highway (Figure 17); two up only 1.2 and 1.5 m in riparian alders along the Buckland River downriver from Buckland; and one in a 6-7-m willow at the junction of Portage Creek and American River. This last nest was in a small, isolated patch of spindly riparian willows and was supported in a fork formed by branches only 2.5-5.0 cm in diameter. The nest and three nearly fledged young were highly conspicuous in this small willow on 24 June 1974, especially since the leaves were only about one-fourth unfurled.

Back-dating from known nest contents shows that egg-laying in early nests begins during the first week of April, although other clutches may not be completed until more than a month later, about 10 May. Clutches of up to seven eggs have been recorded on the Peninsula (seven eggs on 23 April 1968 on Sunset Ck dredge, Teller Highway, R. E. Pegau, ANRS). Incubation lasts 21 days (20.9±1.2 days in 36 nests, Stiehl 1985). Time to fledging has been variously reported as 4 weeks (Pennsylvania, Harlow 1922), about 5 weeks (Interior Alaska, Brown 1974), and 41±3 days (Stiehl 1985). Incubation is performed almost entirely by the female, while the male remains nearby and often brings food to the incubating female—who nonetheless also leaves the nest to care for herself; both parents participate in feeding the young (Harlow 1922, Stiehl 1985).

Earliest fledging on the Seward Peninsula should occur by the end of the first week of June, although many nestlings do not leave their nests until late June and early July. A few broods, probably from renests after earlier failures, do not fledge until mid-July (fledging occurred at a nest on Little Diomede on 14 July 1977, Biderman and Drury 1978). Families remain together in the general vicinity of their nest sites for 3 to 4 weeks after vacating their nests (Brown 1974, Drury et al. 1978, M. H. Dick and L. S. Dick MS).

Ravens are omnivorous, feeding on a wide range of items, e.g., eggs and young from seabird colonies, dead and dying salmon at spawning streams, carrion of all kinds, fish from village drying racks, small mammals, including hares and ground squirrels, tundra berries, occasional invertebrates, and anything they can scavenge from beaches, roadsides, and refuse dumps.

Black-capped Chickadee—*Parus atricapillus*

The Black-capped Chickadee is a rare resident in the forested regions and a very rare visitant and possible breeder elsewhere on the Peninsula. One of two pairs along Fox River below Milepost 68 Council Road responded in a distraught fashion to my "squeaking" on 3 July 1977, indicating that it had a family nearby. An adult in tall alders along Hot Springs Trail 6.5 km northwest of Elim was carrying food in its bill on 2 July 1972 (H. E. Kingery pers. comm.). They were heard "commonly" along the Kwiniuk River during July and August 1973, and a family with five fledglings was seen 8 km up the river on 1 July 1973 (J. H. Lee pers. comm.).

Outside of the breeding season, this chickadee may wander beyond treeline and can be found in Tall Shrub Thicket. One was seen at Bluff during summer 1976 (P. L. Drury pers. comm.); one was collected at the east end of Safety Sound on 22 October 1977 (H. K. Springer, UAM 4175); the species has been noted several times in the Anvil Creek-Glacier Road area near Nome—4 May 1979, 17 April 1982, and February 1983 (N. and D. Levinson pers. comm.), and a pair engaged in wing-fluttering display in dense willows was observed nearby on 10 June 1987 (J. L. Dunn in litt.); two fed in the willows between the Kuzitrin River bridge and Bunker Hill on 11 November 1986 (D. R. Klein pers. comm.); and one passed through Deering on 19 September 1983, three fed among weeds atop Cape Deceit on 6 October 1984, and singles were in Deering on 18 October 1984, 7 October 1987, and 22 April 1988 (J. D. Walters unpubl. notes). The specimen collected on 22 October 1977 and one collected (UAM 2502) at Anvil Creek on 20 October 1969 were both young of the year; age of the other wanderers is unknown.

An unusual irruption of this species onto the treeless portions of the Peninsula occurred in early winter 1969, catching the attention of many local residents (W. L. Foster in litt.). It was most common before 1 December, but fifteen were seen in the Anvil Creek area on 20 December, including UAM 4986, and four were counted during the Audubon Christmas Bird Count in Nome on 29 December. This invasion even reached Wales, where a writer mentioned in his local newspaper that the village was invaded by little black-headed birds that were unknown to the local residents.

Black-capped Chickadees show a strong preference for relatively dense deciduous forests with large trees (Spindler and Kessel 1980). This habitat is scarce on the Seward Peninsula and explains the rarity of this chickadee in the region.

[Siberian Tit—*Parus cinctus*]

The only reports of Siberian Tits from the Seward Peninsula are those of Anthony (1906). In November and December 1904, he reported hearing "a chickadee" on upper Cripple River, west of Nome, and another in "a stunted bunch of willows" on Penny River. In March 1905 in the Imuruk Basin region, he reported (p. 181) that "A few *Parus* were found at long intervals in the willows; their presence being usually announced by their call, and it was not often that one could be seen near enough for identification. I think that all I saw were *P. cinctus alascensis.*"

While the presence of this species would be reasonable, especially in view of specimen-substantiated records from nearby regions (Kobuk, Grinnell 1900a; Nulato, Gabrielson and Lincoln 1959; Noatak, Hines 1963; Koyukuk R, T. O. Osborne, UAM 5000 and 5001), the above statements by Anthony seem inadequate to establish its occurrence on the Seward Peninsula. Hence, until better substantiated, this species should be considered hypothetical.

Boreal Chickadee—*Parus hudsonicus*

Boreal Chickadees are uncommon residents of the forested portions of the Peninsula. During 29 km of walking in the vicinity of Elim on 1 and 2 July 1972, H. E. Kingery and I counted a total of 17 birds. In a 2-h hike in dense spruce forest north of Koyuk on 3 July 1975, F. G. Scheider and I counted 6 Boreal Chickadees, including at least 1 carrying food. At the western edge of spruce at Milepost 68 Council Road on 3 July 1977, I watched 4 birds that appeared to be a family group in spruce forest along the Fox River.

This chickadee favors forest habitats with substantial amounts of spruce, either coniferous forests or mixed deciduous-coniferous forests (Spindler and Kessel 1980), although it will forage in tall shrubs. An immature male (UAM 4172) wandered beyond treeline to Cape Nome, where it was collected by H. K. Springer on 2 October 1977.

Red-breasted Nuthatch—*Sitta canadensis*

A casual fall visitant on the Seward Peninsula, two Red-breasted Nuthatches were observed at Shishmaref on 4 September 1981 by H. C. Jespersen (J. S. Hawkings pers.

comm.). This nuthatch is known for its periodic autumnal irruptive behavior (Bock and Lepthien 1972, Kessel and Gibson 1978), and 1981 was such a year in Alaska (Kessel and D. D. Gibson unpubl. data). This record is the third for this species in Western Alaska, all in the month of September (Kessel and Gibson 1978).

American Dipper—*Cinclus mexicanus*

Rare residents of the Peninsula, scattered individuals, pairs, and families of American Dippers occur along many of the rapidly flowing creeks and rivers that drain the Southern Uplands. During the nonbreeding season, it has been reported in the creek just west of Koyuk (overwintering, H. Kavairlook pers. comm.), at the Sinuk River (25-26 April 1973, Alaska Department of Fish and Game unpubl. notes), the Penny River (22 October 1976, H. K. Springer pers. comm.; 26 April 1980, D. Levinson, Beltz School unpubl. notes), and the Nome River (several observations, including mid-March 1983 photo by R. R. Nelson), and it undoubtedly occurs in other similar drainages that have open, running water throughout the winter. In the Northern Uplands dippers have been reported from near the headwaters of the Inmachuk River by local residents, including in winter 1982-1983 and on 7 February 1986 (J. D. Walters unpubl. notes), and from Serpentine Hot Springs on 19 March 1988 (M. A. Spindler pers. comm.).

The only nests that have been reported have been built under bridges: one, from which an adult bird was flushed, on an I-beam under the Pilgrim River bridge at Milepost 60 Taylor Highway on 7 July 1967, shown to me by the R. Emmons family; and one under the bridge over Sunset Creek, Milepost 9 Teller Highway, that contained five eggs on 4 July 1968 (W. R. Tilton pers. comm.). In addition, a probable breeder flew past me down Divining Creek, a tributary of the Snake River, on 28 June 1977.

Feeding on aquatic insects, both adults and larvae, and on small fish, this unusual bird swims and walks under flowing waters throughout the year to obtain its prey.

Arctic Warbler—*Phylloscopus borealis*

The Arctic Warbler is a common migrant and breeder on the Peninsula. It nests where appropriate habitat exists throughout the Southern and Northern uplands, but it is essentially absent from the Interior and Coastal lowlands, except during migration. A bird of Medium Shrub Thicket (see Table 11), the Arctic Warbler requires habitats with high densities of vegetative matter below the 1-m level and a canopy of medium-height shrubs averaging about 14% (Kessel MS).

The Alaska form (*P. b. kennicotti*) of this Old World species winters commonly in the Philippines and sparingly in the East Indies and Southeast Asia (Parkes and Amadon 1948). The earliest spring migrants reach Alaska in late May (earliest, 24 May [yr?], extralimitally at Mountain Village, Gabrielson and Lincoln 1959; 29 May 1977, Cape Espenberg, Schamel et. al 1979). On the Seward Peninsula and elsewhere, however, they more commonly arrive during the first week of June, with migrants continuing to arrive until mid-June or even later (latest spring migrants, one on 24 June and another on 25 June 1972, Cape and Needle mts, Kessel per. obs.).

Little is known about the breeding biology of this species anywhere in its range, and few data are available from the Peninsula upon which to base nesting chronologies. Most nests are built on the ground in a mossy substrate. Usual clutch size is probably 5-6 eggs and the incubation period about 13 days, judging from data provided for other *Phylloscopus* by Dement'ev and Gladkov (1954). Young stay in the nest about 12 days (Murie 1956). I have seen food-carrying adults by 5 July, and apparent family groups were still present 2-10 August 1973 at Serpentine Hot Springs, where a juvenal was successfully begging food from an adult on 10 August (D. D. Gibson unpubl. notes).

Fall migration is under way by mid-August (two migrants in dunes on Sarichef I, 15 August 1973, D. D. Gibson unpubl. notes), and usually most birds have left by the end of the month (latest, "common" at Golovnin Bay as late as 31 August 1922, Bailey 1926).

Ruby-crowned Kinglet—*Regulus calendula*

The Ruby-crowned Kinglet is an uncommon breeder in the forested regions of the Peninsula. It extends westward to the limit of spruce along the upper Fox River, below Milepost 68 Council Road, where I saw two birds on 3 July 1977, including a probably breeding female that was "very upset" over an intruding jay. The species was fairly common along upper King Creek at Koyuk on 29 June 1975, where F. G. Scheider and I counted 20 birds, including two carrying food. Along upper Hot Springs Trail northwest of Elim, H. E. Kingery (pers. comm.) saw a pair and four singing males during a hike on 2 July 1972. On 16 July 1973, I glimpsed a kinglet in a spruce stand at McCarthys Marsh. During spring migration 1983, several Ruby-crowned Kinglets overshot their breeding range and reached the willow thickets at the base of Anvil Mountain, where J. D. Walters (unpubl. notes) heard one singing on 3 May, saw two birds on 6 May and watched aerial courtship, and saw a single bird on 10 May.

For breeding, this kinglet is restricted to forest habitats that contain substantial amounts of spruce, favoring relatively open forests with a high heterogeneity of tree distribution (Spindler and Kessel 1980, Kessel MS).

The first spring migrants usually arrive in Central Alaska during the last week of April, although in seasonally late years, they may not arrive until the first week of May; the main fall exodus is usually over by late September (Kessel unpubl. data). The season may be somewhat shorter on the Seward Peninsula (earliest, three, 30 April 1986, extralimitally at St. Marys, B. J. McCaffery unpubl. notes).

The Ruby-crowned Kinglet is largely insectivorous, but it will also feed on seeds and berries (Bent 1949). Its ability to search out nonflying insects for food and its use of some vegetative items allows a relatively long season for this kinglet in the Alaska taiga.

Siberian Rubythroat—*Luscinia calliope*

A casual spring migrant, a male Siberian Rubythroat on the lower, rocky slopes of Cape Mountain on 30 May 1983 was closely viewed by M. L. Ward (pers. comm.), and a male was seen briefly in willows along Krueger Creek, Ear Mountain, on 19 June 1987 (R. V. Harris unpubl. notes). This Old World species is a very rare spring migrant in the western Aleutian Islands and has been recorded in spring in the Pribilof Islands; these records are the first for mainland Alaska (Kessel and Gibson 1978).

Bluethroat—*Luscinia svecica*

An Old World bird, the Bluethroat is an uncommon migrant and breeder on the Peninsula. It breeds locally throughout much of the Northern Uplands and, at least in some years, at the western end of the Southern Uplands (one, near the base of Point Spencer spit, between 30 May and 3 June 1980, J. H. Blackam fide D. A. Woodby in litt.; several, including a male in a patch of low willows, near Cape Riley, southwest of Teller, 15 July 1987, J. M. Wright pers. comm.; and several, west of Salmon L in the drainage of Grand Central R, 11 June-19 July 1987, including pair building a nest on 11 June, K. J. Zimmer in litt., and at least three on a gravel bar, 19 July, P. C. Palmer in litt.).

It is a bird of the Low Shrub Thicket habitat, although on the upper Noatak River, Manuwal (1975) believed that tussock tundra was also a critical habitat component. He found two nests placed on the sides of tussocks and noted adults foraging on tussock tundra (=Dwarf Shrub Meadow). However, all birds I have seen during the breeding season have been closely associated with shrubbery, although migrants occur in alpine tundra during postbreeding and migration periods (Bailey 1926, D. D. Gibson pers. comm.)

Alaska's Bluethroats winter in Southeast Asia (Vaurie 1959). The first spring migrants reach the Peninsula in late May (26 May 1975, Tin City, Flock and Hubbard 1979; 26 May 1983, Wales, M. L. Ward unpubl. notes; 27 May 1984, Inmachuk River, J. D. Walters unpubl. notes; 29 May 1987, Wales, P. J. Baicich in litt.). At least 10 migrant males frequented the lower slopes of Cape Mountain on 30 May 1987 and at least 11 males and a female were there the following day (P. J. Baicich in litt.). A similar passage of at least 12 males and a female occurred at Cape Deceit on 1 June 1988; several of the males were singing strongly, two while in flight (J. D. Walters unpubl. notes). Movement continues on the Peninsula to mid-June (Bailey 1926, Kessel and D. D. Gibson unpubl. data).

I watched a male carrying small food at Neva Creek, Milepost 88 Taylor Highway on 22 June 1977, indicating that young had hatched; and on 3-4 July 1971 at Serpentine Hot Springs, S. O. MacDonald and I watched at least two families of fledglings being fed, one well developed by that date. Thus, given a usual clutch of six eggs (Bailey 1948) and a probable incubation period of 13 days and a nestling period of 13-14 days (based on *L. s. cyanecula* of central Europe, Dement'ev and Gladkov 1954), this species begins nesting almost immediately upon arrival. Many Bluethroats were carrying food for young at Taylor on 12 July 1985 (D. L. Wetzel pers. comm.), and a female was still feeding fledglings at Serpentine Hot Springs on 22 July 1968 (D. G. Roseneau and W. R. Tilton pers. comm.).

Fall migration occurs during August. From 3 through 10 August 1973, locally raised juvenals were observed daily at Serpentine Hot Springs, but the adults had apparently departed (D. D. Gibson unpubl. notes). Latest recorded dates in Alaska include the last few days of August (Kessel and Gibson 1978).

Northern Wheatear—*Oenanthe oenanthe*

Wheatears are uncommon migrants and breeders throughout the region. During breeding they are widely distributed in the uplands and foothills of the Highlands, wherever their favored nesting habitat of block-fields occurs adjacent to Dwarf Shrub Mat tundra. During migration they may be found in any of the nonforested portions of the Peninsula, especially along beaches and in other Coastal Lowlands areas.

Alaskan wheatears (*O. o. oenanthe*) winter on the savannas of northern and eastern Africa (Vaurie 1959). Spring migrants arrive in mid-May (earliest, ''some'' seen and one collected 13 May 1922, Wales, Bailey 1943; one on 13 May and seven on 14 May 1984, Cape Deceit, J. D. Walters unpubl. notes). On 27 May 1978 at Wales, 30 were observed by W. J. Erckmann as they arrived across the ice from the west (D. R. Paulson unpubl. notes), and birds were still moving through the Coastal Lowlands at Cape Espenberg 8-9 June 1977 (Schamel et al. 1979).

Nests are built on the ground, usually under a rock. Clutch size in Alaska ranges from five to eight eggs (nine June nests averaged 6.9 ± 1.2 eggs or nestlings, ANRS). Data on length of incubation and nestling periods from the literature are inexact and conflicting, but early hatching occurs in Alaska about 20 June (ANRS). Young leave the nest by early July, some still unable to fly (newly fledged juvenals have been collected as early as 26 June 1951 in the central Brooks Range, Gabrielson and Lincoln 1959). A nonflying youngster was being fed atop a rock at Serpentine Hot Springs on 3 July 1971 (S. O. MacDonald pers. comm.), and I saw a bob-tailed fledgling just capable of flight at Willis Creek on 4 July 1967. A nest still with eggs was collected on 7 July 1929 at Wales, however (Bailey 1943).

Fall migration is under way by the end of July and reaches a peak in mid-August. In 1973 (D. D. Gibson unpubl. notes), three independent juvenals and an adult male were about old mining tailings along the upper Inmachuk Road on 30 July; by 4 August, wheatears had moved out of the higher elevations and were feeding along Hot Springs Creek and the alluvial bars of the upper Serpentine River; and on 15 August, five birds, including one basic-plumaged male, were in *Elymus* dunes near Shishmaref. On 14 August 1969, ''many'' were flocking along the Teller Highway (J. J. Burns pers. comm.), and migrants moved through Cape Espenberg 23-28 August 1976 and 11-28 August 1977 (Schamel et al. 1979). They moved through Wales between 11 and 26 August 1977, peaking 14-17 August at 20-30 birds a day (D. A. Woodby in litt.). Almost all have departed by the end of the month (latest, immature male collected 30 August 1913 at Pilgrim Hot Springs by J. Koren, Thayer and Bangs 1914; one, 4 September 1973, extralimitally at Cape Krusenstern, D. D. Gibson unpubl. notes).

Gray-cheeked Thrush—*Catharus minimus*

The Gray-cheeked Thrush is an abundant breeder throughout the Southern and Northern uplands and the Interior Lowlands of the Seward Peninsula, and during migration it also occurs in various coastal habitats. It is the fifth most common passerine on the Peninsula. A Medium Shrub Thicket bird, this thrush favors habitats for breeding that have a relatively high percent (about 30%) cover of low shrubs in the understory (Kessel MS). It requires a closed canopy of at least medium-height shrubs, either deciduous or coniferous; but, where available, it also uses Tall Shrub Thicket habitats that contain a high cover of low shrubs (ibid.).

Gray-cheeked Thrushes winter in South America and migrate through North America to Alaska in spring via the Mississippi Flyway, judging from data provided by the American Ornithologists' Union (1983). In most years first arrivals reach Interior Alaska between 15 and 25 May (Kessel unpubl. data), and they appear to arrive on the Seward Peninsula about a week later (earliest, 18 May [yr?], extralimitally at Mountain Village, Gabrielson and Lincoln 1959; 24 May 1985 and 25 May 1988, Inmachuk R, J. D. Walters unpubl. notes; 26 May 1975, Wales, Flock and Hubbard 1979). Migration peaks at Wales about 6-10 June, perhaps birds moving to breeding grounds in northeast Siberia; and migration is essentially complete by the middle of the month (latest, one, 14 June 1976, Wales, D. D. Gibson unpubl. notes).

Most nests reported from the Peninsula have been placed in a vertical crotch about 0.8-1.2 m up in a willow shrub, but one was found on top of a window ledge inside an abandoned cabin (D. G. Roseneau and W. R. Tilton unpubl. notes). Clutch size in eight Peninsula nests ranged from 3 to 5 eggs, with an average of 3.9 ± 0.8 eggs. Incubation lasts 12 days (Jehl and Hussell 1966), and nestlings remain in the nest 11-13 days (Wallace 1939). Back-dating from nest contents indicates that egg-laying began about 5 June 1977 (Kessel pers. obs.) and at least by 8 June 1983 (R. and B. Mearns unpubl. notes). Thus, hatching occurs during the last third of June and fledging occurs in early July (earliest, two fledglings, 1 July 1977, Kessel pers. obs.). Some renesting apparently occurs in the event of an early failure, because I found a nest with three warm eggs on 7 July 1967 and a nest in which young had just hatched on 18 July 1973.

The Gray-cheeked Thrush is primarily a ground feeder, feeding on ground insects and larvae and on berries (Bent 1949, Grinnell 1900a).

Postbreeding movements may begin by late July (Shields and Peyton 1977), but the main fall exodus occurs during the third week of August. Most birds have left by the end of the month (latest, 8 September 1899, Nome R, Grinnell 1900b; male collected 13 September 1913, Nome, J. Koren unpubl. notes).

Swainson's Thrush—*Catharus ustulatus*

The Swainson's Thrush may be a very rare breeder at the southeast base of the Peninsula, where the forests are densest and where F. G. Scheider and I independently identified the call notes of two of these thrushes in a dense patch of White Spruce north of Koyuk on 3 July 1975. This species favors forests with closed and deep canopies and a relative openness in the low-dwarf shrub layer, i.e., up to 1.1 m (Kessel MS)—a habitat largely lacking on the Seward Peninsula.

Elsewhere on the Peninsula, this thrush is a casual spring migrant. One was reported at Wales on 8 and 10 June 1977 (D. A. Woodby and K. V. Hirsch unpubl. notes) and on 6 June 1983 (M. L. Ward unpubl. notes), and it has been seen extralimitally at Cape Krusenstern (one, 2 June 1977, P. G. Connors in litt.) and at Gambell, St. Lawrence Island (one, 31 May 1983, J. L. Dunn in litt.).

Hermit Thrush—*Catharus guttatus*

The Hermit Thrush is a rare breeder along the Norton Sound coastline from Koyuk to Sledge Island, usually occurring in shrubbery with a dense canopy cover and often associated with rock faces, such as those along creek banks and coastal bluffs: Koyuk—one, 30 May 1981 (D. A. Woodby in litt.); just east of Rocky Pt—one singing from shoreline alder, 9 July 1987 (J. M. Wright pers. comm.); Bluff—one, 6 June 1976 (W. H. Drury and P. L. Drury pers. comm.), two singing males, 19 July 1983, and present in alder annually 1984-1987 (E. C. Murphy pers. comm.); Cape Nome—singing male, 8 June 1982 (J. L. Dunn in litt.); Basin Creek, Milepost 15 Taylor Highway—one, 29 May 1970 (D. G. Roseneau and W. Walker pers. comm.), one, 8 July 1976 (W. H. Drury and P. L. Drury pers. comm.); Sledge I—five, 19 July 1984 (G. V. Byrd in litt.), several, one carrying food into rock rubble, 12 July 1987 (J. M. Wright pers. comm.). One in alder at Breving Lagoon on 3 August 1980 (D. A. Woodby in litt.) may not have been a local breeder.

Eye-browed Thrush—*Turdus obscurus*

Accidental on the Peninsula, a male and two female Eye-browed Thrushes were carefully observed by P. G. DuMont (unpubl. notes) for more than an hour, sometimes at 30 m, as they fed and flew about near Wales on 13 June 1975. This Asiatic thrush is a casual to very rare migrant in western Southwestern Alaska (Kessel and Gibson 1978).

American Robin—*Turdus migratorius*

Robins are fairly common breeders on the Peninsula, although they are common throughout the Interior Lowlands and Southern and Northern uplands east of 166° W. They are rare farther west but have nested at Wales (Bailey 1943), and I counted three birds, probably breeders, in shrubby draws at Ear Mountain, 22-23 June 1974.

This thrush is primarily a bird of forested regions, but it extends its breeding habitat to Tall Shrub Thicket and sometimes even to the taller Medium Shrub Thicket. Where these habitats are nearby, robins will use rock outcrops and tors for nesting, even in areas of alpine tundra. For example, I counted 17 robins, including two stubby-tailed fledglings, in 10 km of hiking in the tor-tundra habitat about Serpentine Hot Springs on 3 July 1971. Robins favor habitats with high spatial heterogeneity (Spindler and Kessel 1980), and studies in the forested regions of eastern North America have found that 75% of nests are at forest edges or openings (Young 1955, Knupp et al. 1977).

Robins winter as far north as Southcoastal Alaska (Kessel and D. D. Gibson unpubl. data) and are early migrants to their more northern breeding grounds. Arrival dates are strongly affected by spring weather conditions, but first migrants usually arrive on the Seward Peninsula during the first week of May (earliest, one, 25 April 1973, Milepost 10 Teller Highway, Alaska Department of Fish and Game unpubl. notes; one found dead, 1 May 1979, Nome, D. Levinson, Beltz School unpubl. notes). Birds continue to arrive until mid-May (flock of 12 birds, 14 May 1987, Deering, J. D. Walters unpubl. notes).

While primarily a tree-nester in other parts of its North American range, the American Robin on the Seward Peninsula builds most nests on nonvegetative substrates, e.g., buildings in towns, villages, and mining camps; abandoned railroad cars, mining dredges, and even the tops of vehicle tires; bridge girders; beach drift-wood; and rock tors and cliff faces. At Bluff they nest in the occasional stunted spruce on the tundra (E. C. Murphy pers. comm.). Nest-building takes about 7 days (Young 1955), with some egg-laying beginning on the Seward Peninsula by mid-May but most apparently occurring between 20 May and 10 June. Nests still with eggs in July (e.g., 3 warm eggs, 12 July 1967, East Fork Solomon R, Kessel pers. obs.; 4 eggs, 12 July 1985, Taylor, D. L. Wetzel pers. comm.) are undoubtedly renestings from earlier failures.

Clutch sizes from 16 Seward Peninsula nests averaged 3.8±0.8 eggs, range 3-6, mode 4. Incubation usually lasts 12 to 13 days and young leave the nest between 13 and 15 days of age, some before they can fly (Young 1955). Fledging on the Penin-sula begins as early as mid-June (nearly fully developed nestlings, 10 June 1978, Taylor Highway, T. G. Tobish in litt.; fledglings, 14-16 June 1980, Koyuk, D. A. Woodby un-publ. notes) and is common through mid-July.

Summer foods consist primarily of ground insects and larvae, supplemented, especially in spring and fall, with berries.

Judging from events in Interior Alaska (Kessel unpubl. data), fall migration on the Seward Peninsula has begun by the last week of August, but the main exodus is dur-ing September with perhaps an occasianal individual remaining into October.

Varied Thrush—*Ixoreus naevius*

A fairly common breeder on the Seward Peninsula, the Varied Thrush breeds only in the Southern Uplands west to about 165° 20′ W and along the Pilgrim River in the Interior Lowlands. This distribution pattern appears to be the result of birds ex-tending their range beyond the spruce forests of the southeastern portions of the Peninsula, where they are abundant (107 birds enumerated about Elim, 1-2 July 1972, and 90 about Koyuk, 28 June-3 July 1975, Kessel pers. obs.), westward in the Southern Uplands to the Nome River valley and northwestward, via the lowland area between the Bendeleben and Kigluaik mountains, to the Pilgrim River. The Varied Thrush has also been observed as a very rare spring migrant at the western tip of the Penin-sula (one each on 15 May 1970 and 19 May 1975 and up to three between 29 May and 10 June 1978, Wales and Tin City, Flock and Hubbard 1979 and D. R. Paulson unpubl. notes; one on 30 and 31 May 1987 at Wales, P. J. Baicich in litt.) and as a summer visitant at Serpentine Hot Springs (one seen 23 and 24 June 1987, moving through tall willows, R. V. Harris pers. comm.). It is accidental in spring extralimitally on Wrangel Island, USSR (female, 11 June 1983, Stishov et al. 1985).

Varied Thrushes favor heavily shaded habitats, occurring in greatest numbers where there is both a heavy tree canopy and a heavy shrub canopy (Kessel MS). This habitat characteristic is best provided on the Seward Peninsula in the spruce forests, where an understory of alder is frequently present, also. West of spruce, Varied Thrushes continue to favor patches of habitat with tree height vegetation, i.e., Balsam Poplars, even though small (e.g., the Basin Ck outwash at Milepost 15 Taylor Highway with poplars 3.7 m in height and only 6.4 cm dbh). On a boat trip down the Pilgrim River from the Taylor Highway bridge to Pilgrim Hot Springs on 6 July 1971, I found Varied

Thrushes in every small patch of Balsam Poplars, which occurred at river bends and had alders in the understory, and in the mature poplar forest at Pilgrim Hot Springs. I have also seen them at several sites along the Taylor Highway (Mileposts 23-25, 34, 45-46) and at Cape Nome in dense patches of tall alders with no tree-height vegetation.

This thrush winters as far north as the coastal forests of Southcoastal Alaska (Isleib and Kessel 1973, MacIntosh 1986). The species seems to lack the migratory precision of most passerines, but usually the first spring migrants arrive in Interior Alaska between 22 April and 7 May, being preceded on average by a few days by the robin; movement usually peaks during the first week of May (Kessel unpubl. data). Early arrivals probably do not reach the Seward Peninsula until the first week of May (earliest, one, 4 May 1988, Deering, and two separate birds, 10 May 1983, slopes of Anvil Mt, J. D. Walters unpubl. notes; but, 1-3 May in 4 yr, extralimitally in the southern Nulato Hills, Gabrielson and Lincoln 1959, H. C. Kyllingstad in litt., B. J. McCaffery unpubl. notes).

Little is known about the breeding biology of this species anywhere in its range. Most nests are built in shrubs or trees; the mean height of 38 Alaska nests (ANRS) was 2.6 ± 1.3 m, with 55% of nests between 1.8 and 3.0 m. The only two nests reported from the Seward Peninsula were placed in shrubs at heights of 0.8 and 1.8 m, respectively. A probable nest in a rock crevice was found on 10 June 1986, when J. L. Dunn (in litt.) watched a male Varied Thrush repeatedly carry food into the crevice, apparently feeding young.

While egg-laying may begin in early seasons as soon as mid-May (earliest, about 9 May 1983, extralimitally at Galena, T. O. Osborne pers. comm.), most egg-laying on the Peninsula probably occurs from the fourth week of May through mid-June. Clutch size in 21 nests from Central Alaska (ANRS) was 4.0 ± 0.7 eggs, range 3-6, mode 4. Incubation time is probably similar to that of the robin, i.e., 12-13 days; and, based on a single record from the Kenai Peninsula, nestlings fledge at 13 or 14 days of age (M. A. Miller, ANRS). Hence, most fledging on the Peninsula should occur between the fourth week of June and mid-July, which is in agreement with limited field observations (earliest, fledglings seen 19 June 1973, extralimitally on the lower Noatak R, Manuwal 1974).

Food of the Varied Thrush consists largely of ground-dwelling invertebrates and berries (Bent 1949), the latter especially during early spring and in fall.

While some fall movement may begin by the third week of August, based on observations from Western and Interior Alaska, the main exodus gets under way during the last week of August and the first week of September and continues through September (Kessel unpubl. data). A few stragglers may remain into October.

Yellow Wagtail—*Motacilla flava*

The Yellow Wagtail is a common and widespread breeder, occurring throughout the Peninsula and on the offshore islands, wherever open, shrubby habitats exist. It is the sixth most common passerine of the region.

This wagtail favors open Low Shrub Thicket (see Table 11), especially where irregulatities in the substrate provide some vertical relief, e.g., vegetated tussocks and hummocks, faces of solifluction terraces, cut banks along rivulets and creeks, and broken or disturbed ground along roadsides or about mining operations and ditches.

The Alaska breeding form of this Palearctic species is the Beringian *M. f. tschutschensis* that winters in the East Indies and migrates north in spring via eastern China (Vaurie 1959). First spring migrants usually reach the Seward Peninsula during the fourth week of May (earliest, 21 May 1964, Wales, Breckenridge and Cline 1967; but extralimitally, 17 May 1985, Kotzebue, Selawik NWR unpubl. notes, and 9 May 1947, Mountain Village, H. C. Kyllingstad in litt.), and migration continues into mid-June, peaking in early June (flocks of 6 to 15 birds on Sledge I, 6-15 June 1950, Cade 1952; small passage at Cape Espenberg, 5-10 June 1977, Schamel et al. 1979; 20-30 birds/day at Deering, 1-4 June 1988 and 4-8 June 1984, J. D. Walters unpubl. notes).

The Yellow Wagtail is a ground-nester, usually concealing its nest deeply under vegetation or under a soil overhang. Most frequently on the Peninsula nests have been found in the sides of sedge tussocks, well hidden by drooping leaf blades, or placed under mats of vegetation overhanging the tops of dirt banks. I found one nest with 5 eggs on 22 June 1973 close to the shoulder of the Inmachuk River road, however, that was set deeply into moss under sedge and a 25-cm-high *Ledum* shrub.

Egg-laying begins in early June (4-egg clutch, 8 June 1977, mouth of Arctic R, J. M. Wright unpubl. notes; 6-egg clutch, 9 June 1983, Solomon, R. and B. Mearns unpubl. notes). Clutch size in 19 nests from Western Alaska (Kessel and D. D. Gibson unpubl. data) was 4.7 ± 0.9 eggs, range 3-6, mode 5. Data from Great Britain for *M. f. flavissima* (Smith 1950) show that incubation begins with the laying of the last egg and lasts 12-13 days. Both sexes incubate and feed the young. The nestling period is about 12 ± 1 days, but the young do not normally fly until the sixteenth day after hatching. Young from early nests hatch by late June on the Peninsula (five 2-day-old nestlings on 23 June 1968, Safety Sound, Kessel pers. obs.; adults carrying food on 23 June 1970, Nome and Milepost 7 Teller Highway, Kessel pers. obs.; and a nest with four 4-day young on 27 June 1975, Buckland, F. G. Scheider pers. comm.); and the first young leave the nests by early July (one juvenal, 29 June 1970, Nome, W. J. Weiss and I. H. Black unpubl. notes; two pairs feeding fledged young on 2 and 3 July 1967, Milepost 53 Teller Highway, and one stubby-tailed and one fully fledged juvenal on 5 July 1969, Milepost 57 Taylor Highway, Kessel pers. obs.). A nest, built in the wall of an old sod igloo at Lopp Lagoon, contained four newly hatched young on 7 July 1922 (Bailey 1943) and probably was a renesting attempt.

Postbreeding flocks, composed largely of merged families, begin to form by late July (flocks of 10-15 first seen 28 July 1976 at Arctic R, Noble and Wright 1977; juvenals first common on beaches at Wales on 31 July 1977, when several flocks were seen, including one of 18 birds, D. A. Woodby in litt.). Fall migration is well under way by early August and continues through the month; it peaked at Wales 14-21 August 1977, with numbers reaching 25-30 birds per day (D. A. Woodby in litt.). Yellow Wagtails are rare by September (latest, one, 10 September 1973, Wales, D. D. Gibson unpubl. notes; one, 16 September 1977, Cape Espenberg, Schamel et al. 1979; and an extreme late migrant came aboard ship 18 October 1970, Bering Strait, Watson and Divoky 1972).

White Wagtail—*Motacilla alba*

An Old World immigrant from eastern Siberia, the White Wagtail is a rare breeder along the coastlines of the Seward Peninsula, where it has been recorded from Bluff (W. H. Drury in litt., E. C. Murphy pers. comm.) to Wales (Peyton 1963, Keith 1967) and Shishmaref (UAM 3126) and on all the major offshore islands, including Chamisso Island (Hersey 1916). Three to four pairs nest annually at both Wales and Nome (Kessel and D. D. Gibson unpubl. data). Several observations, probably of migrants, have been reported from inland sites: single birds at Mileposts 17 and 23 Taylor Highway, 4 and 6 June 1970, respectively (D. G. Roseneau and W. Walker pers. comm.); two birds, about 35 km up the Nome River valley, 8 June 1986, D. E. Wolf in litt.); and an adult female at Serpentine Hot Springs on 5 August 1973 (D. D. Gibson, UAM 2558).

White Wagtails are found primarily about sea cliffs and coastal villages, where they nest in cavities and crevices of rock cliffs, abandoned buildings and dredges, old fuel drums, etc. On St. Lawrence Island, a nest with young was found in the cranial cavity of a walrus skull (19 July 1971, S. R. Johnson, ANRS).

The Alaska population of this wagtail (*M. a. ocularis*) apparently winters in Southeast Asia, Taiwan, and the Philippine Islands (Vaurie 1959). Earliest migrants usually arrive on the Seward Peninsula during the last few days of May (one, 25 May 1968, Nome, D. G. Roseneau and W. R. Tilton unpubl. notes; one 27 May 1978 and one 30 May 1969, Wales, Flock and Hubbard 1979; one 29 May 1983, Wales, M. W. Ward unpubl. notes). Movement continues until mid-June.

Nest initiation begins within 7-10 days of arrival and continues in the population over a period of 3 + weeks. Earliest hatching occurs during the fourth week of June (adults carrying food to the nest, 23 June 1968, Nome, Kessel pers. obs.; six chicks from a seven-egg clutch hatched on 26 June 1972, Wales, Kessel and F. G. Scheider pers. obs.; pair carrying food to nestlings 27 June 1982, Nome, J. L. Dunn in litt.). At the other extreme, a clutch of five eggs was not completed until 30 June 1961 at Wales (Peyton 1963), a bird was carrying nesting material into an oil drum on 1 July 1971 at Nome (S. R. Johnson, ANRS), and a pair was carrying food into a cliff-

face crevice on 1 August 1914 on Chamisso Island (Hersey 1916).

There are few data on fall departures from the Peninsula. Three White Wagtails fed about the Sinuk River bridge, Teller Highway, on 24 August 1969 (W. L. Foster, photo). A pair was at Wales on 9 September 1973 (D. D. Gibson, UAM 2571), and a single bird was heard there on 10 September. Extralimitally, one was seen at Icy Cape on the Chukchi Sea coast on 12 September 1980 (Lehnhausen and Quinlan 1981).

Black-backed Wagtail—*Motacilla lugens*

The Black-backed Wagtail of eastern Asia is possibly casual on the Seward Peninsula. A pair of white wagtails was observed carrying food to six recently hatched young at a nest in the corner of a shed at Milepost 1 Teller Highway on 7 July 1973 (G. Maisel in litt.); a photograph of the male showed it to be a Black-backed Wagtail. This species is a casual spring migrant at St. Lawrence Island (J. L. Dunn and R. W. Stallcup pers. comm.) and a rare spring migrant and casual fall migrant in the western Aleutian and Pribilof islands (Byrd et al. 1978, Gibson 1981, D. D. Gibson unpubl. data).

Brown Tree-Pipit—*Anthus trivialis*

An adult male Brown Tree-Pipit was observed feeding in low sedge-moss tundra at the muddy edge of a pond on the coastal flats 3 km west of Wales Village on 23 June 1972 (Kessel and F. G. Scheider, UAM 3294). The specimen was identified as *A. t. trivialis* by L. L. Short and J. Farrand, American Museum of Natural History, and is the only record of this species in the Western Hemisphere.

Red-throated Pipit—*Anthus cervinus*

An uncommon breeder on the Seward Peninsula, the Red-throated Pipit occurs on the coastal mountains (Cape and York mountains) and offshore islands (Sledge, King, and Little Diomede islands) of the Bering Strait region. In addition, on the top of Cape Deceit on 23 June 1974, I saw a single, probably nonbreeding, full alternate-plumaged male.

The largest populations occur on Little Diomede Island, where, on 26 June 1977, A. Watson and E. Steele counted about 20 birds and reported that they appeared to be nesting on the top of the island (J. O. Biderman in litt.), and on Cape Mountain, where in both 1972 and 1974, I saw an average of about one pair per hour of walking. Between 24 and 27 June 1972, during 38 observer-hours on Cape Mountain and nearby Needle Mountain, F. G. Scheider, H. E. Kingery, and I counted a total of 62 different birds.

The Red-throated Pipit nests where block-fields and Dwarf Shrub Meadow are juxtaposed and seems more abundant at locations exposed to the open coast. It does **not** frequent "moist grassy flats and swampy areas," as described for Europe by Vaurie (1959:70).

The Alaska population of this Old World pipit probably winters in Southeast Asia, the East Indies, and the Philippine Islands (American Ornithologists' Union 1983). The earliest spring migrants arrive on the Seward Peninsula during the last few days of May (first arrivals at Cape Mt on 29 May 1978, Flock and Hubbard 1979; 30 May 1983, M. L. Ward unpubl. notes; 31 May 1964, Breckenridge and Cline 1967; and 31 May 1987, P. J. Baicich in litt.).

Few breeding data are available for this species in Alaska. A nest with eggs at Wales was collected on 29 June 1931 by D. Tevuk (Bailey 1932), and on 24 June 1972, F. G. Scheider found a nest with six eggs next to a rock on Cape Mountain. On 27 June 1972 and again on 30 June 1974, I saw adults carrying small food in their bills, indicating that eggs hatch by late June.

Nothing is known about fall departures from the Peninsula, but three birds were still present at Gambell, St. Lawrence Island, on 11 September 1975 (Kessel and Gibson 1978).

Water Pipit—*Anthus spinoletta*

The Water Pipit is a fairly common breeder on the Seward Peninsula. During the breeding season it is widespread throughout the higher elevations of the Northern and Southern uplands and the lower elevations of the Highlands and on all of the major offshore islands.

Two basic habitat requirements were described by Verbeek (1970:428): (1) the site must become snow-free early enough in the season, and (2) it must have some rough features such as tussocks, tilted rocks, or eroded spots for nest sites. Verbeek also suggested that it may be advantageous for pipits to have a snowbank in their territory, where exposed insects may be more efficiently gathered than in vegetation. On the Seward Peninsula, most Water Pipits breed in the dry Dwarf Shrub Mat habitat of alpine tundras, although a nest along the coast east of the mouth of the Sinuk River that contained five eggs on 22 June 1968 was situated in grass just above tide line (D. G. Roseneau, ANRS).

This pipit winters in western United States and western Mexico (Gabrielson and Lincoln 1959). In early seasons, the first migrants arrive on the Seward Peninsula in early May (earliest, about four birds, 6 May 1983, Anvil Mt, and one, 7 May 1987, Deering, J. D. Walters unpubl. notes; six birds, 9 May 1971, Nome R, Alaska Department of Fish and Game unpubl. notes), but otherwise they may not arrive until mid-May. Individuals continue to arrive over a period of at least 3 weeks, selecting nesting territories as snow melt exposes suitable sites.

Some nesting begins during May (earliest, egg-laying began 11-12 May, based on begging fledglings flying after adults, 12 June 1983, Wales, M. L. Ward in litt.; egg-laying at least by 26 May, based on four nestlings, 11 June 1969, Serpentine Hot Springs, D. G. Roseneau and P. Wright, ANRS). Back-dating from nest contents and other observations, however, indicates that most nesting is not initiated until sometime during the first half of June—perhaps because of snow cover.

Pipits place their grass nest on the ground, in a cavity usually excavated under a rock, clod of dirt or hummock, or overhanging vegetation. Unlike pipits in most other areas, which use only grass (see Verbeek 1970), those of the Seward Peninsula often line their nests with ptarmigan feathers (D. G. Roseneau, ANRS). A study of the breeding ecology of *A. s. alticola* in the Rocky Mountains of Wyoming (Verbeek 1970) found that it took 4-5 days for nest-building after the cavity had been excavated. Eggs were laid on consecutive days. Incubation averaged 14.5 days, and the young stayed in the nest for 14-15 days. The female did all the incubating, but the male brought some food to the incubating female and helped care for the nestlings. Fledglings remained in the vicinity of the nest for about a week and became independent of their parents about 14 days after leaving the nest. *Anthus s. pacificus* on the Seward Peninsula apparently follows much the same schedule, judging from observed dates of eggs, nestlings, and fledglings. Clutches of 64 nests in my records and those of the Alaska Nest Record Scheme from the Seward Peninsula and Central Alaska averaged 5.7±0.7 eggs (range 4-7 eggs); dates of the 4-egg clutches suggest that they were either incomplete or replacement clutches.

Water Pipits are ground feeders, and both adults and young feed almost exclusively on insects (Verbeek 1970).

Postbreeding flocks composed largely of juvenals become increasingly evident on the Seward Peninsula by late July, and thereafter pipits begin leaving the alpine areas and can be found feeding at lower elevations—along river alluvia, pond margins, coastal beaches, etc. Fall migration extends throughout August, with most pipits having left the Peninsula by the end of the month (latest, one, 8 September 1973, beach near Wales, D. D. Gibson unpubl. notes); but one collected, 28 September 1921, extralimitally at Wainwright (Bailey 1948).

Bohemian Waxwing—*Bombycilla garrulus*

Waxwings are uncommon breeders on the Seward Peninsula, where they occur in the forested regions. They are fairly common throughout the taiga of Central Alaska (Kessel and Gibson 1978) and continue to be fairly common at the southeastern base of the Seward Peninsula. They become progressively less common westward, however, and are casual beyond treeline. At Koyuk on 29 June 1975, F. G. Scheider and I counted 19 individual Bohemian Waxwings in a 5-km hike along upper King Creek; and about Elim on 1-2 July 1972, I saw 10 birds while walking about 19 km. At the western extremity of trees on 3 July 1977, I saw two pairs at Bear River and counted at least 13 birds along a 2 km-stretch of the Fox River at Mileposts 71.5 and 68.3, respectively, Council Road. Beyond treeline, an emaciated, dying immature male was picked up on the ice at Little Diomede Island on 16 January 1969 (R. Soolook, UAM 3238).

On the Peninsula, this waxwing occurs primarily in scattered spruce woodlands or, as at Bear River and upper Fox River, in riparian Balsam Poplar stands (Figure 16). These habitats are similar to those used in Interior Alaska, where Spindler and Kessel (1980) found waxwings using open habitats with fairly high tree heterogeneity and with a high cover of dwarf shrub.

Due to the unavailability of preferred food (insects, berries, and seeds of Paper Birch in Interior Alaska), most if not all waxwings on the Peninsula are migratory. Judging from their behavior in Interior Alaska (Kessel 1967), they probably depart during September and return in late April-early May, although single birds were seen 12 October and 24 November 1985 extralimitally at St. Marys (B. J. McCaffery unpubl. notes).

There are few data on the breeding biology of this species on the Seward Peninsula. An adult female collected at Elim on 1 July 1972 (UAM 2518) had a brood patch and at least four discharged follicles in the ovary, and I saw a bob-tailed fledgling along the upper Fox River on 3 July 1977. In Central and Southcoastal Alaska, nests are placed in trees, usually 2-6 m above the ground and most frequently in spruce (ANRS, Kessel pers. obs.). A nesting pair closely monitored at Fairbanks by W. C. Fields (unpubl. notes) took 4 days to build its nest; the female began incubation with the laying of the last egg; the eggs hatched after 15 days of incubation; and the young left the nest, barely able to fly, when 18 days old. Both members of the pair built the nest and fed the young, but the female did all the incubating and brooding.

Northern Shrike—*Lanius excubitor*

A Holarctic species of the northern taiga, the Northern Shrike is an uncommon but widespread breeder throughout much of the Seward Peninsula mainland. Here it occurs most frequently in semi-open country, usually breeding in scattered spruce woodlands or in tall shrubs that penetrate alpine or coastal tundras or grow along creek and river banks in treeless wetlands.

Some Northern Shrikes overwinter in Central Alaska, and it is possible that some may overwinter, too, in the spruce forests at the southeast base of the Seward Peninsula, since one remained extralimitally northeast of St. Marys at least until 16 February 1986 (B. J. McCaffery unpubl. notes). Most shrikes leave the Peninsula during winter, however, because of the unavailability of prey for food. They return in spring with the first small passerine migrants, usually in late April or early May (earliest, male collected, 27 April 1913, Pilgrim Hot Springs, J. Koren unpubl. notes).

Early nests are initiated during the first half of May (seven fresh eggs, 11 May 1905, in nest in small Balsam Poplar near hot springs on south shore of Imuruk Basin, Anthony 1906; nine fresh eggs, 21 May 1913, in nest up 3.7 m in Balsam Poplar tree at Pilgrim Hot Springs, J. Koren unpubl. notes). Nests in Central and Western Alaska are usually placed in spruce trees or in tall riparian willows. Nest heights vary with available substrates, with most nests placed 2-6 m above the ground (ANRS, Murie 1946); in alpine tundra areas, however, nests have been recorded at just over 1 m (ANRS, Cade 1967).

Modal clutch size in Alaska is eight eggs, and incubation, as in many predaceous species, begins before the clutch is complete, with hatching spread over 3-4 days (Cade 1967). Based on data from closely related forms in northern Europe, incubation probably lasts an average of 17 days and is performed largely by the female (Ullrich 1971). Young in Alaska usually fledge 19 or 20 days after hatching (Cade 1967). This breeding timetable would allow fledging on the Seward Peninsula as early as the third week of June. Fledging by this date has been reported extralimitally on the Utukok River in western Northern Alaska (young jumped from nest as observer approached on 18 June 1961, H. Kantner, ANRS), but fledged families have not been reported from the Seward Peninsula until the first week of July—probably because of a lack of observers. A nest 3 m up in a willow at Taylor still contained three partially feathered young during the second week of July 1985 (D. L. Wetzel pers. comm.).

Food of summering Northern Shrikes consists primarily of small passerine birds, voles, and large insects, with proportions varying with availability (Cade 1967): adult passerines early in the season, with adult voles added as snowcover melts, and bumblebees and other large insects added as they emerge with warm weather in late May; young voles and fledgling songbirds are used heavily as they leave their nests. Inexperienced juvenal shrikes subsist first on insects and spiders, then begin catching voles, and finally birds.

Most shrikes probably leave the Peninsula during September and early October, as their food supply becomes progressively depauperate with the departure of migrant passerines and with increasing snow cover in the uplands (latest, one, 31 October 1985, extralimitally at Mountain Village, B. J. McCaffery unpubl. notes).

Orange-crowned Warbler—*Vermivora celata*

The Orange-crowned Warbler is an uncommon breeder on the Seward Peninsula, west to approximately 166° W, where I have observed apparent breeders at the Bluestone River; near the mouth of Tuksuk Channel, west of Imuruk Basin; and along Hot Springs Creek at Serpentine Hot Springs. It is a casual migrant farther west (one, 10-11 June 1977, Cape Espenberg, Schamel et al. 1979; one found dead, 30 July 1977, Wales, K. V. Hirsch and D. A. Woodby in litt.).

The primary habitat of the Orange-crowned Warbler on the Peninsula is Medium Shrub Thicket (Table 11), and the warbler's geographic distribution is largely determined by the occurrence of shrubbery in at least this 1.2-2.4 m height range. While this warbler also uses forest habitats in Interior Alaska, it does not occur in coniferous forests (Spindler and Kessel 1980) and thus is largely absent from the forests of the Peninsula, which are mostly spruce.

Wintering primarily in the southern United States and Mexico (American Ornithologists' Union 1957), spring migrants usually arrive in mid-May (earliest, 15 May 1983, near Nome, J. D. Walters unpubl. notes; but 5 May 1986, extralimitally at St. Marys, B. J. McCaffery unpubl. notes), and movement continues through May.

Nesting apparently does not get under way until mid-June. Nests are placed on the ground. Clutch size in 23 nests from Central Alaska (ANRS) was 5.1 ± 0.7 eggs, range 4-6 eggs. The incubation period is unknown, but is probably about 12 days; young remain in the nest for 10 or 11 days (ANRS). An incubating bird flushed from under my foot as I accidentally stepped on a nest of 5 half-incubated eggs at Milepost 8.5 Glacier Road on 28 June 1977. Food-carrying adults are regular after the beginning of July. Extralimitally on the Noatak River, fledglings were reported between 5 and 8 July 1961 by Hines (1963). On 12 July 1973, where ten food-carrying adults were enumerated along 3 km Goose Creek, a tributary of the Noxapaga River, one female was feeding a barely fledged Fox Sparrow! She was very defensive of this sparrow chick, and there were no defensive Fox Sparrows in the area (D. D. Gibson pers. comm.).

This warbler is probably entirely insectivorous when such prey is available, but under adverse conditions it also feeds on berries, seeds, suet, etc. (Bent 1953).

Judging from migration dates in Interior Alaska (Kessel unpubl. data), almost all Orange-crowned Warblers should have left the Seward Peninsula by the first of September. Extralimitally at St. Michael, Turner (1886:178) reported collecting two "in the month of September."

Yellow Warbler—_Dendroica petechia_

Yellow Warblers are common breeders on the Peninsula, with a distribution closely paralleling that of the Orange-crowned Warbler, i.e., they occur regularly as far west as the Bluestone River, the mouth of Tuksuk Channel, and Serpentine Hot Springs. In addition, however, isolated occurrences have been recorded farther north and west: In the vicinity of North Killeak Lake, during 35 km of walking 28-30 June 1973, D. D. Gibson and I counted 57 individual Yellow Warblers; and along Kreuger Creek near Ear Mountain on 23 June 1974, I saw a singing male that may have been a breeder. Three immatures along the west shoreline of North Devil Mountain Lake on 16-17 August 1973 (D. D. Gibson unpubl. notes) may have been raised in that area.

Distribution on the Peninsula is determined by the presence of Tall Shrub and Medium Shrub thickets. The Yellow Warbler favors Tall Shrub Thicket (Table 11) in open, largely treeless habitats, but beyond the range of tall shrubs it will use medium-height shrubbery, e.g., throughout Imuruk Basin, in the Killeak Lake area, and at Ear Mountain.

The Seward Peninsula form of the species (_D. p. amnicola_) winters in Central America and northern South America (American Ornithologists' Union 1957). It usually arrives in Interior Alaska 16-24 May (Kessel unpubl. data) and perhaps a few days later on the Peninsula (earliest, a singing male, 19 May 1983, Nome, M. L. Ward unpubl. notes; one, 29 May 1978, Utica Ck, Inmachuk R, J. M. Wright unpubl. notes).

Few breeding data from the Peninsula are available, but by back-dating from observed events it appears that nesting does not begin until mid-June, perhaps because of food availability. Nests are usually placed in the V-crotch of a deciduous shrub. Of 34 nests recorded from Interior and Western Alaska (ANRS), 76% were placed 0.9-2.4 m above the ground, 38% at 1.5-1.8 m. Studies of the closely related eastern Yellow Warbler (_D. p. aestiva_) by Schrantz (1943) and Goossen (1978) have shown that nest-building takes 4 days; egg-laying begins as soon as the nest is finished, with one egg laid each day until the clutch is complete; incubation, which often begins before the last egg or two are laid, averages 11 days (range 11-12 days); and the average nestling period ranges from 9.5 to 10.5 days. The female alone builds the nest, incubates the eggs, and broods the young; the male maintains the territory and aids in feeding the young (Schrantz 1943).

The size of 14 completed clutches from Interior and Western Alaska (ANRS, Kessel unpubl. data) averaged 4.9 ± 0.7 eggs, range 3-6, mode (71%) 5. At Nome, one nest was being constructed when found on 12 June 1964 (V. Hoeman, ANRS). In 1973, D. D. Gibson and I first saw food-carrying adults on 10 July at Lava Lake; a female was feeding just-fledged young on 17 July at McCarthys Marsh; several fledged broods on 19 July were being fed by adults at the junction of American Creek and the Niukluk River and still on 30 July along the Inmachuk River; and independent juvenals were present on 3 and 4 August at Serpentine Hot Springs. Given the above-calculated

30-day nesting period, nesting must not have begun until mid-June 1973.

The Yellow Warbler is entirely insectivorous (Bent 1953), which probably accounts for its phenologically late migration and breeding season. I observed an interesting feeding behavior on 12 July 1973, when an adult "hawked" for flying insects over the waters of the Fish River.

The fall exodus must begin as soon as the young become independent and capable of sustained flight. Since there is a major movement of Yellow Warblers in Interior Alaska during the first three weeks of August (Kessel unpubl. data), it is likely that all but stragglers have left the Seward Peninsula by the fourth week of August (latest, 27 August 1899, Nome R, Grinnell 1900b).

Yellow-rumped Warbler—*Dendroica coronata*

The Yellow-rumped Warbler is an uncommon breeder in the forested southeastern quadrant of the Seward Peninsula, extending its breeding range to the western limit of forests along the upper Fox River at 163°43′ W, near Milepost 68 Council Road. I saw two there on 3 July 1977, and 5 km farther NNE at Bear River on that same day, I saw three more, including a food-carrying male. Elsewhere, my field companions and I have seen Yellow-rumped Warblers at Koyuk (two on 29 June and two others on 3 July 1975, including an adult carrying food), Elim (seven on 1 and 2 July 1972, including a food-carrying adult), and McCarthys Marsh (eight adults with at least three families of fledged juvenals in the spruce forest stringers along Fish R on 16 July 1973). A casual spring migrant beyond the forests, one foraged in beach rye at Wales on 31 May 1978 (Flock and Hubbard 1979); one sought the protection of a bulldozer in Deering on 14 May 1984, and two were on the cliffs of Cape Deceit on 24 May 1985 (J. D. Walters unpubl. notes); and, extralimitally, it is a casual migrant to northeast Siberia (Portenko 1973, Stishov et al. 1985). A fall migrant visited Deering on 7 October 1987 (J. D. Walters unpubl. notes).

In Interior Alaska, where this forest-inhabiting warbler is a common breeder, it favors forests with relatively high canopy coverages and hence is most numerous in deciduous and mixed deciduous-coniferous forests, although it uses coniferous forests to a lesser extent (Spindler and Kessel 1980, Kessel MS). The lack of the deciduous tree component on the Seward Peninsula may explain the uncommon status of this bird in the forests of the region, which are predominantly spruce forests of low canopy coverage.

A hardy bird, the Yellow-rumped Warbler winters as far north as southwest British Columbia, and the first spring migrants usually arrive in Interior Alaska between 23 April and 6 May, depending on weather conditions (Kessel unpubl. data). They probably arrive on the Seward Peninsula several days later (earliest, 29 April 1944, extralimitally at Mountain Village, H. C. Kyllingstad in litt.).

There are few data on breeding chronologies on the Seward Peninsula, which may be retarded compared to Interior Alaska because of weather. The earliest fledglings reported from the region were on 25 June 1973 on the lower Noatak River (Manuwal 1974). While this may not be a particularly early date, since there are few observations from the region, it is almost 2 weeks later than early fledging at Fairbanks (Kessel pers. obs.). Thus, nesting may not begin on the Peninsula until the third or even fourth week of May.

The Yellow-rumped Warbler is largely insectivorous, but when insects are not available, it feeds readily on berries and seeds (Bent 1953) and even suet (Kessel unpubl. data). This dietary flexibility allows it to arrive in the Alaska taiga relatively early in the season and to remain relatively late.

Judging from migration in Interior Alaska, where fall movement peaks in most years during the last 10 days of August and the first half of September (Kessel unpubl. data), it is likely that the main exodus from the Seward Peninsula is over by the end of the first week of September (latest, 7 October 1987, above).

Blackpoll Warbler—*Dendroica striata*

A fairly common breeder on the Seward Peninsula as a whole, the Blackpoll Warbler is common in the southeast portions as far west as the drainages of the Fish River and in the Kuzitrin River drainage from the lower Noxapaga River to at least Pilgrim Hot Springs, e.g, I have total counts of 25 adults at Koyuk in 18 km of hiking 29 June and 3 July 1975, 99 about Elim and vicinity during 29 km of hiking 1 and 2 July 1972, 23 at McCarthys Marsh during 10 km of walking on 16 July 1973, 15 on the lower Noxapaga River during 6 km of walking on 12 July 1973, and 42 while boating down 18 km of the Pilgrim River and while at Pilgrim Hot Springs on 6 July 1971. Blackpoll Warblers occur as far west as Tall Shrub Thicket exists; I have seen them in the Southern Uplands as far west as 165°35' W, at Sunset Creek, Milepost 9.3 Teller Highway, and in the Interior Lowlands at 165°17' W, near the mouth of the Kuzitrin River (UAM 3194). In the Northern Uplands, they occur regularly at Buckland, where F. G. Scheider and I counted a total of 13 individuals on 22, 24, and 26 June 1975; and they have been recorded as far west as the Inmachuk River, where 4 singing males were seen on 20 June 1984, 3 on 14 June 1985, and 1 on 3 July 1986 by J. D. Walters (unpubl. notes). It is a casual migrant beyond tall shrubs (one, Wales, 7 September 1973, D. D. Gibson, UAM 2692).

In Central Alaska, the Blackpoll Warbler favors deciduous habitats of either tall shrubs or forests (Kessel MS), and on the Seward Peninsula I have found them primarily in Tall Shrub Thicket of alder or willow, but they also occur in the mature Balsam Poplar forest at Pilgrim Hot Springs.

This species winters in northern and northeastern South America, and its spring migration route takes it across the Caribbean Sea and central United States on its way to Interior Alaska and the Seward Peninsula (American Ornithologists' Union 1983). The first migrants usually arrive in Interior Alaska sometime between 16 and 25 May (Kessel unpubl. data), and, since they travel rapidly during their final days of migration (Lincoln and Peterson 1979), they probably arrive on the Seward Peninsula by the fourth week of May.

Data on breeding biology from the Peninsula are few, but 24 nests from near Soldotna, Kenai Peninsula, Alaska (M. A. Miller, ANRS), provide applicable information. While ground nests have been reported in Northwest Territories, Canada (Bent 1953, Salter and Davis 1974), none has been reported from Alaska. On the Kenai Peninsula, 62% of nests were placed below 0.6 m, 42% below 0.3 m. Average size of 18 completed clutches was 5.1±0.6 eggs, range 4-6, mode (67%) 5. Incubation took

12 days (two nests) and young left the nest when 11 days old (two nests).

On the Seward Peninsula, food-carrying adults become evident by early July (1 July 1972 at Elim; 3 July 1977 at Fox R; 6 July 1971 at Pilgrim Hot Springs), and at McCarthys Marsh on 16 July 1973, D. D. Gibson and I counted at least five families of fledged young. Back-dating from these observations shows that egg-laying on the Seward Peninsula begins by about 15 June.

Blackpoll Warblers are primarily insectivorous birds, although they may take a few seeds and berries, especially in fall (Bent 1953).

Based on observations from Interior Alaska (Kessel unpubl. data), fall migration on the Peninsula is under way by the second week of August, and all but stragglers have probably left by the end of the month (latest, 27 August 1899, Nome R, Grinnell 1900b; 7 September 1973, Wales, D. D. Gibson, UAM 2692).

Northern Waterthrush—*Seiurus noveboracensis*

The Northern Waterthrush is a fairly common breeder on the Peninsula, where it occurs to the limits of Tall Shrub Thicket. I have recorded it as far west in the Southern Uplands as the Penny River (165°40′ W), in the Interior Lowlands to near the mouth of the Kuzitrin River (165°17′ W), and in the Northern Uplands to Hot Springs Creek at Serpentine Hot Springs (164°45′ W). It has been taken extralimitally at Cape Serdtse Kamen, Chukotsk Peninsula (male, 14 June 1879, Portenko 1973). This warbler is more widespread and somewhat more numerous than the Blackpoll Warbler, which uses similar basic habitats.

The Northern Waterthrush has three main habitat requisites (Kessel pers. obs.): (1) a canopy height of at least 2.5 m, (2) dense growth in vegetation layer below 1.0 m, and (3) some standing water, either fluviatile or lacustrine. Hence, on the Seward Peninsula, it is found most frequently in tall riparian alder or willow patches that have understory vegetation; but it is also present in numbers in the mature Balsam Poplar forest at Pilgrim Hot Springs, a forest with a dense ground cover of ferns and umbellifers.

Wintering primarily from Mexico to northern South America (American Ornithologists' Union 1983), the Northern Waterthrush usually reaches Interior Alaska between 12 and 20 May—80% of the time between 12 and 17 May, 33% of the time on either 14 or 15 May (Kessel unpubl. data). It probably reaches the Peninsula 4 to 7 days later, weather permitting, although the earliest report has been 24 May (1978) at Utica Creek, Inmachuk River (J. M. Wright unpubl. notes).

This warbler is essentially a ground-nester, placing its nest among the exposed roots of riparian shrubs or among the rootlets of a fallen tree, usually directly over water and within 0.3 m of the water surface (Eaton 1957). Nests have also been found in the sides of fern tussocks and rotten, moss-covered stumps, under driftwood and fallen logs, etc. (Bent 1953, ANRS). Clutches from six Alaska nests averaged 5.0 ± 0.6 eggs, range 4-6 eggs (ANRS, Bent 1953). Incubation may begin with the laying of the next-to-last egg and lasts 12 days (Eaton 1957). Young stay in the nest for only 9 days, but remain concealed in heavy vegetation for several more days, until they have developed enough to fly and perch fairly well; they continue to be fed by their parents for at least 2 weeks after leaving the nest (ibid.).

On the Seward Peninsula, hatching, as indicated by food-carrying adults, begins in late June (26 June 1975, Buckland), and young leave the nest in early July (3 July 1977, Solomon R, when I watched a youngster too young to fly running down the road). Back-dating from these observed events indicates that egg-laying begins by 8-10 June.

Food, especially during the breeding season, is usually gathered at the margins of standing water; the diet consists largely of small invertebrates, especially aquatic insects (Bent 1953, Eaton 1957).

Postbreeding movement is evident in Interior Alaska throughout August (Kessel unpubl. data), so the fall exodus from the Peninsula must begin almost as soon as the young become independent. While a few stragglers may remain until early September, most waterthrushes have undoubtedly left before the end of August (latest recorded, male collected, 26 August 1913, Marys Igloo on the lower Kuzitrin R, J. Koren unpubl. notes).

Wilson's Warbler—*Wilsonia pusilla*

The Wilson's Warbler is a fairly common, widespread breeder on the Peninsula west to about 166° W, where it occurs regularly at the Bluestone River and where I observed six birds in 1973 in willow draws at Ear Mountain. It also breeds as far north on the Peninsula as North Killeak Lake. In addition, it has been recorded as a spring migrant at Tin City (27 May 1969 and 31 May 1978, Flock and Hubbard 1979) and as a fall migrant at Breving Lagoon (2-7 August 1980, D. A. Woodby unpubl. notes); and I observed a nonterritorial male singing in a patch of protected shrubbery in the Coastal Lowlands along the Arctic River, about 8 km upriver from its mouth on 26 June 1970.

The critical habitat requirement of this warbler is a high density of deciduous vegetation in the vertical profile at the low shrub level, i.e., at 0.6-1.1 m (Kessel MS). Such a dense profile does not usually occur in anything shorter than Medium Shrub Thicket, so the geographic distribution of this species in the western portions of the Peninsula is closely correlated with the presence of this habitat. It also occurs in Tall Shrub Thicket and forests, but is generally more abundant in habitats that lack canopies at the tall shrub and tree layers (ibid.). Wilson's Warblers have not been reported from several regions of the Peninsula where shrubbery of appropriate heights is present, e.g., McCarthys Marsh and Imuruk Basin. Perhaps the vegetative density in the vertical profile of the shrubbery in these areas is inadequate.

The Wilson's Warbler winters primarily in Mexico and Central America (American Ornithologists' Union 1983), and the first spring arrival of males in Interior Alaska varies from 7 to 21 May (Kessel unpubl. data). Weather permitting, they probably arrive on the Peninsula about a week later (earliest reported, two, Anvil Mt near Nome, 22 May 1983, J. D. Walters unpubl. notes; but 16 May 1944, extralimitally at Mountain Village, H. C. Kyllingstad in litt.).

As with many passerines, the female arrives later than the male, and, in California, Stewart (1973) found that pair formation did not begin until about 15 days after the males arrived. In Central and Western Alaska, Wilson's Warblers are ground-nesters; the average clutch size from 23 nests was 5.6 ± 0.6 eggs, mode 6 eggs (Brandt

1943, ANRS). A nest I found on 20 June 1977 near Grand Central River, however, contained 10 eggs! Incubation lasts 12-13 days, and young remain in the nest 8-10 days (Harrison 1951, Stewart 1973); disturbed young that erupted from the nest when 8 days old could not fly (Harrison 1951). On the Seward Peninsula food-carrying adults, indicating that eggs have hatched, are common by 1-3 July (Kessel pers. obs.), so egg-laying probably begins during the second week of June, and young could have left their nests by the end of the first week of July.

While primarily an insectivorous bird (Bent 1953), Wilson's Warblers in Interior Alaska have been observed feeding also on millet seeds and chokecherry berries (Kessel unpubl. data).

If the young stay on territory with the adults until they are 32 days old (i.e., until early August), as they do in California (Stewart 1973), family groups would hardly have disbanded by the time migration begins. The main migratory movement through Interior Alaska extends from mid-August to mid-September (Kessel unpubl. data). There are few fall dates from the Peninsula; the latest recorded date is 27 August 1899 from the Nome River (Grinnell 1900b), but a few birds probably remain into early September.

American Tree Sparrow—*Spizella arborea*

An abundant, widely distributed breeder, the American Tree Sparrow is the fourth most common passerine on the Seward Peninsula. Because of its habitat requirements, however, it is somewhat less widespread than the Savannah Sparrow. As a breeder, it is absent from the Coastal Lowlands and from alpine tundra and other areas of the uplands where there is insufficient growth of low shrubs, e.g., it is only a rare spring migrant at Wales; it is absent from Cape Espenberg and the barrier strips along Lopp Lagoon, Shishmaref Inlet, and Safety Sound; and essentially none occur in the uplands along the Council Road between the Nome River and Cape Nome and the slopes above the Woolley Lagoon system.

The American Tree Sparrow is primarily a bird of Low Shrub Thicket. It avoids forest and tall shrub canopies, but tolerates open Medium Shrub Thicket (Kessel MS). In the upper Susitna River Basin, Central Alaska, it occurred only where low shrub cover was greater than 20%; and the mean low shrub cover at species-present sample sites was $35.3 \pm 27.0\%$ (ibid.).

While most of Alaska's tree sparrows (*S. a. ochracea*) winter in southwestern Canada and the western United States (American Ornithologists' Union 1957), a few winter as far north as Southcoastal Alaska (Kessel and D. D. Gibson unpubl. data). Migrants return to the Seward Peninsula in late April or early May, depending on early spring environmental conditions (earliest, one, 27 April 1988, Deering, and two, 3 May 1983, Nome, J. D. Walters unpubl. notes; 26 April 1944, extralimitally at Mountain Village, H. C. Kyllingstad in litt.).

Nesting apparently does not begin until about the third week of May. Nests are placed on the ground, usually at the base of a low deciduous shrub. Nest-building, which is accomplished by the female, takes about 7 days, and egg-laying does not begin for another several days thereafter (Baumgartner 1937b). The mean size of 76 completed clutches near Eagle Summit, Steese Highway, Interior Alaska, was

4.8±0.6 eggs, range 3-6, mode 5 (J. S. Weeden, ANRS). Data presented by both Baumgartner (1937b) and J. S. Weeden (ANRS) show an incubation period of 12.3 days and a nestling period of 9.5 days. Only the female incubates and broods the young, but the male aids in the care of the nestlings and fledglings (Baumgartner 1937b, Weeden 1966). The young are unable to fly for 4-5 days after leaving the nest and continue to be fed by the parents until they are 3 weeks old (Baumgartner 1968).

In 1977 I first noted food-carrying adults on 18 June near Nome and saw barely fledged young on 26 June at the Bluestone River. Back-dating from these observations indicates that egg-laying began by late May. Observations of young just hatching on 22 and 23 June 1968 and 24 June 1976 indicate that initiation of egg-laying may continue through the first week of June. Most young have fledged by late June-early July.

Food consists largely of invertebrates, especially insects, when they are available during the summer; adults and juvenals also take seeds and berries, especially *Empetrum nigrum* and *Vaccinium* spp. (Baumgartner 1937a, Cooper 1984). Tree sparrows frequently feed on flying insects, jumping and flitting about twigs in pursuit of prey and "hawking" over river waters (Kessel pers. obs.).

Postbreeding flocks of juveniles have begun to form by mid-July; the "tsp" flock note was common at McCarthys Marsh on 16-17 July 1973. The main fall movement through Interior Alaska occurs throughout September, but most tree sparrows have apparently left the Seward Peninsula by mid-September (latest, 10 September 1899, Nome R, Grinnell 1900b; two, 10 September 1983, Inmachuk R, J. D. Walters unpubl. notes; but 17 September 1898, extralimitally on the Hunt R, Grinnell 1900a).

Savannah Sparrow—*Passerculus sandwichensis*

A widespread, abundant breeder throughout the Peninsula, the Savannah Sparrow is the third most common passerine of the region. It is absent only in the Highlands, the forests, and where vegetation is too short, e.g., Dwarf Shrub Mat, Salt Grass Meadow. Its abundance varies markedly among areas, however, undoubtedly correlated with habitat suitability. Densities of up to 12.7 territories/10 ha were recorded at the mouth of the Arctic River in willow-grass meadow habitat (Wright 1979), yet few birds occur in McCarthys Marsh, at Lost Jim lava cone, in the immediate vicinity of Wales, on offshore islands, etc.

The Savannah Sparrow is a bird of open habitats, favoring areas of patchy Low Shrub Thicket with a sedge-grass ground cover (Kessel MS). It will use entirely herbaceous habitats, however, if perch sites and cover at least 0.4 m high are available (Kessel pers. obs.). It breeds, for example, in the *Elymus* dunes of Cape Espenberg and along the *Elymus* barrier strips at Safety Sound and at Shishmaref. Table 11 shows the primary use of Low Shrub Thicket, but also illustrates the tendency of Savannah Sparrows to seek the highest available lookout posts when disturbed.

The Savannah Sparrow of Interior Alaska and the Seward Peninsula (*P. s. anthinus*) winters from southwestern British Columbia and western and southwestern United States to El Salvador, Central America (American Ornithologists' Union 1957). Early migrants arrive during the first third of May (earliest, 6 May 1980, Nome, and 9 May

1981, Golovin, D. A. Woodby in litt.; 9 May 1977, extralimitally at the head of Norton Bay, Shields and Peyton 1979), but the main influx of migrants does not appear until mid-May.

Nesting begins in late May-early June. Sedge- or grass-dominated sites are selected for the nest, usually with some deciduous shrub cover (Wright 1979). Nests are placed on the ground and are normally domed over by adjacent vegetation, usually by sedge or grass blades. Clutch sizes in ten nests from the northwestern parts of the Peninsula in 1977 and 1978 averaged 5.1±0.3 eggs (J. M. Wright unpubl. data), and six clutches from the southern coastline in 1980 and 1981 (D. A. Woodby in litt.) averaged 5.2±1.0 eggs. Dates of full clutches from the northwestern parts of the Peninsula ranged from 8 to 27 June 1977 (J. M. Wright unpubl. data); the first completed clutch on the Akulik-Inglutalik River delta was 3 June 1977 (Shields and Peyton 1979). Incubation has variously been reported as 10 days (Welsh 1975) or 12 days (Jehl and Hussell 1966). Hatching extended from 17 June to 15 July 1977 on the Akulik-Inglutalik River delta, with the hatching peak occurring on 21 June 1976 and 24 June 1977 (Shields and Peyton 1977, 1979). Young in Nova Scotia stayed in the nest 8-11 days (average 9.4 days) and left the nest before they could fly (Welsh 1975). Four nests on the Yukon-Kuskokwim Delta were still occupied on the ninth day after hatching, although some young from one nest had left; three nests checked on the tenth day were empty (R. G. B. Brown, ANRS). Thus, the first young on the Seward Peninsula should be out of the nest by late June, which agrees with my observation of the first bob-tailed young of the season at North Killeak Lake on 28 and 30 June 1973.

Savannah Sparrows are opportunistic feeders, eating insects when they are plentiful in the summer, but also feeding on berries and seeds, especially in spring and fall (Bent 1968, Cooper 1984).

Fall movement is under way by late July and continues throughout August; it peaked at 450 birds/day on 8 August 1977 on the Akulik-Inglutalik River delta (Shields and Peyton 1979). A few birds remain through the first week of September (latest, "uncommon," 13 September 1980, Safety Sound, D. A. Woodby unpubl. notes).

Fox Sparrow—*Passerella iliaca*

The Fox Sparrow is a common breeder on the Peninsula, occurring throughout the Northern and Southern uplands and the Interior Lowlands. It does not inhabit the Coastal Lowlands, except where physiographic relief provides sufficient protection to allow growth of medium-height shrubbery. The species is common in the vicinity of North Killeak Lake, Ear Mountain, and at the head of the Nuluk River, and a few occur in protected bowls near the mouths of the Arctic and Serpentine rivers and at other sites around Shishmaref Inlet (Kessel pers. obs.). It is only a rare migrant at Wales, however (first seen on 15 May 1970, 18 May 1975, 8 June 1978, Flock and Hubbard 1979; one 14-17 June 1978, D. R. Paulson unpubl. notes; one 7 and 8 September 1973, D. D. Gibson unpubl. notes).

This sparrow is basically a bird of Medium Shrub Thicket, but it readily uses Tall Shrub Thicket, too (Table 11). It favors shrubbery with a high density of vegetation in the vertical profile at the 1.6-2.0-m level (medium shrub) and substantial canopy coverage (mean total canopy in species-present plots in Central Alaska was 36-43%

[Spindler and Kessel 1980, Kessel MS]). It uses this combination of habitat features whether or not there is a forest overstory.

Fox Sparrows from the Seward Peninsula and Central Alaska (*P. i. zaboria*) winter primarily in the eastern central and southeastern United States (Gabrielson and Lincoln 1959). In early seasons the first spring migrants probably arrive on the Peninsula by the first week of May (earliest recorded, 8 May 1987 at Deering and 10 May 1983 at Nome, J. D. Walters unpubl. notes; but extralimitally, 29 April 1944, Mountain Village, H. C. Kyllingstad in litt., and 29 April 1980, Ambler, D. K. Wik in litt.).

Males and females arrive together and pair within a week of arrival; egg-laying begins as soon as the nest is complete (Threlfall and Blacquiere 1982). Of 24 nests in Interior and Western Alaska, 75% were built on the ground, and 14 completed clutches averaged 4.1±0.6 eggs, range 3-5, mode 4 (ANRS, Kessel unpubl. data). Incubation lasts a few hours beyond 12 days (one nest each, Threlfall and Blacquiere 1982 and ANRS), although eggs in one clutch in Newfoundland took 13.5 days to hatch (Ryan 1974). Young leave the nest after 9 or 10 days, with well-developed tarsi but with stubby tails and short flight feathers; adults may continue to feed the young for 3 weeks after they leave the nest (Threlfall and Blacquiere 1982). I have seen stubby-tailed fledglings on the Seward Peninsula by the fourth week of June (27 June 1972, Grand Central R), so egg-laying must begin by early June and probably by late May (a nest extralimitally at Ambler contained four eggs on 28 May 1972, D. K. Wik in litt.). Fledged juvenals are common on the Peninsula after the first week of July.

Fox Sparrows are essentially ground feeders, often using a vigorous, two-footed scratching behavior to uncover food items. They feed on terrestrial invertebrates, berries, and medium- to large-sized seeds (Bent 1968).

Fall movement must begin as soon as the young are independent, and it continues through August; numbers peaked (n=6) on 20 August 1976 on the Akulik-Inglutalik River delta, where they did not breed (Shields and Peyton 1977). A few stragglers probably remain at least through the first week of September (latest, 27 August 1899, Nome R, Grinnell 1900b; 8 September 1973, Wales, D. D. Gibson unpubl notes; 30 September 1921, extralimitally at Wainwright, Bailey 1948).

Two dark-plumaged Fox Sparrows were seen on King Island during June 1976 (W. L. Drury pers. comm.); a bird seen at Wales on 7 and 8 September 1973 (above) was dark; and D. R. Paulson (unpubl. notes) thought that the 1978 Wales bird was different from the usual *P. i. zaborea*, describing it as having a "very plain head and back, gray-brown with rusty tail." These reports suggest that *P. i. unalaschcensis* (or another coastal subspecies?) may occur casually on the Peninsula, as it has at Barrow (20 May 1938 and 21 May 1942, Gabrielson and Lincoln 1959) and at Uel'kal', Kresta Bay, USSR (28 June 1961, Portenko 1973).

Lincoln's Sparrow—*Melospiza lincolnii*

The Lincoln's Sparrow is a rare breeder on the Seward Peninsula, where it is at the western extremity of its geographic range. At Elim I counted four birds along Hot Springs Trail near the mouth of Elim Creek on 1 July 1972. One bird was carrying food in its bill and a collected female (UAM 2514) had a brood patch and regressing ovules. The species probably occurs elsewhere in the open taiga of the southeastern portions of the Peninsula, but I saw none when at Koyuk or at McCarthys Marsh. The Lincoln's Sparrow is casual beyond taiga (singing male, Serpentine Hot Springs, 23 June 1987, M. A. Spindler pers. comm.). It is a fairly common breeder in Interior Alaska (Kessel unpubl. data).

Golden-crowned Sparrow—*Zonotrichia atricapilla*

The Golden-crowned Sparrow is fairly common on the Peninsula, where it breeds in the Southern Uplands and the western portions of the Northern Uplands. Ever since 1940 (Bailey 1943), observers almost annually have reported one or two pairs nesting at Wales; and in 1974 I counted six birds along the upper Nuluk River on 28 June and ten birds in the shrubby draws near Ear Mountain between 21 and 23 June. East of Ear Mountain, the only breeding season reports in the Northern Uplands have been of three or four adults at Serpentine Hot Springs 22 June-4 July 1987 (R. V. Harris pers. comm.) and a possibly breeding pair at Cape Deceit 3-15 June 1985 (J. D. Walters unpubl. notes). The species is apparently absent from the Interior Lowlands, although I recorded two birds on 24 June 1971 along Tuksuk Channel, where the Interior Lowlands drain into Grantley Harbor. Golden-crowned Sparrows are common in the Southern Uplands between about 164° and 166° W, and a pair with fledglings was on Sledge Island on 19 July 1984 (G. V. Byrd in litt.).

During migration, the species is more widespread. Between 14 and 31 May 1984 a total of 16 birds was counted moving through Deering (J. D. Walters unpubl. notes), and seven immatures were seen 6-10 August 1973 along Hot Springs Creek at Serpentine Hot Springs, where they had been absent earlier (D. D. Gibson unpubl. notes, UAM 2563). Extralimitally at Wrangel Island, USSR, an adult male was collected on 6 May 1938 and an immature on 6 October 1938 (Portenko 1973).

The primary habitat of the Golden-crowned Sparrow on the Peninsula is Low Shrub Thicket, especially where shrubbery is adjacent to openings of Dwarf Shrub Meadow and Wet Meadow. The species also ranges into habitats that have some medium-height shrub overstory, and it occurs in alpine areas as far as low shrubs extend. Characteristically, it is the last shrub bird to be found as one climbs upward onto the Dwarf Shrub Mat tundra.

While this species winters primarily in the western United States and southern British Columbia (American Ornithologists' Union 1983), it is a rare winter visitant as far north as Southcoastal Alaska, including Kodiak Island (MacIntosh 1986). It is primarily a Pacific Coast migrant (Gabrielson and Lincoln 1959, Bent 1968), arriving on the Seward Peninsula during the second week of May (earliest, about six birds on 10 May 1983, Anvil Mt near Nome, J. D. Walters unpubl. notes). Migrants continue to arrive over a period of at least 2 weeks.

Back-dating from known breeding observations shows that nesting begins by late May (nest of 5 eggs hatched 11 June 1981, Wales, J. L. Dunn pers. comm). The grass nests are usually placed on the ground in a formed depression, but one nest with 3 eggs found 13 June 1968 along the Nome River was placed 30 cm up in a shrub (D. G. Roseneau and W. R. Tilton, ANRS). Clutch sizes in ten nests from the Brooks Range and Western Alaska averaged 4.4±0.7 eggs, range 3-5 (Bailey 1948, ANRS, Kessel unpubl. data). Little is known about the breeding behavior of this sparrow anywhere in its range, but the 3 eggs that hatched from a 5-egg clutch in the Brooks Range did so 11 days after the last egg had been laid (G. and V. Staender, ANRS), indicating an incubation period of 11 or 12 days. The nestling period is probably about 9 days, judging from that of the closely related but somewhat smaller White-crowned Sparrow (see below). Egg dates on the Peninsula have ranged from 28 May to 22 June, and stubby-tailed fledglings are common by early July.

The food of the Golden-crowned Sparrow is primarily vegetative, but, as with other emberizids, nestlings are fed insects. Adult foods, in addition to insects, consist of such items as seeds and seed sprouts, berries, buds, flowers, and new leaves (Bent 1968).

Postbreeding movements begin by the end of July, and most Golden-crowned Sparrows have left the region by the end of August (latest, 10 September 1899, Nome R, Grinnell 1900b).

White-crowned Sparrow—*Zonotrichia leucophrys*

A common, widely distributed breeder, the White-crowned Sparrow ranks as the seventh most common passerine of the region. Except in the Coastal Lowlands and in areas of alpine tundra, where appropriate habitat is lacking, the species breeds over most of the Peninsula. It is even a very rare breeder about Wales Village (nest of 5 eggs, 17 June 1945, Bailey 1948; nest of 5 eggs, 11 June 1981, J. L. Dunn pers. comm.). During migration, it has been recorded on Little Diomede Island (Kenyon and Brooks 1960) and in the Coastal Lowlands (Cape Espenberg, Schamel et al. 1979).

This sparrow is an obligate low shrub bird, selecting habitats with a relatively high cover of dense low shrubs; and, where this habitat exists, it will tolerate taller shrub or forest canopies (Kessel MS). It often uses these taller canopies for observation and singing posts. In the upper Susitna River Basin, Central Alaska, the average cover of low shrub at species-present sites was $36 \pm 28\%$; and the vertical density profile at 0.6-1.0 m was $66 \pm 33\%$ and below 0.4 m was $89 \pm 19\%$ (ibid.).

The White-crowned Sparrow is a rare winter resident as far north as Southcoastal and Southeastern Alaska (Kessel and D. D. Gibson unpubl. data), but most members of the subspecies that breeds in Alaska (*Z. l. gambelii*) winter somewhere in western North or Middle America between southern British Columbia and central Mexico (American Ornithologists' Union 1957). Early spring migrants usually begin arriving on the Seward Peninsula during the second week of May, or any time thereafter that habitat becomes available (earliest, one, 4 May 1988, Deering, J. D. Walters unpubl. notes, and one, 9 May 1978, Nome, N. Levinson, Beltz School unpubl. notes). The first birds to arrive are usually males, and they continue to arrive over a period of 2 or 3 weeks; the females arrive 11-12 days after the males (King et al. 1965, DeWolfe 1968).

Nest-building begins within a few days of the arrival of the females and takes 2-4 days (DeWolfe 1968). Almost all nests are built on the ground (ANRS), but one along the Nome River on 10 June 1968 was located 0.5 m up in a willow shrub (D. G. Roseneau, ANRS). Egg-laying begins within a day or two after the nest is finished (DeWolfe 1968), so laying on the Seward Peninsula could begin during the last week of May. My earliest egg date is about 1 June, however, back-calculated from a stubby-tailed juvenal I saw on 25 June 1977 near Nome; and nests with eggs, some apparently renesting attempts, can be found until early July (latest, nest with 4 eggs, 10 July 1973, Lost Jim lava cone, Kessel pers. obs.). Clutch sizes from nine nests on the Seward Peninsula (Bailey 1948, ANRS, J. M. Wright unpubl. data, Kessel unpubl. data) averaged 4.4 ± 0.5 eggs, range 4-5. Incubation, performed by the female, lasts 12 days, and the young usually remain in the nest for 8 or 9 days (DeWolfe 1968, King and Hubbard 1981). The nestlings are tended primarily by the female, but the male shares parental duties after the young have left the nest (DeWolfe 1968). The young may not become fully fledged until 7-10 days after leaving the nest (ibid.). Fledged young become conspicuous on the Seward Peninsula after 1 July. They become independent of their parents by 28 days of age (ibid.), or beginning in mid-July on the Peninsula.

White-crowned Sparrows feed on a wide variety of insect and vegetable matter, including seeds, berries, blossoms and leaves (ibid.). Nestlings are fed almost entirely on insects.

In Central Alaska, local breeders begin leaving their breeding areas at least by late July, with migration well under way by early August (DeWolfe 1967, 1968), and the same is probably true on the Seward Peninsula. After 30 July 1973 most of the White-crowned Sparrows seen along Inmachuk River and Hot Springs Creek at Serpentine Hot Springs and at Devil Mountain Lakes were immatures, but they were fairly common at least until 10 August (D. D. Gibson unpubl. notes). The main fall exodus occurs during August, however, with few individuals remaining even to the end of the month (latest, one, 8 September 1977, Cape Espenberg, Schamel et al. 1979; one immature, 12 October 1985, extralimitally at St. Marys, B. J. McCaffery unpubl. notes).

Dark-eyed Junco—*Junco hyemalis*

The Dark-eyed Junco is an uncommon migrant and breeder on the Seward Peninsula. During breeding it occurs only in the forested southeast portions of the Peninsula, where I have recorded it in the vicinity of Koyuk (seven birds, 29 June and 3 July 1975) and Elim (ten birds, including a pair with a juvenal, 1 and 2 July 1972) and at the western edge of spruce along the Fox River below Milepost 68 Council Road (five birds, including a pair carrying food, 3 July 1977). In all instances, these juncos were in spruce forest or spruce woodland habitats.

As illuminated by Gabrielson and Lincoln (1959) and subsequent observers (Kessel and D. D. Gibson unpubl. data), Dark-eyed Juncos may show up far beyond their forested breeding range, especially during spring migration. They are rare migrants beyond the forests on the Seward Peninsula. Juncos have been recorded at Deering (a movement along the coast 6-22 May 1984, including a maximum of five birds on 8 May; up to two birds 21-25 May 1985; up to three birds 14-28 May and one until 4 June 1986; up to four birds 8-15 May 1987; and one bird 27 April-5 May 1988—all J. D. Walters unpubl. notes), Cape Espenberg (one, 20-22 May 1977, Schamel et al. 1979), Nome (a ''few,'' 22-23 May 1965, S. B. Young unpubl. notes), Ear Mountain (one, 19 June 1987, R. V. Harris unpubl. notes), Sledge Island (one, 10 June 1950, Cade 1952), Tin City (one?, 18 May 1975, Flock and Hubbard 1979), Wales (female collected, 30 May 1913, J. Koren unpubl. notes; several about village, 18-30 May 1922, and one collected there, 30 May 1932, Bailey 1943; one, 1 June 1987, P. J. Baicich in litt.), and Little Diomede Island (male collected, 5 June 1958, Kenyon and Brooks 1960). Farther west, they are casual migrants extralimitally on Wrangel Island, USSR (Portenko 1973, Stishov et al. 1985).

Lapland Longspur—*Calcarius lapponicus*

The Lapland Longspur is an abundant, widespread breeder on the Seward Peninsula, nesting throughout all of the upland and lowland physiographic units. It is second only to the redpoll in abundance among passerines of the region. It is a bird of open habitats, ranging from the offshore islands and coastal barrier strips and lowlands to alpine tundras. Longspurs favor mesic habitats, however, preferably with a shrub component. They are most frequently associated with the ubiquitous Dwarf Shrub Meadow, and, in the damper areas, with hummock-ridge tundra. They commonly feed in this habitat but also in both drier and more moist habitats (e.g., Dwarf Shrub Mat or Wet Meadow, the latter especially by juveniles). If taller shrubs are available, longspurs also use them for observation posts when disturbed. In 1977, Wright (1979) recorded densities at Kitluk River of 13 nests/10 ha in Dwarf Shrub Meadow but lower densities in other habitats.

Alaska's longspurs (*C. l. alascensis*) winter primarily in the western United States and southwestern Canada (American Ornithologists' Union 1957), and they reach the Seward Peninsula in spring via Interior Alaska (West et al. 1968). There is considerable annual variation in the arrival dates of migrants because of early spring environmental conditions. In most years, early migrants arrive on the Peninsula during the first week of May (5 May 1971, Nome, Alaska Department of Fish and Game unpubl. notes; 5 May 1985, Deering, J. D. Walters unpubl. notes; 7 May 1979, near Nome, N. Levinson, Beltz School unpubl. notes), but they may arrive in late April (earliest, 30 April 1988, Deering, J. D. Walters unpubl. notes; and extralimitally, 26 April 1943, Mountain Village, H. C. Kyllingstad in litt., and 27 April [yr?], Cape Thompson, Williamson et al. 1966). Early flocks of migrants are composed almost entirely of males, while later flocks contain progressively higher proportions of females (West et al. 1968); females may not arrive on the breeding grounds for a week or two after the males.

The female begins nest-building soon after arrival. Nests are most often placed in the side of sedge tussocks or small hummocks but may be placed on flat ground. They are usually sheltered by overhanging leaves of sedge or dwarf shrubs. At Cape Thompson, Williamson (1968) found that egg-laying usually began the day the nest was completed; one egg was laid each day until the clutch was complete; incubation, which was performed entirely by the female, began with the laying of the third or fourth egg of a five-egg clutch, so hatching was spread over a 1-3-day period; incubation lasted beween 12 and 13 days; most chicks left the nest after 8-10 days (average 9 days, range 7-11); and young could fly at about 12 days of age.

Back-dating using these chronologies shows that early egg-laying on the Seward Peninsula may begin by the third week of May (two nests with four and five young that hatched 1 June 1978 along the Inmachuk R [J. M. Wright unpubl. notes] would place the beginning of egg-laying as early as 16-19 May, and five other nests either

found by Wright or recorded in the Alaska Nest Record Scheme have clutch dates indicating that egg-laying began at least by 21-26 May). Egg-laying extends over a long period, however, partly because some migrants are still arriving in late May and partly because of renesting attempts. In Norton Sound in 1980 and 1981, two replacement clutches were laid between 5 and 24 June (Woodby and Divoky 1983), and fresh eggs were taken on Mint River near Lopp Lagoon on 11 July 1922 (Bailey 1943). Clutches from 54 nests on the Peninsula, from a range of years and from throughout the breeding season (J. M. Wright unpubl. notes, ANRS, Kenyon and Brooks 1960, Kessel unpubl. notes), averaged 4.6±0.9 eggs range 3-7, mode 4- and 5-egg clutches in equal number. Thirteen clutches from Norton Sound in 1981, including two late nests of 3 eggs, averaged 4.7 eggs (Woodby and Divoky 1983), and clutches from another 32 nests over a 2-yr period at Cape Espenberg averaged 5.2 eggs (Schamel et al. 1979). Clutch sizes are known to vary among years, and they tend to decrease in size as the season progresses (Williamson and Emison 1971, Custer and Pitelka 1977).

The first flying, bob-tailed young on the Peninsula should be present by mid-June, but they do not become common until the third week of June and thereafter. Flocks of juveniles become conspicuous by mid-July, and soon after many move to the lowlands and littoral habitats for feeding (Connors 1978, Schamel et al. 1979, Woodby and Divoky 1983).

Lapland Longspurs are opportunistic feeders, using a wide array of animal and plant matter from on or near the surface of the ground. The diet consists of about 50:50 animal and plant matter, although young are fed almost exclusively animal matter, primarily insects, either larval or adult (Williamson 1968, Seastedt 1980; also cf. Custer and Pitelka 1978, Cooper 1984).

The main exodus of longspurs from the Peninsula occurs during August; it peaked at the head of Norton Bay on 15 August 1977 at a rate of 800 birds/day (Shields and Peyton 1979). Numbers drop sharply after 1 September, but small numbers remain until mid-September (latest, three, 21 September 1980, Safety Sound, D. A. Woodby unpubl. notes; one, 22 September 1977, Cape Espenberg, Schamel et al. 1979).

Snow Bunting—*Plectrophenax nivalis*

The Snow Bunting is a widespread, fairly common breeder and a rare winter visitant on the Seward Peninsula. During the breeding season it occurs in xeric coastal and alpine areas throughout the mainland and offshore islands. In winter it occurs at least along the coast ("common all winter at the Nome city dump and along windswept beaches [Safety Sound, Nome, and Teller]," 1969-1970, W. L. Foster unpubl. notes; adult male collected at Nome city dump, 18 January 1970, W. L. Foster, UAM 3319; four birds, adults and immatures, collected near Solomon, Safety Sound, 15-16 December 1976, H. K. Springer, UAM 3557, 3559, 3561, 3562; one seen, Deering, 17 February 1986, J. D. Walters unpubl. notes).

The primary breeding habitat is cliff and block-fields juxtaposed with dry, low Dwarf Shrub Mat tundra, but these buntings also nest in artificial habitats, such as in buildings, mining dredges, and dredge tailings. I was fascinated, also, to find them breeding in the fractured lava flow south of Lava Lake 9-11 July 1973. They apparently do not nest on the coastal beaches and barrier strips of the Peninsula, however, as they do along the coasts of northwestern and northern Alaska. In winter they frequent the strand communities, especially areas of *Elymus*, where wind reduces the snow cover and exposes feeding sites; and they are found at garbage dumps, which provide shelter as well as food. They may seek cavities or other protected sites for roosting at night or during inclement weather and may burrow into the snow for protection (Bagg 1943, Parmelee 1968).

While a few Snow Buntings winter on the Peninsula, and they are uncommon winter residents on the Yukon-Kuskokwim River Delta and in western Central Alaska (Kessel and Gibson 1978), most of the population apparently spends the winter in southern Canada and the northern contiguous United States (American Ornithologists' Union 1983). They probably migrate through Interior Alaska in spring to reach the Seward Peninsula. This hardy species is the earliest passerine migrant to arrive in Interior and Western Alaska in spring, the earliest males often preceding other species by almost a month. Because of variable weather in late winter-early spring, however, annual dates of arrival on the breeding grounds vary widely. The main movement on the Seward Peninsula usually begins by early April (earliest, "common," 1 April 1971, Nome, Alaska Department of Fish and Game unpubl. notes; two, 2 April 1922, Cape Espenberg, Bailey 1926; 5 April 1982, Nome, D. Levinson, Beltz School unpubl. notes), and in some years movement begins as early as March ("a dozen," 1 March 1905, on Point Spencer spit, Anthony 1906; 40 birds, 1 March 1986, Kuzitrin R bridge, and five, 2 March 1986, near Bunker Hill, D. R. Klein pers. comm.; also, extralimitally, single males, 17 March 1922, along the Chukchi Sea coast at Cape Beaufort, and 19 March 1922, Cape Lisburne, Bailey 1926). These earliest migrants are probably birds that have moved up the coast from wintering grounds farther south in Western Alaska. In addition to being variable, spring migration is an extended phenomenon: the males arrive first, preceding the females by 3 or 4 weeks (Bailey 1943, Parmelee 1968); and migration continues throughout May, with numbers appearing to peak in mid-May.

Nesting begins during the fourth week of May ("nesting," 25 May 1969, Milepost 25 Taylor Highway, and 26 May 1969, Sinuk R, D. G. Roseneau unpubl. notes; female gathering nesting material 24 May 1958, and eggs found on 1 June 1953, Little Diomede I, Kenyon and Brooks 1960; two pairs feeding nestlings, 11 June 1983, Milepost 25 Taylor Highway, R. and B. Mearns unpubl. notes), although some nests still have eggs at the end of June (2 eggs, 27 June 1921, King I, Bailey 1926). Nests are built in a protective cavity, e.g., in crevices in cliffs or tors or in buildings, under rocks or boulders in block-fields and dredge tailings, and under rocks in fellfield tundra. Clutch size in 18 nests from Northern and Western Alaska (ANRS, Bailey 1926, Bee 1958, J. W. Helmericks in litt.) averaged 5.3 eggs, range 4-7 eggs.

Nesting chronologies and behavior of Snow Buntings in the North American Arctic have been summarized by Parmelee (1968). He reported that nest-building, which is done solely by the female, takes about 4 days. One egg is laid per day until the clutch is complete; the female usually begins incubation with the laying of the third or fourth egg, so hatching occurs over several days. Incubation varies from 10 to 15.5 days, apparently depending on the attentiveness of the female [and perhaps environmental temperatures?]. The male frequently brings food to the female while she is on the nest, although she also leaves to feed herself. Young remain in the nest or nest cavity for 10 to 17 days; some can fly strongly when 13-14 days old. The male apparently cares for the first to leave the nest, while the female attends the rest of the brood. The young become independent about 2 weeks after fledging and begin forming flocks with other juveniles.

Given the above chronologies, fledglings on the Seward Peninsula should leave their nest cavities by late June-early July. Indeed, I watched parents feeding a fledgling on 2 July 1967 at Crete Creek, Milepost 39 Teller Highway, and I saw a barely fledged youngster on 4 July 1971 at Serpentine Hot Springs.

During winter and early spring, Snow Buntings subsist primarily on various seeds from grasses, sedges, herbs, etc. In summer and fall their diet consists of a mixture of insects, spiders, seeds, and buds, although the young are fed entirely on animal matter, especially various insects and arachnids (Parmelee 1968).

Fall migration becomes obvious by mid-September (Schamel et al. 1979; also, "large flock," 9 September 1980, Feather R, and flocks of 30-50 birds, 21 September 1980, Safety Sound, D. A. Woodby unpubl. notes) and continues through October, with most birds gone by the end of that month (birds left about 1 November 1976-1978, Nome area, H. K. Springer pers. comm.; last seen 22 October [yr?], extralimitally at Cape Thompson, Williamson et al. 1966).

McKay's Bunting—*Plectrophenax hyperboreus*

Restricted as a breeder to the islands of the Bering Sea, the McKay's Bunting is an uncommon to rare migrant and winter visitant along the mainland bordering the Bering Sea between mid-October and late May (Sealy 1972, Kessel and Gibson 1978). On the Seward Peninsula it is a rare winter visitant, feeding along the windblown coastlines. Over the years it has been reported by most ornithologists who have been in the Nome area in winter, including W. L. Foster (unpubl. notes) and G. E. Hall (unpubl. notes), who reported about 20 McKay's Buntings with as many Snow Buntings at the Nome city dump during the winter of 1969-1970 and who collected three adult males (UAM 3131, 3132, 3240), and H. K. Springer (Kessel and Gibson 1978), who reported about 200 McKay's Buntings along the beach at Safety Sound in mid-December 1976 and collected another adult male (UAM 3560). Extralimitally, up to 20 birds frequented the Kotzebue garbage dump 17 February-5 March 1986, 5 were there at least between 19 February and 5 March 1988, and M. A. Spindler saw 23 McKay's Buntings 24 km northwest of Kotzebue on 18 December 1986 (Selawik NWR unpubl. notes).

Earliest fall arrival dates on the Peninsula have been 9 October 1977 (several males at Nome by H. K. Springer, Kessel and Gibson 1978) and 17 October 1913 (two males collected at Nome by J. Koren unpubl. notes). The latest date recorded in spring has been 16 April 1913 at Nome (14 birds of both sexes collected 31 March through 3 April 1913 and a female collected 16 April 1913, all by J. Koren unpubl. notes), although, judging from mainland dates elsewhere (Kessel and Gibson 1978), this bunting probably continues its residency on the Peninsula well beyond that date.

While adult males of the McKay's and Snow buntings are easily identified, the females and young of these two closely related birds often are difficult, if not impossible, to distinguish in the field, so observational data on numbers and behavior of these forms must be treated with caution during their period of overlap on the Peninsula.

Red-winged Blackbird—*Agelaius phoeniceus*

Accidental on the Peninsula, an adult female Red-winged Blackbird was collected on 6 June 1929 at Wales by A. Nagozruk (Bailey 1930). This species is a casual summer and fall visitant in Western Alaska (Kessel and Gibson 1978).

Rusty Blackbird—*Euphagus carolinus*

A fairly common breeder throughout the taiga of Central Alaska, the Rusty Blackbird is an uncommon breeder on the Seward Peninsula, where it is at the western extremity of its breeding range. It occurs primarily in the southeast portions of the Peninsula and in the drainages of the Fish and Kuzitrin rivers, closely paralleling the distribution pattern of the Blackpoll Warbler. Local residents of Koyuk report its regular occurrence there, especially along the Koyuk River; adults and juvenals were reported as "common" along the Kwiniuk and Tubutulik rivers during summer 1973 by J. H. Lee (pers. comm.); and I, with various field companions, have recorded them at McCarthys Marsh (13 during 10 km of walking on 16 July 1973), along American Creek just above its junction with the Niukluk River (five on 19 July 1973), along the Noxapaga River directly west of Lava Lake (one on 7 July 1973), along the lower Noxapaga River (seven, including a fully fledged juvenal, on 12 July 1973), on the Kuzitrin River flats along Taylor Highway (up to three birds on several July visits to that area), along the Pilgrim River (13 between the Taylor Highway and Pilgrim Hot Springs on 6 July 1961), and near the mouth of the Kuzitrin River at about 165°12′ W (five on 28 June 1971). In addition, this blackbird apparently breeds at Buckland, where F. G. Scheider and I counted six adults between 22 and 26 June 1975, and perhaps very rarely as far west in the Northern Uplands as the Inmachuk River, where J. M. Wright (in litt.) recorded a pair in tall shrubs 13 km up the Inmachuk River on 30 May 1978 and a bird about 27 km up the river on 20 June 1978, and where J. D. Walters (unpubl. notes) saw three spring migrants in Deering on 17 May 1985, one on 23 May 1985, and one on 5 May 1986. In the Southern Uplands, a few birds get as far west as the Snake River, where the Teller Highway crosses it at 165°31' W and where a few birds have occurred consistently over the years. The species is a casual spring migrant farther west (one, Wales, 29 May 1987, P. J. Baicich in litt.; female, Cape Chaplin, Chukotsk Peninsula, 7 June 1913, Brooks 1915).

Rusty Blackbirds favor open habitats near water, showing a preference for Tall Shrub Thicket. At 30 species-present sites in the upper Tanana Valley, Interior Alaska, total canopy cover averaged $17 \pm 28\%$ and spatial heterogeneity of shrubs was high (Spindler and Kessel 1978). An absence of enough canopy cover at the tall shrub level probably explains the absence of this species in the northern and western portions of the Peninsula.

This species occurs as a rare winter visitant in Southcoastal and Southeastern Alaska (Kessel and Gibson 1978), but most winter in southern central Canada and northern central and eastern United States (American Ornithologists' Union 1983). Hence, most spring migrants must reach the Seward Peninsula via interior routes through northwest Canada and Interior Alaska. With variations due to weather, the earliest spring migrants probably arrive on the Peninsula during the last few days of April or the first few days of May (earliest, female, 5 May 1986, Deering, and one, 9 May 1983, near Nome, J. D. Walters unpubl. notes; but, extralimitally, 28 April 1980 at Ambler, Kobuk R, D. K. Wik in litt. [only a few days later that year than at Fairbanks], and 30 April [yr?] at Mountain Village (Gabrielson and Lincoln 1959).

The breeding biology of this species is poorly known anywhere in its range, and few data are available from the Seward Peninsula. Fourteen nests in Interior Alaska (ANRS) were mostly placed in a deciduous shrub or small spruce at 1.5 m or below, although several ground nests, placed at the base of a shrub, have been reported (ANRS, Spindler 1976). Clutch size in 10 of these Interior Alaska nests, some visited only once, averaged 4.8 ± 0.6 eggs, range 4-6. Incubation, performed by the female, lasts about 14 days (Kennard 1920), and the male brings some food to her during this period (R. B. Weeden, ANRS; Kennard 1920). Young may leave the nest when 11 days old, but remain in the immediate vicinity of the nest until they can fly at about 13 days of age (Kennard 1920). Fledging on the Peninsula probably occurs in mid-June (parents with fledglings extralimitally on the Noatak R on 19 June 1961 [Hines 1963] and 18 June 1973 [Manuwal 1974]), although some remain in the nest until the end of the month (adults carrying food and fecal sacs 26 June 1970 at Milepost 7 Teller Highway [Kessel pers. obs.]). Using these data for back-dating, it appears that egg-laying begins on the Seward Peninsula by the third week of May.

Summer food of Rusty Blackbirds consists of invertebrates, especially ground beetles, caterpillars, and grasshoppers, as well as seeds of weeds and grasses (Gabrielson and Lincoln 1959), and as fall approaches berries and refuse from garbage dumps are added to their diet.

Where population levels are sufficient, independent juvenals begin forming postbreeding flocks by mid-July, and local migratory movements may begin by the end of July. Judging from patterns in Interior Alaska, migration from the Peninsula is probably under way by mid-August, with the exodus peaking from the last week of August through mid-September (latest, extralimitally, three, 30 September 1983, Noatak, J. D. Walters unpubl. notes; one until 21 October 1978, feeding on dog food scraps at Ambler, D. K. Wik in litt.).

Brown-headed Cowbird—*Molothrus ater*

A "dull-plumaged" Brown-headed Cowbird was seen at Tin City on 26 August 1977 (D. A. Woodby in litt.), and an adult male was present at Wales 16-17 June and 11 July 1978 (D. R. Paulson unpubl. notes). Outside of Southeastern Alaska, where it is rare, this cowbird is a casual migrant and summer visitant throughout much of mainland Alaska (Kessel and Gibson 1978).

Rosy Finch—*Leucosticte arctoa*

The Rosy Finch is a rare breeder on the Peninsula in dry Dwarf Shrub Mat and fellfield, usually with juxtaposed cliff and block-fields. I watched a female feeding two or three fledglings on the outcrop at Milepost 46 Taylor Highway, west of Big Creek, on 7 July 1967; and I collected an adult male (UAM 3109) from along the wind-blown brow of the coastal cliffs west of Lost River on 29 June 1970. The only other reports are of a sighting near Tin City on 26 May 1975 (Flock and Hubbard 1979) and of sightings of single migrants at Deering on 6 and 9 May 1984 (J. D. Walters unpubl. notes).

The specimen from Lost River was identified as *L. tephrocotis tephrocotis* by Johnson (1973) [=part of *L. a. tephrocotis*, American Ornithologists' Union 1957, 1983].

Pine Grosbeak—*Pinicola enucleator*

An uncommon resident, the Pine Grosbeak is confined to the southeast portions of the Peninsula during the breeding season, where its distribution coincides with that of the spruce forests. It has been reported from the vicinity of Koyuk (10 birds, including a female carrying food, along upper King Ck on 29 June 1975, and another 7 birds in spruce habitats northwest of the village on 3 July 1975, Kessel and F. G. Scheider pers. obs.), 8 km up the Kwiniuk River (adult male, 24 June 1973, J. H. Lee), at Elim (5 birds counted in spruce forests, 1 and 2 July 1972, Kessel pers. obs.), and between Mileposts 67.7 and 71.5 Council Road, where the road passes patches of spruce forest that extend up the tributaries of the Fox River (adult male, 15 July 1966, J. J. Burns and R. L. Rausch unpubl. notes; up to 17 birds, 2-3 July 1977, Kessel pers. obs.).

Grosbeaks frequently wander beyond spruce habitats outside of the breeding season, but they rarely occur far from forests. A specimen was taken near Wales, however, on 16 April 1937 (Bailey 1943); two males were obtained at Teller in 1977—an adult on 25 November and an immature on 7 December (H. K. Springer, UAM 4169 and 4170, respectively); groups of seven and eight birds foraged in willows on 12 and 13 November 1986, respectively, along the Kuzitrin River between the bridge and Bunker Hill (D. R. Klein pers. comm.); and two fed in willows on 28 February 1987 5 km south of Deering (J. D. Walters unpubl. notes).

White-winged Crossbill—*Loxia leucoptera*

The White-winged Crossbill is well-known for its nomadic behavior, which, in response to levels of seed production in spruce forests, causes numbers at specific locations to vary widely from year to year. It is a rare resident on the Seward Penin-sula, where it reaches the western extremity of its North American breeding range and where only scattered individuals and pairs have been reported—in contrast to its flocking behavior elsewhere. Summer records include several at Koyuk on 6 June 1976 (Shields and Peyton 1977); an adult male 8 km up the Kwiniuk River on 4 August 1973 (J. H. Lee unpubl. notes); an adult male near Elim on 2 July 1972 (Kessel pers. obs.); two, possibly a pair, at McCarthys Marsh on 16 July 1973 (Kessel and D. D. Gibson pers. obs.); two specimens collected in the Fish River valley on 10 May 1913 (J. Koren unpubl. notes); and a pair at Milepost 68 Council Road on 2 July 1977 (Kessel pers. obs.).

Outside the breeding season, individuals of this erratic species may stray far beyond their usual geographic range and spruce woods habitat, including to islands of the Bering Sea. On the Seward Peninsula, one was observed at Cape Espenberg on 10 August 1977 (Schamel et al. 1979), one flew east along the coast 11 km west of Nome on 26 July 1899 (Grinnell 1900b), one was seen on the beach near Cape Nome on 1 December 1969 (W. L. Foster in litt.), and a dead subadult bird was picked up in Nome on 6 January 1970 (W. L. Foster, UAM 2501).

Common Redpoll—*Carduelis flammea*

The Common Redpoll is a year-round resident of the Peninsula, where it is an abundant breeder and an uncommon to rare winter visitant. Numbers vary widely, however, both seasonally and annually. It is the most abundant summer passerine of the region and is widely distributed throughout the Peninsula during that season, including on all the major offshore islands. In winter, when it may occur anywhere (including King I, 5 February 1968, J. J. Burns unpubl. notes), it is rare beyond the forests.

The primary habitat for redpolls on the Peninsula is Medium Shrub Thicket, with lesser numbers occurring in Low Shrub Thicket (Table 11). When feeding, however, and outside of the breeding season, they may range widely into many other habitats, including meadows and forests.

While a few birds winter on the Peninsula, most migrate to areas that provide bet-ter and more available food resources. The species is largely nomadic outside of the breeding season, with populations shifting locations in accordance with food availability. Kennard (1976) and Troy (1983) have demonstrated a biennial rhythm in redpoll migration in North America that is apparently related to the seed production of birches and other catkin-producing plants, such as willows and alders, upon which redpolls commonly feed. Most Alaska redpoll populations probably move little farther than necessary to obtain adequate food in winter, although some may travel as far as the northeastern United States (Troy 1983).

Spring migration is highly variable in timing and intensity, due undoubtedly to the variety of populations involved, to wherever they may have wintered, and to spring weather conditions. Reflecting these variables, redpolls often arrive in Interior Alaska in waves, the first sometimes as early as late February-early March (Kessel and Springer 1966). Usually migratory movements in Interior Alaska are most conspicuous through the first 3 to 3.5 weeks of April, with some movement continuing into early May (Kessel unpubl. data). The first arrivals on the lower Kuzitrin River were noted on 7 March 1905 by Anthony (1906), but the main movement apparently does not invade the nonforested parts of the Seward Peninsula until mid- to late April ("coming in flocks" by 15 April 1905, lower Kuzitrin R, Anthony 1906; five birds collected 25 April 1913, Nome, J. Koren unpubl. notes; flock of 18 on 25 April 1973, Milepost 13 Teller Highway, Alaska Department of Fish and Game unpubl. notes; 25 birds on 30 April 1983, Nome and vicinity, J. D. Walters unpubl. notes).

Redpoll breeding occurs over an extended time period. As in Interior Alaska (Kessel unpubl. data), occasional residents may begin nesting extremely early. A resident of Marys Igloo, Kuzitrin River, recognizing the unusually early date, reported to A. Nagozruk on 10 April 1928 that one pair of redpolls "had laid their eggs"; these eggs hatched before the end of April (Bailey 1928). Other nests may still contain eggs in mid-July (two nests with three and four eggs, 12 July 1973, upper Noxapaga R, D. D. Gibson unpubl. notes). Such an extended breeding season, i.e., eggs present over a 14-week period, raises the possibility that the redpoll might be one Alaska passerine that could raise two consecutive broods during a single breeding season. Most of the extended season can be accounted for by the variability among the various population units in spring arrival dates and by renesting attempts following failed attempts (Troy and Shields [1979] reported that a banded yearling made three renesting attempts before successfully fledging young). There is no positive evidence for double-broodedness, but on the Akulik-Inglutalik River delta, Troy and Shields (1979) observed one pair that fledged a brood on 18 June 1977 and reappeared on 19 and 20 July with several begging juvenals, "presumably a second brood."

Nests on the Seward Peninsula are usually placed in a crotch of a shrub, often before leafout and often while snow still surrounds the base of the shrub. Occasionally, however, they are placed on the ground, such as one I found with 4 eggs at the base of a 0.5-m willow on 28 June 1973 near North Killeak Lake. The female builds the nest alone, taking about 3 days; she is often attended by the male (Baldwin 1968). Clutch sizes from 26 nests from the unforested portions of the Seward Peninsula (J. M. Wright unpubl. notes, ANRS, Kessel unpubl. notes, various published sources) averaged 4.2 ± 0.7 eggs, range 3-5. Incubation, often beginning prior to clutch completion, lasts for 11 days and is performed solely by the female, although the male may bring food to her while she incubates (Baldwin 1968). The male aids the female in varying degrees in feeding the nestlings, but only the female broods them (ibid.);

nestlings leave the nest at 12-15 days, averaging 14 days (Baldwin and Reed 1954), although Walkinshaw (1948) reported a nest where the young left after only 9 days.

The peak of egg-laying on the Peninsula occurs between the fourth week of May and mid-June, with the peak of fledging occurring between about 20 June and the end of the first week of July. Postbreeding flocks begin forming before the end of June, and they become increasingly conspicuous during July. In 1973, a flock of fledged families, varying from bob-tailed, weak flyers to fully fledged juvenals, fed together at alder cones at North Killeak Lake on 28-30 June; flocks of 35 + birds, adults and juvenals, gathered at the edges of the Lost Jim lava flow 9-11 July; and large concentrations of redpolls, totaling about 550 individuals in flocks of up to 150 birds, mostly juvenals, were present among the alder patches on a mountain slope near American Creek on 18 July.

Diets of redpolls consist largely of seeds, although some insects may be consumed in mid-summer (West and Meng 1968, White and West 1977). The most frequently used seeds are from sedges, grasses, pigweed (*Chenopodium*), Paper Birch, and alder (ibid.).

Most redpolls probably remain on the Peninsula through August. Extralimitally, on the Akulik-Inglutalik River delta, evidence from banded birds indicated that the breeding population remained at least until 24 August 1976 (Shields and Peyton 1977). Migration from the Peninsula is under way throughout September, however, and the species is uncommon thereafter. Anthony (1906) reported that the last redpolls departed Imuruk Basin by 15 October 1905, but W. L. Foster (in litt.) reported that there were "many" until 1 December 1969.

Alaska redpolls are highly variable in their morphologic characteristics, and much time and effort has been spent by ornithologists trying to delineate a more northern, tundra-oriented "Hoary" Redpoll (*C. hornemanni exilipes*) from a taiga-oriented "Common" Redpoll (*C. flammea flammea*). Recently, however, because of an uninterrupted cline in morphologic characteristics, a geographic and ecologic overlap in breeding ranges, a lack of karyotypic differences, and extensive hybridization, Troy (1980, 1985) has recommended merging these two forms into a single taxon, *C. f. flammea*. The "Hoary" and "Common" forms appear to represent population extremes of a single variable species, so, although both extremes are present on the Seward Peninsula, I have followed Troy in treating them as a single taxon and have not attempted to distinguish the forms.

Eurasian Bullfinch—*Pyrrhula pyrrhula*

An adult male Eurasian Bullfinch was observed in Nome in early December 1977 by H. K. Springer (in litt.). This individual was one of four bullfinches recorded in Alaska during fall and winter 1977-1978 (Kessel and Gibson 1978, subsequent unpubl. data), all apparently part of a displaced fall movement. This Palearctic species is a casual migrant on the islands of the Bering Sea and in the western Aleutians and accidental elsewhere in Alaska (Kessel and Gibson 1978).

Literature Cited

Adams, B. 1878. Notes on the birds of Michalaski, Norton Sound. Ibis 1878:420-442.

Alaska Game Commission. 1949. Waterfowl studies, Kotzebue Sound. Federal Aid in Wildl. Restoration Quarterly Progress Rep. 4:19-28, September 1949. Juneau, AK.

Alaska Game Commission. 1951. Migratory waterfowl studies, northwestern Alaska waterfowl surveys. Federal Aid in Wildl. Restoration Quarterly Progress Rep. 5:10-25, June 1951. Juneau, AK.

Alison, R. M. 1975. Breeding biology and behavior of the Oldsquaw (*Clangula hyemalis L.*). Ornithol. Monogr. No. 18. 52 p.

Alison, R. M. 1976. Oldsquaw brood behavior. Bird-Banding 47:210-213.

Allen, A. A., and H. Kyllingstad. 1949. The eggs and young of the Bristle-thighed Curlew. Auk 66:343-350.

Amaral, M. J. 1977. A comparative breeding biology of the Tufted and Horned puffin, Barren Islands, Alaska. M. S. thesis, Univ. Washington, Seattle. 98 p.

American Ornithologists' Union. 1957. Check-list of North American birds. 5th ed. A. O. U., Baltimore, MD. 691 p.

American Ornithologists' Union. 1983. Check-list of North American birds. 6th ed. Allen Press, Inc., Lawrence, KS. 877 p.

Anderson, R. M. 1915. Preliminary list of specimens collected by R. M. Anderson 1913-14, Birds. p. 163-166. *In*: Canadian Arctic Expedition, 1913-14. Can. Dept. Mines, Summary Report, Geol. Survey for 1914. Sessional Paper 26(1503):163-166.

Andersson, M. 1971. Breeding behaviour of the Long-tailed Skua *Stercorarius longicaudus* (Vieillot). Ornis Scand. 2:35-54.

Andersson, M. 1976a. Clutch size in the Long-tailed Skua *Stercorarius longicaudus*: some field experiments. Ibis 118:586-588.

Andersson, M. 1976b. Population ecology of the Long-tailed Skua (*Stercorarius longicaudus* Vieill.). J. Anim. Ecol. 45:537-559.

Anthony, A. W. 1906. Stray notes from Alaska. Auk 23:179-184.

Ashkenazie, S., and U. N. Safriel. 1979. Breeding cycle and behavior of the Semipalmated Sandpiper at Barrow, Alaska. Auk 96:56-67.

Ashmole, N. P. 1971. Sea bird ecology and the marine environment. p. 223-286. *In*: D. S. Farner, J. R. King, and K. C. Parkes (eds.), Avian Biology, Vol. 1. Academic Press, New York, NY.

Bagg, A. M. 1943. Snow Buntings burrowing into snow drifts. Auk 60:445.

Bailey, A. M. 1925. A report on the birds of northwestern Alaska and regions adjacent to Bering Strait, Parts I-VI. Condor 27:20-32, 62-67, 101-109, 164-171, 197-207, 232-238.

Bailey, A. M. 1926. A report on the birds of northwestern Alaska and regions adjacent to Bering Strait, Parts VII-X. Condor 28:31-36, 84-86, 121-126, 165-170.

Bailey, A. M. 1928. Early nesting of the redpoll in Alaska. Condor 30:320.

Bailey, A. M. 1929. Additional notes from Cape Prince of Wales, Alaska. Condor 31:161.

Bailey, A. M. 1930. The Dotterel and other birds from Cape Prince of Wales, Alaska. Condor 32:161.

Bailey, A. M. 1932. Additional records from Cape Prince of Wales, Alaska. Condor 34:47.

Bailey, A. M. 1933. The Baikal Teal from King Island, Alaska. Auk 50:97.

Bailey, A. M. 1942. Siberian Rough-legged Hawk in northwestern Alaska. Auk 59:305-306.

Bailey, A. M. 1943. The birds of Cape Prince of Wales, Alaska. Proc. Colorado Mus. Nat. Hist. 18:1-113.

Bailey, A. M. 1947. Wryneck from Cape Prince of Wales, Alaska. Auk 64:456.

Bailey, A. M. 1948. Birds of arctic Alaska. Colorado Mus. Nat. Hist. Popular Series No. 8. 317 p.

Bailey, A. M. 1971. Field work of a museum naturalist, 1919-1922: Alaska—Southeast; Alaska—Far North. Denver Mus. Nat. Hist., Museum Pictorial No. 22. 192 p.

Baillie, S. R., and H. Milne. 1982. The influence of female age on breeding in the eider *Somateria mollissima*. Bird Study 29:55-66.

Baird, P. A. 1986. Arctic and Aleutian Terns (*Sterna paradisaea* and *S. aleutica*). p. 349-380. *In*: P. A. Baird and P. J. Gould (eds.), The breeding biology and feeding ecology of marine birds in the Gulf of Alaska. Final reports of principal investigators, Environmental Assessment of the Alaskan Continental Shelf, Biological Studies Vol. 45, NOAA-BLM, Juneau, AK.

Baird, P. A., and R. A. Moe. 1978. The breeding biology and feeding ecology of marine birds in the Sitkalidak Strait area, Kodiak Island, 1977. p. 313-524. *In*: Annual reports of principal investigators, Environmental Assessment of the Alaskan Continental Shelf, Vol. 3, NOAA-BLM, Boulder, CO.

Baldwin, P. H. 1968. *Acanthis hornemanni exilipes* (Coues), Hoary Redpoll. p. 400-407. *In*: A. C. Bent, Life histories of North American cardinals, grosbeaks, buntings, towhees, finches, sparrows, and allies. U. S. Nat. Mus. Bull. 237, Part 1. Washington, DC.

Baldwin, P. H., and E. B. Reed. 1954. A chronology of nesting for the Hoary Redpoll (*Acanthis hornemanni*) at Umiat, Alaska in 1953. J. Colo.-Wyo. Acad. Sci. 4:62-63.

Banko, W. E. 1960. The Trumpeter Swan: its history, habits, and population in the United States. N. Amer. Fauna Series No. 63. 214 p.

Barr, J. F. 1973. Feeding biology of the Common Loon (*Gavia immer*) in oligotrophic lakes of the Canadian shield. Ph.D. thesis, Univ. Guelph, ONT. 204 p.

Barry, T. W. 1967. Geese of the Anderson River Delta, Northwest Territories. Ph.D. thesis, Univ. Alberta, Edmonton. 212 p.

Barry, T. W. 1986. Eiders of the western Canadian Arctic. p. 74-80. *In*: A. Reed (ed.), Eider ducks in Canada. Can. Wildl. Serv. Rep. Series No. 47. Ottawa, ONT.

Barth, E. K. 1955. Egg-laying, incubation and hatching of the Common Gull (*Larus canus*). Ibis 97:222-239.

Baumgartner, A. M. 1937a. Food and feeding habits of the Tree Sparrow. Wilson Bull. 49:65-80.

Baumgartner, A. M. 1937b. Nesting habits of the Tree Sparrow at Churchill, Manitoba. Bird-Banding 8:99-108.

Baumgartner, A. M. 1968. Tree Sparrow. p. 1137-1165. *In*: A. C. Bent, Life histories of North American cardinals, grosbeaks, buntings, towhees, finches, sparrows, and allies. U. S. Nat. Mus. Bull. 237, Part 2. Washington, DC.

Bean, T. H. 1882. Notes on birds collected during the summer of 1880 in Alaska and Siberia. Proc. U. S. Nat. Mus. 5:144-173.

Bédard, J. 1966. New records of alcids from St. Lawrence Island, Alaska. Condor 68:503-506.

Bédard, J. 1969a. Feeding of the Least, Crested, and Parakeet auklets around St. Lawrence Island, Alaska. Can. J. Zool. 47:1025-1050.

Bédard, J. 1969b. The nesting of the Crested, Least, and Parakeet auklets on St. Lawrence Island, Alaska. Condor 71:386-398.

Bee, J. W. 1958. Birds found on the Arctic Slope of northern Alaska. Univ. Kansas Publ., Mus. of Nat. Hist. 10:163-211.

Bellrose, F. C. 1980. Ducks, geese & swans of North America. 3rd ed. Stackpole Books, Harrisburg, PA. 540 p.

Bengtson, S.-A. 1966. [Observations on the sexual behavior of the Common Scoter, *Melanitta nigra*, on the breeding grounds with special reference to courting parties.] Vår Fågelvärld 25:202-226.

Bengtson, S.-A. 1970. Location of nest-sites of ducks in Lake Myvatn area, northeast Iceland. Oikos 21:218-229.

Bengtson, S.-A. 1972a. Breeding ecology of the Harlequin Duck *Histrionicus histrionicus* (L.) in Iceland. Ornis Scand. 3:1-19.

Bengtson, S.-A. 1972b. Reproduction and fluctuations in the size of duck populations at Lake Myvatn, Iceland. Oikos 23:35-58.

Bent, A. C. 1919. Life histories of North American diving birds. U. S. Nat. Mus. Bull. 107, Washington, DC. 245 p.

Bent, A. C. 1921. Life histories of North American gulls and terns. U. S. Nat. Mus. Bull. 113, Washington, DC. 345 p.

Bent, A. C. 1929. Life histories of North American shore birds. Order Limicolae (Part 2). U. S. Nat. Mus. Bull. 146, Washington, DC. 412 p.

Bent, A. C. 1937. Life histories of North American birds of prey. Order Falconiformes (Part 1). U. S. Nat. Mus. Bull. 167, Washington, DC. 409 p.

Bent, A. C. 1942. Life histories of North American flycatchers, larks, swallows, and their allies. U. S. Nat. Mus. Bull. 179., Washington, DC. 555 p.

Bent, A. C. 1949. Life histories of North American thrushes, kinglets, and their allies. U. S. Nat. Mus. Bull. 179, Washington, DC. 453 p.

Bent, A. C. 1953. Life histories of North American wood warblers. U. S. Nat. Mus. Bull. 203, Washington, DC. 734 p.

Bent, A. C. 1968. Life histories of North American cardinals, grosbeaks, buntings, towhees, finches, sparrows, and allies. U. S. Nat. Mus. Bull. 237, Washington, DC. 1889 p.

Bente, P. J. 1981. Nesting behavior and hunting activity of the Gyrfalcon, *Falco rusticolus*, in south central Alaska. M.S. thesis, Univ. Alaska, Fairbanks. 103 p.

Bergman, R. D., and D. V. Derksen. 1977. Observations on Arctic and Red-throated loons at Storkersen Point, Alaska. Arctic 30:41-51.

Bergman, R. D., R. L. Howard, K. F. Abraham, and M. W. Weller. 1977. Water birds and their wetland resources in relation to oil development at Storkersen Point, Alaska. U.S. Fish and Wildl. Serv. Resource Publ. 129, Washington, DC. 38 p.

Biderman, J. O., and W. H. Drury. 1978. Ecological studies in the northern Bering Sea: Studies of seabirds in the Bering Strait. p. 751-838. *In*: Annual reports of principal investigators, Environmental Assessment of the Alaskan Continental Shelf, Vol. 2, NOAA-BLM, Boulder, CO.

Bledsoe, A. H., and D. Sibley. 1985. Patterns of vagrancy of Ross' Gull. Amer. Birds 39:219-227.

Blomqvist, S., and M. Elander. 1981. Sabine's Gull (*Xema sabini*), Ross's Gull (*Rhodostethia rosea*) and Ivory Gull (*Pagophila eburnea*). Gulls in the Arctic: a review. Arctic 34:122-132.

Bock, C. E., and L. W. Lepthien. 1972. Winter eruptions of Red-breasted Nuthatches in North America, 1950-1970. Amer. Birds 26:558-561.

Boekelheide, R. J. 1980. Arctic Terns: Breeding ecology and sea-ice relationships on an arctic barrier island. M.S. thesis, Univ. California, Davis. 101 p.

Boise, C. M. 1976. Breeding biology of the Lesser Sandhill Crane—A preliminary report. Proc. International Crane Workshop 1:126-129.

Boise, C. M. 1977. Breeding biology of the Lesser Sandhill Crane, *Grus canadensis canadensis* (L.), on the Yukon-Kuskokwim Delta, Alaska. M.S. Thesis, Univ. Alaska, Fairbanks. 79 p.

Brandt, H. 1943. Alaska bird trails. Bird Research Foundation, Cleveland, OH. 464 p.

Breckenridge, W. J. 1966. Dovekie on Little Diomede Island, Alaska. Auk 83:680.

Breckenridge, W. J., and D. Cline. 1967. Sandhill Cranes and other birds from Bering Strait, Alaska. Auk 84:277-278.

Brooks, W. S. 1915. Notes on birds from East Siberia and arctic Alaska. Bull. Mus. Comp. Zool. 59:361-413.

Brown, L., and D. Amadon. 1968. Eagles, hawks and falcons of the World. Vol. 2. Country Life Books, Hamlyn Publishing Group Ltd., Middlesex, England. 945 p.

Brown, P. W., and M. A. Brown. 1981. Nesting biology of the White-winged Scoter. J. Wildl. Manage. 45:38-45.

Brown, P. W., and C. S. Houston. 1982. Longevity and age of maturity of White-winged Scoters. J. Field Ornithol. 53:53-54.

Brown, R. G. B., N. G. B. Jones, and D. J. T. Hussell. 1967. The breeding behaviour of Sabine's Gull, *Xema sabini*. Behaviour 28:110-140.

Brown, R. N. 1974. Aspects of vocal behavior of the Raven (*Corvus corax*) in interior Alaska. M.S. thesis, Univ. Alaska, Fairbanks. 139 p.

Browning, M. R. 1977. Geographic variation in Dunlins, *Calidris alpina*, of North America. Can. Field-Nat. 91:391-393.

Bundy, G. 1976. Breeding biology of the Red-throated Diver. Bird Study 23:249-256.

Byrd, G. V., and R. H. Day. 1986. The avifauna of Buldir Island, Aleutian Islands, Alaska. Arctic 39:109-118.

Byrd, G. V., D. D. Gibson, and D. L. Johnson. 1974. The birds of Adak Island, Alaska. Condor 76:288-300.

Byrd, G. V., J. L. Trapp, and D. D. Gibson. 1978. New information on Asiatic birds in the Aleutian Islands, Alaska. Condor 80:309-315.

Cade, T. J. 1952. Notes on the birds of Sledge Island, Bering Sea, Alaska. Condor 54:51-54.

Cade, T. J. 1955. Variation of the Common Rough-legged Hawk in North America. Condor 57:313-346.

Cade, T. J. 1960. Ecology of the Peregrine and Gyrfalcon populations in Alaska. Univ. Calif. Publ. Zool. 63:151-289.

Cade, T. J. 1967. Ecological and behavioral aspects of predation by the Northern Shrike. Living Bird 6:43-85.

Cannings, R. J., and W. Threlfall. 1981. Horned Lark breeding biology at Cape St. Mary's, Newfoundland. Wilson Bull. 93:519-530.

Chapman, L. B. 1955. Studies of a Tree Swallow colony (third paper). Bird-Banding 26:45-70.

Clark, R. J. 1975. A field study of the Short-eared Owl, _Asio flammeus_ (Pontoppidan), in North America. Wildl. Monogr. No. 47. 67 p.

Coachman, L. K., K. Aagaard, and R. B. Tripp. 1975. Bering Strait, the regional physical oceanography. Univ. Washington Press, Seattle. 172 p.

Conant, B., J. G. King, and H. A. Hansen. 1985. Sandhill Cranes in Alaska: A population survey 1957-1985. Amer. Birds 39:855-858.

Conant, B., and F. Roetker. 1987. Alaska-Yukon waterfowl breeding population survey, May 14 to June 14, 1987. U. S. Fish and Wildl. Serv., Juneau, AK. 25 p.

Connors, P. G. 1978. Shorebird dependence on arctic littoral habitats. p. 84-166. _In_: Principal investigators' reports, Environmental Assessment of the Alaskan Continental Shelf, Vol. 2, NOAA-BLM, Boulder, CO.

Connors, P. G. 1983. Taxonomy, distribution, and evolution of golden plovers (_Pluvialis dominica_ and _Pluvialis fulva_). Auk 100:607-620.

Connors, P. G., and C. S. Connors. 1985. Shorebird littoral zone ecology of the southern Chukchi Coast of Alaska. p. 1-57. _In_: Final reports of principal investigators, Environmental Assessment of the Alaskan Continental Shelf, Biological Studies Vol. 35, NOAA-BLM, Anchorage, AK.

Connors, P. G., J. P. Myers, and F. A. Pitelka. 1979. Seasonal habitat use by arctic Alaskan shorebirds. Studies in Avian Biol. 2:101-111.

Conover, H. B. 1926. Game birds of the Hooper Bay Region, Alaska. Auk 43:162-180, 303-318.

Conover, [H.] B. 1944. The North Pacific allies of the Purple Sandpiper. Field Mus. Nat. Hist. Zool. Series 29:169-179.

Cooch, F. G. 1965. The breeding biology and management of the Northern Eider (_Somateria mollissima borealis_) in the Cape Dorset area, Northwest Territories. Can. Wildl. Serv. Wildl. Manage. Bull. (Series 2) 10:1-68.

Cooney, R. T. 1977. Zooplankton and micronekton studies in the Bering-Chukchi/Beaufort Seas. p. 275-363. _In_: Annual reports of principal investigators, Environmental Assessment of the Alaskan Continental Shelf, Vol. 10, NOAA-BLM, Boulder, CO.

Cooper, B. C. 1984. Seasonal bird use of alpine and subalpine habitats in the upper Susitna River Basin, Alaska. M.S. thesis, Univ. Alaska, Fairbanks. 112 p.

Cramp, S. (chief ed.). 1980a. The birds of the western Palearctic. Vol. 1. Ostrich to ducks. Corrected reprinting. Oxford Univ. Press, New York, NY. 722 p.

Cramp, S. (chief ed.). 1980b. The birds of the western Palearctic. Vol. 2. Hawks to Bustards. Oxford Univ. Press, New York, NY. 695 p.

Cramp, S. (chief ed.). 1983. The birds of the western Palearctic. Vol. 3. Waders to gulls. Oxford Univ. Press, New York, NY. 913 p.

Cramp, S. (chief ed.). 1985. The birds of the western Palearctic. Vol. 4. Terns to Woodpeckers. Oxford Univ. Press, New York, NY. 960 p.

Custer, T. W., and F. A. Pitelka. 1977. Demographic features of a Lapland Longspur population near Barrow, Alaska. Auk 94:505-525.

Custer, T. W., and F. A. Pitelka. 1978. Seasonal trends in summer diet of the Lapland Longspur near Barrow, Alaska. Condor 80:295-301.

Dall, W. H., and H. M. Bannister. 1869. List of the birds of Alaska, with biographical notes. Trans. Chicago Acad. Sci. 1, Part 2:267-310.

Darlington, P. J. 1957. Zoogeography: The geographical distribution of animals. John Wiley & Sons, New York, NY. 675 p.

Dau, C. P. 1987. Birds in nearshore waters of the Yukon-Kuskokwim Delta, Alaska. Murrelet 68:12-13.

Dau, C. P., and S. A. Kistchinski. 1977. Seasonal movements and distribution of the Spectacled Eider. Wildfowl 28:65-75.

Davis, R. A. 1972. A comparative study of the use of habitat by Arctic Loons and Red-throated Loons. Ph.D. thesis, Univ. Western Ontario, London. 290 p.

Day, R. H. 1980. The occurrence and characteristics of plastic pollution in Alaska's marine birds. M.S. thesis, Univ. Alaska, Fairbanks. 111 p.

Day, R. H., K. L. Oakley, and D. R. Barnard. 1983. Nest sites and eggs of Kittlitz's and Marbled murrelets. Condor 85:265-273.

Dean, F. C., and D. L. Chesemore. 1974. Studies of birds and mammals in the Baird and Schwatka mountains, Alaska. Biol. Pap. Univ. Alaska No. 15. 80 p.

DeGange, A. R., and A. L. Sowls. 1978. A survey of the Chamisso Island National Wildlife Refuge, 11-14 August 1977. Admin. Rep., Office of Biol. Serv., Coastal Ecosystems, U. S. Fish and Wildl. Serv., Anchorage, AK. 29 p.

Delacour, J. 1951. Preliminary note on the taxonomy of Canada Geese, *Branta canadensis*. Amer. Mus. Novitates 1537. 10 p.

Delacour, J. 1954. The waterfowl of the world. Vol. 1. Country Life, Ltd., London, England. 284 p.

DeLong, R. L., and M. C. Thompson. 1968. Bar-tailed Godwit from Alaska recovered in New Zealand. Wilson Bull. 80:490-491.

Dement'ev, G. P., and N. A. Gladkov (eds.). 1951. Birds of the Soviet Union. Vol.3. Translated Israel Program for Scientific Translations, 1969. National Tech. Info. Serv., U. S. Dept. of Commerce, Springfield, VA. 756 p.

Dement'ev, G. P., and N. A. Gladkov (eds.). 1952. Birds of the Soviet Union. Vol. 4. Translated Israel Program for Scientific Translations, 1967. National Tech. Info. Serv., U. S. Dept. of Commerce, Springfield, VA. 683 p.

Dement'ev, G. P., and N. A. Gladkov (eds.). 1954. Birds of the Soviet Union. Vol. 6. Translated Israel Program for Scientific Translations, 1968. National Tech. Info. Serv., U. S. Dept. of Commerce, Springfield, VA. 879 p.

Derksen, D. V. and W. D. Eldridge. 1980. Drought-displacement of Pintails to the arctic coastal plain, Alaska. J. Wildl. Manage. 44:224-229.

Derksen, D. V., M. W. Weller, and W. D. Eldridge. 1979. Distributional ecology of geese molting near Teshekpuk Lake, National Petroleum Reserve-Alaska. p. 189-207. *In*: R. L. Jarvis and J. C. Bartonek (eds.), Management and biology of Pacific Flyway geese: a symposium. Oregon State Univ. Book Store, Inc., Corvallis.

DeWolfe, B. B. 1967. Biology of White-crowned Sparrows in late summer at College, Alaska. Condor 69:110-132.

DeWolfe, B. B. 1968. *Zonotrichia leucophrys nuttalli* Ridgway, Nuttall's White-crowned Sparrow, p. 1292-1324, and *Zonotrichia leucophrys gambelii* (Nuttall), Gambel's White-crowned Sparrow, p. 1324-1338. *In*: A. C. Bent, Life histories of North American cardinals, grosbeaks, buntings, towhees, finches, sparrows, and allies. U. S. Nat. Mus. Bull. 237, Part 3. Washington, DC.

Divoky, G. J. 1976. The pelagic feeding habits of Ivory and Ross' gulls. Condor 78:85-90.

Divoky, G. J. 1977. The distribution, abundance and feeding ecology of birds associated with the Bering and Beaufort Sea pack ice. p. 525-573. *In*: Principal investigators' reports, Environmental Assessment of the Alaskan Continental Shelf, Vol. 2, NOAA-BLM, Boulder, CO.

Divoky, G. J. 1978. Identification, documentation and delineation of coastal migratory bird habitat in Alaska. I. Breeding bird use of barrier islands in the northern Chukchi and Beaufort seas. p. 482-548. *In*: Annual reports of principal investigators, Environmental Assessment of the Alaskan Continental Shelf, Vol. 2, NOAA-BLM, Boulder, CO.

Divoky, G. J. 1979. Sea ice as a factor in seabird distribution and ecology in the Beaufort, Chukchi and Bering seas. p. 9-17. *In*: J. C. Bartonek and D. N. Nettleship (eds.), Conservation of marine birds of northern North America. Wildl. Res. Rep. 11, U. S. Fish and Wildl. Serv., Washington, DC.

Divoky, G. J. 1984. The pelagic and nearshore birds of the Alaskan Beaufort Sea. p. 397-513. *In*: Final reports of principal investigators, Environmental Assessment of the Alaskan Continental Shelf, Biological Studies Vol. 23, NOAA-BLM, Juneau, AK.

Dixon, J. S. 1933. Nesting of the Wandering Tattler. Condor 35:173-179.

Dorogoi, I. V. 1983. [Biology of the Buff-breasted Sandpiper (*Tryngites subruficollis* Vieill.)]. Byul. Mosk. o-va Ispytatelei Prirody. otd. biol. 88:50-55.

Drent, R., G. F. van Tets, F. Tompa, and K. Vermeer. 1964. The breeding birds of Mandarte Island, British Columbia. Can. Field-Nat. 78:208-263.

Drewien, R. C. 1974. Ecology of Rocky Mountain Greater Sandhill Cranes. Ph.D. thesis, Univ. Idaho, Moscow. 70 p.

Drury, W. H. 1961a. Studies of the breeding biology of Horned Lark, Water Pipit, Lapland Longspur, and Snow Bunting on Bylot Island, Northwest Territories, Canada. Bird-Banding 32:1-46.

Drury, W. H. 1961b. The breeding biology of shorebirds on Bylot Island, Northwest Territories, Canada. Auk 78:176-219.

Drury, W. H. 1976a. Seabirds on the south shore of Seward Peninsula, Alaska. p. 477-554. *In*: Principal investigators' reports, Environmental Assessment of the Alaskan Continental Shelf, Vol. 2, NOAA-BLM, Boulder, CO.

Drury, W. H. 1976b. Waterfowl and shorebirds of coastal habitats on the south shore of Seward Peninsula, Alaska. p. 555-598. *In*: Principal investigators' reports, Environmental Assessment of the Alaskan Continental Shelf, Vol. 2, NOAA-BLM, Boulder, CO.

Drury, W. H., J. O. Biderman, J. B. French, and S. Hinckley. 1978. Ecological studies in the northern Bering Sea: Birds of coastal habitats of the south shore of Seward Peninsula, Alaska. p. 510-613. *In*: Annual reports of principal investigators, Environmental Assessment of the Alaskan Continental Shelf, Vol. 2, NOAA-BLM, Boulder, CO.

Drury, W. H., C. Ramsdell, and J. B. French. 1981. Ecological studies in the Bering Strait Region. p. 175-487. *In*: Final reports of principal investigators, Environmental Assessment of the Alaskan Continental Shelf, Biological Studies, Vol. 11, NOAA-BLM, Juneau, AK.

Drury, W. H., and B. B. Steele. 1977. Studies of populations, community structure and ecology of marine birds at King Island, Bering Strait region, Alaska. p. 75-149. *In*: Annual reports of principal investigators, Environmental Assessment of the Alaskan Continental Shelf, Vol. 5, NOAA-BLM, Boulder, CO.

Dzinbal, K. A. 1982. Ecology of Harlequin Ducks in Prince William Sound, Alaska, during summer. M.S. thesis, Oregon State Univ., Corvallis. 89 p.

Dzinbal, K. A., and R. L. Jarvis. 1984. Coastal feeding ecology of Harlequin Ducks in Prince William Sound, Alaska, during summer. p. 6-10. *In*: D. N. Nettleship, G. A. Sanger, and P. F. Springer (eds.), Marine birds: their feeding ecology and commercial fisheries relationships. Can. Wildl. Serv. Special Publ. for Pacific Seabird Group. Minister of Supply Services Canada, Ottawa, ONT.

Dzubin, A. 1979. Recent increases of Blue Geese in western North America. p. 141-175. *In*: R. L. Jarvis and J. C. Bartonek (eds.), Management and biology of Pacific Flyway geese: a symposium. Oregon State Univ. Book Store, Inc., Corvallis.

Eaton, S. W. 1957. A life history study of *Seiurus noveboracensis* (with notes on *Seiurus aurocapillus* and the species of *Seiurus* compared). Science Studies Vol. XIX, St. Bonaventure Univ., St. Bonaventure, NY. 36 p.

Edgell, M. C. 1984. Trans-hemispheric movements of Holarctic Anatidae: the Eurasian Wigeon (*Anas penelope* L.) in North America. J. Biogeography 11:27-39.

Eisenhauer, D. I., and C. M. Kirkpatrick. 1977. Ecology of the Emperor Goose in Alaska. Wildl. Monogr. 57. 62 p.

Eisenhauer, J. H., and J. Paniyak. 1977. Parasitic Jaegers prey on adult ptarmigan. Auk 94:389-390.

Eldridge, W. 1982. Waterfowl migration surveys of Kotzebue Sound and subsistence harvest observations. Admin. Rep., U. S. Fish and Wildl. Serv., Anchorage, AK. 53 p.

Ellis, D. H. 1979. Development of behavior in the Golden Eagle. Wildl. Monogr. 70:1-94.

Emlen, J. T. 1954. Territory, nest building, and pair formation in the Cliff Swallow. Auk 71:16-35.

English, T. S. 1966. Net plankton volumes in the Chukchi Sea. p. 809-815. *In*: N. J. Wilimovsky and J. N. Wolfe (eds.), Environment of the Cape Thompson region, Alaska. Div. of Tech. Info., U. S. Atomic Energy Commission, Washington, DC.

Environmental Data Service. 1971. Climatological data summaries (unpublished): Candle, Council, Golovin, Moses Point, Shishmaref, Teller, Tin City, Wales, and

White Mountain, Alaska. National Oceanic and Atmospheric Administration, Anchorage, AK.

Environmental Data Service. 1977. Local climatological data, annual summary with comparative data, Nome, Alaska. National Oceanic and Atmospheric Admin., Asheville, NC. 4 p.

Erckmann, W. J. 1981. The evolution of sex-role reversal and monogamy in shorebirds. Ph.D. thesis, Univ. Washington, Seattle. 319 p.

Erikson, D., M. Davidson, and J. Klein. 1983. Birds of Kachemak Bay, Alaska [a checklist]. Pratt Mus., Homer, AK. 2 p.

Evans, R. M. 1970. Oldsquaws nesting in association with Arctic Terns at Churchill, Manitoba. Wilson Bull. 82:383-390.

Evermann, B. W. 1913. Eighteen species of birds new to the Pribilof Islands, including four new to North America. Auk 30:15-18.

Fay, F. H. 1961. The distribution of waterfowl to St. Lawrence Island, Alaska. Annual Rep. Wildfowl Trust 12:70-80.

Fay, F. H., and T. J. Cade. 1959. An ecological analysis of the avifauna of St. Lawrence Island, Alaska. Univ. Calif. Publ. Zool. 63:73-150.

Fenneman, N. M. 1946. Physical divisions of the United States: U. S. Geol. Survey Map, scale 1:7,000,000.

Fisher, J. 1952. The Fulmar. Collins, London, England. 496 p.

Fleming, R. D., and D. Heggarty. 1966. Oceanography of the southeastern Chukchi Sea. p. 697-754. *In*: N. J. Wilimovsky and J. N. Wolfe (eds.), Environment of the Cape Thompson region, Alaska. Div. of Tech. Info., U. S. Atomic Energy Commission, Washington, DC.

Flock, W. L. 1972. Radar observations of bird migration at Cape Prince of Wales. Arctic 25:83-98.

Flock, W. L. 1975. Bird migration at Cape Prince of Wales: Radar and visual observations. Admin. Rep., U. S. Fish and Wildl. Serv., Anchorage, AK. (Attached as Appendix, p. 276-319. *In*: Principal investigators' reports, Environmental Assessment of the Alaskan Continental Shelf, 1976, Vol. 4, NOAA-BLM, Boulder, CO.)

Flock, W. L., and J. D. Hubbard. 1979. Environmental studies at the Bering Strait. p. 713-769. *In*: Annual reports of principal investigators, Environmental Assessment of the Alaskan Continental Shelf, Vol. 1, NOAA-BLM, Boulder, CO.

Ford, E. R. 1934. Rufous-necked Sandpiper nesting in Alaska. Auk 51:232.

Ford, E. R. 1936. Kittlitz's Murrelet breeding at Wales, Alaska. Auk 53:214-215.

Forsell, D. J., and P. J. Gould. 1981. Distribution and abundance of marine birds and mammals wintering in the Kodiak area of Alaska. FWS/OBS-81/13. Office of Biol. Serv., U. S. Fish and Wildl. Serv., Washington, DC. 81 p.

Friedmann, H. 1932. The birds of St. Lawrence Island, Bering Sea. Proc. U. S. Nat. Mus. 80(2912):1-31.

Friedmann, H. 1934. The Siberian Rough-legged Hawk in Alaska. Condor 36:246.

Gabrielson, I. N., and F. C. Lincoln. 1959. The birds of Alaska. Stackpole Co., Harrisburg, PA. 922 p.

Gibson, D. D. 1981. Migrant birds at Shemya Island, Aleutian Islands, Alaska. Condor 83:65-77.

Gill, R. E. 1978. Autumn migration of Dunlin and Western Sandpipers from the Alaska Peninsula. p. 97-114. *In*: Annual reports of principal investigators, Environmental Assessment of the Alaskan Continental Shelf, Vol. 3, NOAA-BLM, Boulder, CO.

Gill, R. [E.] 1979. Shorebird studies in western Alaska, 1976-1978. Wader Study Group Bull. 25:37-40.

Gill, R. E., and C. M. Handel. 1980. First record of the Common Cuckoo from mainland North America. Condor 82:472.

Gill, R. E., and C. M. Handel. 1981. Shorebirds of the eastern Bering Sea. p. 719-738. *In*: D. W. Hood and J. A. Calder (eds.), The eastern Bering Sea shelf: oceanography and resources. Vol. 2. Office of Marine Pollution Assessment, NOAA, Juneau, AK.

Gill, R. E., C. M. Handel, and L. A. Shelton. 1983. Memorial to a Black Turnstone: An exemplar of breeding and wintering site fidelity. N. Amer. Bird Bander 8:98-101.

Gill, R. E., M. R. Petersen, and P. D. Jorgensen. 1981. Birds of the northcentral Alaska Peninsula, 1976-1980. Arctic 34:286-306.

Gollop, J. B., and W. H. Marshall. 1954. A guide to aging duck broods in the field. Mississippi Flyway Council Tech. Sec. Rep. 9 p. (mimeo). [see more readily available S. D. Schemnitz (ed.), 1980:186-187, Wildlife techniques manual, 4th ed., Wildlife Society, Washington, DC].

Goossen, J. P. 1978. Breeding biology and reproductive success of the Yellow Warbler on the Delta Beach Ridge, Manitoba. M.S. thesis, Univ. Manitoba, Winnipeg. 81 p.

Gorman, M. L. 1974. The significance of habitat selection during nesting of the eider *Somateria mollissima mollissima*. Ibis 116:152-154.

Gorman, M. L., and H. Milne. 1972. Creche behaviour in the Common Eider *Somateria m. mollissima* L. Ornis Scand. 3:21-25.

Gould, P. J., D. J. Forsell, and C. J. Lensink. 1982. Pelagic distribution and abundance of seabirds in the Gulf of Alaska and eastern Bering Sea. FWS/OBS-82-48. Biol. Services Program, U. S. Fish and Wildl. Serv., Anchorage, AK. 249 p.

Grinnell, J. 1900a. Birds of the Kotzebue Sound region, Alaska. Pacific Coast Avifauna 1:1-80.

Grinnell, J. 1900b. Notes on some birds of Cape Nome, Alaska. Condor 2:112-115.

Guignion, D. 1968. Clutch size and incubation period of the American Eider (*Somateria mollissima dresseri*) on Brandypot Island. Naturaliste Canadien 95:1145-1152.

Hagar, J. A. 1966. Nesting of the Hudsonian Godwit at Churchill, Manitoba. Living Bird 5(1966):5-43.

Hall, G. E., and E. A. Cardiff. 1978. First North American records of Siberian House Martin, *Delichon urbica lagopoda*. Auk 95:429.

Hamilton, R. D. 1948. The range of the northern Cliff Swallow in Alaska. Auk 65:460-461.

Handel, C. M. 1982. Breeding ecology of the Black Turnstone: A study in behavior and energetics. M.S. thesis, Univ. California, Davis. 96 p.

Hanna, W. C. 1940a. Rufous-necked Sandpiper nesting on Seward Peninsula, Alaska. Condor 42:122-123.

Hanna, W. C. 1940b. Siberian Peregrine Falcon in North America. Condor 42:166-167.

Hanna, W. C. 1947. *Cuculus canorus* on the North American continent. Condor 49:42.

Hanna, W. C. 1961. Second specimen of the Dovekie from Alaska. Condor 63:338.

Hansen, H. A. 1960. Annual waterfowl report, Alaska—1960. Waterfowl Investigations, U. S. Bureau of Sport Fisheries and Wildlife, Juneau, AK. 28 p.

Hansen, H. A., and D. E. McKnight. 1964. Emigration of drought-displaced ducks to the Arctic. Trans. N. Amer. Wildl. Conf. 29:119-127.

Hansen, H. A., P. E. K. Shepherd, J. G. King, and W. A. Troyer. 1971. The Trumpeter Swan in Alaska. Wildl. Monogr. 26. 83 p.

Harlow, R. C. 1922. The breeding habits of the Northern Raven in Pennsylvania. Auk 39:399-410.

Harrington, B. A. 1982. Untying the enigma of the Red Knot. Living Bird Quarterly 1:4-7.

Harrington, B. A., and R. I. G. Morrison. 1979. Semipalmated Sandpiper migration in North America. p. 83-100. *In*: F. A. Pitelka (ed.), Shorebirds in marine environments, Studies in Avian Biol. No.2.

Harris, S. W. 1967. Summer birds of the lower Kashunuk River, Yukon-Kuskokwim Delta, Alaska. Murrelet 47:57-65.

Harrison, H. H. 1951. Notes and observations on the Wilson's Warbler. Wilson Bull. 63:143-148.

Hatch, S. A. 1979. Breeding and population ecology of Northern Fulmars (*Fulmarus glacialis*) at Semidi Islands, Alaska. M.S. thesis, Univ. Alaska, Fairbanks. 125 p.

Hawkins, L. L. 1986. Nesting behaviour of male and female Whistling Swans and implications of male incubation. Wildfowl 37:5-27.

Hawksley, O. 1957. Ecology of a breeding population of Arctic Terns. Bird-Banding 28:57-92.

Hays, H. 1973. Polyandry in the Spotted Sandpiper. Living Bird 11(1972):43-57.

Headley, P. C. 1967. Ecology of the Emperor Goose. Draft M.S. thesis, Univ. of Alaska (Dept. Wildl. Manage.), Fairbanks. 106 p.

Henny, C. J. 1973. Drought-displaced movement of North American Pintails into Siberia. J. Wildl. Manage. 37:23-29.

Hersey, F. S. 1916. A list of the birds observed in Alaska and northeastern Siberia during the summer of 1914. Smithsonian Misc. Collections 66:1-33.

Hersey, F. S. 1917. The present abundance of birds in the vicinity of Fort St. Michael, Alaska. Auk 34:147-159.

Hickman, G. R. 1979. Nesting ecology of Bank Swallows in interior Alaska. M.S. thesis, Univ. Alaska, Fairbanks. 78 p.

Hildén, O. 1964. Ecology of duck populations in the island group of Valassaaret, Gulf of Bothnia. Annales Zoologici Fennici 1:153-279.

Hildén, O., and S. Vuolanto. 1972. Breeding biology of the Red-necked Phalarope *Phalaropus lobatus* in Finland. Ornis Fennica 49:57-85.

Hill, G. A. 1922. With the Willow Ptarmigan. Condor 24:105-108.

Hill, G. A. 1923. The migration of the King Eider at Synuk, Alaska. Condor 25:103-104.

Hines, J. Q. 1963. Birds of the Noatak River, Alaska. Condor 65:410-425.

Holmes, R. T. 1966. Breeding ecology and annual cycle adaptations of the Red-backed Sandpiper (*Calidris alpina*) in northern Alaska. Condor 68:3-46.

Holmes, R. T. 1970. Differences in population density, territoriality, and food supply of Dunlin on arctic and subarctic tundra. p. 303-319. *In*: A. Watson (ed.), Animal populations in relation to their food resources. British Ecol. Soc. Symposium No. 10.

Holmes, R. T. 1971a. Density, habitat, and the mating system of the Western Sandpiper (*Calidris mauri*). Oecologia (Berl.) 7:191-208.

Holmes, R. T. 1971b. Latitudinal differences in the breeding and molt schedules of Alaskan Red-backed Sandpipers (*Calidris alpina*). Condor 73:93-99.

Holmes, R. T. 1972. Ecological factors influencing the breeding season schedule of Western Sandpipers (*Calidris mauri*) in subarctic Alaska. Amer. Mid. Nat. 87:472-491.

Holmes, R. T. 1973. Social behaviour of breeding Western Sandpipers *Calidris mauri*. Ibis 115:107-123.

Holmes, R. T., and C. P. Black. 1973. Ecological distribution of birds in the Kolomak River-Askinuk Mountain region, Alaska. Condor 75:150-163.

Holmes, R. T., and F. A. Pitelka. 1968. Food overlap among coexisting sandpipers on northern Alaskan tundra. Systematic Zool. 17:305-318.

Holtán, L. H. 1980. Nesting habitat and ecology of Aleutian Terns on the Copper River Delta, Alaska. M.S. thesis, Oregon State Univ., Corvallis. 85 p.

Hopkins, D. M. 1955. Northern Seward Peninsula; southern Seward Peninsula. p. 120-124. *In*: D. M. Hopkins, T. N. V. Karlstrom, and others, Permafrost and ground water in Alaska. U. S. Geol. Survey Prof. Paper 264-F.

Hopkins, D. M., and R. S. Sigafoos. 1951. Frost action and vegetation patterns on Seward Peninsula, Alaska. U. S. Geol. Survey Bull. 974-C:50-101.

Hopkins, J. P., and D. M. Hopkins. 1958. Seward Peninsula. p. 104-110. *In*: H. Williams (ed.), Landscapes of Alaska, their geologic evolution. Univ. Calif. Press, Berkeley, CA.

Hudson, G. E. 1957. Birds observed in the Kotzebue Sound area of Alaska during the summer of 1956. Murrelet 38:26-29.

Hudson, T. 1977. Preliminary geologic map of Seward Peninsula, Alaska. U. S. Geol. Survey Open File Map OF77-167-A.

Hultén, E. 1968. Flora of Alaska and neighboring territories, a manual of the vascular plants. Stanford Univ. Press, Stanford, CA. 1008 p.

Humphrey, P. S., and K. C. Parkes. 1959. An approach to the study of molts and plumages. Auk 76:1-31.

Hunt, G. L., B. Burgeson, and G. A. Sanger. 1981a. Feeding ecology of seabirds of the eastern Bering Sea. p. 629-647. *In*: D. W. Hood and J. A. Calder (eds.), The eastern Bering Sea shelf: oceanography and resources. Vol. 2. Office of Marine Pollution Assessment, NOAA, Juneau, AK.

Hunt, G. L., P. Gould, D. J. Forsell, and H. Peterson. 1981b. Pelagic distribution of marine birds in the eastern Bering Sea. p. 689-718. *In*: D. W. Hood and J. A. Calder (eds.), The eastern Bering Sea shelf: oceanography and resources. Vol. 2 Office of Marine Pollution Assessment, NOAA, Juneau. AK.

Hunt, G. L., B. Mayer, W. Rodstrom, and R. Squibb. 1978. The reproductive ecology, foods, and foraging areas of seabirds nesting on St. Paul Island, Pribilof Islands. p. 570-775. *In*: Annual reports of principal investigators, Environmental Assessment of the Alaskan Continental Shelf, Vol. 1, NOAA-BLM, Boulder, CO.

Hussell, J. T. H., and G. W. Page. 1976. Observations on the breeding biology of Black-bellied Plovers on Devon Island, N. W. T., Canada. Wilson Bull. 88:632-663.

Irving, L. 1960. Birds of Anaktuvuk Pass, Kobuk, and Old Crow. U. S. Nat. Mus. Bull. 217. 409 p.

Irving, L., C. P. McRoy, and J. J. Burns. 1970. Birds observed during a cruise in the ice-covered Bering Sea in March 1968. Condor 72:110-112.

Isleib, M. E. 1979. Migratory shorebird populations on the Copper River Delta and eastern Prince William Sound, Alaska. p. 125-129. *In*: F. A. Pitelka (ed.), Shorebirds in marine environments. Studies in Avian Biol. No. 2.

Isleib, M. E., and B. Kessel. 1973. Birds of the North Gulf Coast-Prince William Sound region, Alaska. Biol. Pap. Univ. Alaska, No. 14. 149 p.

Jaques, F. L. 1930. Water birds observed on the Arctic Ocean and the Bering Sea, in 1928. Auk 47:353-366.

Jehl, J. R. 1979. The autumnal migration of Baird's Sandpiper. p. 55-68. *In*: F. A. Pitelka (ed.), Shorebirds in marine environments. Studies in Avian Biol. No. 2.

Jehl, J. R., and D. J. T. Hussell. 1966. Incubation periods of some subarctic birds. Can. Field-Nat. 80:179-180.

Jenkins, D., A. Watson, and G. R. Miller. 1963. Population studies on the Red Grouse, *Lagopus lagopus scoticus* (Lath.) in north-east Scotland. J. Animal Ecol. 32:317-376.

Johnsgard, P. A. 1978. Ducks, geese, and swans of the World. Univ. Nebraska Press, Lincoln. 404 p.

Johnsgard, P. A. 1981. The plovers, sandpipers, and snipes of the World. Univ. Nebraska Press, Lincoln. 493 p.

Johnson, A. W., L. A. Viereck, R. E. Johnson, and H. Melchior. 1966. Vegetation and flora. p. 277-354. *In*: N. J. Wilimovsky and J. N. Wolfe (eds.), Environment of the Cape Thompson region, Alaska. Div. of Tech. Info., U. S. Atomic Energy Commission, Washington, DC.

Johnson, D. H., D. E. Timm, and P. F. Springer. 1979. Morphological characteristics of Canada Geese in the Pacific Flyway. p. 56-80. *In*: R. L. Jarvis and J. C. Bartonek (eds.), Management and biology of Pacific Flyway geese: a symposium. Oregon State Univ. Book Store, Inc., Corvallis.

Johnson, L. L. 1971. The migration, harvest, and importance of waterfowl at Barrow, Alaska. M.S. thesis, Univ. Alaska, Fairbanks. 87 p.

Johnson, O. W., and P. M. Johnson. 1983. Plumage-molt-age relationships in "over-summering" and migratory Lesser Golden-Plovers. Condor 85:406-419.

Johnson, R. E. 1973. The biosystematics of the avian genus *Leucosticte*. Ph.D. thesis, Univ. California, Berkeley. 536 p.

Johnson, S. R. 1976. Spring movements and abundance of birds at Northwest Cape, St. Lawrence Island, Bering Sea, Alaska. Syesis 9:31-44.

Johnson, S. R. 1984. Prey selection by Oldsquaws in a Beaufort Sea lagoon, Alaska. p. 12-19. *In*: D. N. Nettleship, G. A. Sanger, and P. F. Springer (eds.), Marine birds: their feeding ecology and commercial fisheries relationships. Can. Wildl. Serv. Special Publ. for Pacific Seabird Group. Minister of Supply Services Canada, Ottawa, ONT.

Johnson, S. R., W. J. Adams, and M. R. Morrell. 1975. The birds of the Beaufort Sea. LGL Ltd. rep. to Can. Wildl. Serv. 310 p.

Johnson, S. R., and W. J. Richardson. 1981. Beaufort Sea barrier island-lagoon ecological process studies: Final report. Birds, Part 3. p. 109-383. *In*: Final reports of principal investigators, Environmental Assessment of the Alaskan Continental Shelf, Biological Studies Vol. 7, NOAA-BLM, Juneau, AK.

Jones, N. G. B. 1972. Moult migration of Emperor Geese. Wildfowl 23:92-93.

Jones, R. D. 1965. Returns from Steller's Eiders banded in Izembek Bay, Alaska. Annual Report Wildfowl Trust 16:83-85.

Kaufman, D. S., and D. M. Hopkins. 1986. Glacial history of the Seward Peninsula. p. 51-77. *In*: T. D. Hamilton, K. M. Reed, and R. M. Thorson (eds.), Glaciation in Alaska—the geologic record. Alaska Geological Society, Anchorage.

Keith, G. S. 1967. New bird records from Alaska and the Alaska Highway. Can. Field-Nat. 81:196-200.

Kennard, F. H. 1920. Notes on the breeding habits of the Rusty Blackbird in northern New England. Auk 37:412-422.

Kennard, J. H. 1976. A biennial rhythm in the winter distribution of the Common Redpoll. Bird-Banding 47:213-237.

Kenyon, K. W. 1961. Birds of Amchitka Island, Alaska. Auk 78:305-326.

Kenyon, K. W., and J. W. Brooks. 1960. Birds of Little Diomede Island, Alaska. Condor 62:457-463.

Kessel, B. 1967. Late-autumn and winter bird records from interior Alaska. Condor 69:313-316.

Kessel, B. 1979. Avian habitat classification for Alaska. Murrelet 60:86-94.

Kessel, B. 1984. Migration of Sandhill Cranes, *Grus canadensis*, in east-central Alaska, with routes through Alaska and western Canada. Can. Field-Nat. 98:279-292.

Kessel, B., and D. D. Gibson. 1978. Status and distribution of Alaska birds. Studies in Avian Biol. No. 1. 100 p.

Kessel, B., and H. K. Springer. 1966. Recent data on status of some interior Alaska birds. Condor 68:185-195.

Kessel, B., H. K. Springer, and C. M. White. 1964. June birds of the Kolomak River, Yukon-Kuskokwim Delta, Alaska. Murrelet 45:37-47.

Kiff, L. F. 1981. Eggs of the Marbled Murrelet. Wilson Bull. 93:400-403.

King, J. G. 1973. A cosmopolitan duck moulting resort; Takslesluk Lake, Alaska. Wildfowl 24:103-109.

King, J. G., and C. P. Dau. 1981. Waterfowl and their habitats in the eastern Bering Sea. p. 739-753. *In*: D. W. Hood and J. A. Calder (eds.), The eastern Bering Sea shelf: its oceanography and resources. Vol. 2. Office of Marine Pollution Assessment, NOAA, Juneau, AK.

King, J. G., and J. I. Hodges. 1979. A preliminary analysis of goose banding of Alaska's Arctic Slope. p. 176-188. *In*: R. L. Jarvis and J. C. Bartonek (eds.), Management and biology of Pacific flyway geese: a symposium. Oregon State Univ. Book Store, Inc., Corvallis.

King, J. G., and C. J. Lensink. 1971. An evaluation of Alaskan habitat for migratory birds. Admin. Rep., U. S. Bureau Sport Fish. and Wildl., Washington, DC. 46 p.

King, J. R., D. S. Farner, and M. L. Morton. 1965. The lipid reserves of White-crowned Sparrows on the breeding ground in central Alaska. Auk 82:236-252.

King, J. R., and J. D. Hubbard. 1981. Comparative patterns of nestling growth in White-crowned Sparrows. Condor 83:361-369.

Kistchinski, A. A. 1975. Breeding biology and behaviour of the Grey Phalarope *Phalaropus fulicarius* in East Siberia. Ibis 117:285-301.

Knupp, D. M., R. B. Owen, and J. B. Dimond. 1977. Reproductive biology of American Robins in northern Maine. Auk 94:80-85.

Koren, J. 1910. Collecting on Tchonkotsk Peninsula. Warbler 6:2-16.

Kozlova, E. W. 1957. *Charadriiformes*, suborder *Alcae*. Fauna of USSR, Birds, Vol. II, no. 3. Translated Israel Program for Scientific Translations, 1961. Office Tech. Serv., U. S. Dept. of Commerce, Washington, DC. 140 p.

Kuchel, C. R. 1977. Some aspects of the behavior and ecology of Harlequin Ducks breeding in Glacier National Park, Montana. M.S. thesis, Univ. Montana, Missoula. 163 p.

Kuerzi, R. G. 1941. Life history of the Tree Swallow. Proc. Linnaean Soc., New York, 52-53:1-52.

Kyllingstad, H. C. 1948. The secret of the Bristle-thighed Curlew. Arctic 1:113-118.

Lehnhausen, W. A., and S. E. Quinlan. 1981. Bird migration and habitat use at Icy Cape, Alaska. Admin. Rep., Office of Special Studies, U. S. Fish and Wildl. Serv., Anchorage, AK. 298 p.

Lensink, C. J. 1969. The distribution of recoveries from White-fronted Geese (*Anser albifrons*) banded in North America. U. S. Bur. Sport Fisheries and Wildl., Bethel, AK. 63 p.

Lensink, C. J. 1973. Population structure and productivity of Whistling Swans on the Yukon Delta, Alaska. Wildfowl 24:21-25.

Leschner, L. L., and G. Burrell. 1977. Populations and ecology of marine birds of the Semidi Islands. p. 13-109. *In*: Annual reports of principal investigators, Environmental Assessment of the Alaskan Continental Shelf, Vol. 4, NOAA-BLM, Boulder, CO.

Lincoln, F. C., and S. R. Peterson. 1979. Migration of birds. Circular 16, Rev. ed., U. S. Fish and Wildl. Serv., Washington, DC. 119 p.

MacDonald, S. D. 1970. The breeding behavior of the Rock Ptarmigan. Living Bird 9:195-238.

MacInnes, C. D. 1962. Nesting of small Canada Geese near Eskimo Point, Northwest Territories. J. Wildl. Manage. 26:247-256.

MacIntosh, R. 1986. Bird list, Kodiak National Wildlife Refuge and Kodiak Island Archipelago [Alaska]. Kodiak Nat. Wildl. Refuge, U. S. Fish and Wildl. Serv., Kodiak, AK. 2 p.

MacLean, S. F., and R. T. Holmes. 1971. Bill lengths, wintering areas, and taxonomy of North American Dunlins, *Calidris alpina*. Auk 88:893-901.

Maher, W. J. 1970. Ecology of the Long-tailed Jaeger at Lake Hazen, Ellesmere Island. Arctic 23:112-129.

Maher, W. J. 1974. Ecology of Pomarine, Parasitic, and Long-tailed jaegers in northern Alaska. Pacific Coast Avifauna 37. 148 p.

Manuwal, D. A. 1974. Avifaunal investigations in the Noatak River Valley. p. 252-325. *In*: S. B. Young (ed.), The environment of the Noatak River Basin, Alaska. Contrib. Center for Northern Studies No. 1. 584 p.

Manuwal, D. A. 1975. The status of the Bluethroat (*Luscinia svecica*) in North America. Murrelet 56:5-7.

Martin, M., and T. W. Barry. 1978. Nesting behavior and food habits of Parasitic Jaegers at Anderson River Delta, Northwest Territories. Can. Field-Nat. 92:45-50.

Martinez, E. F. 1974. Recovery of a Semipalmated Sandpiper at Prudhoe Bay, Alaska. Bird-Banding 45:364-365.

Maxson, S. J., and L. W. Oring. 1980. Breeding season time and energy budgets of the polyandrous Spotted Sandpiper. Behaviour 74:200-263.

Mayfield, H. F. 1973. Black-bellied Plover incubation and hatching. Wilson Bull. 85:82-85.

Mayfield, H. F. 1979. Red Phalaropes breeding on Bathurst Island. Living Bird 17(1978):7-39.

Mayhew, W. W. 1958. The biology of the Cliff Swallow in California. Condor 60:7-37.

Mayr, E. 1946. History of the North American bird fauna. Wilson Bull. 58:3-41.

McGregor, R. C. 1902. A list of birds collected in Norton Sound, Alaska. Condor 4:135-144.

McKnight, D. E. 1962. A population study of waterfowl on the Tetlin-Northway area of interior Alaska. M.S. thesis, Washington State Univ., Pullman. 89 p.

McLenegan, S. B. 1889. Exploration of the Kowak River, Alaska: Ornithological notes. p. 109-125. *In*: M. A. Healy, Report of the cruise of the Revenue Marine Steamer *Corwin* in the Arctic Ocean in the year 1884. Government Printing Office, Washington, DC.

McRoy, C. P., S. W. Stoker, G. E. Hall, and E. Muktoyuk. 1971. Winter observations of mammals and birds, St. Matthew Island. Arctic 24:63-65.

Melchior, H. R., (ed.). 1979. Biological survey of the Bering Land Bridge National Monument. Revised Final Report (U. S. National Park Serv.), Alaska Cooperative Park Studies Unit, Univ. Alaska, Fairbanks. 286 p.

Mickelson, P. G. 1975. Breeding biology of Cackling Geese and associated species on the Yukon-Kuskokwim Delta, Alaska. Wildl. Monogr. 45. 35 p.

Milne, H. 1974. Breeding numbers and reproductive rate of eiders at the Sands of Forvie National Nature Reserve, Scotland. Ibis 116:135-152.

Mindell, D. P. 1983. Nesting raptors in southwestern Alaska: status, distribution, and aspects of biology. U. S. Bureau of Land Management-Alaska Tech. Rep. 8. 67 p.

Moss, R. 1973. The digestion and intake of winter foods by wild ptarmigan in Alaska. Condor 75:293-300.

Moss, R. 1974. Winter diets, gut lengths, and interspecific competition in Alaska ptarmigan. Auk 91:737-746.

Murdoch, J. 1885. Birds. p. 104-128. *In*: P. H. Ray, Report of the International Polar Expedition to Point Barrow, Alaska. Washington, DC.

Murie, A. 1946. Observations on the birds of Mount McKinley National Park, Alaska. Condor 48:253-261.

Murie, A. 1956. Nesting records of the Arctic Willow Warbler in Mount McKinley National Park, Alaska. Condor 58:292-293.

Murie, O. J. 1924. Nesting records of the Wandering Tattler and Surf-bird in Alaska. Auk 41:231-237.

Murie, O. J. 1929. Nesting of the Snowy Owl. Condor 31:3-12.

Murie, O. J. 1936. The birds of St. Lawrence Island, Alaska. p. 361-376. *In*: O. W. Geist, Archaeological excavations at Kukulik. Misc. Publ. Univ. Alaska, Fairbanks.

Murie, O. J. 1959. Fauna of the Aleutian Islands and Alaska Peninsula. N. Amer. Fauna No. 61. 406 p.

Murphy, E. C., A. M. Springer, and D. G. Roseneau. 1986. Population status of Common Guillemots *Uria aalge* at a colony in western Alaska: results and simulations. Ibis 128:348-363.

Myres, M. T. 1957. Clutch size and laying dates in Cliff Swallow colonies. Condor 59:311-316.

Myres., M. T. 1958. Preliminary studies of the behavior, migration and distributional ecology of eider ducks in northern Alaska, 1958. Interim Progress Rep. to Arctic Institute of North America. 14 p.

National Ocean Service. 1985. United States coast pilot 9, Pacific and Arctic coasts Alaska: Cape Spencer to Beaufort Sea. 12th ed. National Oceanic and Atmospheric Admin., Rockville, MD. 363 p.

Neimark, L. M. 1979. Zooplankton ecology of Norton Sound, Alaska. M.S. thesis, Univ. Alaska, Fairbanks. 93 p.

Nelson, E. W. 1883. Birds of Bering Sea and the Arctic Ocean. p. 57-118. *In*: Cruise of the Revenue-Steamer *Corwin* in Alaska and the N. W. Arctic Ocean in 1881. Government Printing Office, Washington, DC.

Nelson, E. W. 1887. Birds of Alaska. p. 35-222. *In*: H. W. Henshaw (ed.), Report upon natural history collections made in Alaska between the years 1877 and 1881. No. III, Arctic Series, Signal Service, U. S. Army. Government Printing Office, Washington, DC.

Nelson, J. W., and A. L. Sowls. 1985. Breeding seabird survey of Chamisso Island and southern Kotzebue Sound, 8-20 August 1981. Admin. Rep., U. S. Fish and Wildl. Serv., Alaska Regional Office, Anchorage. 37 p.

Nettleship, D. N. 1968. The incubation period of the Knot. Auk 85:687.

Nettleship, D. N. 1973. Breeding ecology of turnstones *Arenaria interpres* at Hazen Camp, Ellesmere Island, N.W.T. Ibis 115:202-217.

Nettleship, D. N. 1974. The breeding of the Knot *Calidris canutus* at Hazen Camp, Ellesmere Island, N.W.T. Polarforschung 44:8-26.

Niebauer, H. J. 1981. Recent short-period wintertime climatic fluctuations and their effect on sea-surface temperatures in the eastern Bering Sea. p. 23-30. *In*: D. W. Hood and J. A. Calder (eds.), The eastern Bering Sea shelf: oceanography and resources. Vol. 1. Office of Marine Pollution Assessment, NOAA, Juneau, AK.

Noble, R. E., and J. M. Wright. 1977. Nesting birds of the Shishmaref Inlet area, Seward Peninsula, Alaska, and the possible effects of reindeer herding and grazing on nesting birds. Admin. Rep., Alaska Coop. Wildl. Res. Unit, Univ. Alaska, Fairbanks. 202 p.

Norton, D. W. 1972. Incubation schedules of four species of calidridine sandpipers at Barrow, Alaska. Condor 74:164-176.

Nysewander, D. R., D. J. Forsell, P. A. Baird, D. J. Shields, G. J. Weiler, and J. H. Kogan. 1982. Marine bird and mammal survey of the eastern Aleutian Islands, summers of 1980-81. Admin. Rep., U. S. Fish and Wildl. Serv., Alaska Regional Office, Anchorage. 134 p.

Oakley, K. L. 1981. Determinants of population size of Pigeon Guillemots *Cepphus columba* at Naked Island, Prince William Sound, Alaska. M.S. thesis, Univ. Alaska, Fairbanks. 82 p.

Oring, L. W., and M. L. Knudson. 1973. Monogamy and polyandry in the Spotted Sandpiper. Living Bird 11(1972):59-73.

Orth, D. J. 1967. Dictionary of Alaska place names. U. S. Geol. Survey Professional Paper 567. Government Printing Office, Washington, DC. 1084 p.

Osborne, T. O., and L. Y. Osborne. 1986. A Ross' Gull incursion into Interior Alaska. Murrelet 67:63-64.

Palmer, R. S. 1962. Handbook of North American birds. Vol. 1, Loons through flamingos. Yale Univ. Press, New Haven, CT. 567 p.

Palmer, R. S. 1967. Species accounts. p. 143-267. *In*: G. D. Stout (ed.), The shorebirds of North America. Viking Press, New York, NY.

Palmer, R. S. 1976. Handbook of North American birds. Vol. 2 and 3, Waterfowl. Yale Univ. Press, New Haven, CT. 521 p. and 560 p., respectively.

Palmer, W. 1899. The avifauna of the Pribilof Islands. p. 355-431. *In*: D. S. Jordon, The fur seals and fur-seal islands of the North Pacific Ocean, Part 3. Commission on fur-seal investigations, U. S. Treasury Dept. Government Printing Office, Washington, DC.

Parkes, K. C., and D. Amadon. 1948. The winter range of the Kennicott Willow Warbler. Condor 50:86-87.

Parmelee, D. F. 1968. *Plectrophenax nivalis nivalis (Linnaeus)*, Snow Bunting, p. 1652-1675. *In*: A. C. Bent, Life histories of North American cardinals, grosbeaks, buntings, towhees, finches, sparrows, and allies. U. S. Nat. Mus. Bull. 237, Part 3. Washington, DC.

Parmelee, D. F. 1970. Breeding behavior of the Sanderling in the Canadian High Arctic. Living Bird 9:97-146.

Parmelee, D. F., and S. D. MacDonald. 1960. The birds of west-central Ellesmere Island and adjacent areas. Nat. Mus. Can. Bull. No. 169. 103 p.

Parmelee, D. F., H. A. Stephens, and R. H. Schmidt. 1967. The birds of southeastern Victoria Island and adjacent small islands. Nat. Mus. Can. Bull. 222, Biol. Series No. 78. 229 p.

Patten, S. M. 1980. Interbreeding and evolution in the *Larus glaucescens-Larus argentatus* complex on the south coast of Alaska. Ph.D. thesis. Johns Hopkins Univ., Baltimore, MD. 219 p.

Petersen, A. J. 1955. The breeding cycle in the Bank Swallow. Wilson Bull. 67:235-286.

Petersen, M. R. 1976. Breeding biology of Arctic and Red-throated loons. M.S. thesis. Univ. California, Davis. 55 p.

Petersen, M. R. 1979. Nesting ecology of Arctic Loons. Wilson Bull. 91:608-617.

Petersen, M. R., and M. J. Sigman. 1977. Field studies at Cape Peirce, Alaska, 1976. p. 633-693. *In*: Principal investigators' reports, Environmental Assessment of the Alaskan Continental Shelf, Vol. 4, NOAA-BLM, Boulder, CO.

Peterson, R. T., and J. Fisher. 1955. Wild America. Houghton Mifflin Co., Boston. 434 p.

Peyton, L. 1963. Nesting and occurrence of White Wagtails in Alaska. Condor 65:232-235.

Pitelka, F. A. 1950. Geographic variation and the species problem in the shore-bird genus Limnodromus. Univ. Calif. Publ. Zool. 50:1-108.

Pitelka, F. A. 1959. Numbers, breeding schedule, and territoriality in Pectoral Sandpipers of northern Alaska. Condor 61:233-264.

Pitelka, F. A., R. T. Holmes, and S. F. MacLean. 1974. Ecology and evolution of social organization in arctic sandpipers. Amer. Zool. 14:185-204.

Pitelka, F. A., P. Q. Tomich, and G. W. Treichel. 1955a. Breeding behavior of jaegers and owls near Barrow, Alaska. Condor 57:3-18.

Pitelka, F. A., P. Q. Tomich, and G. W. Treichel. 1955b. Ecological relations of jaegers and owls as lemming predators near Barrow, Alaska. Ecol. Monogr. 25:85-117.

Platt, J. B. 1976. Gyrfalcon nest site selection and winter activity in the western Canadian arctic. Can. Field-Nat. 90:338-345.

Platt, J. B. 1977. The breeding behavior of wild and captive Gyrfalcons in relation to their environment and human disturbance. Ph.D. thesis, Cornell Univ., Ithaca, NY. 164 p.

Porsild, A. E. 1951. Plant life in the Arctic. Can. Geographical J. 42:120-145.

Portenko, L. A. 1972. Birds of the Chukchi Peninsula and Wrangel Island. Vol. 1. Translated and published for the Smithsonian Institution, 1981. National Tech. Info. Serv., U. S. Dept. of Commerce, Springfield, VA. 446 p.

Portenko, L. A. 1973. [Birds of the Chukotsk Peninsula and Wrangel Island. Vol. 2]. Izdatel'stvo "Nauka," Leningrad. 323 p.

Potocsky, G. J. 1975. Alaskan area 15- and 30-day ice forcasting guide. U. S. Naval Oceanographic Office Special Publ. 263. 190 p.

Preble, E. A., and W. L. McAtee. 1923. A biological survey of the Pribilof Islands, Alaska. Part I. Birds and mammals. North Amer. Fauna No. 46:1-255.

Pruett-Jones, S. G. 1980. Team-hunting and food sharing in Parasitic Jaegers. Wilson Bull. 92:524-526.

Racine, C. H., and J. H. Anderson. 1979. Flora and vegetation of the Chukchi-Imuruk area. p. 38-113. *In*: H. R. Melchior (ed.), Biological survey of the Bering Land Bridge National Monument. Revised Final Rep. (U. S. National Park Serv.), Alaska Cooperative Park Studies Unit, Univ. Alaska, Fairbanks.

Ramsdell, C., and W. H. Drury. 1979. Ecological studies of birds in the northern Bering Sea: Seabirds at Bluff; Distribution of birds at sea; Movements of birds in the Bering Strait. p. 600-712. *In*: Annual reports of principal investigators, Environmental Assessment of the Alaskan Continental Shelf, Vol. 1, NOAA-BLM, Boulder, CO.

Reynolds, J. D. 1987. Mating system and nesting biology of the Red-necked Phalarope *Phalaropus lobatus*: what constrains polyandry? Ibis 129:225-242.

Reynolds, J. D., M. A. Colwell, and F. Cooke. 1986. Sexual selection and spring arrival times of Red-necked and Wilson's phalaropes. Behav. Ecol. Sociobiol. 18:303-310.

Ridley, M. W. 1980. The breeding behaviour and feeding ecology of Grey Phalaropes _Phalaropus fulicarius_ in Svalbard. Ibis 122:210-226.

Roberts, H. A. 1963. Aspects of the life history and food habits of Rock and Willow ptarmigan. M.S. thesis, Univ. Alaska, Fairbanks. 108 p.

Roseneau, D. G. 1972. Summer distribution, numbers, and food habits of the Gyrfalcon (_Falco rusticolus_ L.) on the Seward Peninsula, Alaska. M.S. thesis, Univ. Alaska, Fairbanks. 124 p.

Rutter, R. J. 1969. A contribution to the biology of the Gray Jay (_Perisoreus canadensis_). Can. Field-Nat. 83:300-316.

Ryan, A. G. 1974. An incubation period and a nestling period for the Fox Sparrow. Can. Field-Nat. 88:230-231.

Sage, B. L. 1971. A study of White-billed Divers in arctic Alaska. Brit. Birds 64:519-528.

Sainsbury, C. L., C. E. Hedge, and C. M. Bunker. 1970. Structure, stratigraphy, and isotopic composition of rocks of Seward Peninsula, Alaska. Amer. Assoc. Petroleum Geologists Bull. 54:2502-2503.

Salomonsen, F. 1967. Migratory movements of the Arctic Tern (_Sterna paradisaea_ Pontoppidan) in the southern ocean. Danske Videnskabernes Selskab Biologiske Meddelelser 24:1-42.

Salter, R., and R. A. Davis. 1974. Surveys of terrestrial bird populations in Alaska, Yukon Territory, Northwest Territories, and northern Alberta, May, June, July, 1972. p. 36-384. _In_: W. W. H. Gunn and J. A. Livingston (eds.), Bird distribution and populations ascertained through ground survey techniques, 1972. Canad. Arctic Gas Study, Ltd., Biol. Rep. Series, Vol. 12, LGL Ltd., Environmental Research Assoc., Edmonton, ALB.

Samuel, D. E. 1971. The breeding biology of Barn and Cliff swallows in West Virginia. Wilson Bull. 83:284-301.

Sanger, G. A. 1986. Diets and food web relationships of seabirds in the Gulf of Alaska and adjacent marine regions. p. 631-771. _In_: Final reports of principal investigators, Environmental Assessment of the Alaskan Continental Shelf, Biological Studies Vol. 45, NOAA-BLM, Anchorage, AK.

Sauer, E. G. F., and E. K. Urban. 1964. Bird notes from St. Lawrence Island, Alaska. Bonner Zool. Beitr. 15:45-58.

Schamel, D. 1977. Breeding of the Common Eider (*Somateria mollissima*) on the Beaufort Sea coast of Alaska. Condor 79:478-485.

Schamel, D., and D. [M.] Tracy. 1977. Polyandry, replacement clutches, and site tenacity in the Red Phalarope (*Phalaropus fulcarius*) at Barrow, Alaska. Bird-Banding 48:314-324.

Schamel, D., and D. M. Tracy. 1985. Replacement clutches in the Red-throated Loon. J. Field Ornithol. 56:282-283.

Schamel, D., and D. M. Tracy. 1987. Latitudinal trends in breeding Red Phalaropes. J. Field Ornithol. 58:126-134.

Schamel, D., D. [M.] Tracy, P. G. Mickelson, and A. Seguin. 1979. Avian community ecology at two sites on Espenberg Peninsula in Kotzebue Sound, Alaska. p. 289-607. *In*: Final reports of principal investigators, Environmental Assessment of the Alaskan Continental Shelf, Biological Studies Vol. 5, NOAA-BLM, Boulder, CO.

Schorger, A. W. 1947. The deep diving of the loon and Old-Squaw and its mechanism. Wilson Bull. 59:151-159.

Schrantz, F. G. 1943. Nest life of the eastern Yellow Warbler. Auk 60:367-387.

Scott, D. 1977. Breeding behaviour of wild Whistling Swans. Wildfowl 28:101-106.

Sealy, S. G. 1967. Spring bird phenology on St. Lawrence Island, Alaska. Blue Jay 25:23-24.

Sealy, S. G. 1968. A comparative study of breeding ecology and timing in plankton-feeding alcids (*Cyclorrhynchus* and *Aethia* spp.) on St. Lawrence Island, Alaska. M.S. thesis, Univ. British Columbia, Vancouver. 193 p.

Sealy, S. G. 1969. Incubation and nestling periods of the Horned Puffin. Condor 71:81.

Sealy, S. G. 1972. Additional winter records of the McKay's Bunting. Can. Field-Nat. 86:386-388.

Sealy, S. G. 1973. Breeding biology of the Horned Puffin on St. Lawrence Island, Bering Sea, with zoogeographical notes on the North Pacific puffins. Pacific Sci. 27:99-119.

Sealy, S. G., and J. Bédard. 1973. Breeding biology of the Parakeet Auklet (*Cyclorrhynchus psittacula*) on St. Lawrence Island, Alaska. Astarte 6:59-68.

Sealy, S. G., J. Bédard, M. D. F. Udvardy, and F. H. Fay. 1971. New records and zoogeographical notes on the birds of St. Lawrence Island, Bering Sea. Condor 73:322-336.

Searing, G. F. 1977. Some aspects of the ecology of cliff-nesting seabirds at Kongkok Bay, St. Lawrence Island, Alaska, during 1976. p. 263-412. _In_: Principal investigators' reports, Environmental Assessment of the Alaskan Continental Shelf, Vol. 5, NOAA-BLM, Boulder, CO.

Seastedt, T. R. 1980. Diets of young Lapland Longspurs in arctic and subarctic Alaska. Condor 82:232-233.

Seguin, A. C. 1981. Pacific Eider breeding biology and habitat use on the Seward Peninsula, Alaska. M.S. thesis, Univ. Alaska, Fairbanks. 130 p.

Selkregg, L. L. (ed.). 1977. Alaska regional profiles, northwest region. Univ. Alaska Arctic Environmental Information and Data Center, Anchorage. 265 p.

Senner, S. E., and P. G. Mickelson. 1979. Fall foods of Common Snipe on the Copper River Delta, Alaska. Can. Field-Nat. 93:171-172.

Senner, S. E., G. C. West, and D. W. Norton. 1981. The spring migration of Western Sandpipers and Dunlins in southcentral Alaska: numbers, timing, and sex ratios. J. Field Ornithol. 52:271-284.

Serventy, D. L., V. Serventy, and J. Warham. 1971. The handbook of Australian sea-birds. A. H. & A. W. Reed Ltd, Sydney, NSW. 254 p.

Shepherd, P. E. K. 1955. Migratory waterfowl studies, nesting and banding, Selawik area. Alaska Game Commission, Federal Aid in Wildl. Restoration Quarterly Progress Rep. 10:34-56, September 1955. Juneau, AK.

Shields, G. F., and L. J. Peyton. 1977. Avian community ecology of the Akulik-Inglutalik River delta, Norton Bay, Alaska. p.150-205. _In_: Principal investigators' reports, Environmental Assessment of the Alaskan Continental Shelf, Vol. 5, NOAA-BLM, Boulder, CO.

Shields, G. F., and L. J. Peyton. 1979. Avian community ecology of the Akulik-Inglutalik River delta, Norton Bay, Alaska. p. 608-710. _In_: Final reports of principal investigators, Environmental Assessment of the Alaskan Continental Shelf, Biological Studies Vol. 5, NOAA-BLM, Boulder, CO.

Shuntov, V. P. 1972. Sea birds and the biological structure of the ocean. Translated Agence Tunisienne de Public-Relations, Tunis, Tunisia, 1974. National Tech. Info. Serv. TT-74-55032, U. S. Dept. Commerce, Springfield, VA. 566 p.

Sjölander, S. 1978. Reproductive behaviour of the Black-throated Diver Gavia arctica. Ornis Scand. 9:51-65.

Sjölander, S., and G. Ågren. 1972. Reproductive behavior of the Common Loon. Wilson Bull. 84:296-308.

Sjölander, S., and G. Ågren. 1976. Reproductive behavior of the Yellow-billed Loon, *Gavia adamsii*. Condor 78:454-463.

Skeel, M. A. 1976. Nesting strategies and other aspects of the breeding biology of the Whimbrel (*Numenius phaeopus*) at Churchill, Manitoba. M.S. thesis, Univ. Toronto, ONT. 152 p.

Skeel, M. A. 1983. Nesting success, density, philopatry, and nest-site selection of the Whimbrel (*Numenius phaeopus*) in different habitats. Can. J. Zool. 61:218-225.

Sladen, W. J. L., and A. A. Kistchinski. 1977. Some results from circumpolar marking programs on northern swans and Snow Geese. Trans. Intern. Congr. Game Biol. 13:498-507.

Smith, R. I. 1968. The social aspects of reproductive behavior in the Pintail. Auk 85:381-396.

Smith, R. I. 1970. Response of Pintail breeding populations to drought. J. Wildl. Manage. 34:943-946.

Smith, S. 1950. The Yellow Wagtail. New Naturalist Monograph. Collins, London, England. 178p.

Sorokin, A. G. 1979. [A new suborder (Trochili) in the avifauna of the USSR.] (in Russian). Ornithologiya 14:197-198.

Sowls, A. L., S. A. Hatch, and C. J. Lensink. 1978. Catalog of Alaskan seabird colonies. FWS/OBS-78/78. Biol. Services Program, U. S. Fish and Wildl. Serv., Anchorage, AK. 32 p.

Spaans, A. L. 1979. Wader studies in Surinam, South America. Wader Study Group Bull. 25:32-37.

Spindler, M. A. 1976. Ecological survey of the birds, mammals, and vegetation of Fairbanks Wildlife Management Area. M.S. thesis, Univ. Alaska, Fairbanks. 258 p.

Spindler, M. A., and B. Kessel. 1980. Avian populations and habitat use in interior Alaska taiga. Syesis 13:61-104.

Springer, A. M. 1974. Effects of seasonal, geographic and dietary changes on pollutant levels in Long-tailed Jaegers, *Stercorarius longicaudus* [Seward Peninsula, Alaska]. M.S. thesis, Univ. Alaska, Fairbanks. 19 p.

Springer, A. M. 1975. Observations on the summer diet of Rough-legged Hawks from Alaska. Condor 77:338-339.

Springer, A. M., E. C. Murphy, D. G. Roseneau, C. P. McRoy, and B. A. Cooper. 1987. The paradox of pelagic food webs in the northern Bering Sea: I. Seabird food habits. Continental Shelf Research 7:895-911.

Springer, A. M., E. C. Murphy, D. G. Roseneau, and M. I. Springer. 1985a. Population status, reproductive ecology, and trophic relationships of seabirds in northwestern Alaska. p. 127-242. _In_: Final reports of principal investigators, Environmental Assessment of the Alaskan Continental Shelf, Biological Studies Vol. 30, NOAA-BLM, Anchorage, AK.

Springer, A. M., and D. G. Roseneau. 1977. A comparative sea-cliff bird inventory of Cape Thompson vicinity, Alaska. p. 206-262. _In_: Principal investigators' reports, Environmental Assessment of the Alaskan Continental Shelf, Vol. 5, NOAA-BLM, Boulder, CO.

Springer, A. M., and D. G. Roseneau. 1978. Ecological studies of colonial seabirds at Cape Thompson and Cape Lisburne, Alaska. p. 839-960. _In_: Annual reports of principal investigators, Environmental Assessment of the Alaskan Continental Shelf, Vol. 2, NOAA-BLM, Boulder, CO.

Springer, A. M., and D. G. Roseneau. 1985. Copepod-based food webs: auklets and oceanography in the Bering Sea. Marine Ecology Progress Series 21:229-237.

Springer, A. M., D. G. Roseneau, E. C. Murphy, and M. I. Springer. 1984. Environmental controls of marine food webs: Food habits of seabirds in the eastern Chukchi Sea. Can. J. Fisheries and Aquatic Scis. 41:1202-1215.

Springer, A. M., D. G. Roseneau, E. C. Murphy, and M. I. Springer. 1985b. Population and trophics studies of seabirds in the northern Bering and eastern Chukchi seas, 1982. p. 59-126. _In_: Final reports of principal investigators, Environmental Assessment of the Alaskan Continental Shelf, Biological Studies Vol. 30, NOAA-BLM, Anchorage, AK.

Springer, H. K. 1966. Unusual bird records from Hooper Bay, Alaska. Condor 68:600-601.

Steele, B. B., and W. H. Drury. 1977. Waterfowl and shorebirds of coastal habitats on the south shore of Seward Peninsula, Alaska. p. 1-178. _In_: Annual reports of principal investigators, Environmental Assessment of the Alaskan Continental Shelf, Vol. 3, NOAA-BLM, Boulder, CO.

Stewart, R. M. 1973. Breeding behavior and life history of the Wilson's Warbler. Wilson Bull. 85:21-30.

Stiehl, R. B. 1985. Brood chronology of the Common Raven. Wilson Bull. 97:78-87.

Stishov, M. S., V. I. Pridatko, and V. V. Baranyuk. 1985. [New data on birds of Wrangel Island](in Russian). Byul. Mosk. o-va Ispytatelei Prirody. otd. biol. 90:42-48.

Stocek, R. F. 1970. Observations on the breeding biology of the Tree Swallow. Cassinia 52:3-20.

Stone, W. 1900. Report on the birds and mammals collected by the McIlhenny Expedition to Pt. Barrow, Alaska. Proc. Acad. Nat. Sci. Phila. 1900:4-49.

Strang, C. A. 1976. Feeding behavior and ecology of Glaucous Gulls in western Alaska. Ph.D. thesis, Purdue Univ., West Lafayette, IN. 146 p.

Stresemann, E. 1949. Birds collected in the North Pacific area during Capt. James Cook's last voyage (1778 and 1779). Ibis 91:244-255.

Sutton, G. M., and D. F. Parmelee. 1955a. Breeding of the Semipalmated Plover on Baffin Island. Bird-Banding 26:137-147.

Sutton, G. M., and D. F. Parmelee. 1955b. Nesting of the Horned Lark on Baffin Island. Bird-Banding 26:1-18.

Sutton, G. M., and D. F. Parmelee. 1956. Breeding of the Snowy Owl in southeastern Baffin Island. Condor 58:273-282.

Sutton, G. M., and R. S. Wilson. 1946. Notes on the winter birds of Attu. Condor 48:83-91.

Swales, B. H. 1926. Ruby-throated Hummingbird near St. Michael, Alaska. Condor 28:128.

Swarth, H. S. 1934. Birds of Nunivak Island, Alaska. Pacific Coast Avifauna 22:1-64.

Swartz, L. G. 1966. Sea-cliff birds. p. 611-678. *In*: N. J. Wilimovsky and J. N. Wolfe (eds.), Environment of the Cape Thompson region, Alaska. Div. of Tech. Info., U. S. Atomic Energy Commission, Washington, DC.

Swartz, L. G. 1967. Distribution and movements of birds in the Bering and Chukchi seas. Pacific Sci. 21:332-347.

Swartz, L. G., W. Walker II, D. G. Roseneau, and A. M. Springer. 1975. Populations of Gyrfalcons on the Seward Peninsula, Alaska, 1968-1972. p. 71-75. *In*: J. R. Murphy, C. M. White, and B. E. Harrell (eds.), Population status of raptors. Raptor Res. Rep. No. 3, Raptor Res. Foundation, Vermillion, SD.

Tacha, T. C., P. A. Vohs, and G. C. Iverson. 1984. Migration routes of Sandhill Cranes from mid-continental North America. J. Wildl. Manage. 48:1028-1033.

Thayer, E. S. 1951. Shishmaref waterfowl project. Alaska Game Commission Federal Aid in Wildlife Restoration Quarterly Progress Rep. 6:3-16, September 1951. Juneau, AK.

Thayer, J. E. 1909. Limonites ruficollis in Alaska. Condor 11:173.

Thayer, J. E., and O. Bangs. 1914. Birds. p. 3-48. *In*: J. E. Thayer, O. Bangs, and G. M. Allen, Notes on the birds and mammals of the arctic coast of east Siberia. Proc. New England Zool. Club 5:1-66.

Thomas, V. G., and S. D. MacDonald. 1987. The breeding distribution and current population status of the Ivory Gull in Canada. Arctic 40:211-218.

Thompson, C. F. 1967. Notes on the birds of the northeast cape of St. Lawrence Island and of the Punuk Islands, Alaska. Condor 69:411-419.

Thompson, D. Q., and R. A. Person. 1963. The eider pass at Point Barrow, Alaska. J. Wildl. Manage. 27:348-356.

Thompson, M. C. 1974. Migratory patterns of Ruddy Turnstones in the central Pacific Region. Living Bird 12(1973):5-23.

Threlfall, W., and J. R. Blacquiere. 1982. Breeding biology of the Fox Sparrow in Newfoundland. J. Field Ornithol. 53:235-239.

Tinbergen, N. 1935. Field observations of east Greenland birds: I. The behaviour of the Red-necked Phalarope (*Phalaropus lobatus* L.) in spring. Ardea 24:1-42.

Townsend, C. H. 1887. Notes on mammals, birds, and fishes obtained at various places between the Aleutian Islands and Kotzebue Sound. Birds, p. 98-101. *In*: M. A. Healy, Report of the cruise of the Revenue Marine Steamer *Corwin* in the Arctic Ocean in 1885. Government Printing Office, Washington, DC.

Troy, D. M. 1980. A phenetic and karyotypic investigation of the systematics of the redpolls *Carduelis f. flammea* and *C. hornemanni exilipes*. M.S. thesis, Univ. Alaska, Fairbanks. 88 p.

Troy, D. M. 1983. Recaptures of redpolls: movements of an irruptive species. J. Field Ornithol. 54:146-151.

Troy, D. M. 1985. A phenetic analysis of the redpolls *Carduelis flammea flammea* and *C. hornemanni exilipes*. Auk 102:82-96.

Troy, D. M., and G. F. Shields. 1979. Multiple nesting attempts by Alaskan redpolls. Condor 81:96-97.

Tuck, L. M. 1961. The murres, their distribution, populations and biology: a study of the genus *Uria*. Can. Wildl. Serv. Monogr. Series No. 1. 260 p.

Tuck, L. M. 1972. The snipes: a study of the genus *Capella*. Can. Wildl. Serv. Monogr. Series No. 5. 429 p.

Turner, L. M. 1886. Birds, Part V. p. 115-196. *In*: Contributions to the natural history of Alaska. No. II, Arctic Series, Signal Service, U. S. Army. Government Printing Office, Washington, DC.

Ullrich, B. 1971. Untersuchungen zur Ethologie und Okologie des Rotkopfwurgers (*Lanius senator*) in Sudwestdeutschland im Vergleich zu Raubwurger (*L. excubitor*), Schwarzatirnwurger (*L. minor*) und Neuntoter (*L. collurio*). Die Vogelwarte 26:1-77.

Urner, C. A. 1923. Notes on the Short-eared Owl. Auk 40:30-36.

U. S. Fish and Wildlife Service. 1978-1987. Alaska-Yukon waterfowl breeding population surveys. Pacific Flyway Waterfowl Reports. U. S. Fish and Wildl. Serv., Portland, OR.

Uspenskii, S. M. 1956. The bird bazaars of Novaya Zemlya. USSR Acad. Sci., Moscow. Translations of Russian Game Reports Vol. 4, 1958, Can. Wildl. Serv., Ottawa, ONT. 159 p.

Uspenskii, S. M. 1965. The geese of Wrangel Island. Annual Report Wildfowl Trust 16:126-129.

Uspenskii, S. M. 1972. Die Eiderenten. A. Ziemsen Verlag, Wittenberg, Lutherstadt. 103p.

Vaurie, C. 1959. The birds of the Palearctic fauna. Vol. 1. Passeriformes. H. F. & G. Witherby, London, England. 762 p.

Vaurie, C. 1961. Systematic notes on Palearctic birds. No. 45, Falconidae: The genus *Falco* (Part 2). Amer. Mus. Novitates 2038:1-24.

Vaurie, C. 1965. The birds of the Palearctic fauna. Vol. 2. Non-Passeriformes. H. F. & G. Witherby, London, England. 763 p.

Verbeek, N. A. M. 1967. Breeding biology and ecology of the Horned Lark in alpine tundra. Wilson Bull. 79:208-218.

Verbeek, N. A. M. 1970. Breeding ecology of the Water Pipit. Auk 87:425-451.

Vermeer, K. 1969. Some aspects of the breeding of the White-winged Scoter at Miquelon Lake, Alberta. Blue Jay 27:72-73.

Wahl, T. R. 1978. Seabirds in the northwestern Pacific Ocean and south central Bering Sea in June 1975. Western Birds 9:45-66.

Wahrhaftig, C. 1965. Physiographic divisions of Alaska. U. S. Geol. Survey Prof. Paper 482. 52 p.

Walker, W. 1977. Chlorinated hydrocarbon pollutants in Gyrfalcons and their prey in Alaska. Auk 94:442-447.

Walkinshaw, L. H. 1948. Nestings of some passerine birds in western Alaska. Condor 50:64-70.

Walkinshaw, L. H. 1949. The Sandhill Cranes. Cranbrook Institute of Sci. Bull. No. 9. Bloomfield Hills, MI. 202 p.

Wallace, G. J. 1939. Bicknell's Thrush, its taxonomy, distribution, and life history. Proc. Boston Soc. Nat. Hist. 41:211-402.

Watson, A. 1957. The behaviour, breeding and food-ecology of the Snowy Owl *Nyctea scandiaca*. Ibis 99:419-462.

Watson, G. E., and G. J. Divoky. 1972. Pelagic bird and mammal observations in the eastern Chukchi Sea, early fall 1970. p. 111-172. *In*: C. I. Merton, et al., An ecological survey in the eastern Chukchi Sea, September-October 1970. U. S. Coast Guard Oceanographic Rep. No. 50.

Weeden, J. S. 1966. Diurnal rhythm of attentiveness of incubating female Tree Sparrows (*Spizella arborea*) at a northern latitude. Auk 83:368-388.

Weeden, R. B. 1959. A new breeding record of the Wandering Tattler in Alaska. Auk 76:230-232.

Weeden, R. B. 1964. Spatial separation of sexes in Rock and Willow ptarmigan in winter. Auk 81:534-541.

Weeden, R. B. 1965a. Breeding density, reproductive success, and mortality of Rock Ptarmigan at Eagle Creek, central Alaska, from 1960 to 1964. Trans. N. Amer. Wildl. Conf. 30:336-348.

Weeden, R. B. 1965b. Further notes on Wandering Tattlers in central Alaska. Condor 67:87-89.

Weeden, R. B. 1965c. Grouse and ptarmigan in Alaska: their ecology and management. Federal Aid in Wildl. Restoration Project Rep., Vol. 5, July 1965, Juneau, AK. 110 p.

Weeden, R. B. 1969. Foods of Rock and Willow ptarmigan in central Alaska with comments on interspecific competition. Auk 86:271-281.

Weeden, R. B., and L. N. Ellison. 1968. Upland game birds of forest and tundra. Wildl. Booklet Series, No. 3. Alaska Dept. Fish and Game, Juneau, AK. 44 p.

Weeden, R. B., and L. Johnson. 1973. New records of Mourning Doves in south-central and interior Alaska. Condor 75:353.

Weeden, R. B., and J. B. Theberge. 1972. The dynamics of a fluctuating population of Rock Ptarmigan in Alaska. Proc. Internat. Ornithol. Cong. 15:90-106.

Wehle, D. H. S. 1980. The breeding biology of the puffins: Tufted Puffin (*Lunda cirrhata*), Horned Puffin (*Fratercula corniculata*), Common Puffin (*F. arctica*), and Rhinoceros Auklet (*Cerorhinca monocerata*). Ph.D. thesis, Univ. Alaska, Fairbanks. 313 p.

Welsh, D. A. 1975. Savannah Sparrow breeding and territoriality on a Nova Scotia dune beach. Auk 92:235-251.

West, G. C., and M. S. Meng. 1966. Nutrition of Willow Ptarmigan in northern Alaska. Auk 83:603-615.

West, G. C., and M. S. Meng. 1968. Effect of diet and captivity on the fatty acid composition of redpoll (*Acanthis flammea*) depot fats. Comp. Biochem. Physiol. 25:535-540.

West, G. C., L. J. Peyton, and L. Irving. 1968. Analysis of spring migration of Lapland Longspurs to Alaska. Auk 85:639-653.

White, C. M. 1968. Diagnosis and relationships of the North American tundra-inhabiting Peregrine Falcons. Auk 85:179-191.

White, C. M., and T. J. Cade. 1971. Cliff-nesting raptors and ravens along the Colville River in arctic Alaska. Living Bird 10:107-150.

White, C. M., and D. G. Roseneau. 1970. Observations on food, nesting, and winter populations of large North American falcons. Condor 72:113-115.

White, C. M., and R. B. Weeden. 1966. Hunting methods of Gyrfalcons and behavior of their prey (ptarmigan). Condor 68:517-519.

White, C. M., and G. C. West. 1977. The annual lipid cycle and feeding behavior of Alaskan redpolls. Oecologia (Berl.) 27:227-238.

Williamson, F. S. L. 1968. *Calcarius lapponicus alascensis* Ridgway, Alaska Longspur. p. 1608-1627. *In*: A. C. Bent, Life histories of North American cardinals, grosbeaks, buntings, towhees, finches, sparrows, and allies. U. S. Nat. Mus. Bull. 237, Part 3. Washington, DC.

Williamson, F. S. L., and W. B. Emison. 1971. Variation in the timing of breeding and molt of the Lapland Longspur (*Calcarius lapponicus*) in Alaska, with relation to differences in latitude. BioScience 21:701-707.

Williamson, F. S. L., M. C. Thompson, and J. Q. Hines. 1966. Avifaunal Investigations. p. 437-480. *In*: N. J. Wilimovsky and J. N. Wolfe (eds.), Environment of the Cape Thompson region, Alaska. Div. of Tech. Info., U. S. Atomic Energy Commission, Washington, DC.

Witherby, H. F., F. C. R. Jourdain, N. F. Ticehurst, and B. W. Tucker. 1943. The handbook of British Birds, Vol. 2 (rev. ed.). H. F. and G. Witherby, London, England. 386 p.

Wolfe, J. A., and E. B. Leopold. 1967. Neogene and early Quaternary vegetation of northwestern North America and northeastern Asia. p. 193-206. *In*: D. M. Hopkins (ed.), The Bering Land Bridge. Stanford Univ. Press, Stanford, CA.

Woodby, D., and G. Divoky. 1983. Bird use of coastal habitats in Norton Sound. p. 353-704. *In*: Final reports of principal investigators, Environmental Assessment of the Alaskan Continental Shelf, Biological Studies Vol. 18, NOAA-BLM, Juneau, AK.

Wright, J. M. 1979. Reindeer grazing in relation to bird nesting on the northern Seward Peninsula [Alaska]. M.S. thesis, Univ. Alaska, Fairbanks. 109 p.

Yonge, K. S. 1981. The breeding cycle and annual production of the Common Loon (*Gavia immer*) in the boreal forest region. M.S. thesis, Univ. Manitoba, Winnipeg. 141 p.

Young, H. 1955. Breeding behavior and nesting of the Eastern Robin. Amer. Midl. Nat. 53:329-352.

Young, S. B. 1971. The vascular flora of St. Lawrence Island with special reference to floristic zonation in the arctic regions. Contrib. Gray Herbarium, Harvard Univ., No. 201. 115 p.

Bird Species Index

Index

321

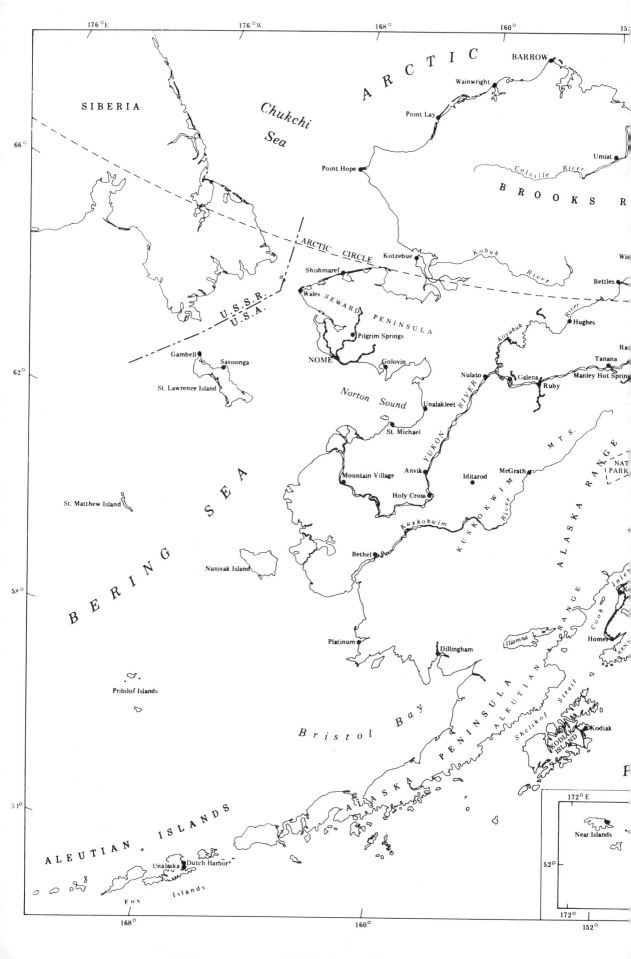